# Heroes of the City of Man

# Heroes of the City of Man

## A Christian Guide to Select Ancient Literature

Peter J. Leithart

*Canon Press*
MOSCOW, IDAHO

Peter J. Leithart, *Heroes of the City of Man: A Christian Guide to Select Ancient Literature*

© 1999 by Peter Leithart
Published by Canon Press, P.O. Box 8741, Moscow, ID 83843
800-488-2034 / www.canonpress.org

04 03 02 01 00 99     9 8 7 6 5 4 3 2 1

Cover design by Paige Atwood Design, Moscow, ID

Printed in the United States of America.

All rights reserved. No part of this publication may be reproduced, stored in a retrieval system, or transmitted in any form by any means, electronic, mechanical, photocopy, recording, or otherwise, without prior permission of the author, except as provided by USA copyright law.

ISBN: 1-885767-55-2

To Woelke,

Adeodatus
Ad Deum datus
Cives alterae
civitatis

# Contents

| | |
|---|---|
| Acknowledgments | 11 |
| Introduction: The Devil Has No Stories | 13 |
| **Section I: Ancient Epic** | |
| Introduction: Ancient Epic | 43 |
| *Pagan Genesis:* Hesiod, *Theogony* | 53 |
| *Fighters Killing, Fighters Killed:* Homer, *The Iliad* | 85 |
| *Son of Pain:* Homer, *The Odyssey* | 147 |
| *Patria and Pietas:* Virgil, *The Aeneid* | 213 |
| **Section II: Greek Drama** | |
| Introduction: Greek Drama | 275 |
| *Blessings of Terror:* Aeschylus, *The Eumenides* | 281 |
| *Riddles of One and Many:* Sophocles, *Oedipus Tyrannus* | 305 |
| *The Contest of Fetters and Thyrsus:* Euripides, *The Bacchae* | 335 |
| *Sophist in the City:* Aristophanes, *Clouds* | 365 |
| For Additional Reading | 391 |

## Acknowledgments

Much of this book was written during a move from Cambridge, England, to Moscow, Idaho, that took place over several months. In writing it, therefore, I was more than usually dependent on the generosity of family and friends who provided housing and other necessities during this period. Thanks to my in-laws, Dan and Margaret Jordan, for giving us a place to land when we first returned from England; to my parents, Paul and Mildred Leithart, for giving us the run of their house for a month; to David and Desiree Smolin, who lent us their home for two months during the summer of 1998; to Colonel and Trinky Grete, who kept me for a week during a summer conference in Florida and let me spread out over a corner of their dining room table while I worked on what became chapter 7. A special thanks to Gilbert and Cindy Douglas and their family, whose generosity is too boundless to enumerate.

I am grateful to the Session of Reformed Heritage Presbyterian Church, Birmingham, Alabama, for permission to teach a class in ancient epic under the auspices of Heritage Academy, which helped me to organize the material in chapters 2–4. The students in my senior Literature Colloquium at New St. Andrews College—Aaron Booth, Michael Collender, Matt Greydanus, Michael Harkin, Courtney Huntington, Heidi McBroom, Holly McBroom, and Aaron Tripp—challenged me with their questions and offered many insights that have greatly improved this work. I have tried to give credit where due and apologize if I have borrowed anything from them without acknowledgment. Thanks to Jim Jordan, who read through the manuscript and made many provocative suggestions. Unfortunately, due to looming deadlines, I was able to incorporate only a few into the book. Wes Callahan was kind enough to read through the manuscript and offer encouragement, and Doug Jones, editor of Canon Press, was cheerful and patient as I slouched toward completion, never breathing a word of complaint.

My immediate family was, as usual, supportive and helpful in ways tangible and intangible. My wife, Noel, and daughter, Lindsey, checked quotations for accuracy, and my oldest son, Woelke, read through the manuscript, correcting factual errors and making stylistic suggestions. As a token of my appreciation and love, I have dedicated this book to him.

Peniel Hall<br>
Moscow, Idaho<br>
Lent 1999

# Introduction:
# The Devil Has No Stories

> Perhaps those poets of long ago who sang
> the Age of Gold, its pristine happiness,
> were dreaming on Parnassus of this place.
>
> The root of mankind's tree was guiltless here;
> here, in an endless Spring, was every fruit,
> such is the nectar praised by all these poets.
> *Purgatorio* 28, 139–144

"What has Athens to do with Jerusalem?" Tertullian exclaimed, and his question has echoed through the following centuries. Tertullian's own answer—"not much"—was not universally shared in the early church. Many of the early apologists, to be sure, expressed their disgust with the loose morality found in the gods of mythology (but then, so did Plato), and Augustine repented of his youthful passion for Virgil and the Roman theater. Yet, Origen and Clement, theologians of Alexandria, were deeply impressed with neo-Platonic philosophy, and Augustine's impressive but incomplete escape from Platonism was the result of tremendous intellectual exertion.

Tertullian's question has taken on fresh relevance today with the rise of classical Christian schools. In its origins, the Christian school movement was largely in line with Tertullian's perspective: Christian schools were founded on the model of Jerusalem rather than Athens. In the last decade, however, many Christian schools have introduced classical elements into their curricula, and among the elements of the classical approach is a renewed attention to classical literature. Jerusalem has moved marginally closer to Athens, and some are beginning to pose Tertullian's question again.

*Heroes of the City of Man* is a book about Athens by an author who resides contentedly in Jerusalem. One of the foundational assumptions of this study is that there is a profound antithesis, a conflict, a chasm, between Christian faith and all other forms of thought and life. Though I appreciate the sheer aesthetic attraction of classical poetry and drama, I have no interest in helping construct Athrusalem or Jerens; these hybrids are monstrosities whose walls the church should breach rather than build. Instead, I have attempted to view Athens from a point securely within the walls of Jerusalem.

An accurate view is possible in spite of the great gulf fixed between the two cities. We have the technology. And, I believe there is profit to be had from this exploration of foreign territory. The purpose of this introduction is to describe the technology and to enumerate some benefits of deploying it.

## The Problem of the Classics

A recent book that pleads for a return to "the classics" provides a starting point for our discussion. According to Victor Davis Hanson and John Heath's *Who Killed Homer?*,[1] the Greek view of the world, which they call "Greek wisdom," is central to Western history and culture. Take away Greeks, and you take away all that is unique and good in our civilization: the autonomy of science and learning from religious and political authority, the civilian oversight of military power, constitutional and consensual government, separation of religion from political authority, faith in the average citizen, private property, freedom of dissent and open criticism of government, religion, and the military.

On purely historical grounds, a number of the details of this sketch are highly questionable. The authors claim that religion and political authority were separated in the Greek city. As evidence, they point out that, unlike many ancient cities, authority in a Greek city-state was not in the hands of a priest-king and that no prophet or seer had power to overrule the decisions of a Greek assembly. Though these points are accurate, there is overwhelming evidence that the Greek city-state was a religious as well as a political organization. Every city was under the patronage of a god, goddess, or founder-hero. At the center of each city was the *hestia*, a common hearth-fire or altar that served as the center for civic festivals. When a Greek city established a colony, fire from the city *hestia* was taken to the new colony so that the altar in the colony burned with the same fire as the mother city. Meetings of the assembly at Athens began with the sacrifice of a pig. From these and many other practices, Zaidman and Schmitt Pantel conclude that Greek civic life was "impregnated" with religion and that there was "no separation between the sacred and the profane."[2]

Hanson and Heath also claim that faith in the average citizen is an inheritance of the ancient Greeks. Perhaps there is some basis for this commonplace, but it must be remembered that citizenship was a very restricted privilege in Greek cities. Rules for citizenship became more stringent with time, and it was ultimately decided that only children of a legally recognized marriage between two Athenian citizens were themselves citizens. As a result, a large proportion of the inhabitants of a Greek *polis* were not citizens but resident aliens. This is not faith in the "common man" but in the "right men."

Putting these inaccuracies to one side, however, Hanson and Heath raise a more fundamental question: Did Greek wisdom build the West? Do we enjoy the freedoms we enjoy because of Greece? Is recovering the wisdom of the Greeks the way to restore our society? For Christians, the clear answer to these questions is a resounding "No." Greeks worshiped and served what are not gods, and idolatry, the Bible assures us, has considerable social and cultural implications. When Paul visited Athens, he did not praise its artistic, literary, or philosophical achievements but was provoked at the countless idolatrous shrines and altars (Acts 17:16). To the extent we share Paul's zeal to see the true God worshiped everywhere, we will react to Greek and Roman literature with similar provocation. Greek thought and culture, founded as it is in idolatry, does not represent "wisdom." It is, at base, folly.

And it is folly that must provoke us, as it did Paul, to opposition. The basic biblical paradigm for dealing with idolatrous religions, their ideas, literature, and practices is unrelenting, total, holy war. Scripture instructs us to make war against the gods of the nations. God leaves us no room for neutrality, no room for borrowing weapons from Greece or from Rome, anymore than we are permitted to borrow some of the "good ideas" found in Hinduism, Islam, or Buddhism. Moses urged Israel in ferocious language to utterly destroy the gods of the Canaanites:

> When the Lord your God shall bring you into the land where you are entering to possess it, and shall clear away many nations before you... and when the Lord your God shall deliver them before you, and shall defeat them, then you shall utterly destroy them. You shall make no covenant with them and show no favor to them.... But thus you shall do to them: you shall tear down their altars, and smash their sacred pillars, and hew down their Asherim, and burn their graven images with fire (Deuteronomy 7:1–5).

> These are the statutes and the judgments which you shall carefully observe in the land which the Lord, the God of your fathers, has given you to possess as long as you live on the earth. You shall utterly destroy all the places where the nations whom you shall dispossess served their gods, on the high mountains and on the hills and under every green tree. And you shall tear down their altars and smash their sacred pillars

and burn their Asherim with fire, and you shall cut down the engraved images of their gods, and you shall obliterate their name from that place (Deuteronomy 12:1–3).

These are fearful instructions, and the New Testament reiterates the same zeal in war against all idols (2 Cor. 6:7; 10:3–6; Eph. 6:10–20). Armed with the sword of the Spirit, the church is to destroy the gods of the nations until Jesus is acknowledged as king over all. Vanquishing "Greek wisdom" is as much a fundamental goal in the church's evangelistic mission as throwing down modern secularism is.

According to some Christians, the Bible forbids us to study Baalistic and Canaanite mythologies, and the Greek myths are more humane, more decent, less crude, and thus closer to Christian teaching than ancient Palestinian myths. Zeus is an idol, but by this argument, he is not as bad as Baal. This argument will be convincing only to those who have been reading expurgated versions of Greek and Roman mythology, of the kind one finds in Edith Hamilton's popular and seductive books. In the past several decades, classical scholars have found that the literature and culture of archaic and classical Greece is profoundly indebted to the literature and language of the Ancient Near East, and from Greece these influences were passed on to early Rome. Greeks apparently learned how to write from the Phoenicians and adapted the Phoenician alphabet. Artistic styles and crafts were introduced from the East. Religious beliefs and practices were also transferred from the region around Palestine to the Greek peninsula. Temples apparently did not exist in Greece until the "orientalizing revolution" of the eighth century (750–650), and many of the rituals of Greek religion were borrowed from the same cultures.[3] Borrowed from the East, Greek mythologies are quite as brutal and savage as the stories of Baal and Molech, as will become evident in our study of Hesiod's *Theogony* (chapter 1). As the visions of Daniel 7 suggest, Greece and Rome were, like Assyria and Babylon before them, bestial powers.

The passages from Deuteronomy thus raise a sharp question for Christian study of the ancient classics. Given the fact that the classics are idolatrous through and through, why should we want to preserve them? Why should we keep alive the memory of Greek gods? Should we be studying the exploits of heroes who served these gods? Should we not instead throw all of Homer, Aeschylus, Sophocles, and Virgil into one flaming heap in the town square? Wouldn't Moses?

A part of the answer to these questions is that Christians have no more moral duty to read and study Greek and Roman literature than ancient Israelites had a duty to study the myths of Baal and Asteroth. Nor should Christian schools or home schoolers think that they can have a good Christian education only if the "classics" are prominent in the curriculum. The goal of Christian education is to train a child to be faithful in serving God and His kingdom in a calling, and certainly this goal can be achieved by a student who never cracks the cover of a Homeric epic. Given the appalling ignorance of the Bible among evangelical Christians today, mastering Scripture must be an overwhelming priority in all Christian education. If one must choose between studying Leviticus or Livy, Habakkuk or Homer, Acts or Aeschylus, the decision is, to my mind, perfectly evident, and the point holds even if the non-biblical literature were Christian. The genealogies of 1 Chronicles 1–9 are vastly more important to study than Dante, Shakespeare, Milton, or Dickens.

But, of course, students and teachers are not always faced with a stark either/or choice. Assuming a student has a strong grounding in Scripture, there may be good reasons for taking up a study of other literature. And a few texts of Scripture demonstrate that it is not necessarily sinful for believers to study pagan literature. Daniel and his three friends learned the language and literature of the Chaldeans (Dan. 1:4), which undoubtedly focused on Chaldean mythology. In the New Testament, Paul occasionally reveals that he knew some of the literature and philosophy of the Greeks and Romans. In Acts 17:28, he quotes a Greek poet, and some have suggested that the phrase "kicking against the goads" in Acts 26:14 comes from Aeschylus, though it might well have been a proverbial saying. In both cases, the context of these passages is important. Daniel learned Chaldean literature while in exile, and this helped to prepare him for a high profile position in an alien land. Paul quotes the Greek poets to the philosophers on Mars Hill as part of his effort to "win some" by becoming all things to all men. Both Daniel and Paul insisted that true insight and wisdom come from Yahweh, the God of Israel, not from Marduk or Apollo (see Dan. 2:28; 1 Cor. 2:6–16). Neither studied "the classics" in order to discover guidance and wisdom for a godly life. They used their knowledge of pagan literature to achieve the purposes of God. Daniel and Paul turned the weapons of Babylon and Greece against their makers, and thus Babylon and Greece fell into the pit they had dug (Ps. 7:16).

God, in short, calls us to war against the idols, but the Bible teaches a variety of strategies and tactics in war. The shrines of the Canaanites were to be utterly destroyed, and the gold and silver of their idols was not to be used, "for it is an abomination" (Deut. 7:25). Yet when the Israelites left Egypt, they received gold and silver from the Egyptians (Ex. 12:35–36), and this gold and silver was used to build the tabernacle at Sinai. Later, David gathered the plunder from his wars with the Philistines and others and gave it to Solomon to build the temple (1 Chr. 22:6–16). Citing these biblical examples, St. Augustine concluded that the church likewise was permitted to "plunder the Egyptians," using the achievements of pagan society to construct God's house and city. This is much easier to do with technology than with literature and philosophy. Whether or not the computer or the software was invented by a Christian, Christians can use computers for the advancement of Christ's kingdom. Plundering ideas is trickier, since the ideas must simultaneously be plundered and purged, received and rejected. With ideas and literature, the confrontation between the Bible and paganism will be more intense, but with great care and wisdom, we can plunder even pagan literature and make it work for us. As Proverbs says, the wealth of the wicked is stored up for the righteous (Prov. 13:22).

More specifically, pagan literature can be used as a weapon for Christian warfare because it gives insight into the works and ways of the enemy. Greek poets and philosophers are enemies of Christ and His church, and they are not remote enemies. The Heroic Age ended some three thousand years ago, but our inner cities, our television and movie screens, and our courtrooms are filled with characters who live by the creed of Achilles. To combat these enemies effectively, it helps to know them from the inside, and literature gives us unique insight into the unbelieving heart.

Moreover, by giving us a glimpse of a world largely untouched by God's truth, Greek and Roman literature help us identify the effect that the gospel has had on the world. Reading Greek and Roman literature, for example, highlights the difference between a world formed by polytheism and a world that worships the One Living God. This theological disagreement has enormous practical significance, but let me highlight one aspect. If the gods are as the Greek myths depict them, then, as Hesiod's work suggests, warfare and conflict are the ultimate reality. Gods and goddesses compete and fight with one another, promoting the good of their favorites and opposing their enemies among men. Peace is inherently impossible in a polytheistic world. This, I will suggest, is responsible for the despair that C. S. Lewis said pervades the Homeric epics. Homer vividly depicts the horror and waste of war (as well as its glories and beauties), but he can see no way of life other than war. How could he? If the gods themselves are at war, how can we expect peace on earth—ever?

In a polytheistic world, a semblance of peace can be established in one of two ways. On the one hand, one god might be powerful enough to force the others into submission. But here cosmic war is replaced by cosmic tyranny; power flows to the one with the biggest gun. On the other hand, in

Homeric epic, and even more in Virgil's *Aeneid*, Fate comes to the fore as the ruling force, and this gives some unity and harmony to the world. Individual gods might be at war, but Fate calmly works out the destiny of each man. But Fate is a mysterious, unapproachable, impersonal force. No one prays to fate or worships it (him). Classical epic thus leaves us with three fundamental theological options: Heaven rings with the petty squabbling of adolescent gods, which means the world is not under control at all, *or* heaven and earth are ruled by a heavenly Führer, *or* things are governed by an impersonal and faceless power that grinds along, indifferent to humanity or justice. Take your pick: chaos, totalitarianism, or determinism. Whichever you choose, the world is a pretty grim place, with no hope for redemption. Homer and Virgil powerfully render this world, and thus they give us insight into the horror of life under the cruel gods.

By contrast, the Bible proclaimed from the beginning that there is one God, Yahweh, who created the world good and rules all things. Violence and evil are not written into the fabric of creation but are due to sin and His righteous judgment on sin, and therefore there is hope of redemption from evil. Ultimate reality is *not* a gaggle of gods, nor an autocrat, nor an impersonal Fate. Rather, ultimate reality is Three Persons in an eternal communion of love. Above us is a God who is love, whose love overflows in creating a world He did not need and in redeeming a world that had turned from Him. Heaven is not a battlefield or a prison; it is a dance hall filled with song. And, one day, earth will join in.

In a similar way, Greek and Roman literature highlight by way of contrast the Christian view of creativity and culture (Hesiod); the hero and heroism (Homer and Virgil); the relation of city and family (Aeschylus); fate, sin, and responsibility (Sophocles); the conflict of reason and emotion (Euripides); and the social effects of philosophical skepticism (Aristophanes). None of these poems or plays teach the wisdom of Christ in a direct way. Rather, by wrestling to evaluate these books biblically, we are led to discover biblical truth that we might otherwise have overlooked. Pagan literature can, rightly used, give us an important entry into the mind and culture of fallen humanity, and even sharpen our understanding of the Christian worldview. Given that our world has abandoned the Christian foundations of our civilization, we will increasingly be confronted with a variety of paganism. Modern paganism is not the same as ancient paganism, but pagan practices and habits of thought and life are being revived. Studying this literature can make us more aware of our enemies' habits and prepare us to wage skillful and victorious war against them. What we should refuse to do is embrace our enemies as friends.

By this argument, studying the mythologies of India, Africa, China, or American Indians would serve as well. Yet, the intended audience of this book lives in a civilization that has been shaped more by stories from Greece and Rome than by the Bhagavad Gita or the tribal mythologies studied by anthropologists. In addition to the "negative" use of Greco-Roman literature described above, then, there is a more "positive" use: Knowledge of the classics is necessary to understand contemporary thought and culture. Freud formulated a psychological theory using the Oedipus myth; the contemporary moral philosopher Alasdair MacIntyre has revived a version of the "virtue ethics" found in Homer, Plato, and Aristotle; James Joyce's *Ulysses* follows the *Odyssey* in some detail, with the not insignificant difference that it is set in Dublin rather than the islands of Greece. If we want to have a sense of our historical situation, it will help to do some grappling with the classics.

Knowledge of Greek and Roman literature is, moreover, important to appreciate fully the literature and culture of the Christian West. Shakespeare is full of classical allusions, as are Dante, Spencer, and Milton, and a knowledge of Greek and Roman literature enhances our understanding and enjoyment of this later literature. Sometimes, the allusions are for comic effect, as when Shakespeare in *Troilus and Creseida* shows us the Homeric heroes sitting around discussing whether they will come off well when Homer writes his epic. Watching the changing interpretations of classical literature provides a window into the changes in the mentality of Western writers and thinkers. Tennyson's *Ulysses* describes an aging but very Victorian Odysseus who itches to go on another voyage, for "'tis not too late to seek a newer world." His poem tells us a great deal about Tennyson and his age but very little about Homer's Odysseus, who was not a restless adventurer but a displaced homebody. W. H. Auden's haunting poem *Achilles' Shield* uses a Homeric motif to explore the horrors of modern war and totalitarianism. A reader with no knowledge of Homer will miss most of the point of these poems.

Of course, students can gain general knowledge of the stories of ancient Greece and Rome by reading adaptions and summaries. For many students, this kind of exposure will be sufficient, and far safer than detailed treatment of the works themselves. As James Jordan has said, pagan literature "can be a kind of intellectual pornography, since the sinful mind of man quite naturally resonates to the themes in Greek and Roman literature."

## On Reading Homer

I have argued that it is permissible for Christians to study ancient pagan literature, provided it is done within a sound biblical framework and is intended to equip the student to serve God more faithfully. This, of course, raises questions about how it is to be done. Like many things, the best way to explain how to read is to offer a reading, and thus *Heroes of the City of Man* as a whole provides my fuller answer to these questions, but here I will make some sketchy introductory comments.

As an entry into the discussion, let me indulge for a few moments in a venerable authorial practice: answering a critic. Two years ago, Canon Press published my study of Shakespeare, *Brightest Heaven of Invention*. In the introduction to that book, I suggested that Christians can begin to grasp extra-biblical literature by fitting these stories into the "master story" the Bible tells. As medieval writers put it, the Bible is the "epitome" of all books, containing a key to all other books and stories. Tragedies, specifically, are "fall stories," similar to the biblical stories in Genesis 3 or 1 Samuel 13–15, while comedies are "redemption stories," similar in structure to the overall redemptive narrative of the Bible. A reader can begin to discern the shape of a story by slotting characters and events into the pattern of biblical stories. All heroes may be compared to the true Hero, Jesus Christ; all damsels in distress are comparable to Christ's Bride, the church; all rescues are acts of salvation; all weddings anticipate the feast of the Lamb; and all villains, serpent-like, spread their several varieties of poison.

Not everyone found this convincing or even helpful. In a review published in the January 1998 issue of *First Things*, Margaret Boerner, who teaches in the Humanities Program at Villanova University, suggested my approach was misleading, even dangerous. She complained of the disservice I rendered with my insistence "especially to inexperienced readers that [Shakespeare] was painting Christian allegory by the numbers." She found my basic argument "muddled": "If, as Christians believe, God has chosen to reveal Himself in the stories of the Old Testament and the Master Story that culminates in the New Testament, then it may be that real life is divinely arranged in the structures of a story, though that takes us into deep theological waters. But do we really want to say that it necessarily follows that *all* stories are divine? Are we really prepared to hold that there are no stories that do not explicitly and deliberately retell the Christ-event?"

Well, now. Boerner's review is inaccurate in several respects. First, she misrepresents the intent of my discussion of the Bible's master story, which was in part pedagogical. In *Brightest Heaven of Invention*, I compared learning new stories to learning a new language, in which we match up what we know with what we do not. Let me follow that analogy another step or two to clarify the point. No two languages, of course, are completely identical. Flash cards will say the Hebrew word *dabar* means *word*, but in the Old Testament *dabar* is also used where we would use the English word *thing*. *Word* and *dabar*, as linguists would say, do not have the same "range of meaning." Vocabularies thus do not match up in a one-to-one manner. Structurally, too, languages cannot be superimposed on one another. Even similar languages like Greek and Latin diverge in many ways. Only the beginning student of Hebrew automatically substitutes *word* whenever he sees *dabar*; only the neophyte Greek scholar thinks a noun in the dative case is always an indirect object. Despite these complexities, it would be a foolish teacher who failed to build a bridge from the known language to the unknown.

Writing an introduction to Shakespeare for Christian students, I worked from known stories to unknown. Boerner no doubt has great facility with Shakespeare, but his plays are forbidding to many. By coming to Shakespeare's plays with the structure and imagery of the Bible in mind, Christian readers can begin to find their way through the plays without feeling they are in a completely alien world. Once they set foot on the shores of Elizabethan drama, they will find other flora and fauna—borrowings from classical mythology, ancient history, British history, Renaissance science, and Elizabethan folklore. Building a pedagogical bridge from the Bible to Shakespeare does not mean the countries are the same. If they were, there would be no need for the bridge in the first place. But without *some* bridge, timid students will not attempt the treacherous passage to Shakespeare at all. My suggestion that Shakespeare's plays fit into a "master story" was thus an effort to help precisely those inexperienced readers that Boerner thinks will be damaged by my book.

There is more to the story than pedagogy, however. Though Shakespeare is not John Bunyan, the imaginative universe in which he operated was infused with Christian imagery, clipped and pasted from the Bible, medieval exegesis of Scripture, the church fathers, and the liturgy of the

Church of England. As E. M. W. Tillyard shows in his classic little book, *The Elizabethan World Picture*,[4] Shakespeare, along with other Elizabethan poets and writers, represents the world as a great chain of being, or, better, a network of chains of beings. Each realm of the universe—the planets, the animal kingdom, the plant world, the human commonwealth—has a proper hierarchical order, and each hierarchy mirrors the others. This conception of the world provided poets with a readily available system of imagery and symbolism. The lion, as king of beasts, is a fitting symbol of the king of the commonwealth, and the sun, as chief among planets, is comparable to the eagle, most noble among birds. Disorder in the commonwealth is, by the same principles, described as disorder among the planets or in nature. Hence, the Duke of Burgundy in Act 5 of *Henry V* laments the effects of war on France, "the best garden of the world," and Hamlet expresses his disgust with life by describing Denmark as "an unweeded garden." For an Elizabethan, this world picture was not merely literary but rooted in theology and Scripture. As Tillyard says, English poets inherited and simplified a medieval world picture that was "solidly theocentric" and derived from "an amalgam of Plato and the Old Testament." For purely historical reasons, then, it is appropriate to interpret Shakespeare in the light of Scriptural patterns of imagery and plot.[5] An Elizabethan hearing "garden" references would, among other things, think of Eden.

Some of Boerner's specific criticisms are misleading. She attributes to me, for instance, the view that Henry V is a "Christ figure." On the one hand, this is strict historical interpretation. Virtually every medieval king was considered a Christ figure,[6] and Shakespeare's Henry explicitly associates himself with this tradition in Act 1: "I am a Christian king," he tells the French embassy. On the other hand, far from suggesting this Henry-as-Christ-figure provides a complete interpretation of the play, most of my chapter on *Henry V* sought to demonstrate that Shakespeare was profoundly suspicious of Henry's French campaigns. The "allegorical" suggestion that Henry is a "Christ figure," then, provides ironic and even tragic background for an account of very unchristian wars. The patriotic melody on the surface of the play is met by a skeptical counter-melody that checks and, in the end, overwhelms the first.[7] Further and more generally, I am hardly the first writer to suggest the presence of "archetypal" patterns and symbolisms running throughout apparently unrelated works.[8] Understanding literature, even the most self-consciously allegorical literature, is never as simple as finding direct correspondences between this and that. At the same time, stories, scenes, motifs, and images have, as Boerner would surely agree, family resemblances that make comparison a fruitful exercise. I would not, for example, argue that there is a direct literary connection between the disciples sleeping in Gethsemane and the astonishing failure of Beowulf's men to wake up during the hero's clamorous battle with Grendel. Yet, drowsiness at the peak of battle, whether we are talking about warriors or disciples, symbolizes a moral sluggishness, which in turn highlights the hero's strenuous heroism. Taking note of these parallels in no way implies the author of Beowulf is explicitly and deliberately writing allegory (though there are in fact some indications that he was).

But a pox on defensive nit-picking! Despite distortions, Boerner's fundamental charge is accurate: What she seems particularly to dislike in my book was my effort to interpret Shakespeare theologically. As she suspected, I do see Christ everywhere and in everything, as the One in Whom all things, including Western literature, consist. Shakespeare's plays are among the "all things" that Paul says are created "for Christ" (Col. 1:16–17). If there is offense in taking Paul quite literally and pressing his global affirmation into crannies of the academy that would rather not hear from an apostle, it is an offense for which I cannot apologize. Pressing Paul's point is a straightforward and unavoidable demand of discipleship.

But exactly *how* is Shakespeare "for Christ"?—aye, there's the rub. And if a Shakespeare "for Christ" irritates, how much more Homer?

Thus, we return to the present book, which, even without Boerner's review, would demand that the issues raised in *Brightest Heaven* be revisited. If the argument that Shakespeare can be read through the filter of the Bible is "muddled," then certainly an effort to read Homer through a biblical framework is infinitely more so. Shakespeare presumably had read the Bible and was familiar with the liturgy of the Church of England. We thus begin with the possibility that he is alluding to biblical patterns when he has Hamlet's ghost call Claudius a "serpent" or that he has the Eucharist in view when Petruchio refuses to let his shrewish bride eat at his table. Those interpretations may not be convincing, and they may not be true, but they are *possible*. When Homer has Penelope call the suitors "vipers," the argument has leaped to the far side of muddle: By what logic can that imagery and these stories be examined in the light of the "master story" of Scripture? Had Homer read Moses?

## Our Stories and the Story of God

Several sorts of arguments can be made for the approach to ancient pagan literature found in *Heroes of the City of Man*. As in *Brightest Heaven*, my goal is in part pedagogical. I hope to make ancient literature more accessible to Christian students by pointing out parallels with the Bible. Thus, I compare Hesiod's account of the origin of the world with that of Genesis; I explain Greek sacrifice by reference to Leviticus; I interpret the hospitality theme in the *Odyssey* in the light of a theology of food and feasting; I call Odysseus's unveiling to the suitors an "apocalypse"; when I describe Penelope as a patient and faithful bride awaiting the return of her husband, I intend for readers to catch the biblical resonances.

Yet, this pedagogy is not a mere "teaching device," but is grounded in theological and historical considerations. Let me develop each of these in turn. Again, it will be helpful to begin with one of Boerner's criticisms. She claims that I confused "the absolutely hypothetical nature of fiction and the freedom of creation granted to human imagination with what Leithart undoubtedly holds is the *true* story of God's actions in history." But I do not confuse the two; instead, I simply deny that the human imagination is capable of anything "absolutely hypothetical" or that we have an absolute freedom in creation.

Below I develop a theological argument for that conclusion, but it is important to see that this theological argument seeks to answer a question raised by *literature*, a question that has occupied Christian scholars such as Northrop Frye and C. S. Lewis, as well as non-Christian thinkers like Joseph Campbell and Carl Jung. That question concerns the odd recurrence of plots, patterns of imagery, and characters in stories that originate in widely different places and times—the question of the "archetype." To take one example: The world over, stories with happy endings end with weddings. "They lived happily ever after" is almost invariably preceded by "They were married." Why? To say "Weddings are happy occasions" is not sufficient, for many other things (getting a new job, watching a winter sunset, throwing a toddler in the air—and catching him) can also be happy occasions. To say that it reflects our wish for a better world merely raises the further questions of why humans are so incorrigibly wishful and why marriages should so frequently symbolize this wishfulness. Explaining this phenomenon in terms of the dynamics of marriage—the union of "opposites," the beginning of a new home, and so on—gets us closer to a real explanation, but we still want to ask why our imaginative search for harmony and new life is so often symbolized in *this* manner rather than another. The point can be made from a different angle: Try to imagine a *better* happy ending than a wedding. I believe we find imaginative satisfaction in stories that end with weddings because we live in a world that will end with a wedding. The Bible tells the story of history, a story that is mysteriously "built into" the structure of our minds and practices, so that even writers who resist this story cannot help but leave traces of it—faint and distorted as they may be—on every page.

Two lines of argument support this. First, there is the question of creativity. Human creativity is never the creativity of the Creator but always that of a creature. Though it is not quite right to say this places "limits" on our creativity, it does mean that we never produce anything that is absolutely unprecedented. Second, since God has revealed Himself in a particular story, and since His character is inescapably known to all creatures, this story is likewise inescapably known. Let me unpack these two arguments a bit.

The Bible has an exalted view of human creativity, and therefore of the human imagination. In Genesis 1:26–28, we learn that the Lord made Adam and Eve in His image and after His likeness. Commonly, the image of God in man is described in terms of "moral" attributes such as righteousness and holiness, or by reference to "rational" faculties such as the ability to reason and to will freely. Up to Genesis 1:26, however, God has revealed Himself as a Speaker and a Maker, and thus the immediate significance of being made His "image" is that Adam and Eve were created to speak and make. Adam's first task, significantly, is to name the animals (using speech to "make" a classification system—as God did during the creation week), and when Eve is born from his side, he composes a romantic poem. To be the image of God is to be a creative speaker and producer of "cultural" products—poems and speeches, houses and bridges, computers and combustion engines.

To say that being God's image means being a maker is not precise enough. Animals, after all, make things: beavers build dams, wasps make nests, rabbits dig labyrinthine warrens. This suggests that all animate creatures reflect God's creativity to some degree. Yet, animal "creativity" is purely functional, instinctual, and repetitive; they make things to meet the needs of survival, and their "creations" are always basically the same. Except in Narnia, beaver homes are not cozy bungalows; there is no Frank Lloyd Wright in the wasp community to introduce more environmentally sensitive architectural fashions; rabbits live in precisely the kind of cold and dark hovels that hobbits avoid. God, by contrast, created a world for which He had no need. He was perfectly God, and perfectly content, before the world was. Freely and in sheer love and goodness, He made something different from Himself. His making was not functional or repetitive or necessary for His survival as God. Rather, God's creativity is shown in creating a profusion of unnecessary things that display an unnecessary beauty—unnecessary things like the wild waste of color on tropical birds, like the unearthly softness of chinchilla fur, like you and me.

The creativity of God's images is like that. To be sure, much human creativity is expended to help us survive or to make survival more efficient and comfortable. But only humans create as God does. Only humans paint and draw for no other reason than to produce paintings and drawings; only humans make instruments and organize sound into music that hails men's souls from their bodies; only humans build homes not only for function but for pleasure and beauty. The difference between human and animal making goes to the simplest forms of human creativity: As Samuel Johnson said, no beast is a cook. None of this is "necessary" to sheer bodily survival. But precisely these extravagances make us human.

So, human creativity is real and it is profoundly creative. Yet, it is always the creativity of a creature, who is completely dependent upon the creating Spirit of God for his every breath. The Bible makes it clear that nothing a creature imagines or produces is "absolutely hypothetical" or absolutely free. Instead, Paul teaches that "of Him and through Him and to Him are all things" (Rom. 11:36). The Lord rules and brings into being every created thing and every event of history, and because they ultimately come from Him, every thing and every event bears the stamp of His character. God's character is manifested not only in the things He directly created, but also in things that human beings have made. Even what evil men and women produce cannot escape His comprehensive government. He reveals His delicate glory in the lilies and in the detailed brushwork of a van Eyck; His majesty in mountains and in the vertiginous heights of a cathedral ceiling; and His wrath in the destructiveness of a hurricane and in the horrors of war and civil strife. He has created us so we can create worlds in our imagination and construct them in words and paint and stone, but we imagine and construct those worlds within a world that is what the Bible says it is. We can imagine and write about a world where God is not, but this imagining and writing reveals the God who is.

God's sovereign rule as Creator does not form a limit on human creativity. On the contrary, we are creative only because the Creator is at work in us, only because "of Him and through Him and to Him are all things." In fact, far from imposing a limit on human creativity, God's inexhaustible creativity implies that human beings are in important respects inexhaustibly creative as well. Despite our limitations in space, time, and ability, God's infinite creativity is expressed in many ways through ours. Think of numbers. Even if I write down numbers from now until the day I die, twenty-four hours a day, I will never reach the end of the sequence. On the day I die, any ten-year-old could write down a number that I have never thought of, much less written. This may not seem like a good example of human creativity, since we often think of numbers as being "out there" ready to be discovered or named. That is debatable, but let me suggest another example: There is no limit to the ways I can arrange letters into words and words into meaningful sentences. With a few moments' reflection, I can create a sentence that no one has ever said or written in the history of the world (e.g., "My father is cool" or "His nose hairs make him especially handsome"). And I can keep doing that every day until I die and never empty the tank filled with sentences that might be written.

Though it is not correct to think of God's work as a limit on human creativity, the fact that we are creatures means that our creativity is the creativity of a created being, rather than the creativity of a Creator. And that means not only that our creativity is dependent upon His, but also that nothing we create is absolutely original. I can write a number that not even Albert Einstein thought of, but I can never think of or write a number that God has not thought of. I can write a sentence that never crossed Shakespeare's mind, but I will never utter a sentence that God does not know before it is on my tongue. God knows not only the number I write and the sentence I utter before I write and utter, but He knows and has eternally planned that I will write or utter it. Yet for all that, *because* of all that, my utterances and writings and makings produce something new. This is what it means to be a creative creature.

So much for the first thread of theological argument. I have argued that, in general, human creativity is not "absolutely free" but always preceded by and dependent upon God's creativity. This helps to explain why storytellers from the beginning of time seem continually to be repeating the same stories, though repeating them differently. It is because we are creatures who image our Creator in all we say and write and make. The second thread has to do with stories more specifically. Part of our inescapable imaging of God lies in the fact that the stories we tell inevitably reflect the story that God is telling in the history of the world. A number of points need to be considered to demonstrate this conclusion.

First, the Bible teaches that God reveals His character in creation, in history, and in Scripture. If we wish to know God, we have to seek Him as He has revealed Himself through these media. We cannot know God by peeking "behind" the screen of history and Scripture; we come to know Him *through* His words and works. History, Scripture, and creation are the "books" of God, and if we would know Him we must open the books. There is a fuller revelation in one or another of God's books. For example, we know about God's provision in Christ from Scripture rather than from creation. Yet it is the same God who writes to us in each. Each book, in fact, is large enough to include the others. If we open God's book of creation, we realize that the creation is not static but in motion, that creation has a history; thus God's revelation in creation includes His revelation in history. And since Scripture exists in history, it too forms a chapter in God's books of creation and history. History is the story of God's actions, which manifest His character, and Scripture is largely a record of those actions, that story.

Above, I said that we cannot speak, make, or act without imaging God. Now, we need to add that the God imaged in our speaking and making is not some abstract and unknown character, some God-in-general, but the God revealed in the story revealed in creation, history, and Scripture. If we cannot help but manifest God's character in our creations (including our story-telling), and if the character of God manifested in our creations is known through a story, it follows that we cannot help but retell His stories in our own. God's story tells of a good creation, marred by a rebellion and a curse, which is overcome by the coming of a Redeemer to restore the world. All other stories are contained in that basic story. This does not at all mean that every writer is self-consciously and deliberately writing Christian allegory. It means that, every writer tells stories that reflect in some way God's story.

To summarize:

1. God reveals His character in the story of history and Scripture.
2. We image God's character in all we make and do, including our artistic creations.
3. Since God's character is known by a story, we image God's story in all we do.
4. Therefore, our artistic creations image God's story.
5. Therefore, our stories reflect God's story.

There is thus some analogy between writing and other arts. A painter may wish to rebel against the created realities of light and color and paint, but those same created realities prevent his rebellion from ever being total. His rebellion is constrained by the materials he works with. A composer may wish to overthrow the created realities of sound, but those created realities oppose him. With writing, language itself provides some constraint; a poet who completely rebels against linguistic rules will be incomprehensible, and thus not a poet at all. Yet, writing is somewhat different, since the materials a writer works with exist largely within his imagination; the novelist does not deal with physical realities like paint and sound waves. Yet because of the way God created and governs the world, and because knowledge of the Creator and Governor of the world is inescapable, the rebellion of the imaginative writer is constrained. Somewhere, even in the stories of the most self-consciously rebellious storyteller, God's story shines through.

### Hesiod, Homer, and Moses

Above, I offered theological arguments in favor of a Christian reading of ancient pagan literature. In addition, various historical arguments can be advanced. The first arises from a biblical understanding of ancient history. The stories, imagery, and symbols of ancient literature can be understood from the viewpoint of Scripture because those stories and images were influenced by knowledge of the events recorded in Scripture. God promised Adam that He would send the seed of the woman to deliver humanity from the serpent, and from Adam that promise passed from generation to generation until the flood. Along the way, the story was distorted and half-forgotten, but the cultural memory of the promise at Eden's gate was never erased. After the flood, God reiterated His promises to Noah, and as the head of a new human race, Noah also passed on the promises of God to his sons, and they to theirs. These divine promises form the basis of the story of Scripture, and in various distorted forms they find their way into mythologies from around the world.[9] If Genesis is what Christians say it is, an accurate record of the ancient world, then all the peoples of the ancient world necessarily had at least indirect contact with Adam and/or Noah and with the stories of Eden and the flood.[10] Myths concerning a magical tree guarded by a serpent are recollections of Eden, Pandora is a distorted Eve, and hope for a delivering Hero was inspired by God's promise of the serpent-crushing Seed.

A second set of historical arguments has to do with the way Christians in the past have dealt with the inheritance of the pagan classics. Though it is often thought that the Renaissance recovered classical learning, much of this learning remained available during the Christian Middle Ages. In *The Discarded Image*, C. S. Lewis provides an excellent summary of the medieval debt to classical philosophy, cosmology, and literature, and many of the stories told in the medieval Christian world were derived from the legends of the pagan tribes of northern Europe. Poets and scholars combined Christian and pagan elements in a variety of ways, but in many cases Christians were clearly making an effort to set Greco-Roman and other pagan stories into a biblical framework.

A good illustration of the medieval Christianization of Greek stories is the treatment of Achilles. In Dante's *Inferno*, Achilles appears in Canto V among the lustful, with Dido, Cleopatra, and Helen. Virgil points him out to the pilgrim: "See great Achilles yonder, who warred with love, and that war was his last." Readers of Homer's *Iliad* will be perplexed. Achilles' great sin in the *Iliad* is not lust but wrath.

Yet, Dante's treatment is typical of the Medieval interpretations of Achilles. Sexual passion was more a key to his life and death than his rage. The *Ilias Latina*, a Latin summary of Homer's epic, was the main medieval source for the story of the *Iliad*, and this document describes how Achilles is led to act badly because he is desperately in love with his war bride, Briseis. Agamemnon's folly is also sexually induced, since he refuses to return Chryseis out of passion. Medieval writers also highlighted Achilles' love for Polyxena, a part of the Trojan War myth not found in Homer. Polyxena was daughter of King Priam and Queen Hecuba of Troy. She was watering horses at the well where Achilles killed Troilus, one of Priam's sons, and she caught Achilles' eye. According to one version of the story, she persuaded Achilles to switch to the Trojan side by promising to be Achilles' slave. According to another version, Achilles agreed to abandon the Greeks and fight for the Trojans so that he could have Polyxena. Negotiations were to be conducted in the temple of Apollo, but Paris was hiding behind the god's statue, and shot Achilles in the heel with an arrow as he entered the temple. Lust led directly to Achilles' death. For medievals, the moral of the *Iliad* is the same as the myth of Pandora: Women are dangerous, dangerous, dangerous, and they will sap your fighting spirit.

A remarkable blending of classical and biblical stories is found in the twelfth-century "Roman de Troie" of Benoit de Sainte-Maure, which has Achilles himself refer to Samson, David, and Solomon as examples of men who fell through lust. Another text recasts the story of Achilles and Polyxena so that it matches the story of Samson and Delilah:

> When Polyxena was married to Achilles who loved her exceedingly, she got a message from King Priam her father or Hekabe her mother, saying, "We believe that because you must grieve so greatly for your youthful brother [Hector], whom none dared attack, you must also find out for us the secret place in which Achilles can be breached with steel; and when he is dead and your brother's death is avenged, we will be able to give you to a better husband who is our equal." When Polyxena heard this, she took Achilles in her arms and charmingly challenged him to show her the secret place where he could be harmed by steel; and because there is nothing that woman cannot force men to confess when their dear spouses hold them, he showed her the secret place in the tendon of his heel where he could be harmed by steel. When

Polyxena learned this, she told it to her parents, who subsequently pretended to be having a service in the temple of Apollo... and asked Achilles to join them at the service along with Polyxena their daughter.[11]

Medieval interpretations of the classics are not always commendable and frequently laughable. Using the *Iliad* as a morality tale against sexual sin hardly counts as a fair interpretation of Homer's epic, to put it delicately. Medieval Christians often failed to understand pagan literature on its own terms but instead blithely assumed that it explicitly taught Christian truth.[12] However clumsy their efforts, they realized, rightly, that there are only two alternatives to fitting pagan stories into the biblical story: First, fitting the biblical story into pagan stories or, second, fitting both into some other story. And they recognized, again rightly, that if the Bible was not the "master story," another story would master the Bible.

## Conclusion

Throughout her history, the church's settled conviction has been that the devil has no stories. Satan is not creative but can only parody and ape and distort and misshape the true story. Even the stories that the devil appears to have are not properly his. Hesiod and Homer, Aeschylus and Aristophanes, as much as Moses and Samuel, are "for Christ." We must exercise great care and pray for wisdom in our study of this literature. We must never embrace enemies as friends or treat "Greek wisdom" as sound and true. Yet, it is fully within the rights of Christians, to whom, in Christ, belong "all things" (1 Cor. 3:21–23), to plunder these stories and make what use of them we can. Because some treasures of Athens, purged with fire, may, like the gold of Egypt, finally adorn Jerusalem.

*Notes:*

[1] Subtitled *The Demise of Classical Education and the Recovery of Greek Wisdom* (New York: Free Press, 1998).

[2] *Religion in the Ancient Greek City* (trans. Paul Cartledge; Cambridge: Cambridge University Press, 1994), p. 92. See also Francois de Polignac, *Cults, Territory, and the Origins of the Greek City-State* (trans. Janet Lloyd; Chicago: University of Chicago Press, 1995); Numa Denis Fustel de Coulanges, *The Ancient City: A Study of the Religion, Laws, and Institutions of Greece and Rome* (Baltimore: Johns Hopkins, 1980). An excellent brief summary is found in Christine Sourvinou-Inwood, "What is Polis Religion?" in Oswyn Murray and Simon Price, eds., *The Greek City: From Homer to Alexander* (Oxford: Clarendon Press, 1990).

[3] For a brief but heavily documented study of this, see Walter Burkert, *The Orientalizing Revolution: Near Eastern Influence on Greek Culture in the Early Archaic Age* (trans. Margaret E. Pinder and Walter Burkert; Cambridge, MA: Harvard University Press, 1992). See also Oswyn Murray, *Early Greece* (2d ed.; Cambridge, MA: Harvard University Press, 1993), ch. 6.

[4] (New York: Vintage Books, n.d.).

[5] On the medieval picture, see C. S. Lewis, *The Discarded Image: An Introduction to Medieval and Renaissance Literature* (Cambridge: Cambridge University Press, [1964] 1995). On Shakespeare's use of biblical imagery, see, for example, Nasseb Shaheen, *Biblical References in Shakespeare's History Plays* (Newark: University of Delaware Press, 1989).

[6] On this, see the wonderful study of Ernst Kantorowicz, *The King's Two Bodies: A Study in Medieval Political Theology* (Princeton: Princeton University Press, 1957).

[7] I first encountered this interpretation in Harold C. Goddard, *The Meaning of Shakespeare* (2 vols.; Chicago: University of Chicago Press, 1951), 1.215–268. See also Anthony Brennan, *Henry V* (Twayne's New Critical Introductions to Shakespeare #16; New York: Twayne Publishers, 1992).

[8] "Archetypal criticism" is, in fact, one of the schools of modern literary criticism. For a sophisticated discussion of this, linking Western literature to Scriptural patterns of imagery, see Northrop Frye, *The Great Code: The Bible and Literature* (New York: Harcourt, Brace, Jovanovich, 1982).

[9] On comparative mythology, see the works of Mircea Eliade and Joseph Campbell. Despite the flaws of Campbell's work especially, he has demonstrated the existence of common themes throughout world mythology.

[10] I have dealt with this theme at greater length in an essay, "Did Plato Read Moses?" which is available from Biblical Horizons, P.O. Box 1096, Niceville, Florida, 32588.

[11] Quoted in Katherine Callen King, *Achilles: Paradigms of the War Hero from Homer to the Middle Ages* (Berkeley: University of California Press, 1987), pp. 203–204.

¹² Thus, for example, one medieval commentator interpreted a reference to the "poets" in Cato's *Dystics* as a reference to "Holy Scripture." This example comes from a lecture by Louis Perraud, who teaches classics at the University of Idaho.

# Section I:

# Ancient Epic

## Introduction: Ancient Epic

In modern usage, the word *epic* has come to be a near synonym for *big* and *impressive*. Films like *Ben Hur* are said to have "epic sweep," Bob Costas describes the NBA Finals as an "epic battle," and a political speech may be delivered with "epic grandeur." In literary studies, *epic* sometimes takes on this general connotation. Though they do not conform to standard definitions of epic, both Dante's *Divine Comedy* and Spencer's *Fairie Queene* are sometimes said to be poems on an "epic scale." Frequently, however, the word is used in a more specific sense. Strictly speaking, an "epic" is a long narrative poem that focuses on a single hero who has national or cosmic significance. Epics recount deeds of great valor and include spiritual beings—gods, goddesses, angels, demons—among their casts of characters.

Though Virgil definitely wrote his epic poem, it is commonly believed that the other epics we will examine in the first several chapters originated in performances like that described in Book 8 of the *Odyssey*:

> By now they were serving out the portions, mixing wine,
> and the herald soon approached, leading the faithful bard
> Demodocus, prized by all the people—seated him in a chair
> amid the feasters, leaning it against a central column
>
> . . . . . . . . .
>
> Stirred now by the Muse, the bard launched out
> in a fine blaze of song, starting at just the point
> where the main Achaean force, setting their camps afire,

> had boarded the oarswept ships and sailed for home
> but famed Odysseus's men already crouched in hiding—
> in the heart of Troy's assembly—dark in that horse
> the Trojans dragged themselves to the city
> heights (8.528-531, 559-565).†

This scene illustrates a number of features of ancient epic. Poetry was at that time an oral art, sung or chanted by a bard and sometimes accompanied by a lyre. Some scholars believe that Homer himself wrote or dictated something like the epics we have today, but even if he did write, he was drawing on a tradition of spoken poetry. Poems were not, however, memorized and repeated verbatim. Rather, they were composed on the spot, so that each performance might differ in many details from others. Bards apparently had a mental stock of stories, descriptions, and scenes and could weave them together in countless different ways. The best analogy in the modern world is jazz music, which is usually not written in advance but improvised as it is performed. Bards were "jazz poets."

Epic poets use several standard poetic devises. Epics generally are introduced with a "proem," in which the poet announces the main character and theme of his story and calls on the Muses, goddesses of poetry and speech, to help him do justice to his theme. Most epics, moreover, begin *in medias res*, "in the middle of things." The *Iliad* does not begin like a fairy tale: "Once upon a time there was a man named Achilles." Instead, Achilles rudely bursts onto the page without waiting to be introduced, already in the middle of the Trojan War and already in the middle of an argument with Agamemnon. If we do not know the characters and setting already, we have to read a ways before we can figure out what is going on.

Epic similes are also a characteristic feature of epic poetry. A simile is a comparison of two things, as, for example, "My love is like a red, red rose." Literature scholars distinguish the primary and secondary subjects of similes. The primary subject is the thing that the poet is actually talking about (in this case, "my love"), and the secondary subject is the thing to which the poet is comparing the primary subject ("a red, red rose"). Epic similes expand the *secondary* subject of the simile. Thus, this is *not* an epic simile: "My love, who is very beautiful and delicate and whom I love deeply, is like a rose." That sentence expands the *primary* subject. The following *is* an epic simile (though doubtless a very bad one): "My love is like a red, red rose that blooms from a thorned vine upon the garden trestle, within which a bee, delighted, seeks for nectar." Similes in ancient epic are often reserved for battle scenes and compare warriors to animals, storms, fires, or sometimes to peacetime activities like hunting and fishing. Comparisons are rarely made in the simple form of, "Achilles was like a lion"; more often, they are like this, "Achilles was like a lion doing X and Y and Z." The expansion of the secondary subject (the X, Y, and Z) is not arbitrary, but, as we shall see, it has a specific connection to the action and themes of the poem.

Fixed descriptions or "epithets" are used in epic poetry for characters and things. Achilles is "swift" or "godlike," Hector is "breaker of horses," the Greeks are "long-haired," the sea is often "wine dark," and Dawn is always, always "rosy-fingered." At times the descriptions are appropriate to the scene; Achilles is "swift" while chasing Hector around Troy. Yet, these epithets may have other layers of meaning: Achilles' entire life passes "swiftly" and he is "swift" to react to Agamemnon's insult. In some instances, an epithet may be used for ironic effect. Achilles is called "swift" while sitting among his ships, but this highlights the oddness of his situation—a hero who has renounced battle. Similarly, Hector calls his father "Priam who hurls the strong ash spear" (*Iliad* 6.533), but this comes at the end of a speech predicting the fall of Troy, and, in any case, Priam is now too old to hurl his spear with any effect.

In some instances, the descriptions seem irrelevant to the scene and are used to meet the requirements of poetic meter. Meter in poetry has to do with the rhythm of a poetic line. In English, poetic rhythm is created by standard repeated patterns of stressed and unstressed syllables. Often, the pattern is subdued, but in other poems, such as Tennyson's "Charge of the Light Brigade," the rhythm comes powerfully to the surface. Below, the stressed syllables are capitalized:

> CANnon to RIGHT of them,
> CANnon to LEFT of them,
> CANnon in FRONT of them,
> VOLleyed and THUNdered.

Using emphatic rhythm in this way is appropriate to a poem about the clash and clamor of battle but would normally be out of place in, for example, a love sonnet (unless the poet wanted to suggest that love is a battle, which is true enough).

In Greek poetry, rhythm is created not by patterns of stressed and unstressed syllables but by varying the "length" of a syllable. Here, length literally refers to how long the vowel in each syllable is dragged out in speech: "Ooooo" is a long syllable, and "o" is short. Despite this difference in measuring poetic rhythm, the standard patterns of Greek poetry are much as they are in English. Both of Homer's epics are composed in a meter known as "dactylic hexameter." The word "dactylic" comes from the Greek word for "finger" and is used because the rhythm of a dactyl corresponds to the shape of a human finger. Starting at the hand, follow your index finger to the tip. You will notice, if you have not before, that it is divided into three segments, one longer segment followed by two shorter ones. Dactylic meter, therefore, is a rhythm of "long-short-short." "Hexameter" refers to the number of "dactyls" per line, six in this case ("hex" = six). Thus, a line of dactylic hexameter can be diagrammed as follows (L = long, S = short):

> L-S-S, L-S-S, L-S-S, L-S-S, L-S-S, L-S-S

To get the effect in English, Doug Wilson suggests that you say the word "strawberry" six times. Preferably in private.

Though dactylic hexameter is the bedrock of Homeric poetry, his lines are in reality more complex. Only two complexities can be noted here. First, instead of using dactyls throughout the line, Homer ends each line with two long syllables, called a "spondee." Thus, the line looks like this:

L-S-S, L-S-S, L-S-S, L-S-S, L-S-S, L-L

Two long syllables help to give a sense of completion at the end of each line. Second, there is normally a break in the sense of the line at the midpoint, and often the two resulting halves also break in the middle. In the following example, capitalized letters indicate a long syllable and a vertical line indicates a break in sense:

GO if you WILL | my dear PHOEbus | and WASH from his WOUNDS | the dark BLOODSTAIN

Here you can see the dactylic pattern and the spondee overlaid by a fourfold division of the line.

I began this digression on poetic meter in the middle of a discussion of Homeric "epithets," and it is time to explain why. Standard descriptions of characters do not appeal to us; if a modern novelist described one of his characters as "blue-eyed" every time he appeared, we would begin to think the author lacked imagination. Homer, however, used epithets partly because it helped him compose oral poetry that followed the rhythm of dactylic hexameter. Epithets differ in meter, and therefore one epithet will fit into a particular slot in the poetic line better than others. For example, "Achilles" is a short syllable and a spondee (S-L-L), and thus it can be used at the end of a line that already has nearly five dactyls in it. "Godlike Achilles" is a dactyl and a spondee (L-S-S, L-L), and thus it fits at the end of a line that already has four dactyls (see *Iliad* 1.7). "Swift-footed godlike Achilles" scans as S-L-L, L-S-S, L-L, and this meter limits the number of places it will fit. The general point is that epithets enable an oral poet to compose "on the spot" a poem that stays within a fixed rhythmic pattern.

On a larger scale, ancient poetry often uses "chiastic" or "concentric" patterns. "Chiasm," a term taken from the Greek letter "chi" (X), describes a poem, story, or other piece of writing organized in an A-B-B-A structure. In a chiastically arranged text, the first and last section match either by their similarity or contrast, and the middle two sections match each other in similar ways. The similarity between matching sections can be of several kinds. Sometimes similar imagery is used, sometimes a descriptive phrase or term is repeated, sometimes the same characters appear. Scripture is full of examples of this pattern. If we follow the Hebrew word-order of Psalm 73:3, for example, we find this arrangement:

> A. For I envied
> > B. the arrogant
> > B. the prosperity of the wicked
> A. I saw.

The two A sections describe the Psalmist's reaction to the wicked, while the B sections describe the wicked. Verse 6 is arranged as follows:

> A. Pride
> > B. is their necklace
> > B. like a garment
> A. violence covers them.

Here, the two B sections both employ clothing imagery, while the framing A sections describe the moral character of the unrighteous.

When chiasms are expanded, they are known as concentric or "ring" structures (e.g., A-B-C-D-C-B-A). Matching sections (A-A, B-B, *etc.*) are, as in chiasms, parallel or contrasting, and the central section is often a key turning point (a literary "hinge"). Gordon Wenham, for example, has shown that the entire flood narrative in Genesis 6–9 is arranged concentrically, with Genesis 8:1 ("And Yahweh remembered Noah") at the center. Up to that verse, the waters are rising, everything is being covered, and all living things are dying; after that verse, the waters begin to recede, mountains begin to appear, and new life begins to arise in a new creation.

To illustrate the value of recognizing such structures, let me use an extended biblical example, the story of David and Bathsheba in 2 Samuel 11–12. The story may be outlined as follows:

    A. 11:1: Joab is on the field besieging Rabbah, but David has stayed behind in Jerusalem.
      B. 11:2–5: David sleeps with Bathsheba and she becomes pregnant.
        C. 11:6–25: David arranges for Uriah's death.
          D. 11:26–27: Bathsheba mourns for Uriah.
            E. 12:1–15a: Nathan confronts David.
          D'. 12:15b–17: David mourns for his son.
        C'. 12:18–23: David's son dies.
      B'. 12:24–25: David sleeps with Bathsheba and she becomes pregnant.
    A'. 12:26–31: David goes to Rabbah and finishes the siege, then returns to Jerusalem.

First, this outline clarifies the "boundaries" of a section of text. If we follow the chapter headings of the Bible, we might be tempted to think that the story ends with 11:27, but in fact the same story has been broken up into two chapters. More likely, we might be tempted to think that 12:26–31 is part of a wholly different story, but seeing that it corresponds with 11:1 shows that this episode is integrated into the preceding sequence of events. Second, the central section of this text, Nathan's rebuke of David, forms the key transition in the story. This, with David's penitent response, is the crucial moment, for without Nathan's prophetic rebuke and David's sincere repentance, David's reign is in danger of ending as badly as Saul's did. Third, the "frame" (the "A" sections) sets the context for understanding the point of the entire story.

References to the siege at Rabbah make it clear that David's adultery is not just a private concern. This is not a story merely about personal sin and repentance but about David's failure as the Lord's anointed.

Finally, comparison of corresponding sections can enrich our appreciation of the text. 2 Samuel 11 begins with David remaining behind in Jerusalem while Joab fights at Rabbah; David is negligent in carrying on the Lord's wars. 2 Samuel 12 ends with David going out to Rabbah to claim it and to take the crown of its king. In between, David's faithfulness to his royal calling has been lost and renewed. A more subtle insight comes from comparing the C-D sequence with its corresponding D-C sections. Bathsheba mourns, as we expect, after her husband dies, but David, strangely, mourns *before* his son dies, and afterwards rises from the dust, changes clothes, worships in the Lord's house, and eats a meal. Here we have a shadow of the gospel: David sins and deserves to die, but that judgment is instead carried out on David's son. Since his punishment has been born by his son, David is released and goes out to take Rabbah. So also, by the death of David's Greater Son, we, who also deserve death, are raised from the dust, seated at the Lord's feast, and sent out to conquer. As we shall see, similar insights emerge when we recognize concentric arrangements in Hesiod, Homer, and Virgil.

Hesiod and Homer both produced their epics in the last third of the eighth century B.C. From Hesiod's poems, M. L. West draws these conclusions about his life:

> His father came from the Aeolian city of Cyme on the coast of Asia Minor, just south of Lesbos.... He had been a merchant seaman, but found it difficult to make ends meet and removed to Ascra, an out-of-the-way village on the eastern side of Mount Helicon in Boetia, presumably to make a living off the land. Here, it seems, Hesiod was born and brought up, together with his brother Perses.

About Homer we know even less. Doubts about the very existence of Homer have been raised through the centuries, but the contemporary consensus is that a man called "Homer" did live and was responsible in some way for at least the *Iliad*, though there is more dispute concerning the *Odyssey*. Traditions from the ancient world inform us that Homer was blind and that he was from the island of Chios, off the coast of present-day Turkey. Virgil's life is much better known, but since his historical circumstances are crucial to understanding his poem, I have included a brief sketch of his life in chapter 4.

*Notes:*
  † This is the translation of Robert Fagles (New York: Penguin, 1996).

## *Pagan Genesis:*
## Hesiod, *Theogony*

According to the Greek historian Herodotus, Homer and Hesiod, both poets of the eighth-century B.C., were "the men who created the theogony of the Greeks and gave the gods their names, and described their forms." A "theogony," according to the definition of M. L. West, is a literary work dealing with "the origin of the world and the gods, and the events which led to the establishment of the present order." By this definition, we can see that Hesiod's epic poem covers much of the same ground as the book of Genesis. Both books tell about the origins of the world, the establishment of the present order in heaven and earth, and the arrangement of human life and civilization. One of the key questions that we will examine throughout the chapter is how Hesiod matches up, or fails to match up, to Genesis.

West's definition helps us to see the unity of Hesiod's poem, which sometimes seems little more than a list of names. In essence, Hesiod is telling two parallel stories. In the first story, he describes the origin of the gods in the form of a genealogy. Genealogies were important in the ancient world, and there are several lengthy genealogical passages in the Bible (Gen. 10; 1 Chr. 1–9). *Theogony* traces several sets of descendants, beginning with the original four "gods"— Chaos or Chasm, Earth, Eros, and Tartarus—and climaxing with the Olympians, especially Zeus (whose name is a form of the word for god), along with his siblings, wives, and children. Because many of these gods double as places or things, the genealogy of the gods is also a record of the origin of the visible universe. The other story is known as a "succession myth," because it describes how the leader of each generation of gods is overthrown and succeeded by one of his sons. The succession of chief gods also climaxes with Zeus, and the *Theogony* is largely about his rise to prominence and his success in defending his position. For Hesiod, the triumph of Zeus and the Olympians is a triumph of truth, justice, and the Greek way.

One of Hesiod's techniques for arranging his poem is the ring or concentric construction, which I have described in the introduction to epic literature above. M. L. West has discovered a number of specific passages in Hesiod that are arranged in this manner. At the end of the first section of the prologue or *prooimion*, Hesiod refers to the Muses as those "who with their singing delight the great mind of Zeus father in Olympus" (p. 4).† Several lines follow that describe the content of the Muses's song, and the poet concludes by saying that "they sing of the family of men and of powerful Giants to delight the mind of Zeus in Olympus" (p. 4). Thus, these lines form a unit that begins and ends with references to the Muses' song that delights Zeus. A more complete ring is found in the description of Zeus's battle with the Titans:

   A. The Hundred-Handers, allies of Zeus
      B. The Titans and their prison
         C. The roots of earth and sea
         C. The sources of earth, sea, sky, Tartarus
      B. The Titans and their prison
   A. The Hundred-Handers

After the second A section, a new episode begins, involving a war between Zeus and Typhoeus.

On a larger scale, P. Walcott has pointed out that the poem includes five long stories, usually separated by genealogies or descriptive passages:

*Prooimion* (Prologue)
Earth and first generation of gods
    First story: Kronos overthrows Heaven
Descendants of Night, Pontos, and others
    Second story: Zeus overthrows Kronos
Sons of Iapetos
    Third story: Prometheus
    Fourth story: Zeus v. Titans
Description of Tartarus
    Fifth story: Zeus v. Typhoeus
Zeus established as king
Marriages of Zeus

If we focus on the stories, several structural features of the poem become clearer. First, the stories have an obvious progression, beginning with Zeus's family history, then describing his rise to preeminence, and finally recounting the battles in which he successfully defends and consolidates his power. After these triumphs, Zeus enters his rest by contracting a great number of marriages. Thus, the poem has a "comic" structure, giving a series of conflicts and threats and ending with Zeus distributing the spoils of battle, marrying dozens of wives, and living happily ever after.

Second, from one perspective, the stories are arranged according to an A-A-B-C-C pattern. The first and second stories are closely parallel, since in both a god overthrows his father and seizes power. Stories four and five are similar in that each describes one of the wars of Zeus, and similar details are repeated. To combat the Titans, Zeus enlists the aid of giants with "a hundred arms" springing "from the shoulders—unshapen hulks—and fifty heads grew from the shoulders of each of them" (p. 7; cf. p. 24), while Typhoeus has "a hundred fearsome snake-heads with black tongues flickering" coming "out of his shoulders" (p. 27). Descriptions of the two battles are also very similar. When Zeus fights the Titans, "long Olympus was shaken to its foundations by the onrush of the immortals; the heavy tremors of their feet reached misty Tartarus" (p. 23), and when he battles Typhoeus, "great Olympus quaked under the immortal feet of the lord as he went forth, and the earth groaned beneath him" (p. 28). The central story of the five, concerning Prometheus, is, significantly, the one most directly concerned with human life, which is Hesiod's focus in his *Works and Days*.

From another angle, the five stories are arranged concentrically:

    A. Triumph of children of Earth (Kronos)
       B. Triumph of children of Kronos (Zeus)
          C. Zeus and Prometheus
       B. Triumph of Zeus over brothers of Kronos
          (Titans)
    A. Triumph of Zeus over child of Earth (Typhoeus)

In the discussion below, I do not follow the order of Hesiod's poem. Instead, after a discussion of the *prooimion*, I consider stories 1–2 and 3–4 (Zeus's origins, rise to power, and wars) and then close with a detailed look at the central story, that of Prometheus, which describes the origins of human civilization.

### The Muses

The lengthy *prooimion* of the *Theogony* divides into two sections. Hesiod begins with an invocation of the "Muses of Helicon," but the poem then moves into more strictly autobiographical material that ends on page 4. In the following line, he again invokes the Muses and begins to describe their songs, origins, and functions. This second invocation of the Muse marks a second beginning.

In the first section, Hesiod tells his name and describes himself as a shepherd taught to sing by the Muses. Each of these details raises questions. First, the name *Hesiodos* means "one who emits a voice." Scholars have found no other examples of Greeks named Hesiod, and a number have suggested that the poet is employing a fictitious name that symbolizes his status as a poet. Second, when the Muses come to teach him to sing he is "tending his lambs below holy Helicon" (p. 3). Yet, the autobiographical section comes to an abrupt end with, "But what is my business round tree and rock?" Hesiod is apparently mocking the poetic devices he has been using to this point in the poem, as if to say "I am no shepherd. I have nothing to do with a pastoral landscape. I'm just pretending to be a shepherd because that is what poets are supposed to do."

When the Muses appear, they hardly speak with the melodious voices that we expect and do not even promise to tell the truth:

> Shepherds that camp in the wild, disgraces, merest bellies:
> we know to tell many lies that sound like truth,
> but we know to sing reality, when we will (p. 3).

The Muses give Hesiod a "branch of springing bay to pluck for a staff" and "breathed into me wondrous voice." These gifts, he says, equip him to "celebrate things of the future and things that were aforetime," especially concerning the gods and the Muses themselves (pp. 3–4). The staff is a mark of authority, and Hesiod's initiation as a poet has overtones of investiture as a priest or a prophet. Like Moses on the mount of Yahweh, Hesiod claims that he has been visited by gods and become their mouthpiece.

But what kinds of gods are these? If Hesiod is inspired by Muses who tell lies, is he warning us that we should not really trust what he says? Perhaps Hesiod's intention is to say something about the nature of poetry and of all art. No poetry or art can perfectly and exhaustively depict the world. Poets are always selective, and no painter can capture *every* detail of a scene on canvas. When we add to that the fact that all art employs "tricks" to make the artistic product seem real, it is possible to see why Hesiod's Muses could boast of their ability to "lie." Perhaps the Muses also mean to suggest that it is through these "lies" and tricks that poetry communicates truth. A deeper point emerges here as well, one that is crucial for understanding Greek religion and culture as a whole. Poetry is a gift of the gods, and such gifts are prominent throughout the *Theogony*. Especially in the Prometheus story, relations between gods and men involve giving and withdrawal of gifts, but the Prometheus story indicates that all divine gifts are, like the poetry of the Muses, ambiguous. They both deceive and tell the truth, and they bring both good and evil. Divine gifts, for the ancient Greek, are to be received not with thanksgiving but with a degree of suspicion. This is precisely the serpent's line of temptation to Eve. God, he tells her, commanded her not to eat from the tree of knowledge because He knew that "in the day you eat from it . . . you will be like God" (Gen. 3:5). Before Eve noticed that the fruit was good, she had already, sinfully, begun to distrust God's goodness.

Though the first section leaves a number of ambiguities, already Hesiod announces that the major theme of his own song will be—like the song of the Muses—Zeus and "the rest of the holy family of immortals who are for ever" (p. 3). In these lines, the list of gods runs from Zeus to "Night," which is the opposite of the genealogy of the gods later in the poem. By starting with Zeus in this first "genealogy," Hesiod shows that the king of the gods is his central concern. Though chronologically last, Zeus is the "source" and goal of the gods. This focus is evident also in the second section of the *prooimion*, where Hesiod mentions the two main themes of the Muses' song:

> They celebrate first in their song the august family of gods, from the beginning, those whom Earth and broad Heaven begot, and the gods that were born from them, givers of blessings. Second they sing of Zeus, father of gods and men, how far the highest of the gods he is, and the greatest in power. And again they sing of the family of men and of powerful Giants (p. 4).

Though this list begins with Earth and Heaven rather than Zeus, Zeus is again the main interest. As we have seen above, the second part of the prologue is framed by references to the delight that Zeus takes in the song of his daughters, the nine Muses, and this means that even the songs of Earth and Heaven ring with praise to Zeus. Moreover, Zeus is here depicted as the "mediator" between the early gods and the human race. By its order, the passage (Earth/Heaven—Zeus—men) indicates that Zeus is "father of gods and men."

Hesiod announces the theme of the poem a third time at the end of the *prooimion*. He again mentions the children of Earth and Heaven and Night, the rise of the Olympian gods, and how they "shared out their estate, and how they divided their privileges, and how they gained all the glens of Olympus in the first place." But here he also mentions a desire to sing of the origin of "the earth" and "the rivers, and the boundless sea with its furious swell, and the shining stars and broad firmament above" (p. 6). He will sing not only a theogony, but a cosmogony, the origins of the cosmos. He will sing a pagan Genesis.

The three summaries of the larger poem help us to refine the structure of the *prooimion* as described above:

Invocation of Muses
    Origins, from Zeus to Night
Encounter with the Muses
    Origins, from Earth/Heaven through Zeus to men
Description of the Muses' functions
    Origins, from Night to Zeus

For Hesiod, it seems accurate to say that "of Zeus, and through Zeus and to Zeus are all things." Zeus "mediates" between the ancient gods and the human race partly through the Muses. Hesiod's description of the Muses indicates something about his understanding of the place of poetry in human life. Poetry is a gift from Olympus, originating from Zeus and is an act of praise to the king of the gods. It also brings benefit to men. The Muses are daughters of Zeus and Memory, and through their inspiration the poet is able to "recall" events from the beginning of time. When the poet sings his delightful words about "the famous deeds of men of old, and of the blessed gods," the listener "soon forgets his sorrows and thinks no more of his family troubles" (p. 6). Poetic memory soothes the painful memories of life.

The Muses also have a more public role:

> Whomsoever great Zeus's daughters favour among the kings that Zeus fosters, and turn their eyes upon him at birth, upon his tongue they shed sweet dew, and out of his mouth the words flow honeyed, and the peoples all look to him as he decides what is to prevail with his straight judgments. His word is sure, and expertly he makes a quick end of even a great dispute. This is why there are prudent kings: when the peoples are wronged in their dealings, they make amends for them with ease, persuading them with gentle words (p. 5).

Modern people think poetry is sharply distinct from political life. We read poetry as we listen to music, to escape from the clamor of the public square. For Hesiod and the Greeks, however, poetry and political rhetoric come from the same source. Politicians able to soothe an unruly crowd exercise the same divine gift as the poet who soothes private memories.

In part, this different conception of the role of poetry has to do with a difference in the setting in which poetry existed. Today, poetry is a private thing; we *read* books of poetry, if we read poetry at all, silently to ourselves. By contrast, Hesiod's poetry, like Homer's, was primarily an oral art, chanted or sung in a public setting rather than written for people to read in armchairs. The main setting for the recitation of poetry was the public gathering for a feast. Several times in Homer, we see scenes where poets are asked to recite a story for people gathered in a great hall. Odysseus's account of his travels in *Odyssey* 9–12 is delivered in such a setting, and we shall see that Odysseus tells his tale as a "bard." Though as Christians we cannot accept Hesiod's belief in the Muses, his view that poetry is a public form of speech has much to recommend it. Israel's prophets attacked her sins and delivered Yahweh's offer of mercy; their role was necessarily a public and even political one. Yet, Isaiah, Jeremiah, Ezekiel and the "minor prophets" were all poets, delivering the oracles of God in language of astonishing power and beauty. Taking a more recent example, try to think of the Civil Rights movement without thinking of Martin Luther King, Jr.'s resonant and poetic evocation of a world without prejudice. "I have a dream" is moving poetry. It is also shrewd policy.

*Review Questions.*
  1. What is a "theogony"?
  2. What two main stories does Hesiod's *Theogony* tell?
  3. Describe the concentric arrangement of the passage concerning the battle between Zeus and the Titans.
  4. How are the five major stories of the *Theogony* organized?
  5. Describe the structure of the *prooimion*.
  6. Describe some of the ambiguities of the first section of the *prooimion*.
  7. How does Hesiod make clear that Zeus is the central character of his poem?
  8. Who are the Muses? What is their role?
  9. In what sense do the Muses "lie"? What might this say about the nature of art?
  10. How does Hesiod connect poetry and political rhetoric? How does this differ from the modern view of poetry?

*Thought Questions.*
  1. Read the first book of Ovid's *Metamorphosis*. How does Ovid's account of the origins of the gods differ from Hesiod's? How are they the same?
  2. Read an encyclopedia article on early Greek history. What was happening in the eighth century B.C.? What

period of Greek history does Hesiod fit into?

3. What do the Muses do on Mount Helicon? What does this suggest about their functions? (p. 3)

4. In what kind of setting does Hesiod meet the Muses? Why is this significant? (p. 3)

5. Besides Zeus and Night, what deities are mentioned in the first list of gods? (p. 3)

6. How were the Muses born? (p. 4)

## The Birth and Battles of the Gods

Above, we examined how the five main stories are arranged in the *Theogony*. As Hesiod wrote the poem, however, the stories are embedded in extremely detailed and complex genealogical lists. To understand the stories, it is important to have some grasp of the flow of the genealogies. They are arranged in a series of cycles, each of which covers a related set of generations. A chart, or several, may help. Cycle one, the first set of lists, can be summarized as follows:

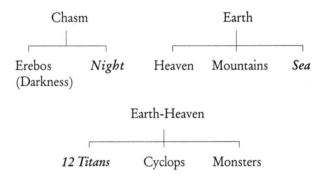

This first genealogical cycle ends with the youngest of the Titans, Kronos, overthrowing his father and taking his position as the chief of the gods.

Cycle two also has a triple structure, and each of the sections matches the corresponding section in the first cycle. Night is one of the children of Chasm in the first cycle, and her children are listed in the first section of the second cycle.

Sea is one of the children of Earth, and his children are listed in the second portion of the second cycle. Kronos's children are the focus of the third section of cycle two. The main difference between the cycles is that the second is much more elaborate:

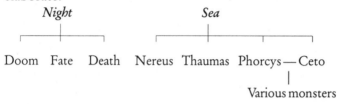

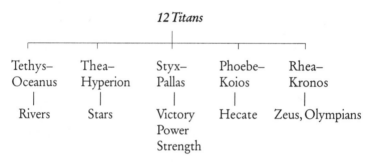

Note that the second cycle, like the first, ends with a change in leadership, when Zeus overthrows Kronos as Kronos had overthrown Heaven. Thus, to summarize:

*First Cycle*
Chasm's children
Earth's children
Heaven and Earth's children
Kronos overthrows Heaven

*Second Cycle*
grandchildren through Night
grandchildren through Sea
grandchildren through Kronos
Zeus overthrows Kronos

A number of parallels between Hesiod's genealogy and the biblical account of creation may be noted. The Bible opens with the words, "In the beginning, God created the heaven and the earth. And the earth was formless and void, and darkness was on the face of the deep" (Gen. 1:1–2). During the first three days of the creation week, the Lord separates night and day, heaven and earth, and waters and sea, and, in the following three days, He fills each realm with suitable creatures. Compare Hesiod:

> First came the Chasm; and then broad-breasted Earth, secure seat for ever of all the immortals who occupy the peak of snowy Olympus; the misty Tartara in a remote recess of the broad-pathed earth; and Eros, the most handsome among the immortal gods.... Out of the Chasm came Erebos [the realm of darkness] and dark Night, and from Night in turn came Bright Air and Day, whom she bore in shared intimacy with Erebos. Earth bore first of all one equal to herself, starry Heaven, so that he should cover her all about, to be a secure seat for ever for the blessed gods; and she bore the long Mountains, pleasant haunts of the goddesses, the Nymphs who dwell in mountain glens; and she bore also the undraining Sea and its furious swell, not in union of love. But then, bedded with Heaven, she bore deep-swirling Oceanus (pp. 6–7).

"Chasm" (Greek, *chaos*), which West describes as a dark "yawning space" beneath the earth, parallels the "deep" of Genesis 1:2. Both Hesiod and Genesis view creation as a series of separations, and the separations are in the same order: Day and night are the first creatures made, and in both texts night precedes day (Gen. 1:1–5); Hesiod's description of Earth "giving birth" to Heaven resembles the Lord's action on Day 2, when He places the firmament between the waters below and waters above, separating the waters of heaven and earth (Gen. 1:6–8); and the birthing of mountains and sea is similar to the separation of waters and land on Day 3 of creation (Gen. 1:9–10).

Hesiod and the Bible, moreover, describe the structure of the resulting cosmos in similar terms. Proverbs 8:30 describes Wisdom as a "master workman" who assisted the Lord in creating and organizing the world. Thus, the world is being pictured as a "cosmic house," often with three stories. The second commandment, for example, forbids bowing to images of anything in "heaven above, earth beneath, or the waters under the earth" (Ex. 20:4). Heaven is the roof, earth is the main floor, and the seas form the (flooded) "basement" of the world. Hesiod's conception is similar. After Kronos forcibly separates Heaven and Earth (see below), the universe is divided into three main regions: heaven, earth, and sea. Children of Heaven and Earth are associated with one or the other of these regions: The children of Oceanus and Tethys are rivers (p. 13), while the children of Hyperion and Thea, as well as those of Kreios and Eurybia, are stars or planets (pp. 13–14). Zeus honors Hecate by giving her "a share both of the earth and of the undraining sea. From the starry heaven too she has a portion of honor" (p. 15). During Zeus's battle with Typhoeus, the whole universe is in an uproar: "All the land was seething, and sky, and sea" (p. 28).

To these Hesiod sometimes adds a fourth region, Tartarus, which is most elaborately described in the account of the war with the Titans. Tartarus is "as far below the earth as heaven is from earth," so that it takes nine days for an anvil to fall from earth to the bottom of Tartarus. It is below the "roots of the earth and of the undraining sea," where "darkness is spread about its neck in three layers." Here the Titans are confined after Zeus's victory, and Poseidon keeps them in Tartarus by fastening "bronze doors" and building a wall (pp. 24–25). Tartarus appears in later Greek mythology as a region similar to the biblical hell.

Despite these similarities between Hesiod and the Bible, the differences are even more striking. The most obvious difference appears immediately. According to Genesis, "God created the heavens and the earth," and throughout the Bible this Creator rules all things. This is different from the Greek myth in three crucial ways. First, Hesiod's myth is not really a creation story, since there is no "creator." Chasm just *is*, and Earth also pops up from nowhere to give birth to the rest of the cosmos. Eros—the god of sexual love—is available to make sure that the various gods unite to form new gods. In Scripture, the formless emptiness of earth in Genesis 1:2 is the product of the Creator's original speech. Thus, second, for the Greeks, the world is as eternal and divine as the gods themselves. In fact, Earth and Heaven are *older* than the Olympian gods, who are not born for two more "generations." As Hesiod's title indicates, he is telling the story of the "origins" of the gods, their birth and their "genealogy." For the Bible, God has no "genealogy," no "origins." He and He alone simply *is*, and there is no other.

Finally, all of this reflects the basic Greek view that the universe is a "great chain of being." There are two ways to think about how God relates to the world. In the Christian view, God is different from the world—"above it." At the same time, He personally and actively controls every detail of history and nature, acting within creation and controlling it without being subject to created limits. In the Greek view, the gods and the world are not basically different from one another but are at different ends of a continuum. Think of a totem pole. At the top of the pole is the god of the tribe, and as you go down you find lower and lower forms of life—men, women (!), large animals, toads, etc. Gods are higher, bigger, stronger, and wiser, but lower beings are of the same "stuff." In *Theogony*, Zeus has more power than other beings, but Zeus is no more "god" than Earth herself. This is why Zeus can have sex with mortal women and why some human beings can rise up to the level of the gods by performing heroic and glorious deeds.

Other differences between Genesis and Hesiod appear as the story progresses. One key difference has to do with the source of creativity and renewal. In Scripture, the source of all creative power is God Himself. When, in the days of Noah, the world was corrupted and needed to be renewed, the Lord Himself sent the flood to cleanse the face of the land. For Hesiod, by contrast, Earth is the fertile source of rebirth. With Heaven, she gave birth to the original order of the world. And, when Heaven mistreats his children, Earth advises Kronos how to overthrow him, and later, when Kronos repeats his father's mistakes, Earth again intervenes to help Zeus. Both Kronos and Zeus are symbolically "children" of Earth. Kronos is "hid away... in a cavern of Earth" (p. 7) and later Zeus is hidden "in a cave hard of access, down in the secret places of the numinous Earth" (p. 17). From this perspective, the *Theogony* is about a succession of worlds given birth by Earth. She is "creator" and "recreator." The gods who renew the order of the world are twice born; emerging from the womb of Earth, they are "of the earth, earthy."

Earth and her children create and organize the world through violence, war, or sex. Earth gives birth without sex to Heaven, but then the two unite (no doubt with the help of Eros) to produce Kronos and his siblings. Heaven hates all his children and jealously refuses to share his sovereignty with them. So he hides them in a dark cavern within their mother, Earth, until Kronos frees them. Kronos tells Earth he is willing to overthrow Heaven, and

> mighty Earth was delighted. She set him hidden in ambush, put the sharp-toothed sickle into his hand, and explained the whole strategem to him.
> Great Heaven came, bringing on the night, and, desirous of love, he spread himself over Earth, stretched out in every direction. His son reached out from the ambush with his left hand; with his right he took the huge sickle with its long row of sharp teeth and quickly cut off his father's genitals, and flung them behind him to fly where they might (p. 8).

By this violent attack on his father, Kronos separated Heaven and Earth, forming the world we now know, with blue sky above and green earth below.

Kronos apparently learns nothing from his own childhood traumas and treats the children he fathers with Rhea in much the same way, swallowing each as they come from Rhea's womb, until Hestia, Demeter, Hera, Hades, and Poseidon have all been swallowed whole. Distraught at her husband's behavior, Rhea runs to Earth and Heaven ("Mom and Dad") to complain. They assure her that Kronos is already fated to receive due punishment, and at their suggestion, Rhea hides her youngest son, Zeus, in a cavern within Earth. To ensure that Kronos has no suspicions, Rhea wraps a stone in a blanket and delivers the substitute to Kronos. Meanwhile,

> Rapidly then [Zeus's] courage and resplendent limbs grew; and when the due time came round, the great crooked-schemer Kronos, tricked by the cunning counsel of Earth, defeated by his son's strength and strategem, brought his brood back up [i.e., he vomited the children he had swallowed] (pp. 17–18).

Having overthrown Kronos who had overthrown his father, Zeus claims supreme kingship, but his claim is tested by three battles. The first is against his "uncles"—the other children of Heaven and Earth, known collectively as Titans. Zeus enlists the help of other monstrous, children of Heaven and Earth who had been confined in the dark recesses of earth—the hundred-armed, fifty-headed giants Obriareos, Kottos, and Gyges. These assault the Titans with rocks, so that Zeus triumphs, confining the Titans below the earth, "down in the misty gloom" (pp. 24–25), while Zeus and the other leading Olympians divide the universe into three sections: Zeus takes the sky and earth, Poseidon the sea, and Hades the underworld.

Unlike his father and grandfather, Zeus is willing to share his domain and honor with his siblings, and with other deities like Styx and Hecate (pp. 14–15). Like a good king, Zeus ascends on high and gives gifts. This is what makes his rule just. So far as Hesiod is concerned, the victory of Zeus as "king and lord" of immortals and humans, is all for the good. But the story of his triumph over the Titans gives cause for alarm. Zeus enlists the aid of some of the monstrous children of Heaven and Earth, who were so loathsome at birth that Heaven put them back in Earth's womb, deep in an unlighted cavern. After driving the Titans into Tartarus, trapped behind Poseidon's bronze doors, the three monsters are appointed as "trusty guardians of Zeus" (p. 25). Zeus brings a peace and justice that depends on monstrous guardians. Olympus rules only with the help of the giants. Their cooperation with darker powers is a major theme of Greek tragedy and is also evident in Virgil's *Aeneid*.

Zeus's second contest is a battle of wits with Prometheus, which we shall examine in the following section. His last battle is with the youngest child of Earth, Typhoeus, a contest between the Olympian "son" of Earth and his monstrous "brother." Again a cosmic battle follows, ringing through heaven, earth, and sea, shaking Olympus, and heating the land until it "seethes." This time, however, Zeus needs no help from his monstrous henchmen. Casting a thunderbolt at Typhoeus, he "scorched all the strange heads of the dreadful monster on every side" so that he "collapsed crippled, and the huge earth groaned" (p. 28).

In each case, the chief god wins or defends his dominion by ambush (as in Kronos's victory over Heaven), trickery (Kronos and Zeus both deceive their fathers to take control), or outright war (Zeus's war against the Titans and Typhoeus). Violence is, for Hesiod, a normal feature of divine life. Hesiod's imagery suggests that even when some part of the world is born sexually, war is involved. He describes the noise of the battle between Olympians and Titans with this striking image: "it seemed just as if Earth and broad Heaven above were coming together, for even such a mighty din would be arising with her being crashed down upon and him crashing down from above" (p. 24). There is little to choose between sex or war; both involve the violent clash of opposites.

This story of a violent succession of gods is not an invention of Hesiod. In a number of details, Zeus's story, especially his triumph over Kronos, closely follows myths from the Ancient Near East, that is, the world of the Bible. In recent decades, classical historians have increasingly acknowledged the similarities between Ancient Greek artistic styles, language, myths, and rituals and those of the Ancient Near East. As the Swiss historian Walter Burkert put it, the

Greeks of the seventh century B.C. (700–600 B.C.) experienced an "orientalizing revolution," a revolution from the East. Hesiod stands close to the beginning of this period, and his work shows more obvious signs of Eastern influence than Homer.

West summarizes the similarities between the Hittite mythologies (which are based on earlier Hurrian stories) and the *Theogony* of Hesiod:

> [In the Hittite myths] there are four generations of rulers instead of three; but the first king, Alalu, is a nonentity. The second, Anu, is the Akkadianized form of the Sumerian An = Sky, and he therefore corresponds to Uranos [Heaven] in name as well as in rank. He had no cult among the Hittites. Like Uranos, he is castrated, and gods are born from his severed members. The third king, Kumarbi, like Kronos, castrates his father and swallows his son, and (probably) a stone. In a Hurrian text from Ras Shamra, Kumarbi is equated with El and the Greeks identified the Phoenician El with Kronos; the "identity" of Kronos and Kumarbi is thus indirectly confirmed. The fourth king is the Weather-god, who is the chief god, corresponding to the Greek Zeus. He survives Kumarbi's attempt to destroy him, and is victorious in a theomachy [war of the gods]. Like Zeus again, he is threatened even after his victory by a prodigious monster, and defeats him.

Genesis 1, in contrast to both the Hittite and Greek myths, contains no hint of conflict. God sovereignly and creatively speaks the world into existence. The world is the product of language, the Word of the Father, not of sex or violence or violent sex. Creation is a sheer gift of love from a Creator who has no need to make the world at all. Of course, the Bible recognizes the reality of evil, but it teaches that the original creation was a place of harmony and peace, a mirror of the eternal communion within the Triune God Himself. Wrath and discord come only because of Adam's disobedience, and in the new heavens and earth they shall be finally eliminated. In the Greek world, salvation from conflict and evil is impossible. Everything is conceived in violence and will always be violent. Zeus forever remains allied to the monsters.

The "comic" epic of Hesiod ends with several of Zeus's marriages. Warfare that ends with marriage is a common motif in literature, from King David killing two hundred Philistines to win the hand of Michal to Prince Charming battling the dragon to rescue Sleeping Beauty to Jesus leading his armies to victory just before the Bride descends from heaven (Rev. 19–21). Linked with this is the "victory-house building" pattern frequently found in Scripture. After David defeats the Philistines, he wishes to build the Lord's house, but instead the Lord promises to build him a house—a house of descendants (2 Sam. 7). Jesus came to defeat Satan in His death and resurrection and is now at work building His church, against which the gates of hell will not prevail. Similarly in this story, Zeus, having defeated the rivals of his throne, begins to build his house, gathering his harem and fathering many children. Having won his victory, Zeus enters into his rest.

Each marriage reveals something about the character and "attributes" of Zeus. Zeus first marries "Metis," whose name means "cunning" or "cleverness." Metis gives birth to Athena or Tritogeneia, who possesses "courage and sound counsel equal to her father's." Unwilling to part with Athena's qualities, "Zeus put her away in his belly first, so that the goddess could advise him of what was good and bad" (p. 29). Zeus is thus (as Homer puts it) "resourceful Zeus," full of cunning, clever disguises, and shrewdness. That is an ambiguous description, for cunning can be a good or bad quality depending upon what one is being cunning about. His second marriage has more positive offspring. From his marriage to Themis ("right order" in nature and society), Zeus fathers the "Watchers"—Lawfulness, Justice, and Peace (p. 29). Thus Zeus, in cooperation with proper order, brings justice and peace to a community. As noted above, the orders of Heaven and Kronos were flawed because each god was willing to kill his children rather than share his realm with them. Zeus establishes right order because he distributes honors (*timai*) to the other Olympians, who share in his rule. Hesiod is moving here from mythology to political thought, and later Greek philosophers adopt his terminology, though they gradually strip away the mythic clothing.

Though there are formal similarities between Zeus's story and stories from the Bible, the end of Hesiod's epic shows that there are tremendous differences between Zeus and Yahweh. The difference is not, however, that Zeus has many brides and Yahweh has none. Rather, the difference is that Zeus has many brides and Yahweh has only one, His church. Yahweh is monogamous, the husband of one wife, while Zeus is a philanderer on a scale that even Bill Clinton will never rival. Surrounded by minor deities, Zeus wants to make sure that he has everything they have. Being the One and only God, Yahweh has all good in Himself, and since He is One, He can have only one Bride. The story of Yahweh ends like the story of Zeus, with a wedding. For the Bible too is a, or rather, *the* "comedy."

*Review Questions.*
    1. Explain the structure of the two cycles of genealogies.
    2. How is Hesiod's account of the origin of the universe similar to Genesis 1?
    3. Describe the "three-decker" universe in Hesiod and the Bible.
    4. What is Earth's role in the reorganization of the world under Kronos and Zeus? How are these two gods "sons" of Earth?
    5. How does Kronos overthrow his father?
    6. How does Zeus come to power?
    7. Describe the two battles of Zeus after he becomes the chief god.
    8. Explain some parallels between Hesiod's myth and the myths of the Ancient Near East.
    9. Why is it appropriate for the *Theogony* to end with a list of Zeus's marriages?

10. Explain the significance of the various "wives" that Zeus takes.

*Thought Questions.*
1. Who are the Cyclops? What is characteristic of them? How did they help Zeus? (p. 7)
2. Who is born from the genitals of Heaven? What is the significance of this? (pp. 8–9)
3. Explain the significance of Aphrodite's names (p. 9).
4. Describe some of the children of Ceto and Phorcys (pp. 11–12).
5. Who is Hecate? What is her relation with Zeus? (pp. 15–16)
6. Compare the descriptions of Styx on pages 14–15 and 26–27.
7. Who are Apollo and Artemis? Whose children are they? (p. 30)
8. Who was Zeus's child by Alcmene? (p. 31)
9. What do all the goddesses on pages 32–33 have in common?
10. Who are Odysseus's children? How does this differ from Homer's Odysseus? (p. 33; see chapter 3)

## Prometheus and the Gifts of the Gods

It is striking that Hesiod nowhere tells how human beings were first made, though in another work, *Works and Days*, Hesiod tells about the five ages of man, another motif borrowed from the East. Originally, "gods and mortal men have come from the same starting point," yet men have gradually degenerated from that origin. First men were made of gold and lived in a Paradise where work and misery did not exist. Why this age came to an end Hesiod does not say. After the golden age came the silver age, during which men suffered because of their own witlessness and crimes. Silver men were eventually put away by Zeus because they refused to pay homage to the Olympians. Bronze men followed and were "a terrible and fierce race, occupied with the woeful works of Ares and with acts of violence." These were "laid low by their own hands." After them came the race of heroes, who lived during the time of the Trojan War, some of whom were given a life on the Isles of the Blessed Ones. Finally, Hesiod himself lived in the "fifth race," a race of iron, that "will never cease from toil and misery by day or night, in constant distress, and the gods will give them harsh troubles." Iron men, like the others, are doomed to be destroyed (*Works and Days*, p. 40).

None of this appears in *Theogony*. Men appear only as marginal characters in the succession wars of the gods. Despite the brevity of his description, Hesiod tells about the origins of basic practices of human life, which are the focus of the stories of Prometheus, the son of Kronos's brother Iapetos (who might be in some way related to the biblical Japheth). This link with biblical genealogies suggests that Hesiod is presenting a garbled version of real history, as recorded in Scripture. Even the titanic characters in Hesiod's work have parallels in the Bible's account of early history. The Bible records that there were giants (Nephilim) in the earth from ancient times (Gen. 6:4), and 2 Peter 2:4 refers to angels being cast into Tartarus, which is the place reserved for Titans in Hesiod's account. Prometheus's genealogy is important to understand his place in Hesiod's world. He is not an Olympian, but he is not a mortal either. In each of the three stories that Hesiod tells, he takes the side of human beings against Zeus, though it seems less out of love for men than out of resentment against the Olympians.

The first story has to do with the origins of Greek sacrificial practice. Sacrifice was central to all ancient religion, including Israel's, and to understand the importance of this story we need to reflect on its meaning. We use the word "sacrifice" to mean "giving up" something that is dear to us. When we help a poor person beyond the expected degree, we act "sacrificially"; a baseball player "sacrifices" his own batting statistics to advance a runner to third; a soldier makes the ultimate "sacrifice" by giving his life for his comrades or country. When applied to religion, we think of "sacrifice" as giving up of an animal or some gift to God or the gods. Though this element is present in ancient understandings of sacrifice, it is not fundamental. Instead, what is crucial is the link sacrifice establishes between God and men, and this connection frequently involves meals. The Hebrew word for sacrifice means "slaughter" and refers to the killing of an animal in preparation for a common meal as well as for a religious ritual. In the Bible, the sacrificial meat that is burned on the altar is called God's "bread" (Leviticus 21:21), and the priest and sometimes the worshiper ate from this same meat. Sacrifice thus had to do with the common meal that God and men share at the Lord's altar, which is also His table. As Jean-Pierre Vernant, a scholar of ancient Greek religion, points out, in Greek the verbs for "butcher" and "sacrifice" are the same. To "sacrifice" means to kill and prepare an animal for a sacred meal.

In both Hebrew and Greek sacrifice, different amounts of sacrificial meat were distributed to different people, depending on a person's place in the community. In the Old Testament peace offering, for example, the fat and inner organs—considered the best portions—were offered to the Lord, the breast and right thigh were given to the priests, and the remainder of the food was given to the worshiper (Lev. 7:28–36). In many Greek sacrifices, the one presiding at the sacrifice received a special portion, as did some of the leading men of the group. Sacrifice was a central part of the religion of the Greek city-state, and again the distribution of the meat reflected rankings within the city. Some feasts were reserved for the leaders of the city, and in many cases non-citizens were not allowed to participate in sacrificial feasts at all. When they did share the meal, they had to accompany a citizen. Feasts provided a small glimpse of the arrangement of the city.

When we put these two features of sacrifice together, we can understand something of the significance of sacrifice to the Greeks. On the one hand, the fact that men shared the same meat as the gods meant that gods and men were table fellows and friends. On the other hand, the way sacrificial flesh was distributed showed that there was also a distance between them. Sacrifice was a reminder of the closeness and the distance of the gods. Each sacrifice told the worshiper that men no longer lived in the golden age, when men sat across from the gods at the same table.

Sacrifice, like the structure of the world itself, is the product of rivalry and trickery, though this time Zeus is on the receiving end of the trick:

> When gods and mortal men were coming to a settlement at Mekone, [Prometheus] had carved up a big ox and served it in such a way as to mislead Zeus. For him he laid out meat and entrails rich with fat in the hide, covering it in the ox's stomach, while for men he laid out the ox's white bones, which he arranged carefully for a cunning trick by covering them in glistening fat.... With both hands [Zeus] took up the white fat; and he grew angry about the lungs, and wrath reached him to the spirit, when he saw the white ox-bones set for a cunning trick. Ever since that, the peoples on earth have burned white bones for the immortals on aromatic altars (p. 19).

Several features of this story are noteworthy. First, the distribution of the sacrificial animal is very different from that in the Bible. In the Old Testament "burnt offering," all the animal's flesh was given to the Lord (Lev. 1), and in other sacrifices the best portions—the fat and internal organs—were always placed on the altar (Lev. 3:3–4; 4:8–10). In Greek sacrifice, the gods are given bones and the fat, while the meat and internal organs are eaten by men. Second, this distribution highlights the distance between the immortal gods and mortal men. According to the Greek conception, men are "bread eaters" and "meat eaters," while the gods feed on ambrosia and in sacrifice receive fat and bones that have been turned into smoke. Meat-eating men become hungry and have to be filled again and again. Their life is necessarily a life of unfilled desire and lack. The fact that Prometheus places the meat in a stomach highlights this aspect of human life. Stomachs constantly need to be filled, and this turns man, in Vernant's words, into a "meat sack."

In *Works and Days*, Prometheus's trick is referred to only in passing, but there Hesiod adds an important detail. As part of the condition of men after the golden age, "the gods keep men's food concealed: otherwise you would easily work even in a day enough to provide you for the whole year without working" (p. 42). Unlike the golden age, when men could find sufficient food without labor, Zeus has now hidden food in the earth. Man has to plant, water, and toil to "uncover" the grain foods "concealed" in the earth. This is Zeus's fitting punishment for Prometheus's trick of "concealing" the meat inside the stomach.

In *Theogony*, Zeus responds to Prometheus's "hiding" of the meat by "hiding" fire: "with his anger ever in mind, [Zeus] would not give to the ash-trees the power of untiring fire for mortal men who live on earth" (p. 20). The parallel of Prometheus's trick and Zeus's response is clearer in *Works and Days*, where Hesiod says that Zeus "concealed fire," and the word in Greek for "concealing" fire is the same as that used for "covering" the bones in fat. Control of fire is one of the unique characteristics of human life. Fire is one of the key lines between civilization and savagery. Man without fire is a beast, forced to eat meat raw, struggling to warm himself, unable to work with metals and materials that are necessary to a technically advanced civilization. Winning the chief portion of the sacrifice was an act of pride, man's attempt (through Prometheus) to better Zeus. Zeus's response reduces man to the level of a beast, without fire, without cooking.

Prometheus again comes to man's rescue, ensuring that humans will not remain at the level of the beasts: "the noble son of Iapetos outwitted [Zeus] by stealing the far-beaconing flare of untiring fire in the tube of a fennel"

(p. 20). Though a great gift to man, fire is ambiguous, both beneficial and dangerous. Moreover, the fire that Prometheus brings to man is not the everlasting fire of Olympus but the "mortal" fire of earth. Like the stomach in which he concealed man's meat, the fire of Prometheus symbolizes the human condition. As Vernant puts it,

> It is a perishable fire, created, hungry, and precarious, like all mortal creatures. To start it requires a seed of fire, kept beneath the ashes or carried in the hollow of a fennel stalk in the Promethean manner. To keep it alive is must be fed. It dies when it is not nourished. Fire's insatiable voracity, which makes it devour everything in its path, would liken it to a wild animal, as many formulas appearing as early as Homer suggest.

With sacrifice, fire indicates man's position in the cosmos. Less than a god because he eats flesh rather than ambrosia, man is more than a beast, for he cooks his food. Centuries later, Samuel Johnson was keeping alive the same perspective: Beasts think and feel, Johnson claimed; but no beast is a cook.

Prometheus's gift of fire transgresses the will of Zeus, who had concealed fire from men. Therefore, Zeus seeks to punish men with his final trap: woman, a "beautiful evil" (Greek, *kalon kakon*). Zeus designed the woman, Ambidexter molded earth into "the likeness of a modest maid," Athena dressed her in a white garment and veil and placed a diadem on her head, and, according to *Works and Days*, Aphrodite "showered charm about her head, and painful yearning and consuming passion." In *Works and Days*, Hesiod names her Pandora, "all gift," which means both that all the gods adorned her and that she brought men every gift. Zeus realized that Prometheus, whose name means "far-sighted," would see through the trap, so he sent Pandora to Prometheus's dim-witted brother Epimetheus, whose name means "shortsighted." Prometheus had already warned his brother not to accept gifts from Zeus, but Epimetheus forgets and accepts Pandora, along with her box full of all the evils of the world. The story ends with Hesiod's brief comment that

> formerly the tribes of men on earth lived remote from ills, without harsh toil and the grievous sicknesses that are deadly to men. But the woman unstopped the jar and let it all out, and brought grim cares upon mankind. Only Hope remained there inside in her secure dwelling under the lip of the jar, and did not fly out, because the woman put the lid back in time by the providence of Zeus the cloud-gatherer who bears the aegis (*Works and Days,* pp. 39–40).

This episode of Pandora's "box" is well-known, but in the context of Hesiod's writings, it manifests a great deal about Hesiod's views of women, marriage, and human life. First, this continues the themes of trickery, concealment, and hiding in the relations of gods and men. Prometheus concealed meat within the stomach, bones within the fat, and fire in the fennel stalk. Zeus responds by concealing food in the earth, hiding fire, and finally by concealing the heart of a "bitch" (*Works and Days*, p. 39) under the guise of a beautiful maiden. Outwardly, she is *kalon* (beautiful) but inwardly she is *kakon* (evil). Second, in *Theogony*, the woman (her name, Pandora, does not appear in this work) is "an affliction for mankind to set against the fire" (p. 20). This indicates several things. Most obviously, the woman is a punishment for Prometheus's theft of fire and is therefore "against" the fire. The phrase also suggests that the woman somehow corresponds to the fire, so that she is a fitting punishment for Prometheus's theft. Like the fire, Pandora is an ambiguous gift, bringing both good and evil. On the one hand, a man must marry. If he does not, he has no chance of an heir and he grows to old age "lacking anyone to look after him." Yet, even if he marries a sensible wife, the bad will compete with the good, and if he gets an awful wife he will live "with unrelenting pain in heart and spirit" (p. 21).

Woman is an affliction also because she is suited only for

prosperity and cannot survive poverty, which is so often the lot of man:

> As the bees in their sheltered nests feed the drones, those conspirators in badness, and while they busy themselves all day and every day till sundown making the white honeycomb, the drones stay inside the sheltered cells and pile the toil of others into their own bellies, even so as a bane for mortal men has high-thundering Zeus created women, conspirators in causing difficulty (*Theogony,* pp. 20–21).

Like the drone bee who sits inside the hive, the woman spends her days within the house. More seriously, she, like the drone, is a belly that consumes the products of man's labor without producing anything. This comparison thus reaches back to Prometheus's original trick. He hid meat in a stomach to keep it from Zeus, and Zeus punishes mankind by hiding a "stomach" in a beautiful woman, a meat sack that is never full. Woman is "set against fire," for like the fire she needs continual feeding.

All this is very different from the biblical picture of the creation of woman. In Genesis 2, the fact that Adam lacks a partner is the one thing in the whole creation that is "not good." Eve is given to Adam as a good gift, a "helper suitable for him," and Adam accepts her for the good gift that she is. The biblical picture of the woman's role in the origin of evil also differs markedly from that of Hesiod. In *Works and Days*, Pandora releases evil, disease, and misery into the world. Though Hesiod is not clear about why or how she does this, later myths said she opened the jar of evils because of her insatiable curiosity. In Genesis 3, Eve first eats the fruit of the forbidden tree, but verse 8 indicates that Adam was "with her" through the whole temptation and refused to intervene to defend her against Satan. Adam, moreover, is clearly wrong to blame Eve for the sin, as Paul makes clear in Romans 5 when he says that sin entered by the disobedience of "one man."

According to Hesiod's story, the only thing left in the jar

after Pandora opens it is hope. What is "hope" doing in the jar of evils? When it is left inside, does this mean that hope is nowhere to be found, since it is locked away in the jar? Or does it mean that hope always remains near to man, staying in its dwelling place? Vernant answers by pointing to the ambiguous nature of the Greek word for "hope" (*elpis*). The word is closer to the English word "expectation," which can either be of good (hope) or of evil (fear). In the light of this, it is clear that, unlike the gods, who have nothing to desire or fear, humans are always accompanied by *elpis*. Expectation, like sacrifice, work, and women, is one of the fundamental constants of human life.

This seems like simple common sense; of course, human life is full of good and evil expectations. Christians, however, are called to live not by common sense but by faith. All of us fear, but fear is not, as Hesiod would have it, a simple constant of human life. We fear because we fail in faith and love, for faith drives out anxiety about tomorrow (Matt. 6:25–34), and "perfect love casts out fear" (1 Jn. 4:18). For the Christian, hope is not ambiguous but fully positive, because we serve a God who can perform what He has promised and who has a constancy of character that Zeus entirely lacks. "Hope," Paul says, "does not disappoint"—not because of any inherent power in our hopes but because "the love of God has been poured out within our hearts through the Holy Spirit" (Rom. 5:5).

Both Hesiod and the Bible describe something like a "fall," but the two accounts are very different. For Hesiod, work and women are necessary features of life after the decline from the golden age. In the Bible, however, God instructed Adam and Eve to "subdue" and "take dominion" before the fall, so that work is part of the original creation. As we have already seen, Eve is given before the fall and marriage is part of the created order. Hesiod, we might say, sees man's fall as a fall into society and civilization; the Bible sees society and civilization as goods of the original world and the fall strictly as a fall into sin, which corrupts man's civilizing efforts.

Hesiod's man falls into civilization, yet the gods do not equip him for the task. Through theft and trickery, man must wrest from Zeus the tools by which civilizations are built. Zeus jealously guards his status at the top of the ladder of being. Not being himself the creator of earth and heaven, Zeus wants to make sure that no one else is a creator either. Yahweh is also a jealous God, who will not share His glory or worship with another. Yet, Yahweh is also the God who is love, the giving God, who gives generously and without reproach (James 1:5–8). In particular, God is the source of all human creativity; though He is Creator—*because* He is Creator—He pours His creating Spirit upon creatures. This is brought out in Exodus 31:1–11, where Yahweh tells Moses that He has given artistic skill to Bezalel and Oholiab so that they can make the tabernacle and its furnishings. Strikingly, this is only the fourth reference to the Spirit of God in the Bible, and it alludes clearly to the Spirit's activity in creation (Gen. 1:2). In Genesis 1, God's Spirit forms a cosmos; in Exodus, the same Spirit equips men with creative skill to form a new world. In both, Scripture reveals a God of love and a view of the world profoundly at odds with Hesiod's pagan Genesis.

*Review Questions.*
 1. What are the "five ages" of man? According to Hesiod, which age are we living in?
 2. What is sacrifice? How does Greek sacrifice symbolize man's relation to the gods?
 3. How does Prometheus trick Zeus into accepting the sacrificial bones?
 4. What does Zeus do in response to Prometheus's first trick? Why makes this such a serious punishment?
 5. What is Zeus's final punishment? How does this punishment fit Prometheus's crime?
 6. How is a woman like fire? How is she like a drone?
 7. Compare Hesiod's view of woman to the biblical view in Genesis 2.

8. What is left inside Pandora's jar? Why?

9. How does Hesiod's view of the "fall of man" differ from the Bible's?

10. In Hesiod's story, how do human beings get the skills necessary for civilization? Where does the Bible say these skills come from?

*Thought Questions.*

1. Who are Prometheus's parents? His siblings? (p. 18)

2. What happened to Menoitios? How does this fit with the rest of the *Theogony*? (p. 18)

3. What happened to Atlas? (p. 18)

4. What is Prometheus's original punishment from Zeus? (p. 18)

5. What kind of ornamentation does Pandora's clothing have on it? Why is this significant? (p. 20)

6. What is the lesson of the experience of Prometheus? (p. 21)

*Notes:*

† I am using the translation of M. L. West in *Theogony & Works and Days* (World's Classics; Oxford: Oxford University Press, 1988). Unfortunately, this edition does not have usable line numbers, so I have been forced to cite the text by page number.

## Fighters Killing, Fighters Killed: Homer, *The Iliad*

According to the myths, the Trojan War broke out as a result of a beauty contest among three goddesses, Hera, Athena, and Aphrodite. During the wedding of Peleus and Thetis, the parents of Achilles, Eris ("Strife") threw a golden apple among the guests, bearing the label, "For the fairest." Each goddess claimed it, and Zeus refused to pass judgment. Instead, he allowed Hermes to take the goddesses to Mount Ida, where Paris, a handsome prince of Troy, was asked to decide. Hera bribed him with promises of power and riches, Athena with glory in battle, but it was Aphrodite's offer that Paris would be given Helen, the most beautiful woman in the world, that got Paris's attention. The only obstacle to the fulfillment of this promise was the fact that Helen was already married to Menelaus, prince of the Greek city of Sparta. Undaunted, Paris visited Sparta, and while Menelaus was traveling to Crete, he seduced Helen and they eloped to Troy. When the Trojans refused to return Helen or punish Paris for his adultery and his offense against Menelaus's hospitality, Menelaus gathered other Greek (or Achaean) princes to lay siege to the city.

Though this story forms the background for Homer's *Iliad*, the epic makes only passing reference it (24.31–36).[1] Nor is there any mention of the most famous incident of the war, that of the Trojan horse (see on the *Aeneid* below). Instead, the *Iliad* records the events of a few weeks during the ninth year of the ten-year siege of Troy (2.345–346). In the Greek original, the first word is *menis* (pronounced MAY-nis), "wrath," and the first line announces that the poem is about the rage of Achilles. Insulted by Agamemnon, brother of Menelaus and leader of the Greek operation, Achilles withdraws from battle, and through much of the story, he sits among his ships, grimly refusing every offer of reconciliation. The *Iliad*'s focus on Achilles is fully justified, since the fortunes of the Greeks and the outcome of the war hinge on him.[2] With their greatest warrior refusing to fight, the Greeks retreat before the Trojans, led by Hector, son of the Trojan king, Priam. Eventually, Achilles relents enough to allow his friend, Patroclus, to enter the battle dressed in Achilles' armor, and Hector kills Patroclus. Achilles' rage turns from Agamemnon to Hector, and he ravages the Trojans, finally killing Hector and then savagely dragging his body around the battlefield. The epic ends with Priam's night visit to Achilles' ship, during which Achilles agrees to return Hector's body to his father for burial.

To understand Achilles' withdrawal from battle, we need to examine what is called the heroic ethic, the heroic ideal, or the heroic way of life. Sarpedon, a Trojan warrior, sums up its main tenants in a speech to Glaucus:

> Ah my friend, if you and I could escape this fray
> and live forever, never a trace of age, immortal,
> I would never fight on the front lines again
> or command you to the field where men win fame.
> But now, as it is, the fates of death await us,
> thousands poised to strike, and not a man alive
> can flee them or escape—so in we go for attack!
> Give our enemy glory or win it for ourselves! (12.374–381).

As is evident from this quotation, heroes viewed death, glory, and immortality in a particular way. Heroes expect no life of bliss after death. Book 11 of the *Odyssey* indicates that the early Greeks believed that the dead continue some shadowy kind of existence in Hades, but this is hardly worthy to be called "life." Death is for all practical purposes the end. And this end is what defines human beings over against the gods. As we have seen from Hesiod's *Theogony*, the gods did not create the world and they do not have complete control over what happens in it. Gods are more powerful than mortals, but this it only a matter of degree; at times in the *Iliad*, heroes fight, wound, and come near to defeating gods. Death is the one absolute boundary between the gods and humans: Men and women are "mortal" while the gods are "immortal" or "deathless." Death is, for the hero, always an imminent end; at his back, every hero continually hears "time's winged chariot hurrying near." As Simone Weil explains, all mortals know that at some point in the future they will die. For the warrior, death looms every morning as the inevitable future, and therefore every day the hero cuts off all hope, erases every future except death. War thus destroys "all conceptions of purpose or goal, including even its own 'war aims.' It effaces the very notion of war's being brought to an end."

Though the hero knows that his life is short and death is the end, he wants to live forever. The only way to achieve "eternal life" is to fill the brief days of life with deeds of such glory that people will remember and celebrate them in song and poetry after the hero is gone. Thus, the Greek word *kleos* refers both to a hero's reputation for glory and to the songs poets sing about him. Living and dying with glory, the hero is no longer a mere man but has become eternal like the deathless gods. In its extreme form, a man guided by this ideal will devote his life to achieving a reputation for courage, strength, and bravery, and he will protect that reputation against all challenges. Just as the deathless gods are completely self-absorbed, so the consistent hero is concerned above all with his own name. The answer to the first question of the hero's catechism is, Man's chief end is to glorify himself forever (see 16.115–119).

Two haunting lines in Book 4 capture the heroic view of war and death:

> Screams of men and cries of triumph breaking in one breath,
> fighters killing, fighters killed, and the ground streamed
> blood (4.522–524; see 8.76–77).

With their matter-of-fact "fighters killing, fighters killed," these lines capture the Homeric sense that the destruction of war is, as C. S. Lewis put it, "all in the day's work." The parallel of the two phrases suggests that the two are indistinguishable: Is there any difference between killing and being killed? For the hero, not much: A hero gains glory by killing, but he can also achieve immortality by a heroic death. The equality between killing and being killed is horrifically captured in the first line, where the screams of the dying and the exultation of their killers harmonize in a chorus of bestial shrieks.

Heroism is a highly individualistic and competitive ideal, for heroes do not even want their friends to surpass them in glory (16.101–106). This overriding desire for *kleos*, however, is softened by an emphasis on the love (*philos*) that a hero is supposed to have for his fellow warriors. This is the thrust of Ajax's appeal to the wrathful Achilles in Book 9:

> Achilles—
> he's made his own proud spirit so wild in his chest,
> so savage, not a thought for his comrades' love—
> we honored him past all others by the ships....
> Achilles,
> put some human kindness in your heart (9.768–781).

Clearly, Ajax believes that consideration for one's fellow warriors is required even of a great hero like Achilles. As the central hero of the epic, Achilles' actions are played out between the poles of *kleos* and *philos*.

Homer's attitude to the heroic ideal is complex. He admires the skill and strength of his characters. With his readers, he stands in awe of the sheer fury that Achilles unleashes during his final rampage. Yet, Homer's epic explores the limits of the heroic ethic, examines its contradictions, exposes its ironies. Homer's presentation of the heroic ideal is made complex by the figure of Hector. Hector is not a wholly different animal from Achilles. Like his Greek counterpart, he seeks to enhance and protect his heroic reputation, and he speaks a number of times of the shame (Greek, *aidos*) he would feel if he were to abandon the fight (see 6.521–533). More than Achilles, however, Hector's heroism has a social and political dimension. As a prince and the greatest of the Trojan warriors, Hector is fighting not so much for personal glory as to protect a city full of women, children, and old men. His *aidos*, shame, is connected not only with protecting his reputation, but also with his recognition of his place in the city and the obligations that this position places on him. Since Hector is who Hector is, it would be shameful for him to act the coward. As Seth Schein points out, true *aidos* includes compassion toward the weak and helpless (22.97–98).

For both Hector and Achilles, heroism imposes a tragic choice. For Achilles, as we shall see, whether he chooses glory or love, he will die. Hector's heroic dilemma is colored in a shade different from that of Achilles, but it is no less tragic. Hector's *philos* is never in doubt; instead, he is caught in the tension between these two dimensions of *aidos*, a choice sharply posed in his final battle with Achilles. Hector has to choose between the appeals of his parents and wife—his obligation to the helpless who huddle within the city walls—and his heroic fear of shame, of losing reputation. Choosing either of them leads to his loss of both; to retreat behind the walls means that he will not be fighting to defend the city, but if he stands to fight Achilles he will die and leave Troy without a protector. Hector and Achilles can avoid disastrous consequences only by renouncing heroism entirely. Neither is willing to do that.

The heroic ideal has been one of the formative influences on Western culture (similar in its influence to the ideal of romantic love that arose in the late middle ages and continues to this day). In different forms, the hero appears as the "great-souled" man of Aristotle's *Ethics*, the rational sage of Stoic philosophy, the Renaissance courtier of Castiglione, but this ideal is not confined to the distant past. The heroic age ended centuries ago, but many modern people operate according to its principles. Inner city gang members who murder because they have been "dissed" are the heirs of Achilles, as is anyone who runs to court to defend every infringement on his "rights." Leaders more concerned with their "place in history" than with ruling justly are seeking a kind of heroic immortality. As I write, America is in the midst of a nightmarish scandal, which has stretched over months because President Clinton has heroically avoided the shame of a forthright confession.

It is important to realize that this ideal is not in any sense a Christian ideal. I do not mean that Christians cannot have heroes, or that "heroic" virtues like courage, strength, and perseverance are unchristian. But the heroic ideal is bound up with a particular religious position, a particular view of one's self, and a particular view of what it means to be courageous, strong, and persevering. It rests on the idea that death is the final end for man, while the Bible teaches we all will exist, either in heaven or hell, for eternity. Heroism encourages self-absorption, where the Bible teaches us to imitate Christ's self-forgetfulness (Phil. 2:5–8). Achilles wants to make sure that Patroclus steals none of his glory; the Christian, like Christ Himself, is to promote the glory, reputation, and well-being of others more than himself (Rom. 12:3; 15:1–2; Phil. 2:4). It would be a useful exercise to compare Hebrews 11, often described as a catalogue of biblical "heroes," with the heroes of the *Iliad*. That one becomes a hero by hoping for things unseen or by patiently waiting for God to fulfill His promises—this would be nonsense to a Greek hero. But patience, obedience, and hope are the essence of biblical heroism.

Much of the book of Jeremiah is an attack on the "heroic" mentality of Jews living at the end of the kingdom of Judah. Jeremiah insisted that the Lord had given the world into the hands of Nebuchadnezzar (27:1-11); to resist

Nebuchadnezzar's conquest of Jerusalem and Judah was to resist God. One after another, Judah's kings rejected Jeremiah's counsel and refused to accept the humiliation of defeat and subjection, and Judah was eventually crushed by Babylonian armies. Jeremiah confronts us with this challenging lesson: Obedience to God sometimes demands giving up not only one's honor but even the political independence of one's homeland. Had Jeremiah been seated on the walls of Troy as Hector waited for his final battle with Achilles, the prophet would have urged him to return to the city and lock the gate tight. During Jesus' lifetime, some compared him to Jeremiah (Matthew 16:14). Like the prophet, Jesus battled Jews who wanted to resist the Gentiles—Romans in this case—with Homeric heroism. Not only the Zealots, who raised militias to fight the Romans, but even the Pharisees were resistant to the presence of unclean Gentiles in the holy land. Jesus' instructions in the Sermon on the Mount assume this context. Jesus is teaching His disciples how to live peacefully as a subject people and warning them not to resist. Each of the first three gospels includes a lengthy chapter in which Jesus prophesies that the rebellious city of Jerusalem will eventually be destroyed because of its resistance to Rome (Matthew 24; Mark 13; Luke 21). Heroic concern for honor is, the Bible clearly shows, disastrous both for the hero and for his city.

Greek heroes need war to achieve immortality, and the *Iliad* is one of the great literary accounts of war. As with the heroic ideal, Homer's attitude toward war and toward the Trojan war in particular is complex. No one in the story has the modern attitude that war is a waste. They accept it as a matter of course, as nothing more than "fighters killing, fighters killed." Yet Homer recognizes the costs and brutalities of war, which he depicts in excruciating detail. The Old Testament is full of war stories, but nowhere in Scripture do we find the kind of graphic descriptions of violent death that fill page after page of the *Iliad*. And Homer is aware of the suffering that war causes, especially to women and children who lose husbands and fathers. Yet, Homer ingeniously shows us another side to war, one that we are often unwilling to admit—its attractiveness, its severe beauties, its thrills. He frequently compares killing and risking death to the excitements of fishing, hunting, and other sports. Even if Homer did not love war, he powerfully shows us why many do.

C. S. Lewis said that beneath the surface of Homer's worldview is not so much sadness as despair, especially despair that the world will ever be different. This despair is inevitable, considering the religious viewpoint of the ancient Greeks. Warfare, after all, not only dominates earth; it rumbles through the heavens as well. Gods and goddesses incited the war from the beginning, and throughout they take sides in battle and keep the war going. Hera and Athena, offended by Paris's preference for Aphrodite, join sides with the Greeks against the Trojans, and Poseidon is also pro-Greek. With Apollo, Aphrodite defends Troy and especially her favorite, Paris. Zeus is somewhat more even-handed, sometimes supporting the Trojans but throughout much of the epic arranging all things to promote the glory of Achilles. Gods often play a direct role in the battle, causing "random" incidents: When an arrow falls short of its target, it is because a god has intervened, and when the tide of battle turns inexplicably, it is because the gods are stirring up one side. Gods kindle human desires and passions, whether for love or for battle. They are the source of all that is irrational and unexplained.

The irrationality of the gods goes to their moral character as well. Zeus is considered the embodiment of wisdom, but he exhibits no ethical consistency. An incessant adulterer, Zeus fathers children randomly with goddesses and humans, a fact that mythologically captures Zeus's fundamental unreliability. How can mortals trust him when he constantly cheats on Hera? Yet, the heroes seem not to notice the fickleness of the gods. In the flush of a day's victory, each side mistakenly assumes that tomorrow will again be a day of victory. At the beginning of the story, the advancing

Greeks refuse to accept terms of peace, certain that Troy is ready to fall. When, a few days later, Hector advances into the Greek camp, he assumes the gods are with him and refuses to return to the city as night falls. On the following day, Patroclus, dressed in Achilles' armor, is on the field and pushes the Trojans back to their walls. Heroes, in Weil's words, "forget to treat victory as a transitory thing." Or, to say the same thing, they forget that the gods cannot be trusted.

In the midst of the warfare that clamors through heaven and earth, the city is a preserve of comparative peace. Homer's poem is organized around the contrasting spaces of the city and the war camp. The world of the city is a complex and highly developed one. Within its walls are all sorts and conditions of humanity: women, the elderly and children, workmen, slaves, and sometimes warriors. As Hector walks through Priam's palace in Book 6, we get a brief glimpse of the refined beauties of Trojan life, now threatened by the Greek siege. Across the battlefield, the Greeks camp among their ships and erect a makeshift trench and wall to protect themselves from the Trojans (7.500–539). Superficially like the walled city, the camp has few of the features of city life—no women (other than war brides, who are more like objects), no children, few elders, no art or architecture. All the men of the camp are young, strong aristocratic heroes. Between these two sites is the "no man's land" of the battlefield, the place where men fight for glory, where the city struggles against the camp. Homer's poem presents the city and its chief protector, Hector, in a positive light, but the doom of Troy broods over the whole poem. In a world of heroes, the city is a temporary holdout against the chaos of continual war. The Trojans will be defeated on the field, Troy's high and windy walls will fall, its homes and palace will burn. City will be absorbed by camp, as all of Troy's women are taken as war brides. Like victory in war, the city is a vapor.

Large sections of the *Iliad* are devoted to fairly repetitive and often grisly descriptions of battle, and it is easy to feel that it is a disorganized poem. In part, both the repetition and the apparent chaos are deliberate literary devices. War scenes are greatly expanded to give the reader a sense of the tremendous scale of battle; instead of describing many years of war, Homer composed intense and lengthy descriptions of a few days of the conflict. The chaos of the text mimics the chaos of war, in which screams of triumph and death can hardly be distinguished. Homer's battle scenes are not, however, realistic. They are more like a series of duels than a real battle; heroes frequently exchange taunts or review their family histories before getting down to business. Here again, the heroic ethic is in the background. One cannot become a hero by sending infantry into battle or by pushing the red button that launches ICBMs. Heroic warfare has to be man-to-man.

Despite the apparent chaos, a number of devices help to unify the epic. First, a "chiastic" arrangement structures the whole poem, beginning with a quarrel and ending with a reconciliation scene. A glance at the connections between Books 1–3 and 22–24 fills out the picture:

>   A. A Trojan priest demands that his daughter be returned, Book 1
>   B. The armies gather for battle, Book 2
>   C. Duel (Paris and Menelaus), Book 3
>   C'. Duel (Hector and Achilles), Book 22
>   B'. Greek armies engage in funeral games, Book 23
>   A'. A Trojan king, Priam, asks Achilles to return his son's body, Book 24

Further, Cedric Whitman has shown that Book 24 reverses the arrangement of Book 1:

Book 1:
>   Rejection of the Trojan priest Chryses; death of many Greeks
>       Council of chiefs and quarrel of Agamemnon and Achilles
>           Achilles appeals to his mother, Thetis
>               Thetis appeals to Zeus
>                   Assembly of the gods, Hera opposing Zeus

Book 24:
> Assembly of the gods, Hera opposing Zeus
> Thetis and Zeus
> Thetis takes Zeus's message to Achilles
> Achilles with Priam: reconciliation
> Funeral of Hector

Books 1–3 and 22–24 thus function like contrasting bookends that hold the rest of the epic together. Whitman explains that the chronology of Book 24 reverses that of Book 1:

> Book I has first the day of Chryses' appeal, followed by nine days of plague, the day of the council and quarrel, and finally a twelve-day gap till the gods return to Olympus; Book XXIV begins with a twelve-day period during which the gods grow steadily more disgusted with Achilles' excesses, followed by the day on which Iris rouses Priam to go to the Greek camp; nine days are then devoted to gathering wood for Hector's pyre, and on the tenth day he is buried.

Thus, the day scheme for Book 1 is, 1-9-1-12; Book 24 reverses this chronology: 12-1-9-1.

By examining the sequence of days, Whitman has arrived at a more comprehensive concentric arrangement:[3]

A. Book 1
  B. Books 2–7: 3 days, one of fighting, one of burial, one for building wall
    C. Book 8: one day of fighting
      D. Book 9: Embassy to Achilles
    C. Books 11–18: one day of fighting
  B. Books 19–23: 3 days: one day of Achilles, one of burial, one for funeral games
A. Book 24

Importantly, in Whitman's arrangement, the embassy of Odysseus, Ajax, and Phoenix to Achilles takes the central position, and we shall see that it is in several senses the turning point of the action. At a number of points, we will return to this scheme, since comparison of the related books is often illuminating. Individual books are also, we shall see, sometimes arranged concentrically.

Homer also employs repeated type scenes that foreshadow later scenes. At several points in the poem, a single warrior comes to the fore in his "hour of supremacy" (Greek, *aristeia*, literally "prowess"). Thus, Diomedes, Agamemnon, and Patroclus have *aristeiai* (the plural form), and all these foreshadow the coming rampage of the supreme Greek, Achilles. As in a musical composition, a theme is introduced, followed by a series of variations that come to a crescendo: "da-da-da-da," followed by "da-da-da-DA" and "da-da-DA-DA!," and finally, with the appearance of Achilles, "DA-DA-DA-DA!!" Similarly, duels between Menelaus and Paris (Book 3) and between Ajax and Hector (Book 7) foreshadow the climactic dual between Hector and Achilles (Book 22). Hector's death has been foreshadowed by two other important death scenes, those of Patroclus and the Trojan Sarpedon, and the deaths of Patroclus and Hector seal Achilles' own, though the latter is not recorded in the poem.

*Review Questions.*
   1. According to the myths, how did the war begin?
   2. What part of the war is the *Iliad* about?
   3. What is the ancient Greek view of death?
   4. Describe the hero's attitude toward death.
   5. What does Homer think of the "heroic ethic"?
   6. What accounts for the "despair" that, according to C. S. Lewis, pervades Homer's epic?
   7. Explain the "geography" of the epic. Why is this spatial division important?
   8. Describe the "chiastic" links between Books 1–3 and Books 22–24.
   9. How are the structures of Books 1 and 24 connected?
   10. Describe some of the poetic techniques that Homer uses to unify the poem.

*Thought Questions.*

1. Look up the Trojan War in a book of Greek myths and summarize some of the events of the war that are not included in the epic.

2. Many legends about Achilles are not found in the *Iliad*. Read about Achilles in a book of mythology and summarize some of these legends.

3. Examine the story of a military leader (e.g., Joshua, David) from the Old Testament. How does his heroism and warfare differ from the Greek heroic ideal?

4. Read an encyclopedia article about warfare in the ancient world. Is Homer's depiction of one-on-one warfare realistic?

5. Read an encyclopedia article about the discovery of the ruins of Troy. Who discovered the location of Troy? How did he do it?

## The Rage of Achilles, Books 1–8

"Rage" (*menis*) is, as I have noted, the first word and a key theme of the *Iliad*. Achilles is enraged because Agamemnon has violated his rights as a prince and equal, treated him as an outcast and underling, and claimed to be greater than Achilles. For Achilles, operating by the heroic ethic, there is no more serious insult. Achilles has been "dissed," and he intends to make Agamemnon, and all the Greeks, pay.

The circumstances of the insult are these. Chryses, a Trojan priest of Apollo, has asked for the return of his daughter, Chryseis, whom Agamemnon has captured and claimed as a war bride. Agamemnon brusquely refuses the demand, but Chryses prays to Apollo, who for nine days (1.61) rains arrows into the Greek camp, causing countless deaths. Desperate, Achilles calls a council to deal with the problem, and the Greeks prevail on Agamemnon to return Chryseis to her father. Enraged, Agamemnon demands that Achilles' war bride, Briseis, be given to him as compensation.

To anyone familiar with the origins of the Trojan war, these incidents sound terribly familiar. Just as Paris abducted Helen from Menelaus and thereby started a war between Greeks and Trojans, so Agamemnon's theft of Briseis instigates a feud that divides the Greek camp. Within the first four hundred lines of the epic, the drama of Paris and Helen is replayed three times:

| *Woman Seized* | *Refusal to Return Girl* | *Rage* |
|---|---|---|
| Chryseis | Agamemnon | Apollo |
| Chryseis | Chryses | Agamemnon |
| Briseis | Agamemnon | Achilles |

Even the length of Apollo's assault on the Greeks is significant; just as the Greeks have besieged Troy for nine years, so Apollo besieges the camp for nine days. Nine days of plague result from a man's refusal to give up a woman, complete with "corpse-fires burning on, night and day, no end in sight" (1.60)—in all these ways, the opening lines of Book 1 present the entire Trojan War in miniature. Within the war between Trojans and Greeks, Greeks are now set against Greeks.

In the light of our discussion of the heroic ideal above, the reaction of Achilles is important to consider. He seems to have loved Briseis in some way. He retreats to his ships mourning for her (2.790–792), and later claims to have "loved that woman with all my heart, though I won her like a trophy with my spear" (9.416–417). Yet, his immediate and dominant reason for withdrawing is that Agamemnon has treated him with contempt and trampled his rights. For him, as for all heroes, honor, glory, and plunder are inseparable. Heroes achieve glory not only by doing great deeds but by gathering hoards of booty, which serves as proof of a hero's victories and enhances his reputation. Agamemnon's seizure of Achilles' war bride is thus an attack on his glory and self-respect (see 1.192–198). His withdrawal is calculated to enhance his reputation: He quits and goes back to the ships to show Agamemnon that the Greeks cannot win without him (1.280–287). When they begin to lose, they will realize that Achilles is the "best of the Achaeans," and if he ever returns to lead the Greeks to victory, he will win eternal fame. In this sense, his rage follows directly from his heroic status. He defends his reputation and beats down anyone who cheats him of his share of the spoils.

Achilles is an ideal hero also in his godlikeness. Seth Schein has pointed out that Achilles is unusual in the number of his connections with the world of the gods. His mother, Thetis, is a minor deity, and Achilles is the only human in the *Iliad* who speaks face-to-face with a god. Since Thetis once slept with Zeus, Achilles has a direct line to the highest Olympian power, a fact reflected in the concentric structure of Book 1:

> Assembly of the Greeks; Agamemnon quarrels with Achilles
> > Achilles appeals to Thetis
> > Thetis appeals to Zeus
> Assembly of the gods; Hera quarrels with Zeus

With Thetis as intermediary, Achilles makes sure that his complaint is heard on high. Achilles' anger, moreover, is described as *menis*, a word normally associated with divine wrath. When he returns to the battle later, his wrath has become "demonic" (in Schein's terms), inspired by the gods, and he is such an unstoppable force that he even fights a river god. Homer gives us a hero who is on his way to achieving the godlike status that all heroes aspire to.

Ideal though he is, Achilles' reaction to Agamemnon's insult is unwise, as the elderly Nestor tells him: "you, Achilles, never hope to fight it out with your king, pitting force against his force" (1.324–325). In Achilles, heroism has been pushed to an extreme, and this extreme is intensified by Achilles' knowledge of his future. Every warrior knows that he will someday die, but Achilles knows from the beginning that he faces a stark choice:

> Mother tells me,
> The immortal goddess Thetis with her glistening feet,
> That two fates bear me on to the day of death.
> If I hold out here and I lay siege to Troy,
> my journey home is gone, but my glory never dies.
> If I voyage back to the fatherland I love,
> my pride, my glory dies...
> True, but the life that's left me will be long,
> the stroke of death will not come on me
> quickly (9.497–505).

Whenever he threatens to leave Troy for home—as he often does (1.201–202)—this prophecy is very much in the back of his mind. Achilles' situation is an intensified form of the classic heroic choice: glory with certain death *versus* a long life without glory.

One of Homer's aims is to trace out the consequences of extreme heroism. One consequence is that Achilles renounces other dimensions of the heroic way of life, specifically the love (*philos*) that a hero is supposed to show for his fellows. Like the kid who won't play unless he is made team captain and worshiped by his teammates, or the youngster who imagines his own death and thinks that *then* everyone will miss him, Achilles goes so far as to ask his mother to secure a Trojan victory. His goal is to increase his reputation as a warrior. When Thetis appeals to Zeus, she makes this explicit: "Come, grant the Trojans victory after victory till the Achaean armies pay my dear son back, building higher the honor he deserves" (1.607–609). Achilles is willing to let his fellow Greeks be slaughtered so long as it increases his *kleos*. The extremity of his heroism thus isolates him from the society of heroes.

Another consequence of Achilles' extreme adherence to the heroic code of glory is more sharply ironic. Achilles has such a fine sense of his own gifts and worth that he withdraws from war when Agamemnon claims superiority. But the battlefield is the only place where he can display his gifts and worth. His heroism is so extreme that he becomes an anti-hero, and when we next see him he is sitting among his ships singing about the great deeds of heroes (9.224–228). Achilles should be providing material for heroic songs, not singing them.

A final point from this initial situation has to do with the role of women in the heroic world. Women are much more prominent in the *Odyssey*, but in the *Iliad* they naturally tend to be on the sidelines. Yet their role is crucial. Greeks and Trojans are fighting over a woman, and so are Agamemnon and Achilles. Fittingly, while the battle rages outside, Helen sits within the city weaving a robe with scenes of the war (3.150–154). Weaving frequently symbolizes fate in ancient literature; the gods or the fates "weave" a man's destiny. Men fight, but the unfaithful woman who caused the war sits within the city weaving slaughter. There is a slight whiff of Hesiod in the air; Helen, Chryseis, and Briseis are Pandoras, women who open the box that unleashes the furies of war. Helen's beauty is, like Pandora's, a "terrible beauty" (3.190). But Homer is not a misogynist, a hater of women, and even Helen is presented with great sympathy. She despises Paris (3.490–510), which says something for her taste in men; she calls herself a "slut" (6.422), which is both brutally honest and pitiable; and she genuinely laments the pain she has caused to good men like Hector (6.420–426). Though Helen is the chief cause of the war, she is also one of its chief victims.

Agamemnon's blunder in handling Achilles infects the entire Greek camp. Whitman's concentric outline of the first half of Book 2 highlights this:

  A. Dream from Zeus
   B. Greek council
    C. Assembly of troops
     D. Greeks rush for ships
    C'. Odysseus reassembles troops
   B'. Greek Council
  A'. Sacrifice to Zeus

During the first assembly of troops (C), Agamemnon foolishly tests his men by telling them they can go home. The Greeks madly rush for the ships: "Shrill shouts hitting the heavens, fighters racing for home, knocking the blocks out underneath the hulls" (2.178–180). This scene occupies the central position in Book 2 and thus is thematically prominent. Odysseus intervenes to hold back the flood and brings the warriors back to order. Disaster is averted, but we are left with grave doubts about Agamemnon's ability to lead the Greeks to victory. The weakness of Agamemnon's leadership becomes clearer by a comparison with Book 23, which matches Book 2 in the epic's concentric structure. There, Achilles presides at the funeral games for Patroclus, and with Achilles in charge the camp is orderly and at peace. Conflicts occur, but Achilles intervenes with justice and firmness to bring them to a quick resolution. Agamemnon is a center that cannot hold, and he offends Achilles, who is, in Book 23 at least, the main centripetal force holding the troops together.

In *Troilus and Cressida*, Shakespeare highlighted the disorder caused by Agamemnon. According to Shakespeare's conception of the world, everything and everyone has its proper place and is held in place by submission to proper authority. If a subordinate rebels, chaos follows, but the same thing happens when a ruler fails to exercise his authority in the proper manner. "The specialty of rule hath been neglected," says Ulysses (Odysseus) to Agamemnon, and when authority or "degree" is "shaked, which is the ladder to all high designs, the enterprise is sick!"

Homer's view is similar. Like most Greeks, Homer assumed that the world was organized into a 'great chain of being.' Every link in the chain had to stay in place. When men tried to rise too high in the chain of being, becoming like gods, they were slapped back into place. On the other hand, men at war, as we shall see, became little more than beasts, slipping down the chain of being. For Homer, man's proper place is right in the middle. In some ways, this idea parallels Christianity. Men are required to submit to the Lord, not seeking to unseat God from His throne, and to subdue the animals under them. The Greek view, however, is timeless and motionless. Being virtuous means staying in your own place, forever. For the Christian, virtue is obedience, and by the grace of God we do not remain where we are but advance from glory to glory.

In Book 2, however, the Greeks are all as blind as Agamemnon. When Thersites says in council that Agamemnon is shamefully leading "the sons of Achaea into bloody slaughter" and has disgraced Achilles, "a greater man," (2.272–273, 279), Odysseus beats him on the head with a scepter and the rest of the troops laugh (2.309–324). Thersites is right, as we already know from Zeus's conversation with Thetis in Book 1. Zeus's plan to arrange the war to bring glory to Achilles unfolds through the epic. This gives a tragic coloring to the Greeks' confidence and casts an ironic light on Hector's decisions. For a time, Zeus holds off his plan, forbidding the gods to participate in the fight as Diomedes drives the Trojans before him (Books 3–7). In Book 8, however, Zeus begins to fulfill Thetis's request. When Hector then advances on the Greeks, he thinks he will continue to win, but this is just part of Zeus's plan to honor Achilles. Hector is a pawn in Achilles' game. So, however, are the Greeks: They will not learn the truth until Zeus has executed his plan, until the Greeks have suffered bloody slaughter.

The parallels between the beginning of the epic and the beginning of the war form the background for the duel between Paris and Menelaus in Book 3. These two were the parties in the initial dispute that has turned into a protracted siege, and so it is appropriate that they fight to see who will take Helen home. Paris functions, moreover, as a foil to other characters. Achilles occupies one end of the heroic spectrum, a man so concerned with his heroic status that he refuses to fight; Paris occupies the other end, for he has no concern for heroic reputation. Initially Paris strides boldly out, but when Menelaus makes his way toward him, "he dissolved again in the proud Trojan lines, dreading Atrides [Menelaus]—magnificent, brave Paris" (3.40–41). Hector calls him a "prince of beauty" whose main gifts are "the fine lyre and these, these gifts of Aphrodite, your long flowing locks and your striking looks" (3.43, 63–64), and warns that Paris will one day fall on the battlefield to "roll and couple" with the dust rather than with Helen (3.65). Paris stands on the side of Aphrodite, of women, of beauty, of art. Against him comes Menelaus, "dear to Ares," the god of war (3.84). The clash of Paris and Menelaus thus becomes a clash of city and camp, beauty and battle, women and men.

His duel with Menelaus confirms that Paris is out of his element. Menelaus takes Paris by the helmet and begins to drag him behind the Greek lines, with the "chin-strap holding his helmet tight . . . gouging his soft throat" (3.430–431). Just in time, Aphrodite intervenes to protect her favorite, snapping the chin strap and whisking Paris to his "bedroom filled with scent" (3.441), where he eventually seduces Helen. Frustrated and enraged, as when Helen first left him, Menelaus vainly searches the Trojan army for his opponent, but Paris is back where he belongs, in the soft and safe world of the bedroom.

Because of Aphrodite's intervention, the duel intended to bring an end to the war is inconclusive. Yet for the moment, the truce stands, for oaths have been taken to Zeus. On Olympus, Zeus considers the alternatives: "do we rouse the pain and grisly fighting once again or hand down pacts of peace between both armies?" (4.17–18). Considering Troy's generosity in sacrifices and wine libations, Zeus thinks of ending the war, preserving Troy, and sending Menelaus home with Helen. Everybody can be happy. But the rage (4.42) of Hera and Athena will not be pacified; Hera reminds Zeus of all the time and effort she has expended planning and executing the destruction of Troy, and Zeus relents, though with the agreement that Hera will have to allow *him* to destroy a city someday. Zeus sends Athena among the Trojan troops to incite Pandarus to shoot an arrow at Menelaus. Outraged at the breach of the pact, Agamemnon condemns all the Trojans as transgressors who will pay dearly for their treachery (4.179–187). The irony of this condemnation is charged, for Agamemnon's fury at the Trojans reminds us of Achilles' rage against Agamemnon's transgression of his rights. Moreover, we are again back at the beginning of the war. Pandarus is another Paris, re-opening Menelaus's wounds and reigniting the conflict.

Spatially as well as thematically, Paris and Achilles occupy extreme positions in the *Iliad*. Though he first appears on the battlefield, Paris belongs in the city and in the bedroom especially; Achilles, meanwhile, is as far from the city as possible, nursing his anger among the ships. Hector stands between these two poles, a middle position symbolized by his movements through the geography of the epic. At the beginning of Book 6, the scene shifts from the battlefield to the city as Hector goes from the field to ask the Trojan women to offer sacrifices and pray for their soldiers. This Book may be outlined as follows:

A. The battle continues, lines 1–83.
B. Hector enters the holy city, lines 84–588.
  1. At the urging of his brother Helenus, Hector returns to the city, lines 84–137.
  2. Glaucus and Diomedes trade pacts of friendship on the battlefield, lines 138–282.
  3. Hector enters the city.
    a. Encounters Trojan women, lines 283–288.
    b. Encounters Hecuba, his mother, lines 289–365.
    c. Encounters Paris and Helen, lines 366–439.
    d. Finds Andromache and his son Astyanax, lines 440–588.
C. Hector returns to the battlefield, lines 589–631.

Apart from Paris, Hector is the only hero who moves across the boundary that separates the battlefield from the city, and unlike his brother, Hector is equally at home in both. Hector's heroism is rooted in his ties to the city that he protects.

One of the strangest aspects of Book 6 is the scene with Diomedes and Glaucus that intervenes between Hector's departure from the field and his entry to the city. Diomedes has been on a rampage, controlling the field like another Achilles (6.110–118). When he jumps from his chariot to square off against Glaucus, he stops to ask if Glaucus is a god dropped down from heaven. Glaucus gives a convoluted explanation of his descent from Bellerophon of Corinth, and Diomedes realizes that his own grandfather, Oeneus, once hosted Bellerophon and exchanged gifts with him. Given these family links, the two agree not to fight one another and exchange armor, though Diomedes gets the better of the deal, anticipating the eventual Greek victory and the stripping of Trojan armor.

Several things in this interlude are noteworthy. First, it highlights the role of gifts and hospitality in ancient Greek culture. Exchanging hospitality and gifts forms a bond between the giver and receiver. These bonds were supposed to be inviolable, binding even future generations to friendship. Against this background, this episode comments on the war itself, which is being fought precisely because Paris breached the rules of hospitality; Menelaus opened his home and table, but not his wife, to the Trojan prince. Moreover, in Book 4, a temporary truce has been violated and the war reignited. Even more pointedly, one episode in the story that Glaucus tells concerns the wife of Proetus, who accused Bellerophon of trying to seduce her; that is, Bellerophon was accused of behaving like a Paris. But the charge was false (6.178–197). If Paris had acted like Bellerophon, or even like Glaucus and Diomedes, there would be no Trojan War. Finally, this exchange is set in the middle of the account of Hector's return to the city. Perhaps it is meant to represent the kind of bonds, formed by gifts, hospitality, and friendship, that characterize the city at peace—the kind of bonds that the war has now rendered quite impossible. Glaucus and Diomedes form a little city in the midst of the battlefield; but that city is a small island in a sea of blood, even more fragile and short-lived than Troy itself.

As Hector enters the city, he encounters only women: first, the wives and daughters of Troy rush at him, begging news of the battle, then he meets his mother, Hecuba, Helen, and, after an anxious search, his wife, Andromache. At the level of the story, this is perfectly logical, for all the men should be out on the field fighting the Greeks. Yet, the prominence of women also reinforces one of the thematic structures of the epic. Cities, and the indoor spaces of the city especially, are the preserve of women, as the field is the place for men. The spatial division of the epic is also a gender division. This is similar to the biblical habit of identifying cities as feminine—"daughter Jerusalem" or the bride-city that descends from heaven in Revelation. Hector's role is to defend the women/city against enemies.

Besides women, Hector meets only Paris, who is in the bedroom polishing his armor, the only man of fighting age who remains in the city (6.377–382). Hector rebukes his brother severely, observing that Paris sits safely within the city while Trojans die around the walls "and all for you" (6.383–391):

> What on earth are you doing? O how wrong it is,
> this anger you keep smoldering in your heart! Look,
> your people dying around the city, the steep walls,
> dying in arms—and all for you, the battle cries
> and the fighting flaring up around the citadel (6.384–388).

Smoldering anger, refusal to fight, lack of concern for his comrades, people dying because of one man's inaction—now, who does *that* sound like? Homer has set things up to show that the two ends of the heroic spectrum curve around to meet. Paris would be more at home singing of heroes than being one, but Achilles is the one we actually see singing. An Achilles who seeks only glory and renown can end up like Paris, who cares not at all for heroic glory. In different senses, both Paris and Achilles are "without shame" (6.414–418; 24.52). Paris is shameless because shame does not sting him into action, while Achilles is shameless because he recoils from every hint of shame and seeks to be filled with nothing but glory. Achilles' effort to purge shame—to be "without shame"—leads him to act as if he had no concern for his reputation—to "shamelessness." Exclusive concern for reputation dissolves into a total lack of concern for reputation. If avoiding shame is your only standard of behavior, you can end up shameless.

Hector, by contrast, is not "shameless." Even Helen, though still attracted to the handsome Paris, recognizes how different he is from his brother:

> I wish I had been the wife of a better man, someone
> alive to outrage, the withering scorn of men.
> This one has no steadiness in his spirit,
> not now, he never will (6.415–418).

Hector is moved by shame only because he is not *only* moved by shame. He acts like a true hero because he is more than heroic. On the one hand, he is itching to return to the field. Helen asks Hector to sit beside her to take a rest, but because he is the kind of man that Helen wishes Paris were, Hector refuses. Hecuba offers him wine, but he refuses to indulge in the delights of the city when battle is calling. Though he refuses and protests his desire to return to the field, he keeps stopping to chit-chat with the women and takes a long time to search through the city for his wife. Torn between the city and the field, even when he thinks of the battle, it is because he knows he is the "lone defense of Troy" (6.428–431; 6.478).

Hector's transcendence of the merely heroic is brought out in the scene with his wife, Andromache, one of the most famous and touching scenes in Homer. In this, their last meeting, Andromache is at the Scaean Gates, "the last point he would pass to gain the field of battle" (6.465). The scene that follows thus takes place on the boundary between the battlefield and the city, and this setting reinforces our view of Hector as a man of both city and camp, a man poised between his sense of duty to Troy and his realization of what the battlefield will bring. He listens sympathetically to his wife's plea that he not return to battle, lest "you orphan your son and make your wife a widow" (6.512). When he replies, "All this weighs on my mind too, dear woman" (6.522), we hear a note of tenderness almost wholly lacking in other heroes. His greatest fear, he says, is that his dear Andromache will be dragged off from her land and forced to live as a slave: "No, no, let the earth come piling over my dead body before I hear your cries, I hear you dragged away" (6.553–555). That tenderness is exhibited also when he reaches down to pick up his young son, who recoils in terror at the sight of his father's helmet. Laughing, Hector removes the helmet, the capstone of his battle gear, picks up the boy, kisses him, and, tossing him in the air, pronounces a blessing. If Achilles tried to remove his helmet, we suspect his head would come off with it.

Hector is an unusually well-rounded hero, but he is still a hero, intent on gaining *kleos*:

> I would die of shame to face the men of Troy
> and the Trojan women trailing their long robes
> if I would shrink from battle now, a coward.
> Nor does the spirit urge me on that way.
>     I've learned it all too well. To stand up bravely,
> always to fight in the front ranks of the Trojan soldiers,
> winning my father great glory, glory for myself (6.523–529).

Praying that his son will be "first in glory among the Trojans," he envisions him coming "home from battle bearing the bloody gear of the mortal enemy he has killed in war—a joy to his mother's heart" (6.569–574). Hector is the best that the heroic world can produce; but he is still a hero. And this will lead to his final tragedy.

Hector's pity for his wife and child makes him more likeable than Achilles, but, as David Gress has pointed out, 'Hector's pity, if pity it is, is strange by Western standards.' He goes on to explain:

> It is a pity limited by his own pride and honor, his KUDOS, which does not permit him to survive and protect his wife and

son, because to do so would be to court shame and to shirk his true destiny as a warrior—even if that destiny brings immediate death. Hector feels no obligation to his wife and child as such; the only obligation he recognizes as unconditional is that he must uphold his reputation as a warrior.... Christian or Western ethical rules of duty to others would have told Hector that his responsibilities as husband and father, especially if disaster was going to strike, outweighed his warrior's pride.

The duel between Menelaus and Paris has been inconclusive, but Hector is still eager to see the war come to an end. So, he challenges the best of the Greeks to meet him in single combat. This second formal duel connects Book 7 with Book 3:

*Book 3*
    Truce
        Helen among the elders of Troy
            Inconclusive duel of Paris and Menelaus
*Book 7*
            Inconclusive duel of Ajax and Hector
        Trojans and Greeks in council
    Truce

The only condition for the truce is that if one of the combatants is killed, his body should be returned for proper burial (7.88–105). This foreshadows the later duel between Hector and Achilles, which ends with Achilles defiling his enemy's body. The Greeks recognize Hector's prowess and shrink from confronting him: "Even Achilles dreads to pit himself against him out on the battle lines where men win glory" (7.130–131). Finally, "Big" Ajax is chosen by lot, but after a lengthy and intense combat, they are parted and the battle ceases for the night. Strangely, Hector suggests that he and Ajax exchange gifts before the night falls:

    Come,
let us give each other gifts, unforgettable gifts,

so any man may say, Trojan soldier or Argive,
"First they fought with heart-devouring hatred,
then they parted, bound by pacts of
friendship" (7.345–349).

Like Glaucus and Diomedes, they agree to cease fighting, bound as they are by gifts.

Each army retreats from the field for the night to eat and sit in council. The Trojans are concerned about Diomedes' advance and are considering ways to bring the siege to an end. Antenor, a Trojan elder, suggests that Helen and her treasures be returned. He recognizes that the Trojans "broke our sworn truce. We fight as outlaws" and therefore cannot expect victory (7.400–404). Paris, who feels no outrage or sympathy concerning the slaughter of Trojans outside the gates, becomes angry, and though he agrees to send back the treasures he stole from the Greeks, he insists "I won't give up the woman!" (7.416). This is not the first time we have heard these words; Agamemnon had said virtually the same thing to Chryses and then to Achilles. As Agamemnon's refusal endangers the Greeks and perpetuates his feud with Achilles, Paris's refusal to give up the woman perpetuates the war.

Yet, Paris's offer to return certain treasures to the Greeks is a concession, and the Trojans approach the Greeks with the proposal, which they hope will "halt the brutal war" (7.456). Diomedes believes it is a move of desperation: "Now, at last, the neck of Troy's in the noose—her doom is sealed" (7.464–465). Agamemnon seconds this response. Success today has given them hope for success tomorrow. But they have failed to reckon with the plan of Zeus, who spends the night plotting "fresh disaster for both opposing armies" (7.552). The next day, Zeus begins to execute his plan, as Hector rises to take glory. Inspired by the gods, he eventually drives the Greeks behind their makeshift wall that separates the camp from the battlefield (see 7.500–510). Before he can destroy "all the Achaean and all their hollow ships" and "turn home to the windy heights of Troy"

(8.578–579), night falls and the battle ends. But the damage is done. Achilles' stock is rising through the roof.

Homer describes the descent of darkness with an exquisitely beautiful passage:

> And so their spirit soared
> as they took positions down the passageways of battle
> all night long, and the watchfires blazed among them.
> Hundreds strong, as stars in the night sky glittering
> round the moon's brilliance blaze in all their glory
> when the air falls to a sudden, windless calm...
> All the lookout peaks stand out and the jutting cliffs
> and the steep ravines and down from the high heavens bursts
> the boundless bright air and all the stars shine clear
> and the shepherd's heart exults—so many fires burned
> between the ships and the Xanthus' whirling rapids
> set by the men of Troy, bright against their walls.
> A thousand fires were burning there on the plain
> and beside each fire sat fifty fighting men
> poised in the leaping blaze, and champing oats
> and glistening barley, stationed by their chariots,
> stallions waited for Dawn to mount her glowing
> throne (8.638–654).

Like the night scene before Agincourt in Shakespeare's *Henry V* ("a little touch of Harry in the night"), the impression of peace that this passage leaves is partly achieved by contrast to the relentless violence of the preceding pages. More than this, the passage gives a feeling of cosmic calm. Stars shining from heaven find an earthly mirror in the fires that dot the landscape, for both heaven and earth are at rest. It is in passages like these that Homer captures the grandeur of war, its thrill and beauties. Like the city, however, night is only a short reprieve from battle. The men sitting beside the fires are still "fighting men" and the stallions champing their oats and barley wait for the dawn, when their masters will champ for a taste of battle and blood. Significantly, the passage takes the Trojan perspective, whose "spirits soared" as their day of victory comes to an end. Knowing that Hector's advance is part of Zeus's plan to exalt Achilles, the reader realizes that the Trojans' sense of the world's harmony is false. For now, Trojan campfires throw their cheerful light against the walls and the stars glitter above, but soon the walls themselves will burn and stars will fall from the sky.

*Review Questions.*
1. Why is Achilles mad? What is significant about the circumstances that lead to Achilles' rage?
2. What is the prophecy concerning Achilles' future? Why is this significant?
3. What are the consequences of Achilles' extreme zeal for his own glory?
4. What is the plan of Zeus? What do the Greeks think will happen? The Trojans?
5. What kind of leader is Agamemnon? How do you know?
6. Why do Paris and Menelaus fight the first duel? What happens during the duel of Paris and Menelaus?
7. How are Paris and Achilles different? How are they similar? What is Homer getting at through these two characters?
8. How is Hector different from both? Why is it significant that he enters the city? How is this reflected in the scene with Andromache?
9. What is the significance of the scene between Diomedes and Glaucus?
10. What is the mood of the nighttime scene at the end of Book 8? What is significant about it?

*Thought Questions.*
1. What kind of relationship did Achilles and Agamemnon have before Agamemnon's insult? (see 1.99–108, 192–202)
2. How is the heroes' conduct in council similar to their conduct in war? How is it different? (see 1.356–358; 2.895–916; 3.179–184)

3. Describe the procedure for sacrifice (see 1.545–566). Compare it to the sacrificial procedures in Leviticus 1–4.

4. What kind of dream does Agamemnon have in Book 2.1–56? How does this dream fit with the rest of the action in Book 2?

5. How do the Greeks and Trojans prepare for the duel between Paris and Menelaus? (3.315–356)

6. How does Agamemnon try to stir Odysseus to battle? How does this fit with larger themes of the poem? (4.405–424)

7. What is significant about the gods entering battle in Book 5? What does this say about the heroes? How do the gods fight?

8. Describe Priam's palace. Why does Homer focus on the bedrooms? (6.288–297)

9. How does the duel between Ajax and Hector end? Why is this significant? (7.326–358)

10. Is Zeus in charge of the war? (see 8.382–565)

## The Love of Achilles, Books 9–17

While the Trojans dream of victory, the Greeks panic, and Panic is, as Homer says, "comrade of bloodcurdling Rout" (9.2). Hector's advance has been devastating, and the Greeks realize their only chance for salvaging their siege is to enlist the help of Achilles. Gathering again for council at a feast (9.106–108), Agamemnon suggests, as he did in Book 2, that everyone go home, but Diomedes opposes this as the plan of a coward. Wise old Nestor suggests a better course, urging Agamemnon to give up his "overbearing anger" and seek reconciliation with Achilles: "late as it is, let us contrive to set all this to rights, to bring him round with gifts of friendship and warm, winning words" (9.130–135). In Book 7, we saw a similar pattern: The Trojans decide in council to make some concessions and seek peace with the Greeks, but Diomedes refuses the offer. Agamemnon's attempts to appease Achilles will meet with a similar response.

And this is hardly surprising, for Agamemnon's "repentance" is severely qualified. He does not take full responsibility for treating Achilles unjustly, attributing his actions to madness, blindness, and inhuman rage (like that of Achilles). Later, when Achilles finally returns to the battle, Agamemnon's confession is even less satisfactory: "But I am not to blame! Zeus and Fate and the Fury stalking through the night, *they* are the ones who drove that savage madness in my heart, that day in assembly when I seized Achilles' prize—on my own authority, true, but what could *I* do?" (19.100–104). Agamemnon's failure to openly confess wrong tells us something about his character, but it reveals a deep fault in the heroic ethic as well. If self-glory is the greatest good, and shame the greatest evil, open confession of sin is simply impossible, for one cannot confess sin without risking shame. If confession is impossible, so is genuine forgiveness; how can you forgive someone who insists, in Clintonesque fashion, "It's not my fault"? And if forgiveness and reconciliation are impossible, then so are friendship, community, and genuine fellowship. The heroic ethic is an ethic for the battlefield and the camp, and even in the camp it is a divisive force. One cannot build a city, or at least a lasting city, on such a basis.

To his credit, Agamemnon is willing to do what Paris is not—return the girl, swearing an oath that he has not slept with her (9.157–161). More than that, he offers gifts to make amends for the offense he caused: tripods, stallions, seven women, the first choice of Trojan spoils. Generous though they are, these gifts have an insulting underside. Gift-giving, as we have seen, is one of the chief means by which ancient Greeks formed personal bonds, yet gift-giving is also a way of asserting one's superiority. If I give you $1 million, it establishes a connection between us, but there is no doubt who is dominant in the relationship. Gifts and bribes are not entirely dissimilar. By giving such rich gifts to Achilles, Agamemnon is implicitly continuing to claim superiority. This is more explicit in his promise to give Achilles one of his own daughters as a bride, to make him "my son-by-marriage" (9.170). That sounds good, until we realize that the original insult was Agamemnon's claim to be greater than Achilles. If Agamemnon becomes his father-in-law, his superiority is established permanently and bindingly. That Agamemnon still intends to demonstrate his superiority to Achilles is shown in the outburst at the end of his speech:

> All this—
> I would extend to him if he will end his anger.
> Let him submit to me! Only the god of death
> is so relentless. Death submits to no one—
> so mortals hate him most of the gods.
> Let him bow down to me! I am the greater king,
> I am the elder-born, I claim—the greater man (9.187–193).

These are hardly conciliatory words. Fortunately, the embassy to Achilles, consisting of Ajax, Odysseus, and Phoenix, has the sense not to repeat Agamemnon's final statements.

As noted above, Book 9 is a central hinge in the structure of the *Iliad*. It stands at the center of the epic, both continuing Homer's development of the issues raised in Book 1 and looking forward to the resolution of the second half of the epic. First, it reveals most pointedly how Achilles' heroism has been transformed into its opposite. Odysseus makes the first appeal to Achilles, and he addresses him as a hero. He reminds Achilles of his father's warning not to lose control of his anger and his promise that by holding his rage in check, Achilles' comrades "will exalt you all the more" (9.313). Odysseus ends his speech by promising that, were he to return, Achilles would be honored "like a god": "Think of the glory you will gather in their eyes!" (9.367–368). Achilles' response is shocking:

> No, what lasting thanks in the long run
> for warring with our enemies, on and on, no end?
> One and the same lot for the man who hangs back
> and the man who battles hard. The same honor waits

for the coward and the brave. They both go down to Death,
the fighter who shirks, the one who works to exhaustion.
And what's laid up for me, what pittance? Nothing—
and after suffering hardships, year in, year out,
staking my life on the mortal risks of war (9.383–391).

His response to Phoenix's story about Meleager is similar. Meleager withdrew from defending his city when he became enraged at his own mother. He was eventually aroused out of his pout to beat back the enemy, but Phoenix points out that by that time the offers of gifts had been withdrawn: "he beat off that disaster . . . empty-handed" (9.729). So Achilles runs the risk of entering "this man-killing war without the gifts," which means that his "fame will flag, no longer the same honor, even though you hurl the Trojans home" (9.735–737). Achilles bitterly asks, "what do I need with honor such as that?" He goes so far as to threaten to leave for home the next morning and advises the others to do the same (9.432–447; 506–510). Knowing the prophecy that Achilles will die a peaceful but inglorious death if he leaves, this threat is a threat to abandon heroism entirely. Achilles is tottering at the edge of anti-heroism, for he is on the verge of choosing life over glory.

Odysseus also appeals to Achilles' sense of duty, his *philos*, to his fellow soldiers. Again reminding Achilles of his father's advice, he urges, "you hold in check that proud, fiery spirit of yours inside your chest! Friendship is much better. Vicious quarrels are deadly—put an end to them, at once" (9.309–312). Burly Ajax, a man of action rather than an orator, brusquely makes the same argument. Achilles is "so savage, not a thought for his comrades' love." Agamemnon's offer was sufficient even if Achilles had lost a brother or a child, but in Achilles "the gods have planted a cruel, relentless fury in your chest" (9.777–778). Achilles, while admitting that Ajax's words are well said, cannot get over the rage that rises whenever he thinks of Agamemnon's treatment: "like some vagabond, like some outcast stripped of all my rights" (9.792–793). Achilles' godlike rage has isolated him from his fellows, and he seems deaf to the imperative of *philos*.

With regard to the plot, the embassy to Achilles has a double significance. On the one hand, Achilles' refusal of Agamemnon's offer ensures that Zeus's plan will go forward, that the Trojans will continue to have success, and that Achilles' honor will be multiplied. On the other hand, the appeals of his friends have some effect. Initially, Achilles threatens to leave the next day; after Phoenix's speech, he wavers and agrees to put off a decision until morning (9.755–756); after Ajax's brief outburst, Achilles gives his final word:

> You go back to [Agamemnon] and declare my message:
> I will not think of arming for bloody war again,
> not till the son of wise King Priam, dazzling Hector
> batters all the way to the Myrmidon ships and shelters,
> slaughtering Argives, gutting the hulls with fire.
> But round my own black ship and camp this Hector
> will be stopped, I trust, blazing for battle
> as he goes—stopped dead in his tracks (9.794–801).

This is still a decision to refrain from battle, but more importantly it is a decision to remain at Troy. Achilles' change of heart, slight though it is, is significant on several levels. Achilles decides for heroism and glory, stepping back from the precipice of an anti-heroic future; he will not be a Paris forever. Given the prophecy that looms over Achilles, a decision to remain at Troy is also a decision for death, albeit a glorious one. What he responds to is not, however, a promise of future *kleos* but an appeal to *philos*. Thus, he begins to be restored not only to his heroic destiny but also to the fellowship of heroes. His godlike isolation begins to melt away. Achilles' positive response to Ajax's appeal foreshadows his later return to battle. Though he lusts for honor, in the end Achilles returns to battle out of love for a fallen friend.

Achilles' rejection of Agamemnon's offer means that the plan of Zeus will move forward, and as it does the battle reaches a peak of intensity. More than any others in the epic,

Books 11–17 depict the twists and turns, the horrors and triumphs of battle. Homer's descriptions of the battlefield and warriors, especially the similes he uses to describe them, help us determine some facets of Homer's view of the war. Many of his epic similes compare warriors to predators. Diomedes goes on a rampage through the Thracian part of the Greek camp:

> As a lion springs on flocks unguarded, shepherd gone,
> pouncing on goats and sheep and claw-mad for the kill,
> so Tydeus' son went tearing into that Thracian camp
> until he'd butchered twelve (10.561–564).

Heroes are bestial even in their clothing: Agamemnon enters the field wearing the "hide of a big tawny lion" and Menelaus walks beside him draped in a leopard skin (10.27, 34), while Diomedes puts on a hide decorated with "the gleaming teeth of a white-tusked boar [running] round and round in rows stitched neat and tight" (10.307–308). Like predators, heroes immediately leap to strip their victims. When a Trojan falls, the Greeks fight to strip his armor as plunder, swarming over him like flies on a fresh pail of milk (16.745–747), while the Trojans protect the body so that it can be taken back to the city for proper burial rites. These descriptions are not offered merely as realistic descriptions of ancient battle but have a thematic purpose. War is an opportunity for eternal glory as men seek godlike immortality, but it also turns its practitioners into something less than human. Battles end with feasts—the predatory feast of slaughter is followed by a sacrificial feast to the immortal, cruel gods (16.185–195).

Homer also compares the heroes to forces of nature, especially fire and water:

> Wild as a swollen river hurling down on the flats,
> down from the hills in winter spate, bursting its banks
> with rain from storming Zeus, and stands of good dry oak,
> whole forests of pine it whorls into itself and sweeps along

> till it heaves a crashing mass of driftwood out to sea—
> so glorious Ajax swept the field, routing Trojans (11.580–585).

Epic similes of this type not only capture the awesome power of the heroes but also show something of the lack of moral grounding for their actions. A river is not guilty of murder when it overflows its banks and floods a city, nor a fire guilty of arson when it burns down buildings. Similarly, a hero is not guilty when he hews down his enemies and devours them; that is just what heroes *do*.[4]

Victims also become something less than human. Pisander and Hippolochus seek mercy from Agamemnon, who rejects their pleas:

> And he pitched Pisander off the chariot onto earth
> and plunged a spear in his chest—the man crashed on his back
> as Hippolochus leapt away, but *him* he killed on the ground,
> slashing off his arms with a sword, lopping off his head,
> and he sent him rolling through the carnage like
> a log (11.166–170).

Ajax kills a Trojan who falls like a cut tree (13.210–215), and when the Greek Meriones hits Harpalion with an arrow, the latter falls, "gasping out life as he writhed along the ground like an earthworm stretched out in death, blood pooling, soaking the earth dark red" (13.753–755).

Yet, as we have mentioned, Homer is also able to capture the thrill that warriors experience in the midst of battle. In part he does this by comparing battle to the games of peacetime—hunting and fishing. Odysseus and Diomedes go after Dolon "as a pair of rip-tooth hounds bred for the hunt and flushing fawn or hare, through a woody glen keep closing for the kill, nonstop and the prey goes screaming on ahead" (10.421–424). When Patroclus comes on the field, he plunges his spear into the head of Thestor and raises him from his chariot, dragging "the Trojan out as an angler perched on a jutting rock ledge drags some fish from the sea, some noble catch, with line and glittering bronze hook" (16.480–485).

Behind the scenes, the changeable gods affect the ebb and flow of battle. In Book 14, Hera seduces Zeus and puts him to sleep so that the Greeks can make a comeback. Just as Helen tries to distract Hector from the business of war, so also Hera takes Zeus's attention from the battle. The only difference is that Hector has more self-control. Homer depicts Hera's seduction as an act of war:

> round her shoulders she swirled the wondrous robes
> that Athena wove her, brushed out to a high gloss
> and worked into the weft an elegant rose brocade.
> She pinned them across her breasts with a golden brooch
> then sashed her waist with a waistband
> floating a hundred tassels, and into her earlobes,
> neatly pierced, she quickly looped her earrings,
> ripe mulberry-clusters, dangling in triple drops
> and the silver glints they cast could catch the heart.
> Then back over her brow she draped her headdress,
> fine fresh veils for Hera the queen of the gods,
> their pale, glimmering sheen like a rising sun,
> and under her smooth feet she fastened supple
> sandals (14.217–229).

This echoes the description of Patroclus and Achilles as they arm themselves for battle (see 16.155–173). Sex is Hera's chief weapon. Zeus falls for the scheme, and takes her away to his own bedroom, surrounded by the clouds. With Zeus distracted, the tide of war turns against the Trojans, and Hector falls.

Overall, however, these books depict a steady Trojan advance toward the Greek ships. Some of the best of the Greek heroes are wounded—Ajax, Odysseus, and Diomedes. Hector finally breaks through the makeshift wall that protects the Greek camp and sets fire to the ships. Achilles' wish is coming true. When he returns, he will be able to win glory over difficult odds; while he sits in his ships, every Greek is aware that they need him. Without Hector knowing it, the plan of Zeus is advancing, a plan that includes his death.

The battle at the wall of the Greek camp is worth pondering for a moment. First, boundaries and walls played a more important role in the ancient world than in our own day. Practically, walls were necessary for defense, but they also had a religious significance. From a biblical perspective, we can note that God created an ordered world largely by forming boundaries: between night and day, waters above and below, sea and land. Setting off boundaries is thus an imitation of God's creative act. When two people take a piece of land and divide it into two territories, a new situation is brought into reality, a "new creation." This explains why forming boundaries must be done with care, justice, and prayer, and it also shows why the Bible warns against setting aside ancient boundary stones.

The religious significance of the wall is brought out at the beginning of Book 12. Homer describes the Greek ramparts:

> The Argive trench could not hold out much longer,
> nor could the rampart rearing overhead, the wide wall
> they raised to defend the ships and the broad trench
> they drive around it all—they never gave the gods
> the splendid sacrifice the immortals craved,
> that the fortress might protect the fast ships
> and the bulking plunder heaped behind its shield.
> Defying the deathless gods they built that wall
> and so it stood there steadfast no long time (12.4–12).

Ancient Greeks believed that no boundary or protection could hold out against the gods, and so all boundaries were sanctified by sacrifice. Because the Greeks neglected this, their wall was doomed to be breached. The battle at the wall of the Greek camp also foreshadows the later battle at the walls of Troy. Though the Trojans had observed proper custom in building their walls, the gods had decreed a doom against them. Their walls were destined to fall.

Even before Hector breaks through, Achilles has begun to take a more active interest in the battle. Standing on "the stern of his looming hollow hull, looking out over the uphill work and heartsick rout of war" (11.708–709), he notices that a wounded warrior is being taken from the field. His *philos* aroused, Achilles sends Patroclus to find out who it is, and Patroclus discovers that Machaon, "the expert healer," has been wounded. Nestor is there as well, and in one of his typically rambling speeches, the old man encourages Patroclus to ask Achilles to let him enter the battle wearing Achilles' armor. The Trojans might flee, thinking that Achilles has returned to the field (11.948–955). Nestor's words appeal to Patroclus, who agrees to the scheme. Before returning to Achilles, however, he takes an arrow from the thigh of a fellow Greek and pours healing ointment on the wound. It is a good omen: Patroclus comes on the scene as the healer of Greek wounds.

So he will be. In Book 16, he returns to Achilles and appeals to him to relent from his rage; Achilles is "cursed in your own courage" (16.34). Patroclus speculates that Achilles is staying back for fear of some prophecy (16.41), but Achilles denies it: "No, no, my prince, Patroclus, what are you saying? Prophecies? None that touch me. None I know of. No doom my noble mother revealed to me from Zeus" (16.57–59). Patroclus may not know it, but we know that he protests too much. Like Odysseus, he appeals to Achilles' loyalty to his wounded fellows, but Achilles is still more concerned with his own wound, the humiliation he received from Agamemnon (16.57–68). Yet he gives Patroclus permission to enter the battle wearing his armor and leading the Myrmidon warriors. This represents an ideal solution for Achilles. He can continue nursing his grudge against Agamemnon and remain at his ships, consistent with his decision in Book 9. Because Patroclus will enter the battle dressed as Achilles, however, any victories that he achieves will partly be attributed to Achilles himself. Achilles can stay outside the battle and still receive glory.[5] It seems the best of both worlds; he has found a way to dodge his heroic dilemma.

Yet, his plan is doomed, overshadowed by the plan of

Zeus. Achilles insists that Patroclus should not attempt to take the walls of Troy himself: "you must not burn for war against these Trojans, madmen lusting for battle—not without *me*—you will only make *my* glory that much less" (16.104–106). Achilles may have seen the folly of heroism in Book 9, but now he is back in heroic form, itching for glory. He is beginning to taste battle, and he wants to make a meal of it. Achilles prays to Zeus that Patroclus will show courage and that he will return safely, but "one prayer the Father granted, the other he denied: Patroclus would drive the onslaught off the ships... but denied him safe and sound return from battle" (16.294–297). Zeus's plan may exalt Achilles, but it will first debase him. Achilles knows that as soon as he enters the battle wearing his armor, he is doomed to die at the windy heights of Troy. As if some infection attached to the armor itself, the same happens to all who wear it— Patroclus, and later Hector.

Patroclus acquits himself well in the battle, driving the Trojans back, inspiring the troops, and cutting off the Trojan retreat. Eventually, Hector and Patroclus face one another and fight like lions over the corpse of Hector's driver Cebriones. On Patroclus's fourth charge, Apollo knocks the helmet from his head, and he is wounded, left on the field for Hector to finish off. With his dying words, Patroclus predicts the death of Hector at the hands of Achilles, but Hector brushes off the threat, takes the armor of Achilles, pulls his spear from Patroclus's chest, and turns on another Greek. Zeus, meanwhile, has confirmed Hector's fate, accusing him of taking Achilles' armor "against all rights" (17.235). Patroclus, the healer of Greek wounds, has died. But from his dying a new Achilles will come forth as the hero who will bring healing.

*Review Questions.*

1. How does Agamemnon try to resolve his quarrel with Achilles? Is his offer a good one?

2. Is Achilles moved by the speeches of his friends? What does he decide? Why?

3. What kind of animals are the warriors compared to? Why?
4. What is significant about the comparison of the heroes to forces of nature?
5. How does Homer capture the thrill of battle?
6. What is significant about Homer's description of Hera's preparations to seduce Zeus?
7. Why do the gods permit the destruction of the Greek wall?
8. What is significant about Patroclus's aid to Machaon?
9. Why does Achilles agree to let Patroclus enter the battle wearing his armor?
10. What restriction does Achilles impose on Patroclus? Why? What does this say about Achilles' attitude toward the war?

*Thought Questions.*
1. What are the Greek princes doing before they meet in council? Why is this significant? (9.103–110)
2. What do Diomedes and Odysseus do during the night in Book 10? Is it a useful exercise?
3. How is Agamemnon wounded? What effect does this have on the battle? (11.288–347)
4. What other Greek heroes are wounded in Book 11?
5. What omen do the Trojans see as they breach the Greek wall? What does it mean? (12.225–266)
6. Which goddesses conspire to distract Zeus from the battle? Why is this significant? (14.236–256)
7. Whose son is Achilles, according to Patroclus? Why does Patroclus say this? (16.39–40)
8. Why does Zeus want to save Sarpedon? How does Hera persuade him otherwise? (16.512–548)
9. What happens to Patroclus's soul when he dies? (16.1001–1009)
10. What is Zeus's view of human life? (17.509–525)

## Enraged Love, Books 18–21

News of Patroclus's death and Hector's seizure of Achilles' armor devastates Achilles:

> A black cloud of grief came shrouding over Achilles.
> Both hands clawing the ground for soot and filth,
> he poured it over his head, fouled his handsome face
> and black ashes settled onto his fresh clean war-shirt.
> Overpowered in all of his power, sprawled in the dust,
> Achilles lay there, fallen (18.24–29).

This description is patterned on earlier descriptions of death. Death descends over the eyes of men struck in battle, and they fall to couple with the dust. Patroclus was impersonating Achilles when he died; now the original Achilles falls in a kind of symbolic death. Achilles' is not merely sympathizing with his friend; he knows that his return to the battle, and his death, is immanent. Eerily, Achilles' slave women gather around him, beating their breasts, as if mourning for their master rather than their master's friend (18.31–35).

Achilles "dies"; the Achilles that rises from the "grave" of mourning is the same and yet different. Grief is only part of Achilles' reaction. He is also enraged, as he has been throughout the story, but now his rage is turned toward Hector and the Trojans (18.394). In fact, grief and rage are indistinguishable in Achilles (see 18.369, 374). Earlier, he lost the will to fight because of Agamemnon's treatment, but now his only purpose for living is to take vengeance upon Hector. He now recognizes that his anger has cost Patroclus his life. If he had not been sitting by the ships "a useless, dead weight on the good green earth," he could have protected his friend. Seeing the effects of his rage against Agamemnon, he wishes that "strife could die from the lives of gods and men and anger that drives the sanest man to flare in outrage" (18.126–127). But these are the words of an outraged man, who is intent on perpetuating strife by taking vengeance. That he is still operating by the heroic ethic is evident, for he fully commits himself to glory: "I'll lie in peace, once I've gone down to death. But now, for the moment, let me seize great glory!" (18.143–144). *Philos* has not only turned his rage to Hector; it has revived his lust for *kleos*.

Meanwhile, the Trojans gather for council. Achilles has been standing in the Greek camp giving out a great war cry. Merely by his cry, and by raising the prospect of his return to battle, he has driven the Trojans into panic. In the council, Polydamas speaks first and, like the Greek Thersites in Book 2, urges the Trojans to retreat to the city before dawn. He realizes that Achilles' rage "will never rest content" to fight it out in the "no man's land" of the battlefield: "*he* will fight for our wives, for Troy itself!" Behind the strong walls of Troy, they will be safe: "Not even *his* fury will let him crash our gates" (18.303, 306, 327). This is sound advice, but Hector treats it with contempt: "Aren't you sick of being caged inside those walls?" Troy is already being plundered, for the Trojans have had to strip down their treasures to support their defensive war. He implies that the other Trojans are cowards, insisting that "I for one, I'll never run from his grim assault"—but Hector will later do precisely that! (18.330–360). The Trojans assent to Hector's strategy, for "Athena had swept away their senses" (18.362). But their senses have already been swept away by the heroic ideal that grips them. Acting as a hero in his passion for glory, Hector dooms himself and his city. Hector does not want to feel the shame, the *aidos*, that comes from being a coward; but he neglects the other aspect of his *aidos*, the need to pity and protect those who remain in the city, the wisdom that retreats to fight another day.

Hera sends Iris to urge Achilles back to the battlefield, warning him that the Trojans are trying to capture the body of Patroclus, in order to cut off his head and stake it by the city: "Yours, the shame will be yours if your comrade's corpse goes down to the dead defiled!" she tells him (18.209–210). Achilles' anger concerning the threat to Patroclus's body will later be expressed in his mistreatment of Hector's. Achilles objects that he has no armor, and Thetis promptly seeks out Hephaestus, the smithy god, to forge a new set. This is one of the great illustrations of Homer's free use of a "type scene." With Achilles ready to return to battle, we expect an arming scene, and do we ever get an arming scene! The description of the shield alone occupies a large part of Book 18. This great expansion of the arming scene is like using italics; Homer signals that *this* arming scene is the climax of the whole epic.

Achilles is no ordinary warrior, and this is no ordinary shield. It is covered with intricate scenes that depict a "world of gorgeous immortal work" (18.564). An entire world in bronze, it includes the sun, moon, and some of the major constellations (18.565–571), and its outermost rim is encircled by "Ocean," which surrounds the earth in Greek cosmology (18.708–709). Within this cosmic setting are scenes from two cities. The first is a city at peace; within it there are weddings, processions and dances, a court, and markets. The second city is under siege, as is Troy, but the city refuses to surrender, just as Hector has refused to retreat. Besiegers and besieged struggle at a river bank, foreshadowing Achilles' later slaughter of Trojans in the river (Book 21). Strife, Havoc, and Death join in and leave the land scattered with corpses.

In addition to the peaceful city, the shield contains other scenes of what Simone Weil called the "brief evocations of peace" in the midst of the relentless mayhem of war that dominates the *Iliad*: a farmer plowing a field, the harvest of a king's grain field, girls and boys gathering grapes from a vineyard. Above all, there is a dancing circle:

> Here young boys and girls, beauties courted
> with costly gifts of oxen, danced and danced,
> linking their arms, gripping each other's wrists....
> A breathless crowd stood round them struck with joy
> and through them a pair of tumblers dashed and sprang,
> whirling in leaping handsprings, leading out
> the dance (18.693–707).

Contemporary popular dance is often a highly individual affair. John Travolta can gyrate around the dance floor whether or not anyone else is there. Each dancer shows off his stuff, lost in his own world, turning everyone else into a spectator. Folk dancing, by contrast, is a communal event and thus a common image of social harmony and peace. Each dancer has his unique place in the dance, and there are leaders and followers. Arm in arm and hand in hand, individual dancers are linked together into a greater whole.

But the evocation of peace has some ironic twists. In the "peaceful" city, two men are quarreling "over the blood-price for a kinsman just murdered" while the elders sit in a "sacred circle" judging the case (18.572–592). It is significant that, unlike Achilles, the men contending in court are not pursuing vengeance by the sword but fighting with words and arguments, the weapons of the city. They have subordinated their rage to the judgment of elders, something that Achilles has refused to do. More generally, the shield shows that violent death has as much a place in the city as on the battlefield. Dancers there may be, but some citizens do not follow the choreography. Later, Homer describes a scene of cattle rumbling from the farmyard to pasture (18.670–685). It is a bucolic scene, as the animals go "along a rippling brook, along the swaying reeds." Yet it is interrupted by the attack of a pair of lions, who drag off one of the bulls, "gulp down the guts and black pooling blood," and fight off the herdsman and gods who try to intervene. Troy's comparative peace has been shattered by the onrush of savage Greeks, who tear Trojans like lions tearing prey.

Some commentators on the *Iliad* suggest that the shield depicts an "ideal" world, but this is not the case. It depicts the world as it is, with its beauties and harmonies, as well as its dangers and cruelties. Homer, however, cannot imagine any other world, and this is what infuses the worldview of the poem with despair and resignation. There is no vision of a world beyond strife. Peace and war lie side by side, both equally essential. At best, strife and murder can be subordinated to the rule of law, but Homer has no hope for a New City that descends from heaven, in which only righteousness and peace will dwell. Even the most serene evocations of peace, we should remember, are forged on a weapon of war.

When Thetis delivers the armor to Achilles, its glory is so great that none can look at it (19.15–23). Dressed in it, Achilles seems a glorious god, "blazing forth," ready to fight alongside Agamemnon. Their "reconciliation" is hardly satisfying, nor does it make Achilles a more appealing character. Though earlier he had professed to love Briseis with all his heart, he now seems to dismiss her entirely: "Agamemnon, was it better for both of us, after all, for you and me to rage at each other, raked by anguish, consumed by heartsick strife, all for a girl?" (19.63–65)—as opposed to something *really* important. Homer says that the Achaeans rejoice that Achilles is "swearing off his rage," but this is not quite true. Rather than giving up his anguish and anger, he intends only to "beat it down ... by force" (19.75–76). In fact, he has not foresworn his rage; he has only redirected it to a new object. Agamemnon, for his part, refuses to accept blame, saying, in essence, the gods made me do it. In the war camp, where only heroes live, this is the only possible kind of reconciliation: Achilles and Agamemnon agree to fight together. They will never, we can be sure, dance together.

Achilles is ready for battle, but Odysseus reminds him that an army needs to eat, and urges him to take a break for a meal. Since it involves a sacrificial shedding of blood, a feast will also be an opportunity to seal his renewed friendship with Agamemnon: "as a peace offering, let [Agamemnon] present you a lavish feast in his tents so you won't lack your just deserts at last" (19.213–215). Agamemnon agrees: "we can seal our binding oaths in blood" (19.229). Achilles will have none of it. In some of the most chilling lines in the poem, he makes clear that he is interested in a different kind of feast, a different slaughter, a different sacrifice: "You talk of food? I have no taste for food—what I really crave is slaughter and blood and the choking groans of men" (19.254–256). Even after Agamemnon has delivered the promised gifts, swearing to Zeus that he has not slept with her, Achilles is not pacified: "no comfort could reach the fighter's heart till he went striding into the jaws of bloody war" (19.370–371). Good thing he has "sworn off his rage" (19.86).

Books 20–22, the *aristeia* of Achilles, have an intricate arrangement. At the beginning of Book 20, Zeus holds council and encourages the gods to interfere with the battle. The gods make a tremendous ruckus, but when they get to earth they do nothing. Then, Achilles meets Aeneas and Hector in succession, but both are rescued by gods before being killed. Books 21–22 follow a similar pattern. Achilles fights the river god Scamander, and this spurs the other gods to join in as they had threatened to in Book 20. Achilles then fights Agenor and Hector, in battles that mirror each other. Both Agenor and Hector deliberate about whether to face Achilles before deciding to fight. In both battles, a god intervenes. Apollo rescues Agenor by taking on the appearance of Agenor and running away, so that Achilles pursues him. While Hector is, like the false Agenor, running from Achilles, Athena helps Achilles by taking the form of Hector's brother and urging him to stand and fight. Thus, Books 20–22 are organized in parallel panels:

*Book 20*
A. Gods threaten to fight
B. Achilles v. Aeneas (god intervenes to end fight)
B'. Achilles v. Hector (god intervenes to end fight)

Books 21–22
A. Gods fight
B. Achilles v. Agenor (Apollo tricks Agenor)
B'. Achilles v. Hector (Athena tricks Hector)

Zeus's main goal in sending the gods into battle is to prevent Achilles from razing the walls, which fate has decreed Achilles will not destroy. Without the gods helping the

Trojans, Achilles will win too easily. Symbolically, the intervention of the gods raises the battle to cosmic proportions. Not only Greeks and Trojans, but the whole universe fights before the walls of Troy in a great pagan Armageddon. No wonder the "whole world quaked" (20.71), as it does in Hesiod's description of Zeus's battle with the Titans (see chapter 1). Some of the exploits of the gods and goddesses appear humorous. Achilles is a terror on the field, but the catfights between Athena and Aphrodite and Hera and Artemis (which ends with Artemis running back to daddy, Zeus) are hard to take seriously (21.437–590). The gods cannot really be terrifying or terrified, for they risk nothing when they enter the fray. Deathless gods cannot be heroic.

We have seen many warriors in battle up to this point, but none like Achilles. His butchery has an almost religious power to it, as he spears Hippodamas "like some bull that chokes and grunts when the young boys drag him round the lord of Helice's shrine" (20.458–460). Homer constructs a horrifying epic simile to capture the power of his charge:

> Over against [Aeneas] came Achilles rearing like some lion
> out on a rampage, and a whole town of men has geared
> for the hunt to cut him down: but at first he lopes along,
> all contempt, till one of the fast young hunters spears him—
> then... crouched for attack, his jaws gaping, over his teeth
> the foam breaks out, deep in his chest the brave heart groans,
> he lashes his ribs, his flanks and hips with his tail,
> he whips himself into fighting-fury, eyes glaring,
> hurls himself head-on—kill one of the men or die,
> go down himself at the first lethal charge (20.194–203).

Deeply wounded when Hector plunged his spear into Patroclus, Achilles now groans and glares against his attacker.

Like the predator, Achilles shows no mercy to his victims. When Troas grasps Achilles' knees and pleads for mercy,

> he'd no idea, thinking *Achilles* could be swayed!
> Here was a man not sweet at heart, not kind, no,

he was raging, wild—as Troas grasped his knees,
desperate, begging, Achilles slit open
his liver (20.527–530).

He storms through the Trojan camp "like inhuman fire raging on through the mountain gorges splinter-dry, setting ablaze big stands of timber ... chaos of fire" (20.554–557). He is no longer a man. He is an elemental force of nature, relentless as death itself.

Before Achilles, the Trojans retreat behind the walls of their city. Hector alone remains outside, watching as the fire spreads across the field.

*Review Questions*

1. What is the significance of Achilles' fall into the dust?
2. Explain how Achilles' rage is involved in Patroclus's death.
3. Why does Hector decide not to retreat behind the walls of Troy?
4. What is significant about the length of Homer's description of Achilles' shield?
5. What is depicted on the shield?
6. How does the shield display the "despair" of the Homeric worldview?
7. What does Achilles say when Odysseus urges him to eat? Why is this significant?
8. Explain the structure of Books 20–22.
9. Explain the lion simile used to describe Achilles.

*Thought Questions.*

1. After hearing of Patroclus's death, what does Achilles think of his rage? (18.113–131)
2. In W. H. Auden's post-World War II poem, "Achilles' Shield," he describes a shield that contains no scenes of peace or of heroic battle but only concentration camps and trench warfare. What is Auden saying by rewriting Homer in this way?

3. How are Achilles' armor and shield linked with his glory as a hero?

4. Why is it significant that Book 20 begins with a council of the gods? (20.15–22)

5. Why must Aeneas be spared? (20.348–356)

6. What is significant about Achilles' battle with the river Xanthus? (21.225–320)

## The Final Feasts, Books 22–24

As noted above, the last three books of the *Iliad* correspond chiastically (in reverse order) to the first three books. Book 22 describes the duel of Hector and Achilles, the duel that resolves the unfinished duel of Paris and Menelaus in Book 3. Book 3, moreover, gave us a first glimpse of Hector, while in Book 22 we see him alive for the last time.

Hector stands outside the city walls, "shackled fast by his deadly fate" (22.6), while Priam and Hecuba urge him to run to safety. Fated he may be, but Hector is having doubts about staying outside the walls. Like Achilles, he "nurses his quenchless fury" (22.115). Like Achilles, he faces the heroic choice between a shameful but long life or a short and glorious death:

> If I slip inside the gates and walls,
> Polydamas will be the first to heap disgrace on me....
> I would die of shame to face the men of Troy
> and the Trojan women trailing their long robes ...
>     So now, better by far for me
> to stand up to Achilles, kill him, come home alive
> or die at his hands in glory out before the
> walls (22.118–131; see 22.359–362).

Even now, however, he considers the possibility of laying down his weapons and trying to negotiate a deal: "I could promise to give back Helen, yes, and all her treasures with her." We know from the previous books that Achilles is not in a conciliatory mood, and Hector knows it too: "He'll show no mercy, no respect for me, my rights—he'll cut me down straight off—stripped of defenses like a woman once I have loosed the armor off my body" (22.136–150). He expects Achilles to treat him the way Agamemnon has treated Achilles. In spite of this, he decides in favor of glory and immortality by fighting Achilles. There is no glory in the city; it is only on the field and in the camp. Achilles and Hector make precisely the same choice.

Yet, Hector's heroic choice has dimensions lacking in Achilles'. He must not only choose between shame and glory, but he must choose between the city and the field, between joining his family and fellow-citizens behind the walls or remaining outside in the vain hope of defeating Achilles. He must choose between the *aidos* of being considered a coward and the *aidos* that would lead him to save himself and protect his people. When Hector chooses to fight, he is thinking like a hero, but he is also motivated by a love for Troy and a sense of responsibility for her protection—a patriotic sentiment that we find in none of the Greeks. As he fights Achilles, he is thinking of the benefit for his city if Achilles were killed: "How much lighter the war would be for Trojans then if you, their greatest scourge, were dead and gone!" (22.339–340). The irony of the situation is like that of the scene in Book 6 with Andromache. Hector, the city's protector, fights to save his wife and city; but to do that he must leave them. As James Redfield puts it, his act of defense requires a kind of betrayal.

Achilles has no such motive. As the Trojans stream back behind the safety of the city walls, Achilles' rage turns against Apollo: "Now you've robbed me of great glory, saved their lives with all your deathless ease" (22.22–23). He warns the watching Greeks not to throw a spear at Hector, fearing that "someone might snatch the glory, Achilles come in second" (22.247). Glory and fury are inextricably mixed in Achilles' heroic temperament. When Hector flees from Achilles, it is the latter's "fury" that drives him on, as both men "race for the life of Hector breaker of horses" (22.169, 171, 193).

When Hector stops running and faces Achilles, he suggests that they swear a pact:

> I will never mutilate you—merciless as you are—
> if Zeus allows me to last it out and tear your life away
> But once I've stripped your glorious armor, Achilles,
> I will give your body back to your loyal comrades.
> Swear you'll do the same (22.302–306).

These are the same terms that Hector demanded in his duel with Ajax, but Achilles' rage permits no oaths: "There are no binding oaths between men and lions—wolves and lambs can enjoy no meeting of the minds—they are all bent on hating each other to the death" (22.310–312). When Achilles delivers the fatal blow with his spear, Hector again begs that Achilles to treat his body with respect and accept the ransom that Priam will offer for its return. Achilles is adamant that he will "shame your corpse while Achaeans bury my dear friend in glory" (22.396–397). Again, his fury rises to terrifying heights:

> Beg no more, you fawning dog—begging me by my parents!
> Would to god my rage, my fury would drive me now
> to hack your flesh away and eat you raw—
> such agonies you have caused me. Ransom? ...
> The dogs and birds will rend you—blood
> and bone (22.407–410, 417).

Like the dogs and birds, Achilles feasts only on slaughter and the choking groans of dying men. Intent on bringing shame to Hector, he drags his body behind his chariot back to the Greek camp, his "dark hair swirling around that head so handsome once, all tumbled low in the dust" (22.473–474). Hair, a natural crown, is associated with glory in ancient literature, but now Hector's glory lies in dust.

Within the city, Hecuba hears that Troy's glory has been laid in the dust and begins to tear her own hair (22.487–488), while Priam is "mad to go rushing out the Dardan Gates" after his son's killer (22.485). They are not only fearful for the future of Troy but see that Troy has lost its "greatest glory" (22.512). When Andromache sees Achilles dragging Hector away, she faints, flinging off her "glittering headdress"—her crown of glory—a gift of Aphrodite (22.550–552). Naturally, her concern is for her young son, who will grow to manhood without a father to protect him from thieves and strangers. Hector's shame, the end of his glory, goes on from generation to generation. Significantly, she describes both her son's and her husband's humiliation using the image of food. While Astyanax once "would only eat the marrow, the richest cuts of lamb," now he would be driven from the banquet (22.581–587, 589). And all this because Hector lies among the Greek ships while "glistening worms will wriggle through your flesh, once the dogs have had their fill of your naked corpse" (22.598–599). As Achilles' hour of glory brings shame to Hector, so Achilles' feast of slaughter robs food from Andromache's table.

Troy is filled with grief, and so is the Greek war camp, though their grief is by now expressed in a more dignified and less desperate way. Patroclus lies in state on his funeral pyre, while all the Greeks drive their chariots around giving "the solemn honors owed the dead" (23.9–10). As part of the funeral arrangements, Achilles sets out a feast and leads in a chant of mourning. The Greeks arm and ride past on their chariots, each casting his hair on the funeral pyre—sacrificing their own glory to honor the glorious dead (23.147–158). Achilles himself has been growing a lock of hair for the river god Spercheus, but he offers it instead on Patroclus's pyre. He had vowed to offer his lock and fifty rams when he returned to his home, but with the death of Patroclus and now Hector, he knows he will never return to fulfill that vow (23.162–174). Sacrifices are heaped up on Patroclus, along with jars of honey and oil, four stallions, two of Patroclus's favorite dogs, and a dozen young Trojans. As Homer says, "Achilles' mighty heart was erupting now with slaughter" (23.202). The funeral is a religious rite, but for Achilles it seems more like a continuation of the battle.

And not only for Achilles. He arranges funeral games for the Greeks: a chariot race, boxing, wrestling, a running race, a duel in full armor, and archery. That these games are infused with the spirit of war is clearest from the chariot race. As Diomedes closes in on Eumelus and is ready to pass him, Apollo suddenly "rages" at Diomedes whose eyes fill with "tears of rage" as he watches Eumelus pull ahead (23.432, 434). Menelaus curses Antilochus as they race to beat one another to a narrow part of the track: "no one alive more treacherous than you! Away with you, madman—damn you!" (23.489–490). When Idomeneus announces that Diomedes is going to win, Little Ajax tells him to stop "blustering, you, you foul-mouthed." Idomeneus responds in kind, calling Ajax stupid, stubborn, bullneck, and betting him that Diomedes is in the lead, and the two nearly come to blows (23.502–547). The ground rules for the duel are little different from the rules of battle: "The soldier who gets in first and cuts a rival's flesh, who pierces armor to draw blood and reach his entrails" is the winner (23.894–895).

Like the battle, the games are opportunities to achieve glory, including expensive prizes: animals, tripods, a silver bowl, gold, iron, and weapons. Warriors receive plunder in their games as in their battles, but their main goal is to show their superiority in warlike games. Epeus, a boxing champion, sums up the attitude in words that remind us of Mohammed Ali: "I am the greatest" (23.746). The parallel between war and games is suggested when Achilles calls off the wrestling match between Ajax and Odysseus (both of whom were severely wounded not long ago—Achilles is the healer!) with the words: "No more struggling—don't kill yourselves in sport!" (23.818). He almost exactly repeats the words of the herald Idaeus, who calls off the duel between Hector and Ajax by saying "don't kill yourselves in combat" (7.322). Even the rewards are similar in both cases. Achilles tells Odysseus and Ajax that "victory goes to both. Share the prizes" (23.819), while Idaeus tells Ajax and Hector that they are equal in glory and the love of the gods: "Zeus who marshals the storm cloud loves you both. You're both great fighters—we all know that full well" (7.323–324). In the heroic world, battles are games—dangerous and deadly, but games nonetheless. Games, conversely, are battles.

But in the midst of this playful war, something has come over Achilles. He is not the same man who was feasting on gore and blood in the previous books. He seems finally to have sworn off rage, having received his fill of slaughter and choking groans. When Little Ajax and Idomeneus nearly come to blows, Achilles intervenes to calm them down (23.548). Is this the same Achilles who has been nursing a grudge against Agamemnon throughout the whole epic? And there is more. Out of pity (23.593), he proposes to give Eumelus second prize, a mare, but the real second-place driver, Antilochus, objects. He suggests that Achilles give Eumelus another prize, and demands to be given his prize, threatening to fight anyone who tries to take the mare from him (23.598–619). Achilles relents and lets Antilochus keep his mare. Pity?! From Achilles!? Can the one who is as relentless as death relent?

Whatever has happened to Achilles has happened to others of the Greeks as well. When the mare has been given to Antilochus, Menelaus springs forward to accuse Antilochus of cheating in the race. Antilochus, who has only just threatened to fight off anyone who tried to seize his mare, backs down: "lord Menelaus—you're my senior, you the greater man. . . . I'll give you this mare I won—of my own accord" (23.651–657). If only, if only: If only Paris had given up his "mare," if only Agamemnon had given up Chryseis without demanding compensation, if only Achilles had given up his, admitting Agamemnon's superiority, the slaughter of the Trojan War could have been avoided entirely. Antilochus provides a moral barometer for the main characters of the epic, and shows them up to be stubborn, senseless.

The generous, just, pitiable Achilles of the funeral games has again disappeared at the beginning of Book 24. While the gods feud about the body of Hector, Achilles is still mourning and fasting, still "eating your heart out here in tears and torment," still full of "heartsick fury" (24.157, 165). Yet, though Achilles intends to defile Hector's body and leave it for the dogs, Apollo intervenes to preserve it. The pro-Greek gods resist him, but he reminds them of Hector's faithfulness in offering "thighs of oxen and flawless, full-grown goats" and rebukes them for favoring Achilles, a "man without a shred of decency in his heart" who has "no shame" (24.40, 47, 52). That description—"no shame"—strikes several notes at once. We recall that this is the same description given to the unheroic Paris. Achilles' lack of shame, his lack of concern for the reproaches of his fellows, led to the death of many Greeks, including his beloved Patroclus. But in the aftermath of his magnificent *aristeia*, another dimension emerges: Achilles has "no shame" because he is filled to the brim with glory.

Zeus accepts Apollo's arguments, decreeing that "Achilles must receive a ransom from King Priam, Achilles must give Hector's body back" (24.94–95). He sends Thetis to give instructions to receive Priam and Hermes to conduct him to Achilles tent. Simultaneously, he sends Iris to tell Priam that Achilles will accept him, though he must bear "gifts to Achilles, gifts to melt his rage" (24.178). Here again we see the contrast of rage/war and gifts; gifts are the means of relation in times of truce and peace. Gifts bind men together in pacts, but we have already seen Achilles refuse pacts and gifts. Agamemnon has tried this before, but in spite of the gifts Achilles' rage burned as hotly as ever. We are not as sure as Iris is that "Achilles is no madman, no reckless fool, not the one to defy the gods' commands. Whoever begs for mercy he will spare with all the kindness in his heart" (24.221–223). Hecuba's assessment seems more accurate: "If he gets you in his clutches, sets his eyes on you—that savage, treacherous man—he'll show no mercy, no respect for your rights" (24.244–246). She expects him to treat Priam the way Agamemnon has treated Achilles, and she suggests that the only fitting vengeance is to "sink my teeth

into his liver, eat him raw" (24.253). Hecuba wishes to be a
female Achilles, sharing his savage diet.

Spurred by the gods and by the reassuring omen of the
eagle (24.373–381), however, Priam makes his way to Achilles, bearing a rich ransom of robes, cloaks, blankets, gold, tripods, caldrons, and a cup. Guided by Hermes, he gets
through the Greek line and finds Achilles at his table, having
just finished his feast (24.557–558). This setting is significant. Achilles has not eaten during the twelve days since the
death of Patroclus; he has fed only on slaughter and rage.
Now his hunger for slaughter is satisfied, and he is returning
to food, to the joy, fellowship, and satisfaction of ordinary
bread, wine, and meat. Their meeting is like something from
a dream described in lovely poetry:

> The majestic king of Troy slipped past the rest
> and kneeling down beside Achilles, clasped his knees
> and kissed his hands, those terrible, man-killing hands
> that had slaughtered Priam's many sons in battle.
> Awesome—as when the grip of madness seizes one
> who murders a man in his own fatherland and flees
> abroad to foreign shores, to a wealthy, noble host,
> and a sense of marvel runs through all who see him—
> so Achilles marveled, beholding majestic
> Priam (24.559–567).

This is one of many Homeric similes that is "appropriately
inappropriate." Achilles is marveling like a man who, having
committed a murder, flees his homeland and finds refuge in
a foreign land. But Achilles, not Priam, is acting as host here.
Yet, on another level, the simile is apt, since Achilles has
killed a man and he now holds the hand of the "host" whose
land he has invaded.

Priam introduces himself by reminding Achilles of his
own father, and he begs for pity. Achilles is overcome with
grief at the thought of his father, and the two weep together,
bound together in sadness and loss: Priam weeping for Hector and Achilles for his father and Patroclus. For a moment at

least, Achilles' pity extends beyond himself and his immediate circle, as he, apparently for the first time, sees the war from Priam's perspective: "Poor man, how much you've borne—pain to break the spirit!" (24.605). Yet he counsels Priam to exercise a kind of Stoic calm and explains human life in terms of the theory of the jars:

> There are two great jars that stand on the floor of Zeus' halls and hold his gifts, our miseries one, the other blessings. When Zeus who loves the lightning mixes gifts for a man, now he meets with misfortune, now good times in turn (24.615–618).

This has a superficial resemblance to the Christian idea of Providence, but it is really very different. According to Achilles' theory, Zeus distributes miseries and blessings arbitrarily. For the Christian, though we cannot always see the reasons for God's dealings, we can be sure that He has His reasons and they are just. Moreover, there is no promise of undiluted blessing in Achilles' universe. The Christian suffers now but is promised a glory beyond imagining, and therefore lives in hope. Achilles suffers now and then dies; and therefore lives in despair. The best one can do is act like a Stoic—accepting with calmness whatever comes along.

Achilles treats Priam with dignity and sympathy, and we almost like him. But the rage is only just beneath the surface. When Priam asks for Hector's body and urges Achilles to "return to your own native land, safe and sound" (24.653–654), he cannot know that Achilles' fate is already sealed, that he will never return home. But the mention of this possibility brings a dark glance and a warning from Achilles: "No more, old man, don't tempt my wrath, not now! . . . Don't anger me now. Don't stir my raging heart still more" (24.655–656). Priam is terrified, but even in his rage, Achilles has become more cautious. He tells his servants to prepare Hector's body away from Priam's sight, fearing that "overwhelmed by the sight of Hector, wild with grief, Priam might let his anger flare and Achilles might fly into fresh rage himself" and violate the laws of hospitality (24.684–687). He does not want to be a Paris all over again.

Achilles and Priam agree to the terms of Hector's funeral. Achilles will make sure that the Greeks refrain from fighting for twelve days (the same period during which Hector's body was defiled, and the same period as the funeral of Patroclus). Then, they seal their pact with a meal together. As Achilles fasted during the time since Patroclus's death, so Priam had fasted and remained sleepless during the twelve days since the death of Hector (24.747–755). After eating with Achilles, he sleeps in the Greek camp, a sign of his trust in the word of Achilles. Achilles' feast of blood and slaughter is ended by sharing a common table with his opponent's father.

The shared feast of Achilles and Priam would have been a wonderful ending, but the epic goes on and closes instead with the return of Hector's body to the city, where Andromache, Hecuba, and Helen mourn in turn. Andromache mourns for the future of her son:

> I cannot think he will ever come to manhood.
> Long before *that* the city will be sacked,
> plundered top to bottom! Because you are dead,
> her great guardian, you who always defended Troy,
> who kept her loyal wives and helpless children safe
> all who will soon be carried off in the hollow ships
> and I with them (24.855–862).

Priam organizes the funeral, which ends with "a splendid funeral feast in Hector's honor, held in the house of Priam, king by will of Zeus" (24.942–943). It is *this* feast, rather than the feast of reconciliation, that closes the epic. And for Homer this is the only possible ending. A funeral feast is not a feast of celebration but of resignation. In the heroic world, the world of continual war, of glory-seeking deeds, no reconciliation, no peace, no feast can possibly be permanent. No battle is raging at the end of the epic, but the final lines are haunted, as the Trojans themselves are, by the expectation of the twelfth day, the day when the battle will resume, when the rage of Achilles, Ajax, Menelaus, and Agamemnon will be rekindled. And the fire of rekindled rage will consume Troy.

There are beauties in the *Iliad* and even an occasional flash of genuine nobility. But the world it depicts is a world that knows nothing of the promise of a Prince of peace, Whose government and peace have no end, Who invites the nations to an eternal banquet that will celebrate a final and total victory in a world without pain, tears, or death. This is the unimagined promise that fills the *Iliad* by its absence.

*Review Questions.*

1. How is the duel of Achilles and Hector related to the first duel between Menelaus and Paris?
2. Explain the dimensions of the heroic choice that faces Hector.
3. What is motivating Achilles?
4. Describe the rites of Patroclus's funeral.
5. What kind of games are played at the funeral? What is significant about them?
6. How is Achilles different during the funeral games?
7. Why is it significant that Achilles is eating when Priam arrives?
8. What is Achilles' theory of the jars? How is it like and unlike the Christian view of Providence?
9. What are the funeral arrangements for Hector?
10. What is the feeling at the end of the epic?

*Thought Questions.*

1. In what ways is Hector, standing outside the walls of Troy, like Achilles? (22.108–131)
2. What do the Greeks do to the body of Hector? Why is this significant? (22.433–441)
3. What does the ghost of Patroclus tell Achilles? What does he tell him about life after death? (23.72–127)
4. To whom does Achilles offer a libation and prayer? (23.242–258)

5. How can Odysseus compete in the funeral games when he has just been wounded in Book 11? (23.844)
6. Why does Hera consider Achilles superior to Hector? (24.66–77)
7. What effect do Priam's gifts have on Achilles? How does this fit with wider themes of the epic? (24.178)
8. What omen does Priam see as he sets out with gifts for Achilles? (24.373–381)

*Notes:*
[1] The line numbering comes from Robert Fagles's translation of the *Iliad* (Penguin, 1991). Line numbers will differ in other translations.

[2] Thanks to my student, Aaron Tripp, for clarity on this point.

[3] Note that Whitman leaves out Book 10, which is often thought to be a non-Homeric addition.

[4] This explanation was suggested by my student, Aaron Tripp.

[5] The significance of this arrangement was made particularly clear to me by a paper written by Michael Harkin.

## Son of Pain:
## Homer, *The Odyssey*

Odysseus (Latin name, "Ulysses") is one of the enduring figures of Western literature. Prominent, though not central, in the *Iliad*, he is the main character in the *Odyssey*, and his exploits are mentioned in Virgil's *Aeneid*. Later, he appears as one of the most famous shades in Dante's *Inferno*; Alfred Lord Tennyson devoted several poems to his adventures; James Joyce followed the *Odyssey* in writing one of the most notorious novels of this century, *Ulysses*; and motifs from the *Odyssey* are found throughout the poems of T. S. Eliot. Famous in Homer's epic for his disguises, Odysseus's literary personality has also gone through many transformations over the centuries. Tennyson's aging Ulysses, for example, complains, "How dull it is to pause, to make an end," and urges his comrades, "'Tis not too late to seek a newer world." This Ulysses is a very Victorian Ulysses, aching to explore the far reaches of the world, to pass through the arch of experience "wherethrough gleams the untraveled world whose margin fades forever and forever when I move"—perhaps even to establish a colony on some African coast.

This, by contrast, is how Homer begins:

> Sing to me of the man, Muse, the man of twists and turns
> driven time and again off course, once he had plundered
> the hallowed heights of Troy.
> Many cities of men he saw and learned their minds,
> many pains he suffered, heartsick on the open sea,

fighting to save his life and bring his comrades home.
But he could not save them from disaster, hard as he strove—
the recklessness of their own ways destroyed them all,
the blind fools, they devoured the cattle of the Sun
and the Sun god blotted out the day of their return.
Launch out on his story, Muse, daughter of Zeus,
start from where you will—sing for our time too (1.1–12).[1]

As these lines make clear, Tennyson's questing, restless, exploring Odysseus is not Homer's Odysseus. Like the Michael Douglas character who goes berserk when he gets caught in an endless Los Angeles traffic jam, Homer's hero is just a guy who wants to get home to his wife and kid.

Homer's second epic tells a story that begins in the aftermath of the Trojan War. It is one of several "return stories" (Greek, *nostoi*) that recount the journeys, adventures, and eventual homecoming of the heroes of the Trojan war. (Several other *nostoi* are told in the course of the *Odyssey*.) Odysseus did not return immediately to Ithaca, the island kingdom over which he ruled, but was blown off the map into a fantastic world of witches, giants, and monsters. Because of his delay, the men of Ithaca competed for the hand of his wife, Penelope, each hoping not only for a new bride but to displace Odysseus from his throne. The "suitors" spend their time at Odysseus's house, slaughtering his animals for meals and drinking his wine. Telemachus, Odysseus's teenage son, does not have the strength or experience to protect his mother and his wealth from Penelope's suitors, so all must wait for the eventual coming of the king. Finally, Odysseus arrives in Ithaca, rescues his wife, avenges himself on the suitors, and restores order in his kingdom.

Because the *Odyssey* tells of a hero's return from the Trojan war, many of the characters of the *Iliad* reappear. In the early books, Telemachus takes a fact-finding trip to Pylos, where he meets old Nestor, and to Sparta, where he spends time with Helen and Menelaus, now reunited. On his journey to the underworld, Odysseus encounters three of his old comrades in arms, Achilles, Agamemnon, and Ajax.

Throughout the epic, moreover, there are references to events of the Trojan war and to the fates of other heroes who returned. Structurally, the plots of the two epics are closely parallel. In both, the hero is most conspicuous by his absence: Achilles spends a good bit of the *Iliad* sulking in his tents, and Odysseus is not at home, where he is needed. In both, the hero's friends and comrades suffer by his absence. In both, the hero's return means terrible destruction for his enemies.

Closely connected as the two epics are, striking differences are also evident, in part because the heroes confront different situations. On the battlefield of Troy, Achilles could rely on his superior strength and skill to mow down the Trojans. Each battle in the *Iliad* is a face-off between two heroes, and the fittest survives. Such tactics simply will not work when you are dealing with Cyclopes and Sirens or trying to steer between the man-eating Scylla and ship-swallowing whirlpool, Charybdis. More than once, Odysseus considers or tries to fight his opponents in the Achillean way. As his ships pass by Scylla, whose six heads poke out from a cliff to devour men, Odysseus puts on his armor and takes a spear in each hand. But it does no good: while everyone is staring in horror at Charybdis, "Scylla snatched six men from our hollow ship" (12.264). The difference between the wartime and post-war situation finds a parallel in recent history. From World War II to 1989, America's overall military strategy was simple: Stop the Soviets. Now that we no longer square off against a mighty opposite, we have other, equally serious, obstacles to overcome, but our methods must be more discriminating. So also, Odysseus's journeys take him to remote mythical lands where the struggle is with magic and monsters rather than other warriors.

Monsters . . . and women and often goddesses are dangerously seductive. Women appear very infrequently in the *Iliad*, though their appearances are significant for various reasons. But women so dominate the action of the *Odyssey* that some suggest that it was written by a woman. Not only do women characters appear frequently, but they are strong and individual personalities. Penelope has wit and cunning to rival her famous husband's; Circe and Calypso both possess powers that challenge the hero; and Nausicaa, the princess of the Phaeacians, is, like her mother Arete, a formidable character. Women are far from being mere window-dressing for the manly action; in fact, women such as Penelope and Circe are clearly superior to the majority of dim-witted and barbarous men around them. This does not make the *Odyssey* a feminist tract, and it does not even mean that the women are portrayed in an especially positive way. As we look carefully at the text, we shall see that there is more than a touch of Hesiod in the *Odyssey*.

Subtle tactics are needed to navigate this world, and Odysseus is the man for the job. As Douglas Frame has pointed out, there is a linguistic connection between the Greek word *nostos* ("return") and the word for "mind," *nous*. Strength is not enough. Only a man whose mind is fully engaged, who does not forget what he is and where he is going, who is full of cunning or *metis*—only such a man will be able to survive and triumph over the dangers of a post-war world. Odysseus is precisely such a man, a different kind of hero for a different time. Achilles bursts into the first line of the *Iliad* in a blazing rage; he is made for war and little else; he will not, cannot, suffer in silence. Odysseus, by contrast, is a "man of twists and turns," who wears disguises and assumes false identities, who adapts himself and waits patiently for his opportunity to strike. Odysseus, for all his prowess in battle, is a man of cunning words. As Helen says in the *Iliad*, Odysseus looks most noble when seated, in the posture of deliberation and story-telling. In the climactic books of the *Odyssey*, he returns to his house disguised as a beggar, and has to endure the mockery and physical abuse of the suitors before the moment arrives for his vengeance. Homer's Achilles assuming a disguise, much less enduring torment from lesser men, is all but unimaginable.

Charles Segal has brought out the difference between

Odysseus and Achilles by attending to the use of the Greek word *kleos*, "heroic fame," in both epics. For Achilles, *kleos* and *nostos*, fame and return, are exclusive of one another. If he chooses to go home, he gains no glory; if he fights for glory, he will never return home. This is not the case for Odysseus, who achieves glory *by* his return. Odysseus's method for achieving glory likewise differs from Achilles'. When he finally reveals himself to the Phaeacians, Odysseus identifies himself as "Odysseus, son of Laertes, known to the world for every kind of craft *(dolos)*—my fame *(kleos)* reaches the skies" (9.21–22). As Segal points out, "A woman can be expected to use *doloi* [deceptions] for her *kleos*, but a hero should win his *kleos* in fair fight on the battlefield." Such would be the case if Odysseus faced other heroes like himself. Faced as he is with superhuman monsters, and often with women and goddesses who are masters of *dolos*, Odysseus's only successful response is to spin more intricate *doloi*.

As in the *Iliad*, Homer continues to be concerned with order and disorder. The Iliad shows that men at war become something less than human. They slip down the chain of being to the level of animals, and when men act like animals, there is no possibility of order among them. The *Odyssey* moves away from the chaos of war toward a restoration of order, especially the order of the household. Homer is showing the kind of character required to establish and maintain order. Not fleet Achilles or even patriotic Hector can bring peace. It takes the wiles and cunning of an Odysseus.

In structure, too, the epics differ. The *Iliad* could have been composed by Achilles, who speaks straight-on; there are few digressions from the simple story line of Achilles' rage. The *Odyssey* is more intricately woven. Beginning with four books in which Odysseus does not even make an appearance (the so-called "Telemachy" or "Telemacheia," because of its focus on Telemachus), the poem then moves to Ogygia, where Odysseus is exiled with Calypso. Books 5–8 describe Odysseus's departure from Ogygia and his arrival at

Scheria, the island of the Phaeacians, but this chronological narrative is interrupted in Books 9–12, where Odysseus tells the Phaeacians the retrospective story of his travels from the Trojan War to the island of Calypso. Books 13–14 take Odysseus from Scheria to Ithaca, but then Book 15 interrupts with an account of Telemachus's return from *his* journey. All this feinting, this moving to and fro, this layering of time, reflects the cunning of its hero.

The proem, quoted above, reveals another parallel between the structure of the epic and the personality of its hero. Achilles is mentioned immediately in the first line of the *Iliad*. In the *Odyssey*, we learn a great deal about the hero in the first twenty-odd lines, but we do not learn his name. Robert Fagles highlights the delay by inserting a teasing ellipsis (...) at the end of line 15: all the survivors of the Trojan War have returned "but one man alone..." We expect the man to be named, but nearly 10 more lines go by before Homer finishes that thought. This pattern of "delayed identification," repeated a number of times in the epic, captures in miniature the plot of the entire story. When the poem begins, no one is certain whether Odysseus is dead or alive, and when he finally shows up at home, he is disguised so that few recognize him. In a number of incidents, he is an anonymous hero, a "nobody," until the final moments. Delay is one of the tactics of this "man of twists and turns" and necessary in a situation in which he is not sure whom to trust. Homer's proem reinforces this tactic by imitating it poetically, playfully delaying and putting us off before speaking the name "Odysseus."

In our study of the *Iliad*, we frequently noted the contrast of city and war camp which, with the "no man's land" of the battlefield, are the main zones in which the epic takes place. The battlefield is the space in which men achieve lasting glory and honor in individual combat with their enemies. When Achilles does finally fight, it is not out of regard for the collective needs of the Greek armies but because of a very personal grudge against Hector. The *Odyssey* is much more concerned with the proper order of the house (Greek, *oikos*) and city (Greek, *polis*). As the opening lines show, the epic is not about a lone adventurer but about Odysseus as a leader of a crew. Odysseus's comrades failed to achieve their *nostos* because they were foolish—they lacked *nous*. Consistent with this concern for the proper order of social life, much of the epic takes place indoors, inside the halls at Sparta, Phaeacia, or Ithaca. Odysseus recounts his adventures after sharing a feast with the Phaeacians, and even the final slaughter of the suitors takes place within Odysseus's palace. Odysseus, unlike Achilles, is needed not merely to achieve his personal glory but to restore proper order to his kingdom. Odysseus's *aristeia* occurs not in the field where "men win fame" but in the hall of feasting.

Geography symbolizes this concern for justice and order. The *Iliad* takes place entirely on the seashore, during a siege before a strongly fortified city. Odysseus's adventures are those of a seafaring hero, and many of the obstacles to his return are obstacles thrown up by the sea ("heartsick on the open sea") or by Poseidon, the god of the sea, his main divine adversary. The sea and its deity thus become a symbol of the chaos that Odysseus must overcome and tame in order to return. When he arrives physically in Ithaca, however, another surging chaos awaits him in the form of the suitors, and Odysseus's triumph over them is the final "voyage" of his journey home. Odysseus has not completed his *nostos* until there is no more sea.

This more politically interested stance is connected with the moral and religious perspective of the *Odyssey*. The *Iliad* is famously a morally ambiguous epic. It is not a story of good guys against bad guys; instead, good and bad guys appear on both sides of the battle lines, and it is not at all clear that the best man wins. This moral complexity (or simple chaos) is reflected in the *Iliad*'s description of the gods. They are at war with one another, and Zeus, far from ruling over all with justice and righteousness, arbitrarily distributes suffering and good as he pleases (see Achilles' analogy of the jars). By contrast, the *Odyssey* is much more "tidy," to use the word of Howard W. Clarke. There are clear good guys—Odysseus and all those who remain faithful to him—and clear bad guys—primarily the suitors but also the various monsters that confront Odysseus on his journeys, which grotesquely mimic the suitors. And the good guy wins a victory in the end, leaving the suitors a bloody mess in the hall at Ithaca.

Religiously, the Zeus of the *Odyssey* is the upholder of right, who avenges wrong and punishes men for their sins. In the proem, this "tidy" moral perspective is already evident. Odysseus's crew was destroyed as punishment for eating the cattle of the Sun: "the recklessness of their own ways destroyed them all" (1.8). Zeus is especially a protector of the stranger and sojourner, and he avenges himself against those who violate the customs of hospitality. Hospitality is one of the key issues in the epic. The suitors are bad guys because they abuse the hospitality and wealth of Odysseus's house, and the worst monsters that Odysseus faces are those who refuse to show hospitality to strangers. Related to this, Henry Fielding said in *Tom Jones* that the *Odyssey* is the "eatingest epic," and one scholar has estimated that nearly one in every thirty lines describes the preparation or eating of food. Food is not just about getting enough fuel to keep your body going. Food has religious connections, for sacrifice is the chief ritual of Greek religion and all meals involving meat are supposed to include sacrifices. Food is connected with social life, for the feast is a model of peaceful and harmonious community, and food is connected with morality and sin, for Odysseus's crew gets into trouble mainly because they eat the wrong things. Food provides the moral and religious standard by which characters are judged. This emphasis on food is fitting for an epic that focuses on a man who insisted in the *Iliad* that dinner should precede battle, a hero who says that his stomach is a tyrant.

When we look at the theme of hospitality more carefully, however, doubts about the theological "tidiness" of the *Od-*

*yssey* begin to arise. Zeus, I have said, is the protector of the stranger and the defender of those who show hospitality. Well, sort of. Through most of the epic, this is the case, but there is a strange scene in Book 13 that calls this into serious question. The Phaeacians have welcomed Odysseus among them, bathed, robed, and feasted him, and, after listening to his tales of woe, have sent him in a magical boat back to Ithaca. One cannot imagine a more hospitable crowd. Yet, as the Phaeacian ship returns home from Ithaca, Poseidon is angry that they have helped his archenemy, Odysseus, and he decides to "crush that fine Phaeacian cutter out on the misty sea" and, just to make sure that the Phaeacians do not have another chance to show hospitality, he will "pile a huge mountain round about her port" (13.169–170, 173).

One would expect Zeus, protector of strangers, to object. Instead, he suggests a better way of getting even with the Phaeacians:

> Here's what seems best to *me*.
> As the people all lean down from the city heights
> to watch her speeding home, strike her into a rock
> that looks like a racing vessel, just offshore—
> amaze all men with a marvel for the ages.
> Then pile your huge mountain round about
> their port (13.175–180).

Promoting hospitality is all well and good, but when hospitality offends the honor of another god, that's just too much. Zeus has not changed all that much from the *Iliad*. He still pours out woes from his jars with scant regard for justice or right.

Further, though Odysseus is a different kind of hero from Achilles, the heroic ethic still shapes his behavior. Odysseus triumphs after and through suffering, but his triumph is still a heroic triumph. The attention given to Odysseus's name and identity indicates this. Odysseus is given to deception and disguise; he hides his name and delays identifying himself. Ultimately, however, he wants to make sure that his name is honored. When the Phaeacians suggest that Odysseus is too much the merchant to participate in games, Odysseus reacts as Achilles would: "I'll compete in your games, just watch. Your insults cut to the quick—you rouse my fighting blood" (8.214–215). In the final massacre of the suitors, Odysseus is, like Achilles, as relentless as death.

Odysseus's name is significant in this connection. In Book 19, Odysseus's old nursemaid, Eurycleia, is washing her disguised master, when she discovers a telltale scar on his leg and knows he is Odysseus. Homer digresses to describe the origin of the scar and the origin of his name. Autylocus, Odysseus's maternal grandfather, had said:

> Just as I
> have come from afar, creating pain for many—
> men and women across the good green earth—so let his
> name by *Odysseus*...
> The Son of Pain, a name he'll earn in full (19.460–464).

Scholars point to the link between this name and the verb *odussomai*, which means "to feel anger toward, to rage or hate." By his very name, Odysseus is thus a virtual twin of raging Achilles. His rage takes the form of suspicion, deception, trickery, very different from the overt raging of Achilles but the same passion drives them both.

Alternatively, some suggest that "Odysseus" is connected to the phrase "creating pain for many." So understood, "son of pain" is double-sided. Through much of the epic, Odysseus suffers as much as he causes suffering. Early in the poem, Athena asks Zeus, "have you no care for him in your lofty heart?" The Greek for "have care" is *odussomai*. (George Dimock renders this, "Why do you odysseus him so, Zeus?") "Much pain has he suffered," we are told. The first time we see him, in Book 5, he is staring out to sea from Calypso's island, weeping for the wife and land he cannot reach, and while he is among the Phaeacians, the songs of his exploits of Troy, performed by the Phaeacian bard

Demodocus, make him weep. Yet, his willingness to suffer pain is a strategy, for all the while he suffers he is waiting for the moment when he can turn the tables and make his foes suffer. In all this, Odysseus is an unusual hero, but he has not abandoned the heroic ideal. Though he may suffer playing "nobody" for a time, the goal is to become somebody, even if he must severely "odysseus" others to do it.

A scarred hero comes somewhat closer to the Christian view of heroism than the scarring hero of the *Iliad*, Achilles. Yet, even as a suffering hero, Odysseus is not Jesus. He does not crush the serpent's head *by* his suffering unto death; he suffers *until* he has the opportunity to crush heads. Odysseus is identified by his scar, but he received this scar during a hunt. The *Odyssey*, despite striking differences with the *Iliad*, is still a Greek heroic epic, and Odysseus is still a Greek hero. We should not expect to find in it a model of Christian heroism or patience.

*Review Questions.*
1. What is a *nostos*?
2. Briefly summarize the plot of the *Odyssey*.
3. Describe the differences between the setting of the *Iliad* and *Odyssey*.
4. Describe the differences between Odysseus and Achilles.
5. What does *metis* mean?
6. Describe the structure of the *Odyssey*, especially in comparison to the *Iliad*.
7. What is the theme of "delayed identification"? How does the "proem" reflect this theme?
8. How does the moral perspective of the *Odyssey* differ from the *Iliad*? What does this say about the difference in the depiction of the gods?
9. How does food figure into the story?
10. What does the name "Odysseus" mean?

*Thought Questions.*

1. Read Dante's description of Ulysses in *Inferno*, canto 26. Is Dante's Ulysses closer to Homer's or Tennyson's?

2. Look back at Hesiod's *Theogony* and find some of the characters from the *Odyssey* (e.g., Cyclops).

3. Find some of the references to Odysseus in the *Iliad*. What does that epic say about him? What kind of character is he? How is he like and unlike the Odysseus of the *Odyssey*?

4. Look up Odysseus in a book of Greek mythology. What other exploits is he known for?

## The Image of His Father, Books 1–4

One of the striking structural features of the *Odyssey* is that the title character does not appear in the first four books. He is stranded on the island of Ogygia with Calypso, a "bewitching nymph" and "lustrous goddess" (1.17) who holds him while he continually pines to return to his wife and home. "Calypso" is related to the Greek verb *kaluptein*, "to hide," and Odysseus begins the epic hidden in several senses. He is hidden from the reader while attention is focused on the situation in Ithaca, an example of the "delayed identification" motif. He is hidden from Penelope and Telemachus who do not even know if he is alive. More symbolically, he is hidden in the sense that he is not fulfilling the heroic demand to perform deeds that bring renown. So long as the suitors run riot in his house, Odysseus is losing reputation as well as material wealth. To be a hero, he must renounce marriage to Calypso and unveil himself in an avenging "apocalypse."

Though Odysseus is absent from the story, his predicament is mirrored in his son's. This is evident from the structure of Books 1–4, the "Telemachy" or "Telemacheia." Book 1 begins with an assembly of the gods on Olympus (1.31–32), and a similar scene is found at the beginning of Book 5 (5.1–4). The repetition of this scene in Book 5 announces, "We're starting over again from the beginning." Both divine assemblies, moreover, discuss the situation of Odysseus, and both end with a god being sent to initiate a resolution to the crisis. Athena is sent off in Book 1 to encourage Telemachus, and Hermes goes in Book 5 to tell Calypso she must release Odysseus. Within Books 1–4, we can discern a "concentric" or "ring" arrangement, with sections marked off by geographic changes:

> Book 1: Telemachus and suitors in Ithaca
> > Books 2–3: Telemachus in Pylos and Sparta
>
> Book 4: Suitors in Ithaca plot Telemachus's death

Thus, the Telemachy leaves Telemachus in the same situation as his father: He is gone from home and all ways of return are threatened by the suitors. When she discovers that Telemachus is gone, Penelope discerns the similarity of father and son: "Why bent on rambling over the face of the earth?—a darling only son! Your father's worlds away, god's own Odysseus, dead in some strange land" (2.402–404).

Book 1 and the first portion of Book 2 also have a concentric arrangement.

> A. Assembly on Olympus, 1.24–112
> > B. Athena and Telemachus, 1.113–376
> >
> > B. Telemachus and Penelope, 1.377–419
>
> A. Assembly in Ithaca, 1.420–2.292

This structure invites us to compare the matching sections, A with A and B with B.

Let's begin with the assembly on Olympus. Poseidon, who has manipulated Odysseus's absence, is himself absent from Olympus on a business trip to Ethiopia. Athena, Odysseus's patron, seizes the opportunity to ask Zeus to help Odysseus get home. Her request interrupts Zeus's ruminations on the *nostos* of another hero of Troy, Agamemnon:

> the father of men and gods was first to speak,
> sorely troubled, remembering handsome Aegisthus,

> the man Agamemnon's son, renowned Orestes, killed.
> Recalling Aegisthus, Zeus harangued the immortal powers:
> "Ah how shameless—the way these mortals blame the gods.
> From us alone, they say, come all their miseries, yes,
> but they themselves, with their own reckless ways,
> compound their pains beyond their proper share.
> Look at Aegisthus now...
> Above and beyond *his* share he stole Atrides' wife,
> he murdered the warlord coming home from Troy
> though he knew it meant his own total ruin.
> Far in advance we told him so ourselves,
> dispatching the guide, the giant-killer Hermes.
> 'Don't murder the man,' he said, 'don't court his wife.
> Beware, revenge will come from Orestes, Agamemnon's son,
> that day he comes of age and longs for his native land.'
> So Hermes warned, with all the good will in the world,
> but would Aegisthus' hardened heart give way?
> Now he pays the price—all at a single stroke" (1.33-52).

Zeus espouses an interesting theology, complaining that mortals blame the gods for the troubles they bring upon themselves. This stands in some tension with Achilles' theology of the two jars at the end of the *Iliad*.

More important here, however, is the example that Zeus refers to: Aegisthus brought punishment upon himself by ignoring the warnings of Hermes, taking Agamemnon's wife Clytemnestra while Agamemnon was fighting at Troy, and then killing Agamemnon on his return. Agamemnon's son, Orestes, took vengeance in turn by killing his mother (see chapter 5 below). That Agamemnon's wife was taken is just, for he had seized Achilles' war-bride at the beginning of the *Iliad*. In the context of the *Odyssey*, the return story of Agamemnon, which is told several times at considerable length, is a warning tale for the main characters. The fact that Athena's request comes in the midst of Zeus's ruminations on Agamemnon indicates that his *nostos* is somehow parallel to Odysseus's. We can fit the main characters of the *Odyssey* into the plot of Agamemnon's return: Clytemnestra = Penelope, Aegisthus = the suitors (cf. 1.47), Agamemnon =

Odysseus, and Orestes = Telemachus. By recalling this story, Zeus raises the critical questions concerning Odysseus's *nostos*: Will Penelope remain faithful to Odysseus, or will she be a Clytemnestra who beds down with one of the suitors? Will Odysseus be betrayed upon his return as Agamemnon was? Will Telemachus, the young son of Odysseus, prove himself as courageous as Orestes, who killed his own mother to avenge his father's murder? The Agamemnon story is an indicator of the tragic potential of the initial situation in Ithaca. Odysseus could end as badly as Agamemnon.

Agamemnon's story is an appropriate warning, then, to Odysseus. This is the way Agamemnon himself uses the story when he speaks to Odysseus in the underworld in Book 11: Though Agamemnon commends Penelope's faithfulness, he is understandably suspicious of wives in general and warns Odysseus not to stumble into a trap. If he wants to achieve his *nostos* safely, he must use his *nous*, every last stratagem of *metis*, and he must meet the *dolos* of women with superior *dolos*. We know from the opening lines of the poem that Odysseus hardly needs this advice. He trusts no one, and all his ways are shrewd.

The story of Agamemnon is told to Telemachus several times in the Telemachy. Telemachus asks about this event while visiting Nestor in Book 3 and is given a typically long-winded account (3.272–352). Menelaus later gives a vivid account of how Aegisthus welcomed Agamemnon home, "feasted him well and then cut him down as a man cuts down some ox at the trough" (4.600–604), which foreshadows the fate of the band of "Aegisthuses" who are besieging Penelope. When Telemachus hears the story from Nestor, he identifies himself with Orestes:

> Oh, Nestor, son of Neleus, Achaea's pride and glory,
> what a stroke of revenge that was! All Achaeans
> will spread Orestes' fame across the world,
> a song for those to come.

> If only the gods would arm me in such power
> I'd take revenge on the lawless, brazen suitors
> riding roughshod over me, plotting reckless
> outrage (3.229–235).

Telemachus's enthusiasm for Orestes' violence makes it easy to miss the radical difference between the two young men. Orestes was avenging a father who had been murdered, but the suitors have not killed Odysseus. Telemachus exaggerates the tragedy of his situation when he compares it with Orestes'.

Or does he? I want to suggest that the situations of Telemachus and Orestes are closer than they appear at first. This is true for several reasons. First, the suitors are acting as if Odysseus were dead, lounging around his house and treating his wife as a widow. There is not much difference between killing Odysseus and acting as if he were already dead. More is going on here, though. As Telemachus says, the suitors are busy "devouring" his house, and, as noted above, the food image is significant. The suitors are abusing the hospitality offered by Penelope and Telemachus, "eating them out of house and home." Elsewhere, Telemachus says they "bleed my household white" (1.292), and in Homer white is the color of dead bones. The imagery suggests that the suitors are trying to "kill" the house of Odysseus. Property and person are not, in Telemachus's mind, sharply distinct. An attack on a man's house and property is an attack on him. This is especially true in the heroic world, in which possessions constitute part of the glory of the hero's reputation.

The prominence of gift-giving also highlights the intensity of the suitors' attack. In heroic Greece, rulers were not elected, and political power was not always passed from father to son. In this semi-feudal system, a prince gained the support and loyalty of powerful nobles by lavishing gifts of land and other wealth on them. A great house like Odysseus's would produce goods to be distributed to the householder's advantage, winning friends and influencing people. Political power flowed to those who used their wealth to establish ties of loyalty and dependence. We still see an element of this even in modern politics. Democratic politicians in the U.S. have the unquestioned support of older Americans because they support social security programs that give tax funds to senior citizens.

Given the political importance of gift-giving in heroic Greece, the plan of the suitors becomes clearer: By devouring Odysseus's substance, they are eroding the basis of his power. Even if he does return, he will have a hard time maintaining the support of the nobility if he cannot provide them with rich gifts. Further, he will not be able to pass on a large enough inheritance for Telemachus to hold power. Thus, as we shall see below, it is important that he not return from Troy empty-handed. "Devouring the house" thus has both personal and political dimensions; it is an attack on Odysseus himself and his reputation, and it is a coup, an attempt to unseat the house of Odysseus from its chief position in Ithaca. Telemachus, it seems, has good reason to use Orestes as a model.

Vengeance against the suitors will be, as the divine council indicates, divine vengeance. As such, it will be appropriate to the crime. The suitors have violated the rules of hospitality of which Zeus is the defender, and Zeus will hold them to account. They have been feasting on another man's wealth, and they will be destroyed in a feast of slaughter. They have been hoping for a wedding celebration, but they will have only a blood wedding (1.308).

Yet, Telemachus is simply not up to the job. This is brought out by the human assembly, which is planned at the end of Book 1 and takes place in Book 2. If the divine council indicates the seriousness of the crisis in Ithaca, the human council emphasizes that only Odysseus can restore order. In several ways, Telemachus's conduct gives hope that he is ready to take an active role in saving his house. He observes the rules of hospitality in his treatment of the visiting Athena (1.144ff); the action begins with Telemachus welcoming a stranger to the house, and the epic will climax with the appearance of another disguised stranger, Odysseus himself. When Penelope asks the bard not to sing of Troy, Telemachus sharply rebukes her and asserts his control over the house:

> Why fault the bard if he sings the Argives' hard fate? ...
> Courage, mother. Harden your heart, and listen....
>   So, mother,
> go back to your quarters. Tend to your own tasks,
> the distaff and the loom, and keep the women
> working hard as well. As for giving orders,
> men will see to that, but I most of all:
> I hold the reins of power in this house (1.403–414).

When the suitors raise their lustful howl of protest, Telemachus also takes them in hand: "You suitors who plague my mother, you, you insolent, overweening... You must leave my palace!" (1.422–430). Telemachus seems to be coming of age, ready to take command. When the assembly meets the next day, however, he seems a younger, smaller man. His angry speech ends in despair: "But now, look, you load my heart with grief—there's nothing I can do!" and, dashing the scepter to the ground, he bursts into tears (2.83–86). He is indeed a "boy" who takes "his stand among the gathered men" (2.37–38).

Books 2–3 describe his "mentoring" into the heroic life that prepares him to later stand at his father's side. The public reason for the trip is to find information about Odysseus from those who might have seen him. But his journey also initiates him into the world of men. As Athena tells him, "You must not cling to your boyhood any longer" (1.341). In this sense, the first books of the *Odyssey* reflect certain "rites of passage" in Greek and other societies, and Athena is the goddess that enables Telemachus to cross the threshold to a new stage of life. Prior to a certain age, boys in many societies are almost entirely surrounded by women—mothers, maids, nurses. At adolescence, they are made members of male society through an initiation ritual that often has three stages. Boys are first physically separated from their mothers; for a time, they are kept in an "in-between" place where they must endure various trials and where they learn certain skills and the lore of the tribe; finally, they are returned to the community, but now they are attached to the society of men. Telemachus's experience goes through these stages: He is physically separated from his mother when he journeys, without her knowledge, to Pylos and Sparta; he remains in those places for a time, learning about the Trojan war from some of its warriors; when he returns to Ithaca in Book 15, he is no longer a boy but a man, ready to assist his father in the defense of his house and kingdom. Given the parallels between Odysseus and Telemachus, moreover, it is possible to see Odysseus's adventures as a similar initiation, a preparation for his heroic return.

Telemachus has never seen a true heroic society in operation, which is to say, he has never seen a proper feast. Feasts picture how society should be ordered—the host offers a portion of meat to the gods, and the guests, arranged according to rank, receive gifts from the host and share a common meal. Right relations with the gods and among men are symbolized and therefore maintained by the feast. A disordered society cannot celebrate a proper feast; the host will not offer thanks to the gods, the guests will not know their rankings, and they will compete for a share of food rather than sharing. Telemachus has seen only the disordered gluttony of the suitors, who slaughter and eat without offering sacrifices to the gods and who prey on another man's house. To correct these defects in his education, Athena suggests that he take a voyage to visit some of his father's comrades. This will expose him to the ways of heroic life and show him how to worship the gods and how to feast. This is why Homer describes the sacrifices that Nestor offers at Pylos in such great detail and why it is fitting that Telemachus arrive in Sparta just in time for a wedding (4.1–23). During his journey, too, Telemachus learns about his peculiar place in Ithacan society. Pisistratus, the son of Nestor, has grown up in the civilized court of his father and knows how to conduct himself. By observing and imitating his behavior, Telemachus begins to learn what it means to be the son of Odysseus.

Telemachus has never known his father, but he learns about him through the exploits that are recounted in Sparta. These stories anticipate the hidden hero's character and foreshadow in some detail Odysseus's return. Helen tells how

> Scarring his own body with mortifying strokes,
> throwing filthy rags on his back like any slave,
> [Odysseus] slipped into the enemy's city, roamed its
>     streets—
> all disguised, a totally different man, a beggar,
> hardly the figure he cut among Achaea's ships.
> That's how Odysseus infiltrated Troy,
> and no one knew him at all...
> I alone, I spotted him for the man he was (4.274–281).

When Odysseus later comes to Ithaca in the guise of a beggar, he is simply up to his old tricks. His victory over the suitors is the continuation of his victory at Troy, also won by cunning.

The last major character in the initial books is Penelope. Like Telemachus and Odysseus, she has her rough "seas" to navigate, and success requires skill and courage. Structurally, by including successive scenes involving first Telemachus and Athena and then Telemachus and Penelope, Book 1 brings out a comparison with Athena. Penelope is a human Athena, who has been able to put off the suitors with a clever ploy. She told them that she would make a choice among the suitors once she finished the funeral shroud for Laertes. Day after day, she wove the shroud, but at night she undid the work, so that it was never finished. This trick is significant on several levels. The loom is typically a woman's instrument; men employ swords and spears, while women work on the loom. Penelope's trick is a typically feminine deception, using the one weapon she has in her armory. Weaving, moreover, is often an image of fate and destiny; the world is pictured in some passages of Scripture as a garment (cf. Psalm 102:25-26), and in pagan literature the fates "weave" the mantle of the world (see 7.233). In the *Iliad*, we see Helen weaving a robe that pictures scenes of the Trojan War, and Penelope is, quite literally, "weaving" the fate of the suitors, for by delaying her decision, she is leaving time for Odysseus to "weave" a web to entrap the suitors. Appropriately, she is working on a funeral shroud, rather than the wedding veil that the suitors hope for. Ironically, the suitors have forced her to finish the web, sealing their own fate. Like her husband, she is a woman of "twists and turns," whose very name is connected with the cunning art of weaving; for the Greek word *pene* means "woof" or "web."

All this is hopeful, but Zeus's recounting of the Agamemnon story raises the question of Penelope's faithfulness to Odysseus: Will she turn out to be a Clytemnestra? The answer of the epic is not as straightforward as it might seem. Like Clytemnestra (11.477), Penelope is a woman who employs deceits (*dolos*, 19.152). Both of them "weave" designs to entrap and eventually destroy men. Penelope's attitude toward the suitors is, moreover, complicated. The trick of the web is ambiguous, for it not only gives Odysseus time to get home but also extends the suitors' courting. If Penelope had made a public announcement that she would not remarry, the suitors would go home. So long as she weaves, she gives encouragement to their hopes, and she continues to receive their attention. At the end of the epic, she will reveal in several ways that she found some pleasure in the suitors, and that she came close to becoming, if not a Clytemnestra, at least a Helen. Yet, as Charles Segal has put it, Penelope, in the final analysis, is using "house-preserving *dolos*," which leads to glory and fame (*kleos*), while Clytemnestra's "house-destroying *dolos*" led to shame (*aischos*). When Penelope first appears, she stands beside a pillar that holds up the roof of the house (1.384-385). This is not merely a bit of descriptive color, but symbolizes what kind of woman Penelope is: Like the pillar, she keeps her husband's house from collapsing.

At the end of Book 4, the scene is set for a replay or a reversal of Agamemnon's *nostos*: Odysseus's palace is filled with prospective Aegisthuses; Penelope uses trickery, though so far she uses it to remain faithful to her husband rather than to betray him; Telemachus is beginning to look like an Orestes in the making. Only the new Agamemnon is missing. Will he step into a trap? Or will he set one?

*Review Questions*
1. Why is Odysseus's appearance in the epic delayed?
2. What is the structure of Books 1–4? What is significant about this structure?
3. Summarize the story of Agamemnon's *nostos*. How does Agamemnon's story relate to the *Odyssey*?
4. How does Telemachus describe the suitors' behavior? Why is that description significant?
5. Explain the personal and political dimensions of the suitors' behavior.
6. What is Telemachus like in the first four books?
7. What does Telemachus learn from his journey to Pylos and Sparta?
8. What trick does Penelope use to keep the suitors at bay?
9. Explain some dimensions of the imagery of "weaving."
10. What is Penelope's attitude toward the suitors?

*Thought Questions.*
1. Whose daughter is Calypso? Why is this significant? (1.62)
2. What is next to the pillar of Odysseus's hall? Why does Homer mention this? (1.147–151)
3. What does Telemachus tell Athena about his parentage? Why is this significant? (1.247–255)
4. To whom does Antinous compare Penelope? Who were they? (2.130–135)
5. What omen does Zeus send in response to Tele-

machus's prayer? What does it mean? What is the suitors' response? (2.164–187, 198–204)

6. How are the endings of Books 1 and 2 similar? How are the beginnings of Books 2 and 3 similar?

7. What is significant about the way that Nestor describes the conquest of Troy? (3.131–135)

8. What happened between Agamemnon and Menelaus at the end of the Trojan war? What does this remind you of? (3.151–175)

9. In Aeschylus's *Agamemnon*, Clytemnestra is as responsible as Aegisthus for Agamemnon's murder, but in the *Odyssey*, she is barely mentioned. Why? (3.212–225)

10. What does Menelaus tell Telemachus about his *nostos*? Why is this important? (4.391–685)

## Hidden Hero, Books 5–8

Book 5 begins where Book 1 began, with a scene on Olympus. Divine initiative has spurred Telemachus to take more active control of his destiny, and now Zeus determines that "the exile must return" bearing "bronze and hoards of gold and robes—more plunder than he could ever have won from Troy" (5.35, 42–43). The hero who has been "calypsoed," hidden on the island of Ogygia, must return displaying the full glory of a hero. These parallels of Books 1 and 5 suggest further connections between the initial situation of Odysseus and the situation in Ithaca, which are developed in the following books.

Calypso is the first of the fantastic creatures we meet and therefore is representative of all. Several features of the situation are noteworthy. Hermes finds her in a cave, a setting of such Edenic beauty and fertility that even Hermes's heart is "entranced with pleasure" as he stands "spellbound" (5.83–84). The enchantment of the setting is important for understanding its significance. As Odysseus will tell the Phaeacians later, he has been traveling through the land of myths and legends. By sending Hermes to release him, Zeus is not only helping to transfer Odysseus geographically from one place to another; he is calling him back from the world of unreal myths to the real world of Ithaca. Since his heroic deeds at Troy, Odysseus has been in "no man's land." And that is no place for a hero.

Though the epic contrasts Ithaca with the mythical world of Odysseus's journeys, it also brings out parallels between them, so that the two worlds illuminate and mirror each other. When Hermes arrives, Calypso is inside her cave, singing and weaving. In the context of the *Odyssey*, Calypso's weaving associates her with Penelope. Just as Penelope has used weaving to delay what she feels is an inevitable decision, so Calypso weaves, hoping she will never have to part with Odysseus, hoping she is weaving his fate. Unlike the suitors, however, Odysseus is a reluctant guest, not a suitor at all. Light may be directed in the other direction as well: If Calypso is a nymph version of Penelope, Penelope has something of the enchantress about her, for she has woven a spell over the suitors.

The parallel of Calypso and Penelope also highlights an important feature of the poem's presentation of women. Odysseus encounters several alluring women in the course of his travels—not only Calypso, but Circe and Nausicaa—and some of his other adventures also involve feminine, though not overtly sexual, threats—the Sirens being the chief example. Sexual temptation is one of the distractions he must overcome if he is to reach Ithaca and deliver his wife, house, and kingdom. Two of these women have magical powers—Calypso and Circe—for Circe turns Odysseus's crew into pigs. Several of the women in this poem are more intelligent than most of the men, but this intelligence is present as another species of witchcraft, another weapon by which women seek to ensnare men and keep them from heroic deeds. However sympathetic his portrayals of women, Homer, like Hesiod, sees women as sources of temptation and a distraction from the proper work of men. Pleasurable to be sure, women can also be dangerous, cunning, too curious, and always potential Pandoras. They are "Calypsos," who weave their designs to keep men "hidden" indoors, at home and in bed.

From a Christian perspective, Odysseus's resistance to sexual temptation leaves a great deal to be desired. The poem makes clear that he is sleeping with Calypso during the seven years of his "captivity" on her island. Even when he refuses to stay with her and professes his undying wish to return home, "withdrawing into the cavern's deep recesses, long in each other's arms they lost themselves in love" (5.250–251). The poet's protest that "he had no choice—unwilling lover alongside lover all too willing" (5.171–172) sounds false. His earlier statement that Odysseus had grown bored with Calypso ("the nymph no longer pleased," 5.170) is probably more accurate, but boredom does not prevent him from taking his pleasure with her. When he encounters Circe and demands that she release his crew from the spell, she is impressed with him and invites him to bed. Suspicious, he responds: "Mount your bed? Not for all the world." But his refusal is only partial: "Not until you consent to swear, goddess, a binding oath you'll never plot some new intrigue to harm me." After she has sworn, "then, at last, I mounted Circe's gorgeous bed" (10.380–382). As long as it's *safe* sex.

Sexual purity in the Christian sense, brilliantly portrayed in Book 3 of Edmund Spencer's *Fairie Queene*, simply is not heroic virtue. Sexual control *is*. In the scene with Circe, it is important that Odysseus refuses to mount her bed until he has assurances that she will release his men from the spell. Later, he will tell Phaeacians how he was tied to the ship's mast so that he would not succumb to the alluring song of the Sirens. His cunning helps him gain control of sexually charged situations, keeps him from being turned into a beast by Circe, and protects him from joining the rotting corpses in the field of the Sirens. Sexual control is an aspect of Odysseus's *metis*.

Calypso's temptation is not, however, mainly sexual. Reminding Odysseus "what pains are fated to fill your cup before you reach the shore," she urges him to "preside in our house with me, and be immortal" (5.228–231). Odysseus refuses. Within the heroic world of the *Odyssey*, this offer has several layers of significance. Immortality is what all heroes pursue. They want their deeds remembered and celebrated forever. Yet, Calypso offers a very un-heroic immortality, not won at the cost of suffering, hardship, and battle, but an immortality that comes simply as a gift. And it would be a very inactive sort of immortality. It is not eternal life so much as eternal stagnation. With Calypso, Odysseus's life would consist of languid days followed by nights of love, but Odysseus has already grown weary of the nymph and her life. In rejecting her offer, he is rejecting one kind of immortality for another. He is embracing his heroic destiny, with all its pain and hardships. He will not seek to escape his name, "son of pain."

Calypso also represents a temptation to forget who he is and the kind of deeds that are expected of such a man. The real temptation for the hero is to renounce his heroic calling. In this way, we can see that Odysseus's choice is very much like that of Achilles in the *Iliad*: A long life of ease in the "hiddenness" of Calypso's cave *versus* a shorter life of strenuous exertion followed by public and eternal glory. Like Achilles, heroic Odysseus can really only choose the latter. In the end, as Seth Schein points out, Calypso's offer represents a kind of death for Odysseus. A hidden hero, one with no name and no deeds, is as good as dead. Immortality without heroic exertion is no life. Here Homer's Odysseus and Tennyson's Ulysses are one, for neither accepts the idea that "to breathe is life."

Odysseus is conscious that he is choosing a mortal, and therefore inferior, life and a mortal wife. Calypso cannot understand: "Much as you long to see your wife, the one you pine for all your days . . . and yet I just might claim to be nothing less than she, neither in face nor figure. Hardly right, is it, for mortal woman to rival immortal goddess?" Odysseus agrees:

> All that you say is true, how well I know.
> Look at my wife Penelope. She falls far short of you,
> your beauty, stature. She is mortal after all
> and you, you never age or die...
> Nevertheless, I long—I pine, all my days—
> to travel home and see the day of my return (5.238–243).

Odysseus chooses to be human rather than to seek to be a god.

Penelope is the main attraction of his return, but she is not the only one. The first time we see Odysseus, he is sitting on the headland looking over the sea "weeping, his eyes never dry, his sweet life flowing away with the tears he wept for his foiled journey home" (5.167–169). He also longs for the "day of my return"—the glorious day of his vengeance. Forlorn lover he may be, but he is also thinking like a hero.

Unfortunately, leaving Calypso means crossing the sea, and Poseidon comes back from his business trip just in time to see Odysseus making his way toward Scheria. He throws a terrible storm that crushes Odysseus's craft and leaves him naked, with nothing, on the shore of Scheria. Odysseus left Ithaca with a fleet of ships and many young nobles fighting alongside. During the war and his attempted return, Odysseus has steadily lost the glory that he possessed when he departed. All but his own ship is lost at sea, eventually the whole crew of that ship is also lost, and the plunder that Odysseus had collected from Troy sinks to the bottom of the sea. When he leaves Calypso's island, he has only the clothes on his back and the raft that he built for his journey home. And now Poseidon has stripped even these last remnants of glory from him. When he is thrown ashore on Scheria, he has literally been stripped naked. This is the furthest depth of his humiliation, his descent into the form of a servant. Journeying through the unreal world of myths brings him no gain.

Scheria is the threshold between the world of myths and the real world. When Zeus determines to send Odysseus to the Phaeacians, he mentions that they are "close kin to the gods themselves" (5.39), and it is later explained that when they have sacrifices the gods join them as guests (7.237–239). Nausicaa gives the geography: Assuring her friends that Odysseus cannot be an invader, she says that "we live too far apart, out in the surging sea, off at the world's end—no other mortals come to mingle with us" (6.223–225). More threateningly, Antinous tells Odysseus that the Phaeacians once lived near the Cyclops!

Their customs are also unusual. Though Nausicaa assures Odysseus that they will show him proper hospitality, Athena tells him "the men here never suffer strangers gladly, have no love for hosting a man from foreign lands" (7.36–37). Phaeacians, Nausicaa tells Odysseus, "care nothing for bow or quiver, only for masts and oars and good trim ships themselves—we glory in our ships" (6.296–298). Antinous concedes "we're hardly world-class boxers or wrestlers" though "we can race like the wind, we're champion sailors too, and always dear to our hearts, the feast, the lyre and dance and changes of fresh clothes, our warm baths and beds" (8.280–283). As Howard Clarke points out, if the Cyclops (whom we meet in the next section) are barbaric, the Phaeacians are "overcivilized." They hardly seem to be part of the same age or world as the heroes of the Trojan war. There is no challenge, no difficulty, all is ease and feasting and warm soft beds. For Odysseus to remain here would be, as much as accepting the offer of Calypso, a rejection of his heroic standing.

The transitional character of the island is symbolized by the strange olive tree under which Odysseus sleeps:

> He set out for the woods and not far from the water
> found a grove with a clearing all around and crawled
> beneath two bushy olives sprung from the same root,
> one olive wild, the other well-bred stock.
> No sodden gusty winds could ever pierce them,
> nor could the sun's sharp rays invade their depths,
> nor could a downpour drench them through and through,
> so dense they grew together, tangling side-by-side (5.525–532).

As Michael Nagler has pointed out, trees, especially olive trees, are important in the imagery of the *Odyssey*. The mast of Odysseus's ship is made of a pine tree (and, significantly, called a *histos*, the same word as "loom"). Grasping a mast saves Odysseus from being swallowed by Charybdis, and the olive-tree bed that stands at the center of Odysseus's house symbolizes his marriage and kingdom. Foreshadowing his return to his olive-tree bed, Odysseus finds refuge and sleeps under an olive tree.

The Phaeacian olive tree is half wild, half cultivated. To see the full significance of this, we should note that Odysseus's adventures in "no man's land" are equally adventures in an uncultivated, uncivilized region of the world. Pierre Vidal-Naquet explains that for Hesiod and Homer, agriculture, sacrifice, prohibition of incest, and cooking food are primary signs of civilized life. Throughout his adventures, Odysseus uses these to gauge the peoples he encounters. His repeated hopes to find "bread-eaters" are usually disappointed. From this angle, he is not so much traveling through never-land as he is visiting a series of barbaric tribes, something like a modern anthropologist. When he lands at Phaeacia, he finds himself under a tree that is half-cultivated and half-wild. He may not be home, where he will delight in the fields of grain, but at least he is not on the island of the Cyclops anymore, either. Phaeacian stands on the border between the uncultivated and the cultivated.

If Scheria is like Ogygia, then the former is no place for a hero. As Odysseus enters the palace of Antinous, he passes walls of bronze crowned with blue glaze that are set with golden doors set on silver door posts. Guarding the doorways are "dogs of gold and silver . . . , forged by the god of fire with all his cunning craft," and in the hall golden boys hold torches to light the feasts (7.98–118). Surrounding the palace are an orchard and gardens that are as luxurious as those around Calypso's cave. Like Hermes gazing at the wonders of Calypso's cave, Odysseus stands before the palace "gazing at all this bounty . . . marveling at it all" (7.157–

158). Like Ogygia, Scheria tempts Odysseus with promises of a long, languid, but ultimately inglorious life. At Scheria too, Odysseus is "calypsoed."

Nausicaa, princess of the Phaeacians, is among the temptations that Scheria presents. Allusions to marriage abound in these books. Athena appears to Nausicaa in a dream and urges her to go to the beach to wash her clothes in preparation for her wedding (6.27–44). Nausicaa is of marriageable age, as both Athena and later Odysseus notice (6.172–177), and she drops hints that Odysseus might be a suitable husband. When he has cleaned and anointed himself, and Athena has "lavished splendor over his head and shoulders," Nausicaa comments to her girlfriends, "Ah, if only a man like *that* were called my husband" (6.270). Later, as she gives him instructions for entering the city without causing a stir, she imagines that the townspeople would speculate, "Now who's that tall, handsome stranger Nausicaa has in tow? Where'd she light on *him*? Her husband-to-be, just wait!" (6.303–304). King Antinous chases away his son Laodamas to make a place for Odysseus in a "burnished chair" (7.201). Clearly, Antinous hopes that Odysseus will permanently occupy the seat of sonship.

Odysseus is seen entering several cities in the *Odyssey*. First, Helen tells the story of his disguised entry to Troy. In Book 7, he enters the city of the Phaeacians, where the story of his entry into Troy is sung (8.559–584), and in later books, he arrives at Ithaca and enters his own house. In every case, he comes in disguise, the "man of twists and turns." The Phaeacians cannot help but recognize his nobility, apparent from his bearing when he first appears in the court. His conduct also marks him out as a hero. When challenged to enter the games, his anger flares and he protests that he is "no stranger to sports . . . I've held my place in the front ranks, I tell you" (8.207–208). To prove the point, he throws a discus further than any competitor and then taunts the Phaeacians: "Now go match *that*, you young pups." In the course of the taunt he reveals that he is a veteran of the Trojan war:

> I'll take on all contenders, gladly, test them head-to-head!
> I'm no disgrace in the world of games where men compete.
> Well I know how to handle a fine polished bow,
> the first to hit my man in a mass of enemies,
> even with rows of comrades pressing near me,
> taking aim with our shafts to hit our targets.
> Philoctetes alone outshot me there at Troy (8.244–250).

Though the Phaeacians know that they are in the presence of a hero, they do not know who he is. This is the pattern of "delayed identification" we have seen at work in various ways already. His identity, however, is revealed by a song; this is appropriate, since heroes live eternally in the songs of the bards. Following dinner, Antinous calls the bard to sing. Among his songs is one about the affair of Ares and Aphrodite, the god of war and the goddess of love. Aphrodite is married to the lame god of fire, Hephaestus but lusts after Ares. They arrange to meet at Aphrodite's bed when they believe that Hephaestus will be gone. Hephaestus, however, has been warned of Aphrodite's betrayal, so he makes a web of chains that will drop on the lovers and hold them fast when they come to the bed. Unsuspecting, Ares and Aphrodite begin making love and the charmed chains fall and catch them like flies in a spider web, while all the gods gather to taunt and laugh at the couple.

Like many mythological stories, this is a revealing episode. It shows that the gods of the Greeks were neither noble nor moral in a Christian sense. Both Ares and Aphrodite were lustful and guilty of adultery, and the other gods, far from condemning, find delight in their predicament. In the *Odyssey*, however, this song strikingly parallels the situation of Odysseus (and, of course, of Agamemnon). Like Ares, the suitors lust after Penelope; like Hephaestus, Odysseus wishes to prevent his wife from being taken from him; we know, though Odysseus does not, that Penelope, unlike Aphrodite, has remained faithful to her "lamed," scarred, suffering husband. More than that, the song ends with Hephaestus triumphing: "Look how limping Hephaestus conquers War, the quickest of all the gods who rule Olympus" (8.373–374), says one of the gods enjoying the spectacle. "The cripple wins by craft," says another (8.375). These are heartening words for Odysseus, the man of craft and guile, for he hopes to catch the suitors in a web.

At Odysseus's request, Demodocus the poet also sings the song of the Trojan horse, Odysseus's own finest hour: "how Odysseus marched right up to Deiphobus' house like the god of war on attack with diehard Menelaus" and "fought the grimmest fight he had ever braved but he won through at last, thanks to Athena's superhuman power" (8.580–584). Hearing the song, Odysseus weeps. Antinous calls a halt to the singing and asks Odysseus point-blank to identify himself. The song, and his reaction to it, confirms that he is a hero of Troy. At the end of the epic, Odysseus will be revealed in rage and slaughter. In the luxurious palace of Antinous, in the flickering lights of the evening feast, things are different. The son of pain whom we first saw weeping on the shores of Calypso's island weeps again as he begins to recount his journey. Song and tears unveil the suffering hero.

*Review Questions.*
1. What does "Calypso" mean? Why is this significant?
2. Why is the enchanting setting of Calypso's home important?
3. How are Calypso and Penelope similar? How are they different?
4. What is Odysseus's attitude toward sex with women other than his wife?
5. What does Calypso offer Odysseus? Why does he refuse?
6. What is Odysseus's condition when he arrives in Scheria? Why is this significant?
7. How is Scheria a transitional stop between the mythical and the real?
8. What does the olive tree represent?
9. Compare Ogygia and Scheria.

10. Why is the story of Ares and Aphrodite told in the *Odyssey*?

*Though Questions.*
1. Why does Calypso think it unfair that the gods make her let Odysseus go home? (5.129–160)
2. Why does Odysseus wish he had died at Troy? (5.338–345)
3. How is Odysseus's landing at Scheria described? (5.497–511) What is significant about this description?
4. How does Odysseus change after he has a bath? How does this reflect the overall story of the epic? (6.247–271)
5. What god do the Phaeacians serve? (6.292–293) How is this ironic?
6. Odysseus gives details about the chronology of his voyage from Ogygia to Scheria. What is the significance of the numbers? (7.298–310)
7. What kinds of names do the Phaeacians have? Why? (8.122–161)
8. What is significant about Love (Aphrodite) and War (Ares) having an affair? What does this say about Homer's view of love? Of war?

## In No Man's Land, Books 9–12

Demodocus, the bard of the Phaeacians, has finished his song, and now Odysseus, "the great teller of tales" takes center stage as the greater bard (9.1). Already Odysseus has been among the Phaeacians for some time without revealing his name, and in his first comments he again teases them by putting off openly declaring his identity. "Now let me begin by telling you my name," he says in line 17, but he actually states his name four lines later. He identifies himself as "Odysseus, son of Laertes, known to the world for every kind of craft—my fame has reached to the skies" (9.21–22). This is the first time in the epic Odysseus has identified himself, and the way he does it is revealing. He is a hero known not for his strength and skill in battle but for his "craft." Though Greek heroes seek for immortal fame above all, Odysseus's self-praise is comparatively rare. The fact that he praises his own achievements shows that he is functioning as both bard and hero.

This identification also shows the complexity of his situation. His fame, he says, reaches to the skies, which means that he has already achieved heroic stature. Demodocus already knows songs about his exploits. Yet, Odysseus has been a "hidden" hero, recently under the power of Calypso and up to this moment "anonymous" among the Phaeacians. For the heroes of the *Iliad*, the challenge was how to gain immortal fame, but this is not quite what Odysseus faces. His name is already immortalized, and in some situations he is all too well-known. His problem is how to survive and triumph over the hostile forces that prevent his homecoming. To do this, he has to avoid identifying himself with the glorified name of Odysseus.[2]

To identify himself, Odysseus tells a series of stories that make up the most famous section of the epic. Being among the most interesting and exciting episodes, these stories are often detached from their context and told as separate stories. Much of the point is lost when this is done. To understand fully the theme of these adventures, we need to note the structure of this section of the epic. William Thalmann has pointed out that the stories as Odysseus tells them are arranged in a concentric or ring structure:

    a. Cicones
        b. Lotus eaters
            c. Cyclops
                d. Aeolus
                    e. Laestrygonians
                        f. Circe
                              Journey to Underworld
                        f. Sirens
                    e. Scylla

                d. Cattle of sun
             c. Charybdis
         b. Calypso
     a. Phaeacians

As in other concentric arrangements (see introduction to epic, above), sections marked with the same letter are related either by some similarity or contrast. In each of the "a" sections, Odysseus enters a city, but there are significant differences between the incidents. Fresh from Troy, he attacks and plunders the city of the Cicones, but he arrives at the city of the Phaeacians destitute and alone, a suppliant seeking guest-gifts. The two "b" sections are connected by the theme of forgetfulness of home, which recurs throughout these stories. The Lotus eaters have no intention of killing Odysseus's comrades but offer them "the lotus to taste." They seem perfectly hospitable, but this "honey-sweet fruit" removes from his men "all desire to send a message back, much less return, their only wish to linger there with the Lotus eaters, grazing on lotus, all memory of the journey home dissolved forever" (9.106–110). For Odysseus himself, Calypso poses the same threat, promising a life of ease that will distract from his heroic destiny. In both, hospitality is not neglected. The problem instead is that the hosts will not let the guests leave; the abuse is an excess of hospitality. Polyphemus the Cyclops and Charybdis the whirlpool are both man-devouring (c), and in both of the "d" sections Odysseus's men violate a prohibition and bring divine wrath upon themselves. In both, moreover, Odysseus falls asleep while his men's curiosity get the better of them (9.35; 12.364).[3] Scylla and the Laestrygonians are man-eating monsters (e), and both Circe and the Sirens (f) sing and tempt Odysseus to neglect his return journey.

    In Thalmann's outline, Odysseus has thirteen adventures, but it is possible that Homer intended there to be only twelve. The Phaeacians represent the first stage of Odysseus's journey out of "no man's land," and therefore ought not be considered an "adventure" on the same scale as the others. Alternatively, one could count Scylla and Charybdis as a single episode, again leaving us with twelve stories. If either of these is a valid suggestion, then the number of episodes is significant. Odysseus has twelve "labors," which reveal him to be as great a hero as the legendary Hercules.

Comparison with Hercules is clearly one of the purposes of Odysseus's journey to the world of the dead that forms the central stanza of Odysseus's song. The importance of this episode is highlighted not only by its central position in the series but also by its length. Most of the adventures cover a portion of a book, but the journey to the underworld covers most of Book 11. It is not entirely clear why Odysseus has to go to the realm of the dead in the first place. Circe tells him that he must meet the blind seer Teiresias, who will give him directions about how to get back to Ithaca, but the famous prophet's directions are very vague. He mentions the cattle of the sun, warning Odysseus not to let his men eat them, but he entirely neglects to mention Scylla, Charybdis, or the Sirens. When Odysseus gets back to Circe, she gives him a detailed itinerary for his return (12.31–121). Why didn't she say anything before? Perhaps we can resolve the problem by saying that Circe was somehow unable to reveal the plans for return until Odysseus had gone to the underworld and emerged again.

Teiresias does give Odysseus a prophecy that he does not receive from Circe, concerning his own future.

> once you have killed those suitors in your halls—
> by stealth or in open fight with slashing bronze—
> go forth once more, you must...
> carry your well-planed oar until you come
> to a race of people who know nothing of the sea,
> whose food is never seasoned with salt, strangers all
> to ships with their crimson prows and long slim oars,
> wings that make ships fly....
> When another traveler falls in with you and calls
> that weight across your shoulder a fan to winnow grain,

> then plant your bladed, balanced oar in the earth
> and sacrifice fine beasts to the lord god of the sea,
> Poseidon (11.136–149).

Poseidon has been the cause of Odysseus's sufferings, and this is the means by which they can finally tame the sea. The idea seems to be that Odysseus is to become a traveling evangelist for the cult of Poseidon, setting up worship of the sea god far from the sea. If he does this, his death will be "gentle, painless death, far from the sea" (11.154). Odysseus thus is promised the best of all worlds. He has won and will win fame and glory in life, but will die the easy death of a non-hero—far from the raging, chaotic sea.

The journey to the dead has several other functions. I suggested above that Odysseus's journeys are being implicitly compared to the labors of Hercules. It is fitting, then, that the climax of Odysseus's journey is an encounter with Hercules, who also entered the underworld and returned. When they meet, Hercules draws a comparison between Odysseus and himself: "Royal son of Laertes, Odysseus famed for exploits, luckless man, you too? Braving out a fate as harsh as the fate I bore, alive in the light of day?" (11.708–710). Odysseus is not only the equal of Agamemnon and Achilles, whom he also encounters in the realm of the shades, but the equal of the great heroes of the distant past.

Agamemnon is there to tell the story of his slaughter, giving details that foreshadow the later blood wedding that we will see at Ithaca:

> I died—a wretched, ignominious death—and round me
> all my comrades killed, no mercy, one after another,
> just like white-tusked boars
> butchered in some rich lord of power's halls
> for a wedding, banquet or groaning public feast....
> if you'd laid eyes on this it would have wrenched your heart—
> how we sprawled by the mixing-bowl and loaded tables there,
> throughout the palace, the whole floor awash with blood
> (11.466–475).

If we have not gotten the point, Agamemnon draws the moral: "even your own wife, never indulge her too far" (11.500). Though he assures Odysseus that he has nothing to fear from Penelope, this brings little comfort from a man so thoroughly fooled by his own wife.

Then there is Achilles, though only a shadow of his former self. The hero who decided for a short life of glory over a long life of ease now recognizes that death holds no glory: "By god, I'd rather slave on earth for another man... than rule down here over all the breathless dead" (11.556–558). Yet he has not changed so much after all, for he asks Odysseus about the exploits of his "gallant son" and appears to find satisfaction in Odysseus's assurance that his son is as lustful for blood and glory as his father.

In its central position, the journey to the dead is a key to the whole series of adventures. The entire sequence is about Odysseus confronting and overcoming death. In a number of adventures—Scylla and Charybdis, the Cyclops, the Laestrygonians, and the Sirens—Odysseus faces the threat of literal death. At other times, the death is metaphorical. We have noted above that Calypso's offer to Odysseus represents a kind of death, an immortality won without effort and without heroic glory. Those adventures that threaten to prevent Odysseus's return to Ithaca—the Lotus eaters and Circe, for example—represent threats of death in the same way. Many in Ithaca believe him to be dead, and even those who keep hope alive regard his absence as a kind of death. Odysseus suffers pain and anonymity (becoming "nobody") and comes near to death on countless occasions but emerges again to conquer the suitors, to restore order, to establish a wedding and a feast. The journey to the underworld encapsulates the journeys of Odysseus; he is singing of his own death and resurrection. This is the initiation that prepares him for his unveiling in Ithaca.

Immediately after his return from the realm of the dead, Odysseus faces the temptation of the Sirens. In one sense, the Sirens are just another obstacle to Odysseus's *nostos*.

Were Odysseus to succumb to their temptation, it would prevent his return: "whoever draws too close... no sailing home for him, no wife rising to meet him, no happy children beaming up at their father's face" (12.46–49). Yet the temptation is subtly different from that of the Lotus eaters or Calypso. The Sirens sing about the Trojan War (12.205–207), and their singing has the same enchanting effect as a bard's song (compare 1.388; 12.45). They appeal to Odysseus as the "Achaea's pride and glory," (12.200), a title that is used only in this place in the *Odyssey* but frequently in the *Iliad*. The Sirens are tempting Odysseus not so much to remain where he is but to turn back to Troy, to transform himself into the Odysseus he was before he went through Hades. To turn back to Troy, to recover his earlier identity, to remain, as Charles Segal puts it, "frozen" in the past, is deadly, for, like the battlefield of Troy, the meadow of the Sirens is strewn with rotting corpses (12.51). Odysseus resists; the old Odysseus was left behind in the realm of the dead; he has become a new man.

In addition to being a record of the experience and temptations of the "dead and risen" hero, the stories symbolize the situation in Ithaca. Odysseus can later face the deadly hostility of the suitors because he has already faced death and returned. More specifically, the behavior of Odysseus's men reflects the conduct of the suitors back in Ithaca. Already in the proem, we were told that despite Odysseus's best efforts, his men were destroyed by their own recklessness, specifically their curiosity concerning the bag of wind (1.7–10). Like the suitors, Odysseus's crew is foolish, they flout Odysseus's command, and they all end up dead. The adventure with Circe particularly brings out the parallels between the crew and the suitors. When the men first see Circe, she is singing and weaving (10.240–245). Singing, she is like the Sirens; weaving, she is like Penelope. Circe turns the crew into swine, and this illumines Penelope's situation, for she too is surrounded by swine. No wonder Odysseus gets on so well with Eumaeus the swineherd when he returns to Ithaca.

Odysseus has been herding swine for ten years!

Odysseus's adventures also reflect the situation in Ithaca in the emphasis on the issue of hospitality, which can be illustrated by the adventure of the Cyclops. According to Odysseus, the Cyclops are

> lawless brutes, who trust so to the everlasting gods
> they never plant with their own hands or plow the soil.
> Unsown, unplowed, the earth teems with all they need,
> wheat, barley and vines, swelled by the rains of Zeus
> to yield a big full-bodied wine from clustered grapes.
> They have no meeting place for council, no laws either,
> no, up to the mountain peaks they live in arching caverns—
> each a law to himself, ruling his wives and children,
> not a care in the world for any neighbor (9.120–128).

As noted above, agriculture, society, political life, and law are closely linked. In order to plant and reap, one has to be sure that no one else is going to attack and steal his produce. Some established ideas of ownership and property are necessary. For trade to take place, there must be some system of laws or courts for resolving disagreements. The fact that the Cyclops do not have agriculture says all that is needed. It means that they are without civilization.

Hospitality is one of the key marks of true civilization in the Homeric world, one that the Cyclops scoff at. Odysseus appeals to Polyphemus by reminding him of obligations to strangers:

> Since we've chanced on you, we're at your knees
> in hopes of a warm welcome, even a guest-gift,
> the sort that hosts give strangers. That's the custom.
> Respect the gods, my friend. We're suppliants—at your mercy!
> Zeus of the strangers guards all guests and suppliants:
> strangers are sacred—Zeus will avenge their rights! (9.300–305).

Odysseus thus places the duty of hospitality on a religious

basis, and the Cyclops' refusal shows that he is not only uncivilized but also impious:

> 'Stranger,' he grumbled back from his brutal heart,
> 'you must be a fool, stranger, or come from nowhere,
> telling *me* to fear the gods or avoid their wrath!
> We Cyclops never blink at Zeus and Zeus's shield
> of storm and thunder, or any other blessed god—
> we've got more force by far' (9.306–311).

Like so many of the people that Odysseus meets, the Cyclops' civilization is defined by its food. Instead of feeding his guests, Polyphemus eats them: "he bolted them down like a mountain-lion, left no scrap, devoured entrails, flesh and bones, marrow and all!" (9.329–330). Likewise, the only "guest gift" that Polyphemus promises Odysseus is that he will kill and eat him last. It is significant, too, that Polyphemus eats men raw, for that is how beasts eat flesh. Civilized men cook flesh and always first offer a portion to the gods. In Ithaca, however, men act like Cyclops, devouring Odysseus's house, neglecting sacrifice, bleeding his house white. They might as well dash his brains out and bolt him down raw. All those who do not feed strangers feed *on* them. Odysseus's response to the threat is appropriate, displaying his *metis*, his craftiness. At first, he considers stabbing the Cyclops in the chest while he sleeps, but that kind of direct confrontation would leave his men stranded in the cave (9.336–343). Instead, Odysseus uses the "weapon" of wine, offering the Cyclops three bowls of strong drink. Polyphemus's perversion of hospitality is defeated by a cunning over-abundance of hospitality.

In its emphasis on hospitality and food, the adventure with Polyphemus is connected with several others. At the palace of Antiphates, king of the Laestrygonians, Odysseus's men are set upon by giants who descended on the ships and "speared the crews like fish and whisked them home to make their grisly meal" (10.135–136). Scylla's six heads seize six of his best men like a fisherman pulling in fish and "she bolted them down raw" (12.277). On the other side is the whirlpool Charybdis who swallows "the sea-surge down her gaping maw" and then "spewed it up" again (12.255, 259–260). The crew's recklessness is shown in connection with diet. Circe "mixed them a potion—cheese, barley and pale honey mulled in Pramnian wine" that contains "wicked drugs to wipe from their memories any thought of home" (10.256–263). When they are turned into swine, it merely makes visible what is already true: They have already acted like pigs in bolting down Circe's food. Though Odysseus warns his crew, they sacrifice and eat the cattle of the Sun, despite the fact that the food behaves oddly while being cooked:

> The cattle were dead already...
> And the gods soon showed us all some fateful signs—
> the hides began to crawl, the meat, both raw and roasted,
> bellowed out on the spits, and we heard a noise
> like the moan of lowing oxen (12.424–428).[4]

Odysseus's adventures might be taken as a series of warnings to "watch what you eat."

Wine is one of Odysseus's weapons against the Cyclops; the other is a disguise. When Polyphemus asks his name, he answers, "Nobody." As a result, when Odysseus pokes a sharp hot pole into the Cyclops' eye, Polyphemus cries to his friends that "Nobody" is attacking and killing him, and they do nothing to help. Not only is this an example of Odysseus's clever tactics, but it is an opportunity for an elaborate pun. Bernard Knox explains:

> The Greek word *outis*, the name Odysseus gives himself, is formed from the normal Greek locution for "nobody"—*ou tis*, "not anybody." This enables Homer to make brilliant use of wordplay that cannot be adequately reproduced in English. When his fellow Cyclops ask Polyphemus why he is making such an uproar and he tells them "Nobody's killing me now by fraud and not by force," they naturally misunderstand it and reply, "*If* nobody's trying to overpower you..."

(9.456–457). But in Greek their reply has a different form for "no one": not *ou tis* but *me tis*, the usual form for use after the word "if." But *me tis*, "not anyone," sounds exactly the same as *meti*, a key word of the *Odyssey*, the main characteristic of its hero: craft, cunning. And Polyphemus is in fact being overpowered by the *metis*, the craft and cunning of Odysseus.

Odysseus "Polymetis"—"of many crafts" (21.306)—uses his *metis*—his cunning anonymity—to overcome Polyphemus.

More abstractly, the contest between Odysseus and the Cyclops is a contest between nature and civilization. Polyphemus is definitely on the side of "raw" nature—without agriculture, without law, without social contact, without an oven. Odysseus overcomes him by forming a weapon, using that fundament of civilized life—fire. When he pokes the sharpened pole into the Cyclops' eye, Homer describes his action as being like a "shipwright" (shipbuilder) and a "blacksmith" (9.430, 438–440). Odysseus's technological *metis* overcomes the raw natural power of Polyphemus.

Given Odysseus's location in "no man's land," "Nobody" is not just another trick. In a very real sense, it describes what Odysseus has become. Though his name is known throughout the world, he is hidden in a shadowy realm of witches and monsters. Odysseus finds this situation frustrating, and as he escapes from the island of the Cyclops, he cannot be restrained from shouting out his name: "if any man on the face of the earth should ask you who blinded you, shamed you so—say Odysseus, raider of cities" (9.560–562). It is as if Odysseus is back on the Trojan battlefield; he has not yet left the old Odysseus behind in the realm of the dead. And his determination to reveal his name backfires. When someone calls your name in a crowded room, you cannot help but turn and look to see who called. Knowing a person's name gives you leverage on him. Once Polyphemus knows the name of his attacker, he can use it in a curse, appealing to his father Poseidon to frustrate Odysseus's plans to go home. Faced with a Cyclops, Odysseus learns, acting like Achilles is simply not an option.

This is a crucial lesson, and the adventure of the Cyclops, like the other adventures, is part of Odysseus's training for his last battle. Like Telemachus in Book 1–4, he is being fashioned into fuller heroic stature. Having honed his *metis* in "no man's land," Nobody is ready to return home, where he will make a name for himself.

*Review Questions*

1. How does Odysseus's situation differ from that of the heroes fighting at Troy?

2. Describe the structure of the stories that Odysseus recites.

3. What is significant about the number of adventures?

4. Why does Circe tell Odysseus to go to the underworld? How does this story reinforce some of the themes of the epic?

5. What is significant about the position of the episode of the Sirens?

6. How does the Circe episode reflect the situation in Ithaca?

7. How does the cannibalism of the Cyclops fit into the epic? What issue is being treated?

8. Explain how food figures into two adventures other than the Cyclops.

9. Explain the pun on "nobody" in the Cyclops episode.

10. How does Odysseus's defeat of the Cyclops symbolize "civilization" triumphing over "nature"?

*Thought Questions.*

1. On what day does Odysseus arrive in the land of the Lotus eaters? What is significant about this chronology? (9.91–95; see 10.32–33; 12.484; 14.273–274)

2. Whom did the sons of Aeolus marry? What is significant about this? (10.1–11)

3. How does Odysseus attract the dead so that he can

speak to them? (10.568–595)
   4. What kind of existence do the dead have? (Book 11)
   5. What women does Odysseus meet in the world of the dead? What do they have in common? What is significant about this? (11.257–377)
   6. What does Alcinous offer Odysseus? Why? (11.378–427)

## His Own Did Not Receive Him, Books 13–18

The second half of the epic is largely a series of "recognition scenes." A recognition scene is one of several "type scenes" frequently used in literature. These frequently involve the reunion of people who have long been separated and include standard recurring elements. One of the parties expresses a wish for the other to appear—and, lo and behold, there he is! Tokens or signs that prove one's identity are also conventional. In Aeschylus's *Libation Bearers*, Orestes and Electra recognize each other by the similarity of their footprints, a scene mocked in Aristophanes' play, *The Frogs*.

Recognition of Odysseus does not come easily. Not only has he been gone for a long time, but he returns in disguise and gradually reveals himself to those who have remained loyal. First, he reveals himself to Telemachus, and together the now-mature young man and his father make plans to dispose of the suitors. Then, he is revealed to his old nursemaid, Eurycleia. He reveals himself to a few loyal household servants. When the moment is right, he reveals himself in all his splendor and strength to the terrified suitors. He is reunited to Penelope and finally to his mourning father, Laertes. Odysseus, who began the epic hidden on Calypso's island, achieves a progressive "apocalypse."

Wendell Berry has pointed out that Odysseus's journey from "no man's land" to home is a movement toward the center of order:

The structure may be graphed as a series of diminishing circles centered on one of the posts of the marriage bed. Odysseus makes his way from the periphery toward that center. All around, this structure verges on the sea, which is the wilderness, ruled by the forces of nature and by the gods. In spite of the excellence of his ship and crew and his skill in navigation, a man is alien there. Only when he steps ashore does he enter a human world. From the shoreline of his island of Ithaca, Odysseus makes his way across a succession of boundaries, enclosed and enclosing.... He comes to his island, to his own lands, to his town, to his household and house, to his bedroom, to his bed.... By these, his homecoming becomes at the same time a restoration of order.

Here we see that the "man of twists and turns" alone can navigate the treacherous voyage to the center, the place around which the world revolves. Only this kind of hero can establish a properly ordered society.

At each stage, Odysseus must show himself by some token or sign. There are obvious reasons for this. He must have some proof beyond his own word that he is indeed the king of Ithaca. This is especially necessary since so many suitors have presented themselves as potential successors to Odysseus. How is one to know if this man is just a cleverly disguised suitor? Penelope is afraid that a god might be deceiving her by taking the form of her husband. More subtly, the need for signs fits with several of the larger themes of the epic. Odysseus is, as we have seen, the man of twists and turns, and other characters also use various kinds of ruses and deceptions. This kind of world makes people wary and suspicious, and absolute proof is needed if one is to win trust. This also relates to the themes of identity, name, and heroism that we have been examining.

Book 13 opens with Odysseus's return to the real world. Scheria was only a midpoint in this return, a borderland between fantasy and reality, between waking and sleeping. Fittingly, the whole Phaeacian sojourn is framed by scenes of Odysseus sleeping. He falls asleep under the olive tree on the shores of Scheria (5.544–547), and the Phaeacians leave him sleeping on the shore of Ithaca (13.127–141). When he wakes, the dreamworld is finally behind him. He is ready to return to reality. The differences between Odysseus's two arrivals are important. When Odysseus struggled ashore at Scheria, he was naked and pennyless, having barely escaped death at sea. Arriving in Ithaca, he is clothed and bears the riches that the Phaeacians have given him. He is no longer "nobody," stripped of glory; he has begun his ascent. This return to glory is also a return to humanity: When he arrived at Scheria, he stalked out to meet Nausicaa like a mountain lion charging a flock (6.142–147), but as he makes way toward Ithaca he is "as a man ach[ing] for his evening meal when all day long his brace of wine-dark oxen have dragged the bolted plowshare down a fallow field" (13.34–36).

True to character, Odysseus is "clothed" not only in Phaeacian garments but in a fictitious identity. The first person he meets on the misty shore of Ithaca is Athena, and when she tells him he is in Ithaca, he tells an elaborate lie about who he is:

> I'm a fugitive now, you see. I killed Idomeneus' son,
> Orsilochus, lightning on his legs, a man who beat
> all runners alive on that long island—what a racer!
> He tried to rob me of all the spoil I won at Troy,
> the plunder I went to hell and back to capture, true,
> cleaving my way through wars of men and waves of sea
> (13.294–299).

Odysseus tells other stories to the swineherd, Eumaeus, and to Penelope. The reasons for the deception are clear. He has returned to his kingdom and cannot guess at first who will be loyal and who is out to kill him. Unlike the gullible Agamemnon, he is a man of twists and turns and realizes he must distrust everyone. Suspicion and deception come naturally to Odysseus, as Athena observes: "Any man—any god who met you—would have to be some champion lying cheat to get past *you*" (13.329–330). Yet the lie contains grains of truth for those with ears to hear. He reveals that he was at Troy, and he will exploit this part of his story throughout the following books. This gives him a basis for saying he knows Odysseus and that he has news of his imminent return. He also says that he has been to "hell and back" to recover his plunder, which is quite literally true. Interestingly, he says he is a fugitive seeking asylum, and in Book 15, Telemachus will welcome a *real* fugitive to the shores of Ithaca and before meeting the other fugitive, his father.

A story is not sufficient cover on Ithaca, however. He needs to have more elaborate clothing to hide his identity. Athena provides this by transforming him into a beggar:

> I will shrivel the supple skin on your lithe limbs,
> strip the russet curls from your head and deck you out
> in rags you'd hate to see some other mortal wear;
> I'll dim the fire in your eyes, so shining once—
> until you seem appalling to all these suitors,
> even your wife and son you left behind at home (13.454–460).

In this disguise, Odysseus will appear in the palace as a supplicant, seeking hospitality. Thus, the disguise picks up on the constant issue of the treatment of strangers. Moreover, Athena makes him look so lowly that the suitors will treat him with contempt, and this will heighten their guilt and justify the merciless slaughter that Odysseus inflicts on them.

In many ways, the story of Odysseus's return to Ithaca reflects themes of the gospel story. The king comes in "disguise" to his own kingdom to reclaim his throne and is mistreated by the nobles of the kingdom. He suffers their mockery and persecution silently, but then reveals himself in power and glory in a day of "resurrection." Even Odysseus's vengeance against the suitors who have been preying on his bride find a parallel in Jesus' "coming" to Jerusalem to destroy the harlot that drinks the blood of his bride (Matthew 24; Revelation 17-18). Still, the two stories diverge subtly. In the gospels, Jesus submits not only to mockery and rejection but even to death, and in His death He achieves His victory. Odysseus, operating by the Greek heroic ethic, suffers silently for a time, but only until he has an opening to take savage vengeance against his persecutors. True, Jesus eventually carries out vengeance against His enemies, but on the cross he prays for their forgiveness. "Forgive them, for they know not what they do" is not part of Odysseus's vocabulary. The cross is not a weapon in his arsenal.

For Odysseus, then, the movement of the last half of the epic is a progress from beggar to king, from humiliation to exaltation. This is not only a personal ascent for Odysseus but effects a reordering of Ithacan society. In a properly ordered society, the king is at the top, and the beggars, though they are to be treated with kindness, are at the bottom. In Ithaca, beggars (suitors) have the run of the palace, while the true king is treated like a beggar. When Odysseus moves from beggar to king, he is also turning the topsy-turvy world of Ithaca right side up. Swine rule Ithaca; Odysseus comes as a beast-master, an Adam who establishes human dominion.

Following Athena's instructions, Odysseus first makes his way to the hut of the swineherd Eumaeus. The fact that a swineherd appears in the epic at all shows how far we are from the *Iliad*, where nearly every character is an aristocrat and a warrior. And Homer takes the time to make Eumaeus a real and thoroughly sympathetic character. His loyalty to Odysseus is shown in the care he has taken to protect and care for the swine (14.9–31). His first words are of his long-lost master:

> Here I sit, my heart aching, broken for *him*,
> my master, my great king—fattening up
> his own hogs for other men to eat, while he,
> starving for food, I wager, wanders the earth,
> a beggar adrift in strangers' cities, foreign-speaking lands,
> if he's still alive, that is, still sees the rising sun (14.44–49).

His words are oddly both true and false. His master *is* a beggar in a land where strangers have been feasting on his wealth, even though he is king and at home.

In an epic where treatment of strangers is the test of good and bad character, Eumaeus shows himself to be a good man by inviting Odysseus to "eat your fill of bread and wine" (14.51). His offer is rooted in his piety. When he slaughters a pig for Odysseus to share he "did not forget the gods" but plucked some tufts from the pig's head to place in the fire as a token offering, along with a prayer for Odysseus's return (14.477–479). At the end of Book 14, Eumaeus passes a further test of loyalty. The beggar tells a story about how Odysseus once provided him with a cloak to sleep in, implying that Eumaeus should imitate his master's generosity. Eumaeus immediately answers "You won't want for clothes or whatever else is due a worn-out traveler" (14.577–578). Eumaeus will do his part in re-clothing the king who had been stripped naked. He is no Cyclops; from his modest possessions, he offers a guest-gift.

Eumaeus's behavior not only reveals something about this loyal servant but also provides a commentary on the situation at the palace. On the one hand, Odysseus's arrival at the swineherd's hut casts light backward on his previous adventures. While the Phaeacian palace was surrounded by a bronze wall and guarded by golden dogs, the swineherd's hut is surrounded by a wall of his own building and real, vicious guard dogs. Odysseus has come from never-never land back into the mundane but familiar world of Ithaca. Yet, though his adventures in fantasy land are over, one of his most challenging tests awaits him on his own soil. As we have seen, his adventures in "no man's land" have toughened him, and taught him the virtue of patience, the necessity of "delayed identification." On the other hand, Eumaeus may be contrasted to the suitors. Though the palace may be more richly endowed and the suitors more noble of birth, the swineherd is more civilized and his hut more welcoming. Finally, the swineherd's reception assures Odysseus that at least some Ithacans have not forgotten him and have kept their lamps lit in anticipation of the bridegroom's return. The master has returned, and finds them so doing.

Homer has gotten his hero back home, and this winds up the travel phase of Odysseus's story (covering Books 5–14). Books 1–4 showed us the education of Telemachus in the ways of heroic society, raising up the son to be a suitable companion to his famous father. But Book 4 ended with the son's fate still hanging in the balance: "the suitors boarded now and sailed the sea-lanes, plotting in their hearts Telemachus's plunge to death" (4.947–948). Before Homer could move forward to the climax of the story, he had to bring Telemachus back into the picture. The parallel between father and son is underscored by the structure of Book 15, which begins with Telemachus's departure from Sparta, switches to the swineherd's hut where Odysseus and Eumaeus trade stories late into the night, and then ends by switching back to Telemachus's arrival at Ithaca.

Like father, like son: Telemachus must go, if not to hell and back, at least from a deadly threat to assured life. All the way home from Sparta and Pylos, he wonders, "would he sweep clear of death or be cut down?" (15.334). Telemachus must be able to overcome another obstacle as well. Like his father on Calypso's island and on Scheria, Telemachus must resist the temptation to bask in the comforts of Sparta and Pylos while he is needed at home. When he accompanies Pisistratus back to Pylos, he shows he has learned this lesson. He refuses to go all the way to Nestor's house because he fears that Nestor, like a well-meaning Lotus-eater, will smother him with hospitality: "Your father's old," he tells Pisistratus, "in love with his hospitality; I fear he'll hold me, chafing in his palace—I must hurry home" (15.223–225). Both father and son must leave "no man's land" behind to return to the field of battle and glory.

Telemachus, like Odysseus, has been instructed to go to Eumaeus's hut, and the swineherd embraces him "as a father, brimming with love, welcomes home his darling only son in a warm embrace . . . home now, in the tenth year from far abroad" (16.19–22). This is an example of a "reverse simile," a comparison that describes a scene in terms that are directly opposite of what is actually taking place. Telemachus has not been away ten years, and Eumaeus is not his father, yet their reunion is compared to the return of a long-lost son. In this case, the simile prepares the way for what happens next. When the swineherd leaves to take a message to Penelope, Odysseus reveals himself to Telemachus; the long-lost father, not the son, has returned. And Telemachus does not immediately welcome his father with a warm embrace: "No, you're not Odysseus! Not my father!" (16.218). It is only after Odysseus explains that Athena's power has transformed him to an old beggar that Telemachus, reacting as Penelope later will, "threw his arms around his great father, sobbing uncontrollably as the deep desire for tears welled up in both" (16.243–245). The first revelation of the king is complete. As in the hall of the Phaeacians, so here in the hut of the swineherd: Tears mark the son of pain.

Eumaeus may sleep with pigs, but the real swine are in the palace. By contrast with the tears and embraces of the swineherd's hut, Odysseus's reception at his house is not unlike his reception by Polyphemus. In both cases, he takes on the guise of a "nobody," an *ou tis*, though this is just one trick from a master of *metis*. As with the Cyclops, too, the suitors show no hospitality. The goatherd Melanthius meets Odysseus and Eumaeus on the way to the palace with harsh words: "Wretched pig-boy, where do you take your filthy swine, this sickening beggar who licks the pots at feasts?" (17.238–239). Twice suitors throw stools at Odysseus. Even Melantho, one of the serving-women, treats him with contempt: "Get out, you tramp—be glad of the good you got—or we'll sling a torch at you, rout you out at once" (19.74–75). Antinous, the leader of the suitors, lashes out at Eumaeus: "Your highness, swineherd—why drag *this* to town? Haven't we got our share of vagabonds to deal with, disgusting beggars who lick the feasters' plates?" (17.412–414). Though he seems to be referring to the real beggars who come to Ithaca for food, Antinous's questions are rich with unintended irony. The palace is indeed full of beggars who lick feasters' plates—the suitors themselves who are begging food from Odysseus's house. When Antinous says he wants to get rid of the beggar, he is pronouncing his own doom (17.447–449).

The connection between the suitors and beggars helps us to understand the boxing match that Odysseus engages in with Arnaeus, a real beggar who tries to protect his turf against Odysseus. Odysseus beats him easily and throws him out the door with the words: "no more lording it over strangers, no more playing the beggar-king for you" (18.122–123). The suitors find enormous comedy in the battle of the beggars, but they are laughing to their own hurt. Only a short time before, Odysseus told Antinous that he looked like a king (17.460). Like all the suitors, he is lording it over strangers and playing the beggar-king, and his fate will be much worse than that of Arnaeus. Homer's description of Arnaeus's wound reminds us of the deaths in the *Iliad*: "Suddenly red blood came spurting out of his mouth, and headlong down he pitched in the dust, howling, teeth locked in a grin, feet beating the ground" (18.112–115).

*Review Questions*
1. What is a "recognition scene"? What is their place in Books 13–19?
2. Explain the similarities and differences between Odysseus's arrival at Scheria and his return to Ithaca.
3. Why is Odysseus transformed into a beggar?
4. How does Eumaeus relate to Odysseus's previous adventures? How does he compare to the suitors?
5. What is significant about the structure of Book 15?
6. How is the return of Telemachus like that of his father?
7. What is a reverse simile? How is the reverse simile used in Book 15?
8. How do the suitors treat Odysseus?

9. What is ironic about Antinous's treatment of Odysseus?

10. What is important about the wrestling match between Odysseus and Arnaeus?

*Thought Questions.*
1. What does Eumaeus think of Helen? (14.79–82)
2. Why must Telemachus hurry back to Ithaca? (15.19–30)
3. What does Helen give Telemachus? Why is this significant? (15.137–143)
4. What omen does Telemachus see as he leaves Sparta? What does it mean? (15.179–199)
5. What story does Eumaeus tell Odysseus? How does it fit into the epic? (15.437–541)
6. What is ironic about Eurymachus's speech to Penelope? (16.481–496)
7. What does Penelope say when she learns that Antinous has struck the beggar? Why is this significant? (17.547)
8. Penelope says that Antinous is "black death itself" (17.554). Considering Odysseus's adventures in "no man's land," why does Antinous not frighten Odysseus?
9. Why is Penelope's warning about the suitors ironic? (17.653–655)
10. Where does Penelope say her glory comes from? (18.284–286)

## Apocalypse, Books 20–24

The suitors clearly have no clue who this beggar is, and in their ignorance, they are less than dogs, for even Argos, Odysseus's dog, recognizes his master upon his return. But does Penelope? It is clear that she values his conversation and advice, since most of Book 19 describes their nighttime conversation. Penelope, finally finding a sympathetic man who has had some contact with her husband, pours out her heart. She tells Odysseus about the trick of the shroud by which she kept the suitors at bay for three years. Odysseus's affection and pity is genuine: "Odysseus's heart went out to his grief-stricken wife" (19.242), and he renews her hope by assuring her that Odysseus is still alive, laden with treasure. Echoing Theoclymenus' prophecy, he swears that Odysseus will return to Ithaca within the month.

Does Penelope suspect who he is? The text does not say for sure, but some commentators believe she does. As we noted above, Helen, who knew Odysseus much less well than Penelope, recognized him when he infiltrated Troy disguised as a beggar. In a strange way, the lies that Odysseus tells are themselves marks of his identity. Penelope, who is herself a master of craft and cunning, might well have recognized her man of "twists and turns" in the elaborate stories he tells. More importantly, Penelope's actions in the subsequent books perhaps suggest that she recognizes him. At the beginning of Book 21, she sets up a contest to determine which suitor she will marry: he must be able to string Odysseus's bow and shoot an arrow through twelve axes. As in many folk tales, the bride sets up a contest to decide who her husband will be. The contest is supposed to lead to a wedding day; Odysseus is there to make sure it is a blood-wedding, crushing the vipers who have tried to seduce his bride (23.33).

This is a change from her earlier promise to accept the wealthiest suitor and changes the terms of their courting. As Bernard Knox observes, Penelope might be credited with great foresight here. She suspects that none of the suitors, who have spent their youth in games and feasting, will be able to meet her challenge, and they will slink away in shame. She is determined she will not accept a weaker man; what she wants is another Odysseus. And that is what she gets—an Odysseus who has been to hell and back. Yet, hers is a puzzling decision: Why does she go ahead with this now? Odysseus in disguise has assured her that her husband is alive and coming home soon, and the prophet Theoclymenus has said that Odysseus is already in Ithaca. Perhaps she recognizes her husband and, without speaking a word about it, they are colluding in the destruction of the suitors.

Interesting as this possibility is, Homer does not explicitly indicate that Penelope recognizes Odysseus, and much of the evidence is against it. During the nighttime conversation between Penelope and the beggar, for example, Homer teases us with the conventions of the recognition scene. Penelope expresses her wish that Odysseus would return:

> Whatever form and feature I had, what praise I'd won,
> the deathless gods destroyed the day the Achaeans
> sailed away to Troy, my husband in their ships,
> Odysseus—if *he* could return to tend my life
> the renown I had would only grow in glory (19.138–142).

The "beggar" assures her that Odysseus is on his way and provides convincing evidence that he has seen Odysseus (19.194–284). In a conventional story, this kind of exchange normally leads to a great unveiling: "And here am I, Odysseus, returned to save you" (said in an artificially deep voice). True to form, however, Odysseus further delays speaking his name, and there is no glimmer of recognition in Penelope. Instead, the scene ends with our expectations of a reunion unfulfilled. The delay is dramatically brilliant, bringing us to the peak of excitement and then easing off. But Homer's artistry takes a surprising further step. Odysseus goes from his conversation with Penelope to take a bath, and during the bath he *is* recognized—not by Penelope but by Eurycleia!

Why then does Penelope decide to choose one of the suitors? To understand this, we have to recognize that Homer's depiction of Penelope's feelings about her situation is more subtle and realistic than it might appear to be. No doubt she is longing for her husband's return. She prays for death partly because it would be better to be with Odysseus under the earth than to continue above ground without him (20.90–91).[5] Yet the dream that she tells Odysseus betrays ambivalence toward the suitors:

> I keep twenty geese in the house, from the water trough
> they come and peck their wheat—I love to watch them all.
> But down from a mountain swooped this great hook-beaked
>     eagle,
> yes, and he snapped their necks and killed them one and all,
> and they lay in heaps throughout the halls while he,
> back to the clear blue sky soared at once.
> But I wept and wailed—only a dream, of course—...
> But down he swooped again and settling on a jutting rafter
> called out in a human voice that dried my tears,
> "Courage, daughter of famous Icarius!
> This is no dream but a happy waking vision,
> real as day, that will come true for you.
> The geese were your suitors—I was once the eagle
> but now I am your husband, back again at last,
> about to launch a terrible fate against them all! (19.604–620).

Odysseus is right in his interpretation: "Destruction is clear for each and every suitor; not a soul escapes his death and doom" (19.628–629). What is intriguing is Penelope's reaction to the fate of her "geese." She loves to "watch them all," and when the eagle slaughters them, she weeps uncontrollably. In Odysseus's absence, at least the suitors provide a pleasing diversion. They may be eating Telemachus out of his inheritance, but Penelope apparently enjoys watching them eat. Just as Odysseus's suffering in exile is eased by his pleasure with Calypso and Circe, so Penelope's journey is not without its joys.

Another important passage occurs after Penelope and Odysseus have been reunited:

> She dissolved in tears, rushed to Odysseus, flung her arms
> around his neck and kissed his head and cried out,
> "Odysseus—don't flare up at me now. Not you,
> always the most understanding man alive!
> The gods, it was the gods who sent us sorrow—
> they grudged us both a life in each other's arms
> from the heady zest of youth to the stoop of old age...."

> Remember Helen of Argos, Zeus's daughter—
> would *she* have sported so in a stranger's bed
> if she had dreamed that Achaea's sons were doomed
> to fight and die to bring her home again?
> Some god spurred her to do her shameless work (23.233–250).

Penelope explicitly compares her situation to Helen's: Just as the gods spurred Helen to her adultery with Paris, so the gods have kept Penelope and Odysseus separate these many years. Implicitly, Penelope is suggesting that she has come close to becoming another Helen. Separated from her husband by the will of the gods, she nearly chose to bed down with another unscrupulous guest, another Paris. Her decision to use the contest of the axes to choose a husband was sincere: She had given up hope that Odysseus would return, and she was ready to settle for another. The final Books of the *Odyssey* do not tell the story of "two clever people working together to foil their common enemies" but the fairy tale story of "the heroic lover coming in the nick of time to rescue the bride from the dragon."

The suitors, not used to war or weaponry, are unable to string the bow, much less shoot the arrow through the axes. Odysseus, still disguised as the beggar, asks for a chance. Antinous dismisses him: "The wine has overpowered you, heady wine" (21.327). His warning that there will be "no end of trouble if you should string that bow" is truer than he can know, as is his story about the Centaur who, drunk with wine, wreaked havoc in the house of Pirithous. Trouble there will be, and Antinous will be the first to feel it. Penelope and Telemachus overrule Antinous to let Odysseus have a try. Penelope even promises him a "shirt and cloak, in handsome clothes" if he can string the bow. Should he prove himself another Odysseus, the beggar will change his rags for garments of glory.

Telemachus dismisses Penelope from the room while Odysseus examines the bow:

> then, like an expert singer skilled at lyre and song—
> who strains a string to a new peg with ease,
> making the pliant sheep-gut fast at either end—
> so with his virtuoso ease Odysseus strung his mighty bow.
> Quickly his right hand plucked the string to test its pitch
> and under his touch it sang out clear and sharp as a swallow's
> cry (21.453–458).

Odysseus has already acted as a bard when he entertained the Phaeacians with the tales of his adventures. By stringing the bow and carrying out his vengeance against the suitors, Odysseus is ensuring that his praises will be sung by poets for ages after. Homer also implies that Odysseus's skill with the bow is a kind of art. Odysseus's bow sings like the Sirens: Both leave the field piled with corpses.

The suitors are celebrating a feast to Apollo, the god of the bow, and they are destined to get their fill of Apollo on this day. Moreover, the fact that the slaughter takes place at a feast picks up on the themes of food and violated hospitality that have been so prominent throughout the poem. Suitors who slaughtered Odysseus's bulls and goats in Odysseus's house are themselves slaughtered there; the white bones of the men who bled Odysseus white will be scattered in the same hall. Homer brings out the connection of the slaughter and the feast by his description of the death of Antinous, the chief of the suitors who is Odysseus's first victim:

> Odysseus aimed and shot Antinous square in the throat
> and the point went stabbing clean through the soft neck and
>     out—
> and off to the side he pitched, the cup dropped from his grasp
> as the shaft sank home, and the man's life-blood came
>     spurting
> out his nostrils—thick red jets—a sudden thrust of his
>     foot—
> he kicked away the table—food showered across the floor,
> the bread and meats soaked in a swirl of bloody filth (22.15–21).

This description also reminds us of Agamemnon's description of his own death at the hands of Aegisthus, though here the tables are turned (!) and the returning hero slaughters those who preyed on his bride.

That arrow through the neck—that reminds us of many death scenes in the *Iliad*. Odysseus is a different man from Achilles, but once he has a clean opening, he strikes as mercilessly as Achilles ever did. When Leodes protests that he only served as prophet to the suitors, the wrath of Odysseus is unfazed: "Only a priest, a prophet for this mob, you say? How hard you must have prayed in my own house that the heady day of my return would never dawn." And with that "Odysseus hacked the prophet square across the neck and the praying head went tumbling in the dust," returning to the dust from which it came (22.337–345). Fortunately, level-headed Telemachus is there to hold his father off. Phemius clasps Odysseus's knees and asks for mercy, and Telemachus quickly says, "Stop, don't cut him down. This one's innocent. So is the herald Medon" (22.376–377).

When the slaughter is done, Odysseus scans the house to find "one and all in blood and dust ... great hauls of them down and out like fish that fishermen drag from the churning gray surf in looped and coiling nets" (22.408–410). Odysseus, who has mastered the sea, masters the surging ocean of suitors. While Agamemnon was caught in a net spun by Aegisthus, Odysseus is more like Hephaestus, who netted Ares by his *metis*. Not only are the suitors slaughtered, but the serving women allied with them are hacked with swords (22.468). This may seem unnecessarily harsh, but it makes sense both in terms of plot and theme. Even more than the suitors, who were not personal servants of Odysseus's house, these women have betrayed him and his queen. Faithfulness in women is a prominent concern in the epic. Clytemnestra, the wife of Agamemnon, was slaughtered by Orestes, her own son, and, though Penelope remains faithful to her husband, faithless women meet Clytemnestra's fate.

Odysseus is strangely slow to celebrate his catch. He

checks Eurycleia when she is about to cry out in victory: "Rejoice in your heart, old woman—peace! No cries of triumph now. It's unholy to glory over the bodies of the dead" (22.435–438). Perhaps this is a lesson Odysseus learned on the island of the Cyclops. Odysseus's unwillingness to broadcast his victory is also seen in the instructions he gives to Telemachus:

> First go and wash, and pull fresh tunics on
> and tell the maids in the hall to dress well too.
> And let the inspired bard take up his ringing lyre
> and lead off for us all a dance so full of heart
> that whoever hears the strains outside the gates—
> a passerby on the road, a neighbor round about—
> will think it's a wedding-feast that's underway (23.147–153).

Even Polyphemus had inquisitive neighbors, so Odysseus is taking no chances that the suitors' cries for help will arouse suspicion. Then, too, it is appropriate that the feast of slaughter that ended the improper feasting of the suitors should yield to a dance and a wedding celebration. For there is, in fact, a wedding underway, as Odysseus and Penelope renew their marriage.

The disguised king has revealed himself to his swineherd, to his son, to his nursemaid, but he has come home chiefly to rescue and be reunited with his bride. Book 23 winds up this loose thread with the scene between Penelope and Odysseus. At first, she, like her son, is cautious, uncertain if this beggar really is her husband:

> A long while she sat in silence ... numbing wonder
> filled her heart as her eyes explored his face.
> One moment he seemed ... Odysseus, to the life—
> the next, no, he was not the man she knew,
> a huddled mass of rags was all she saw (23.106–110).

Telemachus is impatient, but Odysseus is willing to be tested by Penelope's secret signs. Penelope tells Eurycleia to "move the sturdy bedstead out of our bridal chamber," and

Odysseus, for the first time in the story, is tricked, for he knows the bed cannot be moved. This is all the proof Penelope needs:

> the secret sign of our bed, which no one's ever seen
> but you and I and a single handmaid, Actoris,
> the servant my father gave me when I came,
> who kept the doors of our room you built so well (23.254–257).

Just as Odysseus passes the test of the bed, Penelope proves herself to him, for she reveals that, however strong the temptation to become a Helen, had any other man seen her bed, she could not have used this as a test. Through the test of the bed, Penelope has unveiled the hero; he is no longer a beggar, a nobody, but husband, king, Odysseus.

The construction of the bed is not only significant as a secret shared only by Odysseus and Penelope, but because it symbolizes the permanence of their marriage. As Odysseus describes it, "there was a branching olive-tree inside our court," which he cut and shaped "to make my bedpost" (23.214, 223). Their bed, like their marriage, is stable and enduring. Olive trees produce one of the main foods of ancient Greece and thus symbolize fertility, life, and plenty, a fitting sign of their marriage. Living in a palace built around a living olive tree, Odysseus unites nature and culture in one fertile unity. The bed thus symbolizes the work of Odysseus as king. No longer a warrior, the sacker of cities, he is revealed as a restorer of order, as a builder who shapes nature to secure the pleasure, fertility, and future of Ithaca. Branches and poles and trees have been means of Odysseus's salvation. He was saved from shipwreck by grasping one of the timbers of his raft, slept under an olive tree when he landed at Scheria, shielded himself with an olive branch when he approached Nausicaa, and tied himself to a mast to keep from going after the Sirens. These various transformations of the saving tree come to a climax in the bed test, which marks out his home-coming, his final redemption from his trials.

As Book 24 opens, we are again in the underworld, as the suitors arrive and report of Odysseus's deeds. Agamemnon is again recounting his ignoble death at the hands of Aegisthus and Clytemnestra, assuring Achilles that he had died in a more heroic way, when suddenly a group of suitors arrives. It seems they can think of nothing but Penelope's shroud. Amphimedon tells of how Penelope deceived them for three years by promising to marry when the shroud was done, but the shroud, it turns out, was not for Laertes but for them:

> She finished it off. Against her will. We forced her.
> But just as she bound off that great shroud and washed it,
> spread it out—glistening like the sunlight or the moon—
> just then some wicked spirit brought Odysseus back,
> from god knows where, to the edge of his estate,
> where the swineherd keeps his pigs. And back too,
> to the same place, came Odysseus's own dear son....
> The pair of them schemed our doom, our
> deathtrap (24.161–169).

Agamemnon recognizes the scene and rejoices in the faithfulness of Penelope. Because Odysseus had a faithful bride, he, not the suitors, set the deathtrap. Through her faithfulness, Penelope wove a doom for the suitors and ensured that Odysseus's homecoming would not, like Agamemnon's, end in tragedy.

Book 23 brings the hero back to his bride. But the hero is not only a husband but a king, and his return is not only to restore love but also order and justice. Odysseus sees the danger immediately, telling Telemachus:

> When someone kills a lone man in the realm
> who leaves behind him no great band of avengers,
> still the killer flees, goodbye to kin and country.
> But *we* brought down the best of the island's princes,
> the pillars of Ithaca. Weigh it well, I urge you (23.134–138).

Bringing down the pillars of Ithaca is a risky business, not least because the pillars have relatives. Eupithes organizes the suitors' families to attack Odysseus, but just as they are about to join battle, Athena calls a halt: "Let peace and wealth come cresting through the land" (24.537–538).

Like the *Iliad*, the *Odyssey* ends with a reprieve from conflict, but the comic ending feels much more complete in the latter epic. The *Iliad* ends with a funeral feast that we know will be followed by renewed battle. In the *Odyssey*, peace is the final word. Odysseus's return, unlike Achilles', brings resolution. In the hero's absence, the kingdom descended into chaos, while wealth was being wrongly consumed and destroyed. With the hero's return, and the intervention of the goddess, order is restored and things are put back in their proper place. With the hero's return, the disordered feast of the suitors is purged in a feast of battle, and the house becomes what it should be—the site for a continuing feast of bread, wine, and flesh.

*Review Questions*

1. Why do some scholars think Penelope recognizes Odysseus?
2. What in the story suggests that Penelope does not recognize Odysseus?
3. How does Penelope feel about the suitors?
4. Why does Penelope decide to hold a contest for a new husband? Why does she choose the contest of the bow?
5. How is Odysseus's stringing of the bow described? Why?
6. How is the slaughter of the suitors described?
7. What is Penelope's test of Odysseus's identity?
8. Explain the significance of the construction of the bed.
9. What are the suitors complaining about when they arrive in the underworld?
10. What is the final threat to the peace of Odysseus's kingdom?

*Thought Questions.*

1. How does Homer describe Odysseus's restlessness on the night before the battle? (20.27–33)

2. What is ironic about the speech of Philoetius? (20.203–251)

3. Who inspires the suitors to fresh insults? Why? (20.310–333)

4. What story opens Book 21? Why? (21.1–44)

5. What story does Antinous tell? What is significant about it? (21.318–349)

6. What is Penelope's response when told that Odysseus is home and has slaughtered the suitors? (23.63–76)

7. Penelope fears that some cunning man might pretend to be Odysseus (23.242–244). What is ironic about this?

8. How does Odysseus treat his father? Why? (24.241–364)

9. Where is Odysseus when he reveals himself to his father? Why is this significant? (24.243–244)

10. What does Laertes think of the competition between Odysseus and Telemachus? What does this tell about Laertes? (24.566–568)

*Notes:*

[1] Unless otherwise noted, I am using the translation of Robert Fagles (Penguin, 1996). Fagles's line numbering differs from that of most other translations.

[2] Several of the observations in these two paragraphs were suggested by my student, Michael Collender.

[3] Thanks to my student, Michael Harkin, for this observation.

[4] As a matter of policy, my family refrains from eating any food that is still moving around and making animal sounds.

[5] Lattimore is more explicit than Fagles here: "I could meet the Odysseus I long for, even under the hateful earth, and not have to please the mind of an inferior husband" (20.80–83).

## *Patria and Pietas:*
## Virgil, *The Aeneid*

Homer had many imitators in antiquity, but no rivals. The *Iliad* and *Odyssey* were far and away the dominant literary works of the Greek world. It must have seemed arrogant, then, when around 30 B.C. the poet Propertius wrote that "something greater than the *Iliad* is in the making." He was referring to the work of his fellow poet, Publius Vergilius Maro, the author of the epic poem we now know as the *Aeneid*. Despite his audacity, Virgil, which is the English version of his name, did show some humility before Homer, his acknowledged master; for the *Aeneid* consists of only twelve books, in comparison with the Homeric twenty-four.

    Virgil aspired to write an epic on the same scale as the Homeric poems, and even Virgil's story is itself indebted to Homer. Continuing the story of the Trojan war, the *Aeneid* traces the fortunes of Aeneas, a Trojan prince who escapes when Troy is destroyed by the Greeks. Encouraged by prophecies, Aeneas sets out to found a new Troy, though he makes a series of false starts along the way, most dramatically during an extended dalliance with Queen Dido of Carthage, in North Africa. Finally he arrives in Italy. King Latinus has been told that his daughter, Lavinia, will be given in marriage to a foreigner, and he determines that Aeneas is the fulfillment of his hopes. The decision of Latinus enrages Turnus, an Italian prince who has been one of Lavinia's suitors, and he attacks the Trojans. Aeneas eventually leads the Trojans to victory, and the epic ends with Aeneas defeating Turnus in single combat.

Virgil, moreover, organized his poem as a retelling of the Homeric epics in reverse order. The *Aeneid* is divided into two halves, whose beginnings are clearly marked by invocations of the Muse, goddess of poetry. Book 1 begins with a "proem" that refers to the Muses (1.1–19),[1] and near the beginning of Book 7, Virgil again invokes the Muse's aid:

> Be with me, Muse of all Desire, Erato,
> While I call up the kinds, the early times,
> How matters stood in the old land of Latium
> That day when the foreign soldiers beached
> Upon Ausonia's shore, and the events
> That led to the first fight. Immortal one,
> Bring all in memory to the singer's mind,
> For I must tell of wars to chill the blood,
> Ranked men in battle, kings by their own valor
> Driven to death, Etruria's cavalry,
> And all Hesperia mobilized in arms.
> A greater history opens before my eyes,
> A greater task awaits me (7.47–59).

It is as if Virgil is starting a new epic with Book 7.

And that, in a sense, is precisely what he is doing. The plot of Books 1–6 follows the *Odyssey* quite closely. Aeneas makes his entry into the action during a storm at sea, and his first words are a lament:

> Triply lucky, all you men
> To whom death came before your fathers' eyes
> Below the wall at Troy! Bravest Danaan,
> Diomedes, why could I not go down
> When you had wounded me, and lose my life
> On Ilium's battlefield? (1.134–139).

On his way from Calypso's island to the land of the Phaeacians, Odysseus also encountered a storm at sea and wished he could have died at Troy:

> Three, four times blessed, my friends-in-arms
> who died on the plains of Troy those years ago,
> serving the sons of Atreus to the end. Would to god
> I'd died there too and met my fate that day the Trojans,
> swarms of them, hurled at *me* with bronze spears,
> fighting over the corpse of proud Achilles (*Odyssey* 5.338–343).[2]

Shortly after this lament, Odysseus swam ashore and found himself among the Phaeacians, as Aeneas will be blown onto the shores of Carthage. Odysseus recounted his adventures to the Phaeacians, and Aeneas will tell the story of his journey to Queen Dido. As Odysseus lingered to take his pleasure with Calypso and Circe, so Aeneas will dally with Dido for some time, as the queen falls passionately in love with him. Like his Greek counterpart, this Roman Odysseus cannot remain where he is; he must move on to his new home.

Virgil employs these similarities in part to highlight the differences of situation. Generally, the parallels with Odysseus heighten the pathos of Aeneas. Unlike Odysseus's, Aeneas's journey is not a *nostos*, a return. Aeneas has no home to return to but instead must journey to a place he has never known. Specific allusions function in a similar way. Even the two laments quoted above have a very different tone. Aeneas regrets that he did not die in his homeland, before the eyes of his fathers, along with his comrades; Odysseus regrets that he missed "a hero's funeral...my glory spread by comrades" (5.344). Below, we shall see more fully how this reflects a difference between the Homeric and Virgillian conceptions of heroism. As another example of Virgil's use of Homer, when Aeneas arrives in Carthage, he is greeted by this scene:

> There's a spot
> Where at the mouth of a long bay an island
> Makes a harbor, forming a breakwater
> Where every swell divides as it comes in
> And runs far into curving recesses.

> There are high cliffs on this side and on that,
> And twin peaks towering heavenward impend
> On reaches of still water. Over these,
> Against a forest backdrop shimmering,
> A dark and shaggy grove casts a deep shade,
> While in the cliffside opposite, below
> The overhanging peaks, there is a cave
> With fresh water and seats in the living rock,
> The home of nymphs. Here never an anchor chain,
> Never an anchor's biting fluke need hold
> A tired ship (1.217–233).

Here is Homer's description of Odysseus's first glimpse of Ithaca:

> There on the coast a haven lies, named for Phorcys,
> the old god of the deep—with two jutting headlands,
> sheared off at the seaward side but shelving toward the bay,
> that break the great waves whipped by the gales outside
> so within the harbor ships can ride unmoored
> whenever they come in mooring range of shore.
> At the harbor's head a branching olive stands,
> with a welcome cave nearby it, dank with sea-mist,
> sacred to nymphs of the springs we call the Naiads (13.109–117).

These are similar descriptions, but the comparison only serves to emphasize the enormous differences in circumstances. When Odysseus sees this scene, he knows his *nostos* is nearing completion; for Aeneas, Carthage is not home, though he will be tempted to treat it as such.

The "greater history" that begins in Book 7 is a reworking of the *Iliad*, focusing on the war between the Latins and the Trojans and ending with the invading Trojans triumphant. As in the *Iliad*, the conflict originates as a dispute over a woman; Lavinia plays the role of a new Helen. Like the *Iliad*, *Aeneid* 7–12 employs the "absent hero" structure: With Aeneas gone from the field, Turnus is on the verge of defeating the Trojans, but Aeneas returns to battle just in time to win the day. Shortly after, Turnus kills Pallas, a young warrior under Aeneas's protection, and Aeneas battles Turnus to avenge Pallas's death, as Achilles entered the battle in reaction to the death of Patroclus. Virgil's style in the second half of the *Aeneid*, full of epic similes, *aristeiai*, and grisly descriptions of death in battle, mimics the *Iliad*. In more subtle ways, too, the second half of the *Aeneid* is Virgil's *Iliad*. As in Homer's first epic, women are almost wholly absent from Books 7–12. The only women who have prominent roles are Amata, Lavinia's mother, who goes into a frenzy when she learns that her daughter is to marry a Trojan, and Camilla, an Amazon warrior—both women, in short, who do not behave like women. This is in striking contrast to the "Odyssean" half of the *Aeneid*, which includes a very full characterization of Dido.[3]

Though the two halves of the *Aeneid* generally match Homer's epics, Virgil does not handle these parallels in a mechanical fashion. On the one hand, there are Iliadic features in Books 1–6: in Book 2, Aeneas tells Dido about the Trojan horse and the fall of Troy, and Book 5 describes the funeral games for Aeneas's father, Anchises, which parallel the games for Patroclus in Book 23 of the *Iliad*. On the other hand, the whole *Aeneid* has an Odyssean plot. Aeneas, like Odysseus, is on a journey and faces a hostile reception when he arrives at his destination, but overcomes his enemies and wins a bride. When we get to Book 7, we shall examine the Odyssean features of Virgil's *Iliad* more fully.

There are more profound transformations of Homeric epic as well, many of which reflect Virgil's historical situation. We know almost nothing about Homer or his times, but Virgil's lifetime (70–19 B.C.) covered a crucial period of "European" and world history. Before the *Aeneid*, Virgil had gained a literary reputation by writing the *Eclogues* and the *Georgics*, both poetic celebrations of the quiet life of the Italian countryside. The *Aeneid* is a very different kind of poem, and this difference reflects a profound historical shift. During most of the first century B.C., the Roman Republic was wracked by a series of civil wars. Julius Caesar triumphed over Pompey and established a kind of imperial rule, but he was assassinated in 44 and again civil war broke out. Chaotic times made a retreat to a simpler life attractive to many Romans, even if it took place only in the imagination or a poem. This century of misery was brought to a decisive end by the battle of Actium in 31 B.C., where Octavian, the adopted son of Julius Caesar, defeated Antony and took sole control of what was now an empire. Octavian was made "Augustus," and a period of comparative peace and calm followed, known as the *pax Romana*, the Roman peace.

It was during Augustus's reign that Jesus was born in Bethlehem (Luke 2:1). Virgil died before Christ's birth and probably knew little of goings-on in Palestine. But the rise of Augustus filled Virgil, and many other Romans, with hope for a peaceful and prosperous future for Rome and the world. Already in the fourth *Eclogue*, Virgil had written of the birth of a child who would "rule a world at peace" and usher in a golden age, in which, according to Virgil, "the cattle shall not fear the lion." St. Augustine, the Christian bishop of Hippo in North Africa, later said that Virgil was speaking about Christ, and throughout the Middle Ages Virgil was considered a near-Christian poet. For Christians, Virgil was for this reason a superior figure to Homer.

Wherever Virgil got this idea, and whatever he meant by it, the *Aeneid* shows that he saw Augustus as a kind of "messianic" ruler, a "saving" king. The several descriptions of Rome's future in Virgil's epic climax with the reign of Augustus. During Aeneas's visit to the Elysian Fields in Book 6, Anchises shows him the souls of the future heroes of Rome, Augustus prominent among them:

> This is the man, this one,
> Of whom so often you have heard the promise,
> Caesar Augustus, son of the deified,
> Who shall bring once again an Age of Gold
> To Latium, to the land where Saturn reigned
> In early times (6.1062–1067).

Much Greek literature looks back to a better time. For Hesiod, the Golden Age was lost in the past, never to be recovered, and Homer frequently comments on the superiority of the ancient heroes to people of his own day. Virgil, living in the first flush of the Roman peace, wants us to look ahead. In his idolatry, Virgil places Rome and its Emperor, rather than the church and her Sovereign, at the center of world history.

The *Aeneid*, then, is a patriotic epic, celebrating the greatness of Rome. It is a compliment to Virgil's patron, Augustus Caesar, and Rome's political history is alluded to in many episodes. Aeneas's troubled relation with Dido is connected with the Punic Wars between Rome and Carthage, and Aeneas's conquest of Italy and his defeat of Turnus foreshadow the eventual triumph of Augustus, who brought an end to the century of civil war. Yet, though Virgil is a patriotic Roman, he is also profoundly aware of the costs of Rome's imperial expansion. Wherever Aeneas goes, sorrow and death follow. Dido commits suicide when he leaves her, and when Aeneas arrives in Italy he has to battle Turnus. This is made all the more poignant because Dido and Turnus are, for many readers, more likeable and human characters than Aeneas himself. The poem ends on a distinctly odd note, with Aeneas thrusting his sword into the fallen Turnus. This has led some scholars to suggest that Virgil was not really celebrating Augustus at all but subtly criticizing his ruthless methods and the Roman exploitation of conquered peoples.

It is unlikely that this was Virgil's intent. One indication of his favor for Rome is found in his depiction of non-Roman peoples and ways. Modern readers are probably more attracted to Dido than Virgil's first readers would have been, who might well have associated Dido with the real-life African queen who had so recently figured in Roman history—Cleopatra, who allied with Antony in the struggle against Octavian. Like most Romans, Virgil preferred the simplicity of King Evander's hut (Book 8) to the more than oriental splendor of Dido's temple and palace. Throughout the poem,

Virgil, unlike Homer, describes the conflict of Greece and Troy as one between Europe and Asia. Though the Asiatic Trojans are the founders of Rome, they can be so only after undergoing a profound transformation.

We need to inspect the nature of this transformation further before being able to understand Virgil's political stance. The transformation from nostalgia to the Roman emphasis on the future takes place in Aeneas himself. Through the first five books, Aeneas is an Odyssean hero, weeping for home, and the tragedy is that he has no home to weep for. Book 6 is a transitional book in this respect as in so many others. The Sibyl of Cumae leads Aeneas through the underworld, and Anchises shows him the future greatness of Rome. This so fires Aeneas's imagination and zeal that when he emerges from the realm of the dead, he has truly left old Troy behind and accepted his destiny to found a new Troy. Now he can say, "Let the dead bury their dead."

This change in the outlook of Aeneas is part of a larger transformation of heroic ideal. We have already seen two styles of heroism in Homer. Achilles represents an extreme example of the heroic ideal of pursuing personal glory and reputation. Odysseus is as concerned about glory as Achilles, but his means for achieving it are very different. Odysseus is the cunning hero, who adopts disguises, tells lies, and endures suffering and insults, biding his time until he can string his bow. In certain respects, Aeneas is similar to both Achilles and Odysseus. Like Achilles, he can be a savage and merciless warrior, and like Odysseus he is a suffering hero. But Aeneas is not Greek but Trojan and on his way to becoming a Roman. Like Hector, he is more concerned with protecting his community than with personal glory. The proem of the *Odyssey* mentions that Odysseus is a prince striving to bring a whole fleet of ships back to Ithaca, but by the time he appears in the epic, all his men are dead and he returns to Ithaca utterly alone. Aeneas could not consider this a successful enterprise. His mission is to "found a city." Aeneas suffers because "so hard and huge a task it was to found the Roman people" (1.48–49). His sufferings are the labor pains of Rome's birth.

Aeneas, like Achilles, is concerned with glory, but the conception of glory is affected by the forward-looking character of the epic. In Roman legend, Aeneas was the one who bridged Troy and Rome, but the founding of the city actually took place some three hundred years after Aeneas, with Romulus and Remus, and the full glory of Rome did not emerge until Augustus. Aeneas is destined to die shortly after reaching Italy and defeating the Latins; Jupiter tells Venus in Book 1 that after subduing the "Rutulians," a native people of Italy, "he'll pass three summers of command in Latium, three years of winter quarters" before his son Ascanius takes his place (1.358–360). Thus, he is founding a city that he will never see and helping to achieve glory for people who will not live until many generations later. He is "father Aeneas," the founder of a race. Aeneas is more Abraham than Achilles.

In keeping with his different mission, Aeneas has heroic qualities different from either Homeric hero. He is neither "swift" nor "a man of twists and turns" nor *polymetis*. Instead, his outstanding heroic quality is *pietas*, the Latin word that is the source of our English word "piety." This word, however, meant something quite different for Virgil than it does for us. When we say someone is "pious," we mean he is devoted to God, but the word often carries the connotation that the pious person is unconcerned about the rough business of public life—fighting wars, administering justice, founding cities, and so on. For the Romans, and for Christians at least until the time of the Reformation, "piety" meant devotion to one's duty, whether to God or to others. A "pious" person is one who fulfills the responsibilities imposed by his position or his destiny, and these responsibilities normally have public and political dimensions.

Aeneas's famous escape from Troy provides a visual summary of his *pietas*. Carrying his father on his back, leading his son, Ascanius or Iulus, by the hand, and bearing the gods of Troy, Aeneas begins his journey to a new city. The fact that he carries the gods and the fact that they are gods of the old *city* indicate that for Aeneas and Virgil, the religious and public dimensions of *pietas* are inseparable. In the ancient world, cities—including Rome—were religious as well as political organizations. Every city had at least one patron god or goddess, and sometimes the name of the city was derived from the deity (e.g., Athens from Athena). If he is going to found a new Troy, he must bring the gods of Troy with him. To be founder of a city, Aeneas must also be a priest.

*Pietas* also requires proper respect for the fathers, and Aeneas literally bears the burden of the past as he leaves the burning city behind. His relationship to his father is a key issue especially in the first half of the *Aeneid*. Anchises represents the past, but he is also constantly urging Aeneas to embrace his future. Thus, *pius* Aeneas leaves Troy holding the hand of his son, representing his future, and this too is an aspect of *pietas*. In this respect, *pietas* is connected with the theme of *fatum*, "fate" or "destiny." Though still a religious idea in Virgil, fate has also become a political idea. Aeneas is "fated" to be the founder of a people and Rome is "fated" to be great. Aeneas is initially reluctant to pursue his destiny, and throughout the early books he looks nostalgically back to his old home. Through his experience in Carthage and in Book 6, he becomes reconciled to his destiny; only then does he really take Iulus by the hand and lead him forward.

Opposition to *fatum* is called *furor*. In a general sense, this word means "madness" or "frenzy," and it can take various forms. Passionately in love with Aeneas, Dido is full of *furor* (4.95), and Turnus, gripped by lust for slaughter, is possessed by a "madness" for war (7.629–647). They are "mad" not only because their emotions and actions are excessive, but also because they resist Aeneas's fated destiny. *Furor* turns those it possesses against fate and tempts them to neglect their responsibilities. *Furor*, in short, breeds *impietas*. If Aeneas is to remain *pius* and achieve his destiny, he must resist *furor* in all its forms, even when it resides within himself. He must master his passion for Dido, and he must subordinate his battle rage to the purposes of fate. The conflict between *pietas/fatum* and *furor* also takes place at the divine level, where Juno represents the overwhelming power of madness. She inspires Dido's love for Aeneas and sends the fury Allecto to stir Turnus into a hysteria for war. In each case, her aim is to resist the destiny that Jupiter has decreed for Aeneas.

There is yet another front in the war between *furor* and *pietas*. In Book 1, Juno gets Aeolus to stir up a storm, which is a natural symbol of *furor*. Neptune calms the storm, and in the first simile of the epic Virgil compares Neptune's action to a political act:

> When rioting breaks out in a great city,
> And the rampaging rabble goes so far
> That stones fly, and incendiary brands—
> For anger can supply that kind of weapon—
> If it so happens they look round and see
> Some dedicated public man, a veteran
> Whose record gives him weight, they quiet down
> Willing to stop and listen.
> Then he prevails in speech over their fury
> By his authority, and placates them.
> Just so, the whole uproar of the great sea
> Fell silent, as the Father of it all,
> Scanning horizons under the open sky,
> Swung his team around and gave free rein
> In flight to his eager chariot (1.201–215).

A Roman of Virgil's time would undoubtedly have recognized Augustus in that public man who subdues the riot of civil war. For Virgil, the Roman peace was not merely a political achievement but a cosmic event, depending on the conquest of *furor impius*, "unholy Furor" (1.395).

Thus, the *Aeneid* plays out the conflict of piety and madness at several interrelated levels:

| Level | Pietas/Fatum | Furor | Result of Triumph of Piety |
|---|---|---|---|
| Divine | Jupiter | Juno | Calm in heaven |
| Personal | Aeneas | Aeneas | *Pius* Aeneas |
| Story | Aeneas | Dido/Turnus | New Troy |
| Sexual | Male | Female | Harmony |
| Historical | Augustus | Civil War | Empire |

As we shall see below, Virgil develops this conflict in ways that reflect his complex evaluation of Rome's imperial achievement. Yet, from what we have said, it is clear that Virgil believes that Rome's enemies—Carthage and the Italians—challenged Rome because of their mad opposition to fate. Though these enemies have a certain nobility, they are not *pius*; if they were, they would submit to Rome without a struggle.[4]

Especially at the divine level, this conflict and its resolution form one of the structural principles of the *Aeneid*. In Book 1, Juno deliberately opposes the will of Jupiter, and she initiates another attack on Aeneas in Book 7. In Book 12, she finally submits to Jupiter's will (12.1095–1123), a happy resolution that Jupiter meets with a smile (12.1125). Furor is defeated on Olympus, and shortly after, Aeneas triumphs over the madness of Turnus. Jupiter's smile also links this scene with Book 1. While Juno is stirring up the storm at sea, Aeneas's mother, Venus, flees to Jupiter to ask him to confirm her son's destiny. Jupiter "smiled at her, the father of gods and men, with that serenity that calms the weather" (1.344–345), and he goes on to assure her that Aeneas will found an "empire without end" (1.375). The entire *Aeneid* is played out between Jupiter's two smiles. From a Christian perspective, it is important to notice that Juno, with all her passion and rage, remains at Jupiter's side at the end of the epic. Like Homer, Virgil believes that there is *furor* in heaven, and this makes his hopes for peace on earth a mere fantasy. Only a worldview in which heaven is a place of peace and harmony is capable of offering a true gospel of ever-increasing "government and peace."

Aeneas's situation also forms an important framing device. When we first see him in the midst of Juno's storm, he feels "his knees go numb and slack" (1.131–132). The Latin here is *solvuntur frigore membra*, his "members were dissolved with cold." These very words are repeated in the final lines of the poem, but there they refer not to Aeneas's fear but to the death of Turnus. As Aeneas plunges his sword into his enemy, Turnus's body, according to Fitzgerald's translation, "slackened in death's chill" (12.1296), but in Latin this is the same phrase as found in Book 1. Fearful Aeneas, wishing for death in the face of Juno's *furor*, has become triumphant Aeneas, defeating the fury of his Italian rival. Moreover, the location of Aeneas's conflict with *furor* changes over the course of the epic. Books 1–6 focus on Aeneas's conflict with his own *furor*—his passion for Dido, his despair and self-pity when things go wrong, his wish to return to Troy. If Aeneas is to achieve his destiny and face the dangers of founding the Roman people, he must become wholly *pius*. Having gained control of his own passions, Aeneas is prepared for the external conflict that dominates Books 7–12, in which Aeneas battles not his own *furor* but the madness of Turnus.

These links between Books 1 and 12 are part of a larger concentric structure (see the introduction to epic, above), one that overlays the *Odyssey–Iliad* arrangement of the epic. We have already noted that Books 1 and 7 are linked by the invocation of the Muse. Brooks Otis has pointed out that the two books are roughly arranged in reverse order. Book 1 moves from chaos to calm, while Book 7 moves from peace to war, and in both cases Juno plays a prominent role:

*Book 1:*
    Juno's anger at Aeneas
        Storm at sea
            Neptune calms sea

*Book 7:*
            Aeneas arrives peacefully in Italy
        Juno stirs up Amata and Turnus
    War between Trojans and Latins

Otis goes on to suggest a more comprehensive outline of the epic:

    A. Book 1: Juno, Storm, Calm
      B. Book 2: Defeat of Trojans
        C. Book 3: Wandering of Aeneas
          D. Book 4: Tragedy of Dido
            E. Book 5: Funeral Games
              F. Book 6: Journey to the Underworld
    A. Book 7: Peace, Juno, War
              F. Book 8: Aeneas and Evander
            E. Book 9: Night raid of Nisus and Euryalus
          D. Book 10: Death of Pallas
        C. Book 11: War with Latins
      B. Book 12: Victory of Trojans
    A. Juno's reconciliation.

Some correspondences are more obvious than others, but there are a sufficient number of striking parallels to suggest that Virgil consciously arranged his story as Otis suggests. Book 12, which describes a Trojan victory on foreign soil, reverses the Trojan defeat on their own soil recounted in Book 2. Dido's death in Book 4 matches the death of the young warrior, Pallas, in Book 10. In both Books 5 and 9, Nisus and Euryalus play prominent roles, and in both the Trojan ships are threatened by fire. Books 6 and 8 contain prophetic glimpses of the future glories of Rome, the first coming from Anchises and the second depicted on Aeneas's shield. Aeneas's relationship with Italian king Evander (Book 8) furthermore recalls his relationship with his dead father (Book 6). According to this arrangement, the key transition comes as Aeneas passes through the underworld. Even more than in the *Odyssey*, Aeneas's death and resurrection transform the hero into a new man. Further correspondences will be noted as we examine each section.

On his deathbed, Virgil asked the executors of his estate to destroy the unfinished manuscript of the *Aeneid*. Generations of school children have cursed Augustus for overturning Virgil's will and refusing his dying request. But the request itself is a puzzle. Had Virgil realized that he had not equaled Homer? Was he dissatisfied with his creation? Had he become disenchanted with Augustus, whom he had celebrated in the poem? Did his epic, perhaps, subtly criticize Augustus, something he now regretted? Whatever the reasons, the fact is that the *Aeneid*, like its hero, was rescued from the flames and founded a literary tradition that stretches from the first century B.C. through Dante and Milton and into the twentieth century.

*Review Questions.*
1. Summarize the story of the *Aeneid*.
2. Why does Virgil invoke the Muse for a second time in Book 7?
3. How do Books 1–6 follow the *Odyssey*? How do Books 7–12 follow the *Iliad*?
4. How does Virgil's *"Iliad"* overlap with his *"Odyssey,"* and vice versa?
5. How does the *Aeneid* reflect Virgil's historical situation?
6. Explain how Aeneas is different from the Homeric heroes.
7. What is *pietas*? How does Aeneas symbolize *pietas* in his escape from Troy?
8. What is *furor*? How is the conflict of *pietas* and *furor* reflected on various levels in the *Aeneid*?
9. How are the structures of Books 1 and 7 similar? How are they different?
10. Explain the concentric structure of the *Aeneid*. What role does Aeneas's journey to the underworld play?

*Thought Questions.*
1. Read an encyclopedia article about Rome during the first-century B.C., and describe the events during Virgil's lifetime.
2. Read an article about the Punic Wars and write a brief account of those conflicts.

3. John Calvin says that the sum of Christian piety involves love and fear of God, which leads to willing service to Him. Is Calvin's use of "piety" closer to Virgil's or our use of the word?

4. Read Virgil's Fourth *Eclogue*. What is the poem about? Compare the prophecies of Isaiah 11.

5. Read the first two cantos of Dante's *Inferno*. Describe the character of Virgil in that poem.

## Carthage Is Not Ithaca, Books 1–4

These books form a single coherent and carefully structured story, so much so that many readers feel that Virgil's work peaks too early. After the drama and passion of Books 1–4, everything that follows seems anticlimactic. Virgil, however, obviously believed that the episode in Carthage belonged at the beginning, rather than at the end. In part, Virgil wishes to highlight the later *pietas* of his hero by depicting his early failures and to set off his true mission from the tempting settlement in Carthage. From one angle, these books provide a small preview of the entire epic. They are arranged in a roughly chiastic pattern:

> Book 1: Aeneas arrives at Carthage; Dido introduced
> Books 2–3: Aeneas recounts his travels
> Book 4: Aeneas departs; Dido kills herself

As Books 1–4 concern Aeneas's resistance to the *furor* of Dido's love, so the entire epic will be concerned with Aeneas's triumph over all madness and his submission to destiny.

The opening paragraphs of the epic highlight Juno's role. She is still smarting from the "judgment Paris gave," which left her with an "eternal inward wound" (1.40, 54). More than that, she knows that Trojans are destined someday to overthrow the "Tyrian" (founded by Phoenicians from Tyre) city of Carthage, one of her favorite cities, and she fears that

Aeneas will be the one to overthrow it. Juno's knowledge of the future wars between Rome and Carthage (the Punic Wars) puts an extra layer of significance upon these books. The relationship of Aeneas and Dido represents the later conflicts of the two great cities of the Western Mediterranean.

We have already noted that Virgil's description of the landing at Carthage draws from Homer's description of Odysseus's landfall at Ithaca. Reading the *Aeneid* through Homeric eyes leads us to ask, Might Carthage be Aeneas's Ithaca? Might Dido be his Penelope? Virgil, however, has already told us that the hero of his tale is destined for Italy (1.3) and that he will bring the gods of Troy within the "high walls of Rome" (1.12). If this is not a home-coming, why has Virgil described it in these terms?

This same ambiguity is evident in Virgil's descriptions of the city of Carthage itself. As Aeneas enters the gates—enveloped, like Odysseus, in a mist—he admires the bustling civilization that has blossomed in North Africa under Dido's leadership:

> Aeneas found, where lately huts had been,
> Marvelous buildings, gateways, cobbled ways,
> And din of wagons. There the Tyrians
> Were hard at work: laying courses for walls,
> Rolling up stones to build the citadel,
> While others picked out building sites and plowed
> A boundary furrow. Laws were being enacted,
> Magistrates and a sacred senate chosen.
> Here men were dredging harbors, there they laid
> The deep foundation of a theatre,
> And quarried massive pillars to enhance
> The future stage (1.576–587).

Aeneas responds, with a touch of envy and sadness, "How fortunate these are whose city walls are arising here and now!" (1.595–596). He sees in Dido's achievement a picture of what he is destined to achieve but has not.

Aeneas is even more encouraged by the temple that the Carthaginians are constructing, whose walls are decorated with scenes of the Trojan wars. "Sighing" and with "cheeks grown wet with tears," Aeneas relives the battles he lately fought: Achilles and Diomedes on their rampages, the mourning women of Troy, Hector dragged around the city walls behind raging Achilles' chariot. He even sees himself in the midst of the battle. Aeneas concludes, in one of the most famous lines of the epic, that the people of Carthage know of the Trojans and their sufferings, and have sympathy for them: *sunt lacrimae rerum*—literally, "there are the tears of things," which Fitzgerald translates "they weep here for how the world goes" (1.628–629). Since the Carthaginians know the sufferings of Troy so well, Aeneas is sure they will treat him well: "This fame insures some kind of refuge" (1.630–631).

And then there is Dido, every inch a queen. When she appears she looks like Diana, surrounded by nymphs, "with her quiver slung on her shoulders, in her stride she seems the tallest, taller by a head than any" (1.680–683). It is not only Dido's physical appearance that impresses Aeneas. She is the chief of a vigorous people and an emerging civilization:

> In such delight she moved
> Amid her people, cheering on the toil
> Of a kingdom in the making. At the door
> Of the goddess' shrine, under the temple dome,
> All hedged about with guards on her high throne,
> She took her sea. Then she began to give them
> Judgments and rulings, to apportion the work
> With fairness, or assign some tasks by lot (1.685–692).

When some Trojans approach Dido asking for asylum, she is reassuring and hospitable. "Cast off your fear, you Teucrians, put anxiety aside," she tells the Trojans, adding that she will send out a party to search for Aeneas (1.762–763, 780–786). Maybe this is Ithaca after all. It seems too good to be true.

Which it is. Carthage and Dido give Aeneas a taste of what is in store for him. He too will lead a people in constructing a city and a civilization, and like Dido he will pass judgments and assign tasks. But he will not do it in Carthage. Carthage, for all is virtues, is not Ithaca, and any start Aeneas makes here is doomed to be a false start. Virgil signals this in a number of subtle ways. The temple that so impresses Aeneas, and whose walls depict the Trojan war, is dedicated to Juno (1.602, 606). This is the temple that Dido enters, and where she sits to rule her kingdom (1.687–690), so that when Dido takes her seat in Juno's temple, she becomes the living icon of the queen of the gods. Not only is Juno the arch-enemy of Troy, but she is, as we noted above, the divine personification of that *furor* that Aeneas must subdue in order to establish Rome. By associating Dido with Juno from the beginning, Virgil foreshadows the disorder that Dido will experience and cause in later books. Aeneas misinterprets the pictures on the temple walls: If they adorn the walls of a temple of Juno, they can hardly show any sympathy for the Trojans.

Virgil's introduction of Dido is also significant. Aeneas first sees her while he is looking at one of the pictures on the temple walls, a picture of Penthesilea, leading a battalion of Amazons—a tribe of women warriors—into battle against the Greeks, a "girl who dared fight men" (1.672). While he gazes at the Amazon warrior, "the queen paced toward the temple in her beauty, Dido, with a throng of men behind" (1.676–677). Like a scene from a movie where one character's face dissolves into the face of another, identifying the two characters, Penthesilea dissolves into Dido. The threat that Dido represents is heightened by Virgil's comparison of Dido and Diana, for Diana is a huntress, who appears "with her quiver slung on her shoulders" (1.681–682). Dido is an Amazon, a woman in a man's world who dares to fight not only men but the will of Jupiter.

"Diana the huntress"—that is an appropriate comparison. Before Dido is introduced, Virgil initiates a hunting motif that runs through the first four books. When Odysseus arrives at Circe's island, he goes hunting to provide food for his crew and follows with a reassuring speech (*Odyssey* 10.146–195). Similarly, Aeneas goes hunting to secure food for his men and shoots seven stags and then encourages his men to perseverance (*Aeneid* 1.247–283). A hunt seems harmless enough, even necessary, but the Homeric allusion is foreboding. After Odysseus's hunting expedition, his men encounter a powerful witch who turns them to swine and erases all desire to continue their journey (*Odyssey* 10.260). Aeneas's hunting expedition leaves us expecting he will meet another Circe who will turn him into a pig, unconcerned with his "homecoming."

As the story progresses, the hunting motif becomes more ominous. After listening to Aeneas's tale of his woes, Dido's heart is filled with longing, "a wound or inward fire eating her away" (4.2–3). Though it arises from a different passion, Dido's wound associates her with Juno, who suffers an eternal wound of Paris's judgment. More explicitly, Virgil describes Dido's passion as follows:

> Unlucky Dido, burning, in her madness
> Roamed through all the city, like a doe
> Hit by an arrow shot from far away
> By a shepherd hunting in the Cretan woods—
> Hit by surprise, nor could the hunter see
> His flying steel had fixed itself in her;
> But though she runs for life through copse and glade
> The fatal shaft clings to her side (4.95–102).

Just in case we have not gotten the point, Dido's love for Aeneas is sealed when, during a *hunt*, it begins to rain and they retreat into a cave (remember Calypso!). Landing on the shores of Africa, Aeneas kills a stag to feed his men; he does not realize that other victims will follow.

Dido's passion is a product of the unlikely alliance of Venus and Juno, but the arrows that wound her are Ascanius and the stories she hears from Aeneas. Virgil is paying homage to Homer here; a large and famous chunk of the *Odyssey* records the tales that Odysseus tells the Phaeacians. Dido's reaction is partly the result of her deep sympathy for the sufferings that Aeneas has endured. Venus has told Aeneas that Dido too is an exile, forced to leave her homeland because her brother, Pygmalion, killed her rich husband, Sychaeus, out of greed for his wealth. Pygmalion hid his crime from Dido for a long time, but finally Sychaeus appeared to her in a dream and urged her to flee to a new land, where she would build a new Tyrian civilization (1.455–506). Aeneas cannot help but recognize his own experience in Dido's, and she finds her sorrow reflected in his:

> My life
> Was one of hardship and forced wandering
> Like your own, till in this land at length
> Fortune would have me rest. Through pain I've learned
> To comfort suffering men (1.858–861).

Virgil includes the story of Troy's fall not only because of its inherent interest but also because it serves the purposes of his epic. From the time Aeneas awakes to find Troy in flames (2.360–376) through the end, Book 2 has a roughly concentric structure:

A. Hector appears to Aeneas in a dream; he tells him to leave (2.385–397)
  B. Aeneas puts on armor and tries to fight
    C. Aeneas sees Priam killed and thinks of his family (2.612–740)
A'. Aeneas begins to attack Helen; Venus intervenes to tell him to leave (2.811–812)
    C'. Aeneas goes to his father, who refuses to leave the city until an omen appears
  B'. Aeneas returns to the city to find his wife, Creusa
A". Creusa's ghost appears to tell Aeneas to leave (2.1007–1025)

Initially, Aeneas acts like a Homeric hero, going through an Iliadic and then an Odyssean phase. Like another Achilles, he rages in fury against the treachery of the Greeks. He is acting out of *furor* (2.421–426) not only in his anger but also in the fact that he refuses to bow to the destiny that Hector, Venus, and Creusa reveal to him. Then he puts on Greek armor, and, like another Odysseus, fights in disguise (2.519–530). He realizes the hopelessness of his Homeric efforts when he sees King Priam, the embodiment of Troy, fall before Achilles' son Pyrrhus. As the king goes, so goes the city, and for the first time Aeneas seriously thinks about leaving. Though forced to accept his fate, he needs another reminder from Venus before he returns to his family. Anchises at first refuses to leave, but once he sees a flame on Iulus's head, a sign that Jupiter confirms with a thunderclap (2.888–897), he submits to Jupiter's will and urges Aeneas to leave. Throughout Aeneas's journeys, Anchises will play a crucial role, acting as his son's conscience, urging him to continue his journey until his destiny is achieved.

Virgil's description of the sign on Iulus's head is the capstone of a thread of imagery that began with the tale of the Trojan horse. "A tongue of flame" appears, snake-like, "licking his fine hair, playing round his temples" (2.892–893). Earlier, another sign involving young men was given. When the Trojan priest Laocoon warns the Trojans not to accept the Greek horse and throws his spear into the horse's belly, Neptune sends twin snakes with "burning eyes, fiery and suffused with blood, their tongues a-flicker out of hissing maws," which "enveloped one of his two boys, twining about and feeding on the body" (2.288–293). Two signs are given, one involving snakes described as flames and the other involving a flame that is described as a snake. The Trojans misinterpret the first sign, believing that Laocoon is being punished for desecrating the horse, and this mistake leads to the death of Troy. Anchises, on the other hand, rightly interprets the sign of Iulus and sets off on a journey that will end with Troy's rebirth.

Virgil pushes the imagery further, however. Just as Laocoon issues his warning and launches his spear into the belly of the horse, several Trojans show up with a Greek captive, Sinon, who assures them that the Greeks really have gone for good. Sinon's name is similar to the Latin word for a snake's coils (*sinus*) and the word for the undulating motion of a snake (*insinuat*). Sinon is a snake, a deceiver, like all Greeks. When the snakes come out of the sea to capture Laocoon, fear "slithered" (*insinuat*) into the Trojans' hearts. The snakes then slither away to the temple of Minerva, which is the place where the horse is going to be taken. Snakes/deceivers are associated with the horse, which is, of course, the main deception. When the horse "delivers" its deadly children from its womb, Pyrrhus, Achilles' son, makes his way through Priam's palace and the temple of Troy

> As a serpent, hidden swollen underground
> By a cold winter, writhes into the light,
> On vile grass fed, his old skin cast away,
> Renewed and glossy, rolling slippery coils,
> With lifted underbelly rearing sunward
> And triple tongue a-flicker (2.614–619).

Troy is overthrown by treacherous Greek serpents, but a serpent-like flame promises deliverance and a new beginning.

Book 2 shows an Aeneas reluctant to leave old Troy behind, slow to embrace his future. Book 3 is little better, for the story of his journeys is a tale of repeated false starts. At each landing, the story is much the same: The Trojans land and offer sacrifice, but a plague or disaster of some sort forces them to leave, and they are given a prophecy of their future final landing. We should continually recall that Aeneas is telling these stories to Dido. Like the stories Odysseus tells the Phaeacians, Aeneas's tales are as much commentary on the present as they are a recounting of the past.

Many of these places are like old Troy, defiled and cursed by the transgression of Paris. Others, such as Buthrotum, are built on nostalgia. Buthrotum is a Trojan settlement, ruled by Helenus, son of Priam, who is now married to Andromache, widow of Hector. After the Trojan War, Andromache is initially taken by Achilles' son, Pyrrhus, but in something of a reversal of the war, Helenus receives the Trojan woman back. When Aeneas arrives, Buthrotum looks like home, even a "new Troy," but it is still too much the old one. Andromache has not been able to adjust to her exile. She offers sacrifices beside a "thin replica" of the Trojan river Simois at a tomb that is "called Hector's" where "she had blessed twin altars for her tears" (3.412). *Sunt lacrimae rerum* in Buthrotum as in Carthage, but in Buthrotum Aeneas does not see anything like the dynamic effort to found a new city that he witnesses in Carthage. Instead of building as Dido does, Helenus and Andromache have constructed a miniature replica of their old city (3.476–479). Helenus and Andromache are living in the past, and this is not Aeneas's fate. He must be transformed from a Trojan into a Roman.

After hearing Aeneas's story, Dido is inflamed with love. She first resists it, remembering her oath that she would never remarry, but her sister Anna counters by talking of the glory that would come to Carthage if Aeneas were king: "Sister, what a great city you'll see rising here, and what a kingdom, from this royal match! With Trojan soldiers as companions in arms by what exploits will Punic glory grow" (4.65–70). Dreams of glory "set [her] free of scruple" and Dido gives herself entirely to her passion. Instead of enhancing the glory of Carthage, Dido's passion diminishes it. After her encounter with Aeneas in the cave, about which Virgil is very discreet, Dido considers herself married to Aeneas, and she completely forgets her public duties:

> Towers, half-built, rose
> No farther; men no longer trained in arms
> Or toiled to make harbors and battlements
> Impregnable. Projects were broken off,
> Laid over, and the menacing huge walls
> With cranes unmoving stood against the sky (4.120–126).

Aeneas also forgets himself in his love for Dido. When Mercury sees him,

> He found Aeneas
> Laying foundations for new towers and homes.
> He noted well the swordhilt the man wore,
> Adorned with yellow jasper; and the cloak
> Aglow with Tyrian dye upon his shoulders—
> Gifts of the wealthy queen, who had inwoven
> Gold thread in the fabric (4.353–359).

Instead of new Troy, he is busy building new Tyre. Instead of the simple Roman toga, he is wearing garments of more than oriental splendor.

Just what you'd expect from a Trojan—that is what King Iarbas thinks of Aeneas's courtship of the queen. Dido has previously rebuffed Iarbas's offers of marriage, and he is enraged that she is now willing to make Aeneas "master in her realm." To Iarbas, Aeneas is just another Paris, who steals another man's wife (4.291). In Virgil's Iliad, several of Aeneas's opponents will charge him with being another Paris, but in both cases the parallel is less than exact. When Aeneas meets Dido, she is neither married nor given in marriage.

Like Dido, Aeneas is forced to choose between achieving his destiny, between *pietas*, and following his personal desire to stay with Dido. This choice is forced on him when Mercury comes to issue a sharp rebuke. What a waste: Aeneas, father of the Roman race, builds the walls of a city his descendants will later destroy. The key appeal, however, is to Aeneas's duty to his son: "think of Ascanius, think of the expectations of your heir" (4.373–374). Mercury's words inflame Aeneas but not with love for Dido; now he "burned only to be gone, to leave that land of the sweet life behind" (4.384–385). But Mercury is not the only prick to Aeneas's conscience. Anchises has appeared to him in dreams, urging him to move on (4.487–488). During the journey from Troy, Anchises has molded Aeneas's unformed *pietas*, and even in death he continues to lead the Trojan expedition.

*Pietas* toward Anchises and Ascanius demands that Aeneas leave, but it is important to see that he is genuinely torn by the decision. After Dido unleashes the fury of her frustrated love, she faints, leaving Aeneas "at a loss, alarmed, and mute with all he meant to say" (4.541–542). He knows she is sick with love, but

> Duty-bound (*pius*)
> Aeneas, though he struggled with desire
> To calm and comfort her in all her pain,
> To speak to her and turn her mind from grief,
> And though he sighed his heart out, shaken still
> With love of her, yet took the course heaven gave him
> And went back to the fleet (4.545–551).

Some scholars see that *"pius"* as sarcastic: Look at the straight-laced Aeneas, acting like a prude, leaving behind the beautiful Carthaginian queen to follow his destiny. This is not Virgil's view, however. Aeneas is acting piously here, turning his back on his own pleasure in order to do his duty.

There are several other dimensions to this decision. In suppressing his own desire to public duty, Aeneas is a model Roman and a model Stoic. Overlaying this is Virgil's opposition of East and West. The East is the land of splendor, luxury, and passion; the West is the land of simplicity, duty, and reason. Dido is given to the "charms of Carthage" because she is a "Phoenician," an Asian (4.479–480). But Aeneas insists that in Italy "is my love" (4.478). In his own person, Aeneas is acting out the cosmic battle that surrounds the epic. His passion for Dido is from Venus/Juno; it is feminine, a principle of irrationality and disorder. By choosing to follow his destiny, Aeneas is choosing to follow Jupiter's principle of order. Though romantics might wish that Aeneas and Dido could live happily ever after, the whole structure of the epic requires that he leave.

This is one episode where many commentators see subtle criticism of Rome and Augustus. Virgil shows us Aeneas going on to establish a city of future glory, but he leaves behind a city that has stopped in its tracks, ruled by a suicidal queen, and both of these consequences are at least partly Aeneas's responsibility. As we have seen above, Virgil is not a postmodern Roman liberal who sees nothing good in the Roman empire. But the story of Dido shows that he was deeply sensitive to the costs and tragic choices that empire-building demands. He admires Rome's walls, but he wants us to know that when those walls arise, they are already stained with the blood of Dido.

*Review Questions.*
1. Describe the concentric arrangement of these books.
2. How does Virgil hint that Carthage might be Aeneas's new home? How does he indicate that it is a false home?
3. How does Dido's life parallel Aeneas's? How is this connected to Aeneas's reaction to the busy work going on in Carthage?
4. What does Aeneas find on the walls of the temple? What does he think this means? What is ironic about this?
5. How does Virgil signal that Dido is a threat to Aeneas?
6. Describe the structure of Book 2. What is happening to Aeneas in this book?
7. What is the theme of Aeneas's journeys in Book 3?
8. Trace the hunting imagery through Books 1–4.
9. What happens to Dido when she is gripped by love for Aeneas? How does this reflect the themes of *pietas* and *furor*?
10. Why does Aeneas leave Dido? Does Virgil think this was a good thing to do?

*Thought Questions.*
1. Juno's anger at Paris is called a "wound" (1.54). In the light of the rest of Books 1–4, what is significant about that description?
2. Whom does Aeneas meet when he lands on the shores of Carthage? (1.411–434) How is she dressed? What is significant about her dress?
3. Aeneas sees Achilles on the walls of the temple of Juno. What is he doing? What does Virgil think of Achilles? (1.645–652)

4. Who is responsible for deceiving the Trojans? Does Virgil consider this man a hero? (2.55–70)

5. According to Sinon, what happened when the Greeks seized the Palladium, the statue of the Trojan Minerva? (2.230–267)

6. How did the Trojans get the horse into the city? Why is this ironic? (2.311–335)

7. How is the inside of the horse described? Why? (2.317, 327, 344–359)

8. Whom does Aeneas find when he tries to build an altar in the land of Mars? Why is this significant? (3.28–101)

9. Who spreads stories about Dido's "marriage" to Aeneas? What effect does this have? (4.227–296)

10. How does Aeneas defend himself when Dido accuses him of betrayal? (4.403–499)

## Return to Daylight, Books 5–6

Throughout the first four books, the *pietas* of Aeneas has been less than obvious. He has not been successful in combating the *furor* of Dido or in overcoming his own reluctance and discouragement. In response to the storm of Book 1, he despairs of his destiny, wishing nostalgically that he had died at Troy, and at Carthage he allows himself to fall under the spell of Dido's romantic *furor*. As he leaves Carthage, he "kept his eyes upon the city far astern, now bright with poor Elissa's pyre" (5.3–5). This perfectly captures the state of Aeneas's soul: He is still looking back—to Carthage, to Buthrotum, to Troy. In the Old Testament, one of the common words for repentance is "turn." In this sense, Aeneas needs to repent; he must stop looking back and begin vigorously to pursue his destiny.

Between Troy and Carthage, Anchises was able to turn his head and point him forward, but Anchises is now dead. In his current state, Aeneas is not yet ready for landfall in Italy. The gods agree; Neptune's wind forces him off course for one last stop—at Sicily, where Anchises died and was buried.

If Aeneas is going to achieve the *pietas* required to be the founder of the Roman people, his father's guidance has to be restored. Thus, in Book 5, the funeral games, an act of *pietas* toward Anchises, is part of a process that will confirm Aeneas's *pius* submission to fate. Book 6 takes this even further, as Aeneas's journey through the underworld culminates in an encounter with Anchises, which lights a fire of piety in Aeneas that does not go out through the rest of the epic. As Brooks Otis puts it, Aeneas's escape from Dido is also "the renewal of his bond with Anchises." Renewing this sacred bond from the past, Aeneas turns toward the future. Going forward begins with going back.

Brooks Otis has noted that Books 2–5 alternate between Anchises and Aeneas. After the introductory Book 1, Books 2 and 4 focus on Aeneas at Troy and Carthage, and Books 3 and 5 highlight the role of Anchises, first as the guide during Aeneas's journeys and then as the object of funeral games. Father and son finally come together in a climactic and decisive encounter in Book 6. Other structural factors are also at work. As noted above, Book 5 shows that Virgil, although following a Homeric pattern, felt free to use his sources with some freedom. Books 1–6 of the *Aeneid* draw their inspiration mainly from the *Odyssey*, but the funeral games at Sicily in Book 5, and the Trojan women's attack on the ships, come straight from the *Iliad*. Just as Achilles presided at the funeral games of his friend Patroclus, so Aeneas, implicitly another Achilles, presides at the funeral games for his father. As an Iliadic scene inserted into an Odyssean context, Book 5 anticipates the *Iliad* of Books 7–12. Just as the funeral games for Patroclus in the *Iliad* display the prowess of the warriors who have been fighting, these funeral games anticipate the exploits of the warriors who will fight when the Trojans reach Italy. The games are a "mimic battle."[5]

In some cases, the games anticipate the war in considerable detail. One episode illustrates this point and also highlights the reasons for Virgil's transformations of the Homeric stories. During the running race in *Iliad* 23,

Odysseus, who is trailing little Ajax, prays for Athena to help him win:

> and Athena heard his prayer,
> put spring in his limbs, his feet, his fighting hands
> and just as the whole field came lunging in for the trophy
> Ajax slipped at a dead run—Athena tripped him up—
> right where the dung lay slick from bellowing cattle
> the swift runner Achilles slew in Patroclus' honor.
> Dung stuffed his mouth, his nostrils dripped muck
> as shining long-enduring Odysseus flashed past him
> to come in first by far and carry off the cup
> while Ajax took the ox (*Iliad* 23.856–865).

A very similar event takes place in the Trojan footrace in the *Aeneid*. Nisus is in the lead, far ahead of the second-place Salius, who leads Nisus's close friend Euryalus by a head. As they come into the home stretch

> Nisus stumbled by bad luck, in gore—
> A slippery place where beasts had been cut down
> And blood gushed on the turf soaking the grass.
> Elated, with the race as good as won,
> He staggered there and could not hold his feet
> On the trodden ground, but pitched on it headlong
> In the mire and blood of offerings (5.418–424).

Nisus falls, but he "did not forget Euryalus, his beloved." From the ground Nisus trips Salius, allowing Euryalus "to win first place amid applause and cheers" (5.426–433). Unlike Odysseus, Nisus is not concerned only with his victory and glory, but he seeks to help his companion.

What is a comic incident in Homer thus becomes something much more serious in Virgil. Nisus and Euryalus appear again in Book 9, where, impatient with staying behind the Trojan fortifications, they venture out on a nighttime raid of the Latin camp. (Note, above, the connection between Books 5 and 9 in the concentric structure of the epic.) Again, Virgil is borrowing from the *Iliad*, for this episode reminds us of the nighttime sortie of Odysseus and Diomedes (*Iliad* 10), but he alters Homer's story and uses it for his own purposes. Like the Greek heroes, this Trojan pair slaughters the enemy at will. Euryalus cannot resist taking a helmet from one of his victims, a fateful error. As he tries to return to the Trojan base, his helmet betrays him "glimmering back, as he had not foreseen, dim rays of moonlight" (9.528–529). Nisus is well on his way to escape, but he realizes his friend is in trouble, and we know from the footrace that he will go back to help Euryalus. Odysseus and his companions have a successful night attack, while that of Nisus and Euryalus ends tragically as both are killed. Yet in Virgil's view they are "fortunate, both!" (9.633) not only because Virgil will immortalize them in verse but also because they die together, and because they die out of love for one another. It is no accident that in Book 5 Nisus slips in blood rather than dung; in Book 9, having returned to save his friend, he will again lie in a pool of blood.

Book 5 has connections not only with Book 9, but also with Book 1. At the very beginning of the epic, the human action is circumscribed by the actions of several gods: Juno stirs up a storm, Neptune intervenes to pacify the winds, Venus appeals to Jupiter, and the latter, smiling, assures her that Aeneas's fate is secure. At the end of Book 5, all of these characters reappear, in much the same roles. Juno again is stirring up a "storm" against the Trojans, Aeneas prays to Jupiter, Venus appeals on behalf of her son, and Neptune quells the effects of Juno's fury. As we have seen, Juno also creates havoc in Book 7 and is finally pacified in Book 12. Thus, from this angle, Books 1–5 are set off as a distinct section of the epic, while Book 7 begins another large section. Book 6 marks the key transition in the story. Thus, we can diagram the structure of the epic in this way:

>Book 1: Beginning of Part 1—Juno, Neptune, Venus, Jupiter
>Book 5: End of Part 1—Juno, Jupiter, Neptune, Venus
>>Book 6: Transition to Part 2
>
>Book 7: Beginning of Part 2—Juno
>Book 12: End of Part 2—Juno and Jupiter

This outline complements the concentric arrangement described above.

In Book 5, Juno's *furor* creates a frenzy among the Trojan women. She sends Iris, disguised, who rushes among the women. Her first appeal has a familiar ring: "'Miserable women that we are,' she said, 'whom no Achaean hand dragged out to death under the walls of our old fatherland'" (5.803–805). The women echo Aeneas's own complaint from Book 1, where he lamented that he had not died at Troy. In the hysteria of the Trojan women, Aeneas sees the foil of his own despair. Iris also urges the women to consider Sicily their new home: "Who prevents our building here a town for town-dwellers?" (5.815–816). Again, Aeneas must confront a desire to end the journey prematurely, which has been his constant temptation. Sicily is one more in a series of temporary stops that threatens to become permanent. As the women set fire to the ships, the threat becomes acute.

Just as important as the women's *furor* is the reaction of Aeneas. His prayer to Jupiter reflects his continuing uncertainty about the future: Either save the ships or strike me dead, he prays (5.890–899). Jupiter immediately sends a rain that douses the fire, but Aeneas is not yet satisfied. "Stunned by the mischance" he "turns this way and that," and again doubts the whole project of new Troy: "Should he forget the destiny foretold and make his home in Sicily, or try again for Italy?" (5.908–913). The prophet Nautes, however, suggests the alternative of leaving behind those who were "too weary of your great quest" under the command of Acestes. Thus the "mischance" becomes an advantage, since those who are unprepared for the looming battle in Latium are left behind. Only the strongest and most ambitious remain in this purged community of Trojans. Following Nautes's advice, Aeneas "marked with a plow the limits of the town and gave home sites by lot," while Acestes "took pleasure in his new realm, proclaiming an assembly and giving laws to the senate now convoked" (5.983–989). False home though it is, yet like Carthage, Sicily gives Aeneas a taste of the true.

Aeneas is leaving behind those who are not ready for the war; but he himself is not ready for the war. He must therefore leave himself behind. He must be turned into something other than what he is, and, fittingly, Anchises reappears to turn him. Anchises has been the focus of attention throughout Book 5, but in his visionary appearance to Aeneas, the father insists that showing proper piety to the past means moving toward the future that Anchises envisioned. Particularly important here is the way Anchises connects Aeneas's journey through the underworld to the future war in Italy:

> Embark for Italy chosen men, the bravest.
> In Latium you must battle down in war
> A hard race, hard by nurture and by training.
> First, however, visit the underworld
> The halls of Dis, and through profound Avernus
> Come to meet me, son (5.947–952).

If old Troy is to be left behind in favor of new Troy, old Aeneas must die and a new Aeneas be born.

In addition to its relation to the development of Aeneas's *pietas*, his journey through the underworld serves several purposes. Obviously, Virgil is still drawing on Homer. If Homer's Odysseus must go through the underworld to get home, then Virgil's new Odysseus must also go through hell and back. Like Homer too, Virgil wants to associate Aeneas with some of the greatest of ancient heroes, not only Hercules but Theseus. Theseus was famous for going into the labyrinth constructed by Daedalus, killing the Minotaur, and returning. When Aeneas arrives at Cumae, he finds a temple to Apollo built by the same Daedalus (6.22–30). Aeneas's entry into the underworld parallels Theseus's entry into the labyrinth.

Though Virgil is drawing on Homer, here as elsewhere he also has his own agenda and themes. A descent to the underworld is an Odyssean theme, but Book 6 also foretells the second, Iliadic, half of the *Aeneid*. The ancient prophetess of Cumae, the Sibyl, who will guide Aeneas through the underworld, first prophesies of his future:

> The Dardan race will reach Lavinian country—
> Put that anxiety away—but there
> Will wish they had not come. Wars, vicious wars
> I see ahead, and Tiber foaming blood.
> Simois, Xanthus, Dorians encamped—
> You'll have them all again, with an Achilles,
> Child of Latium, he, too, goddess-born....
> The cause of suffering here again will be
> A bride foreign to Teucrians, a marriage
> Made with a stranger (6.130–142).

Aeneas has just fled from Achilles and from Troy, but he is heading into a replay of the same war. Unlike the Trojan war, however, the Italian war will not end in destruction for the Trojans, nor in a hopeless, despairing standoff. It will be the means for establishing Rome, which will bring universal peace and justice. War leading to peace—this prophecy is definitely Roman rather than Greek.

The other great transformation of the Homeric descent is the importance that this journey has in the development of Aeneas. Far more emphatically than Odysseus, Aeneas emerges from the underworld a new man. From this point, he is no longer guided by Anchises, and he no longer doubts the prophecies of his destiny. He goes into the underworld still uncertain about and somewhat resistant to his fate; he emerges as *pius* Aeneas. He goes into the underworld still a Trojan; when he emerges, he is Roman through and through.

That this journey is Aeneas's death to old Troy and his rebirth to new Troy is suggested by his encounters in the underworld. Brooks Otis has mapped Virgil's underworld as follows:

Descent → region of unburied | River Styx | region of shades ⟨ Tartarus / Elysium

Aeneas meets three principal characters in the underworld, each associated with a particular episode in his past, who appear in reverse chronological order. First, he encounters the one most recently dead, Palinurus, the pilot who fell asleep at the helm and drowned at the end of Book 5. Unburied, Palinurus is not allowed to cross the Styx for 100 years, and though he pleads with Aeneas to sneak him across, the Sibyl insists that there is no changing the decree. After crossing the Styx, Aeneas meets Dido and is surprised to find her among the dead:

> Dido, so forlorn,
> The story then that came to me was true,
> That you were out of life, had met your end
> By your own hand. Was I, was I the cause?
> I swear by heaven's stars, by the high gods,
> By a certainty below the earth,
> I left your land against my will, my queen.
> The gods' commands drove me to do their will (6.613–621).

Dido will hear none of it: "At length she flung away from him and fled, his enemy still" (6.634–635). As in his encounter with Palinurus, Aeneas learns that the past is fixed. As Lady Macbeth said, "What's done cannot be undone." Aeneas's final encounter is with Deiphobus, the second Trojan husband of Helen, who married her after Paris died in battle. Thus, Aeneas meets one person from his journey (Palinurus), one from Carthage (Dido), and one from Troy (Deiphobus). Crucially, though his pity is aroused at each stage, Aeneas tears himself away and moves on to the Elysian fields, where he finds Anchises. Aeneas leaves the past behind, so that Anchises can show him a vision of the future.

At Lethe, the stream that causes forgetfulness, Aeneas sees "souls of a thousand nations" covering the land, and Anchises tells him they are "souls for whom a second body is in store" (6.943, 955–956). Aeneas is appalled:

> Must we imagine,
> Father, there are souls that go from here
> Aloft to upper heaven, and once more
> Return to bodies' dead weight? The poor souls,
> How can they crave our daylight so? (6.965–969).

He is still the same Aeneas that we met in Book 1, wishing he had died on the plains of Troy. But this is the key transitional scene in the epic, for Aeneas, who doubts that anyone could so crave to return to daylight, will himself emerge from Dis to lead his party on to Italy.

Anchises is the agent for the transformation of his son into the father of a nation. In the second half of the epic, Aeneas's *pietas* is no longer revealed in his personal struggles with doubt and passion but in his leadership of the Trojan project in Italy. Anchises effects this transformation by divulging the secrets of the world's origin and future, which, for Virgil, is identical to the future of Rome. Anchises' theology is what we would call "pantheism," the idea that the whole universe is divine:

> the sky and lands and sheets of water,
> The bright moon's globe, the Titan sun and stars,
> Are fed within by Spirit, and a Mind
> Infused through all the members of the world
> Makes one great living body of the mass (6.973–977).

Linked with this is an idea of reincarnation. Even the lowest creatures of the sea receive energy from a heavenly source, though this is "poisoned or clogged" by flesh and body, which imprison the spark of the spirit in darkness. At death, the distresses of life are not relieved; in the underworld, every soul is punished and purged for its sins during life. Some enter into the Elysian fields, until the stains of life have been worn away and the "soul's heaven-sent perception" has become clear, but at length the memories of "other souls" are washed clean and they are sent back into a body.

Though Anchises evidently intends this as an answer to

Aeneas's question, it is not clear that it helps. Anchises' answer to Aeneas's question—why would a soul want to return to daylight?—seems to be that the souls have no choice and they forget how painful it was the first time anyway. What follows is, it seems, a more satisfying answer. The souls that Aeneas sees are reentering bodies in order to participate in the building of the great empire of Rome, and the following lines preview Roman history. As in Jupiter's description of the Roman future in Book 1, Anchises sees Roman and world history culminating with Augustus. Readers of the *Aeneid* know from Book 1 the destiny in store for Aeneas. But Aeneas himself does not know his destiny in detail until Book 6. Once he has seen the greatness of what lies ahead, he is ready to move on to Italy. Now, he can answer his own question; he returns to the daylight to initiate the "empire without end."

Yet, there are dark corners in this preview. When Anchises sees the souls of Caesar and Pompey ("that pair"), he cries out, "Sons, refrain! You must not blind your hearts to that enormity of civil war" (6.1120–1121). Rome may achieve the greatness promised to Aeneas, but it will be at the cost of much blood. I have said that Anchises' preview of Roman history ends with Augustus, but that is not quite true. Strictly, it ends with Marcellus, who married the daughter of Augustus in 25 B.C. and was designated as his successor, but he died two years later at the age of twenty. Anchises' mourns the lost promise:

> Never will any boy of Ilian race
> Exalt his Latin forefathers with promise equal to his
> .   .   .   .   .   .   .
> Child of our mourning, if only in some way
> You could break through your bitter fate. For you
> Will be Marcellus. Let me scatter lilies,
> All I can hold, and scarlet flowers as well,
> To heap these for my grandson's shade at least,
> Frail gifts and ritual of no avail (6.1188–1202).

Typical Virgillian melancholy: After the greatness of Augustus, there is only a young man's grave strewn with lilies.

Marcellus is one example of a theme that frequently punctuates the *Aeneid*. One of the scenes that Aeneas sees depicted on Juno's temple in Carthage is the death of Troilus:

> And on another panel
> Troilus, without his armor, luckless boy,
> No match for his antagonist, Achilles,
> Appeared pulled onward by his team: he clung
> To his warcar, though fallen backward, hanging
> On to the reins still, head dragged on the ground,
> His javelin scribbling S's in the dust (1.646–658).

Marcellus, like Troilus, is a "pitiable boy," overcome by an unequal opponent. Virgil seems to take a melancholy delight in the pathos of youthful death, but these two pitiable boys also foreshadow the death of Pallas, another youth fallen in unequal battle (Book 10).

Empire imposes other costs too. Aeneas has already learned that he must renounce love for the sake of destiny, and Anchises enumerates other things that must be rejected:

> Others will cast more tenderly in bronze
> Their breathing figures, I can well believe,
> And bring more lifelike portraits out of marble;
> Argue more eloquently, use the pointer
> To trace the paths of heaven accurately
> And accurately foretell the rising stars.
> Roman, remember by your strength to rule
> Earth's peoples—for your arts are to be these:
> To pacify, to impose the rule of law.
> To spare the conquered, battle down the proud (6.1145–1154).

To achieve her destiny, Rome must leave arts and sciences to others. This is a striking statement, coming as it does from a *poet*. Yet, Rome has its arts that no one who had lived through the Civil Wars of the first century B.C. would despise. Among these is the art of war, but Roman war is very different from the heroic warfare of Homer. Roman war has peace as its goal, the peace of order and the rule of law. In the context of the epic, this sets out not only Rome's mission, but the ideal to which Aeneas must conform in the coming Italian conflict. In Virgil's *"Iliad,"* we shall see whether he lives up to it, whether he has in fact become a "new Aeneas."

*Review Questions.*
   1. Explain the alternation of "Anchises" and "Aeneas" books in the first half of the *Aeneid*. Why does Anchises play such a prominent role in Book 5?
   2. How does Virgil transform the running race from the *Iliad*? What is significant about the changes? How does this episode mimic the later warfare of Books 7–12?
   3. What is the structural significance of the appearance of Juno, Jupiter, Neptune, and Venus in Book 5?
   4. What appeal does Iris make to the Trojan women?
   5. How does Aeneas react to the burning of the ships? What does this say about him?
   6. What is Nautes's advice? How does this help the Trojans?
   7. Describe Virgil's conception of the underworld.
   8. Whom does Aeneas encounter in his journey through the realm of the dead? What is significant about these encounters?
   9. What does Anchises show Aeneas in the Elysian fields? Why? What effect does this have on Aeneas?
   10. In what ways does Virgil show the costs of Rome's "empire without end"?

*Thought Questions.*
   1. Compare and contrast the funeral games in Book 5 with those in *Iliad* 23.
   2. What happens during the boat race? What does this foreshadow at the end of Book 5? (5.218–238)

3. Aeneas is described as "fatherly" in 5.443. What is significant about that description?

4. How does Aeneas calm Salius's anger at losing the running race? (5.434–463)

5. What does Eryx do after Aeneas stops the boxing match with Dares? Why? How does this fit with other events during the games? (5.618–626)

6. What does Aeneas have to find before he can go into the world of the dead? Why? (6.205–217)

7. Aeneas must bury a dead companion before going to the underworld (218–225). Why?

8. How does Aeneas's journey to the underworld differ from Odysseus's in *Odyssey* Book 11?

9. In the *Odyssey*, Odysseus tells about his journey to the realm of the dead, but in the *Aeneid* the poet describes it. How does this make a difference in the story?

10. What happens in Tartarus? (6.717–838)

## The Fury of Hell, Books 7–9

Throughout the *Aeneid*, the thematic conflict is between the various forces allied with fate and those allied with madness or *furor*. Beginning in Book 7, as mentioned above, this conflict is carried out on a different plane. Books 1–6 trace the conflict between *pietas* and *furor* within Aeneas himself; his piety is tested by the various false homes and particularly by the love of Dido. At the end of his odyssey, however, Aeneas finally deals with his Trojan past and embraces his Roman future. From this point, the conflict is no longer within the hero but now takes on a public form in the Italian war. For this reason, Virgil considers the second half of the epic to be a "greater work." Were Virgil writing the Proverbs, the comparison of Proverbs 16:32 ("he who rules his spirit is better than he who captures a city") would apparently have been reversed.

For this public and military setting in *Aeneid* 7–12, Virgil draws on the first Homeric epic. As we saw above, the Sibyl predicted the *"Iliad"* situation of the latter part of the *Aeneid*. Beginning in Book 7, we find ourselves in the midst of another Trojan war. Since this marks the beginning of a new stage of the epic, Virgil again invokes the Muse (7.47), and again we shall see Juno stirring up a storm, this time not on the sea but among the people of Italy. Armies of men again fight over a woman, and again we see warriors killing, warriors killed, and hear the mingled cries of anguish and exultation.

Yet, Virgil continues the Odyssean themes as well. Reading Books 7–12 through the lenses of the *Odyssey*, we have the following correlations: Aeneas is a new Odysseus, Lavinia a new Penelope, and Turnus the false suitor that Aeneas must overcome. From this Odyssean perspective, moreover, Aeneas's coming to Italy is a *nostos*, a home-coming. Early in the epic, Apollo tells the Trojans to go to the "self-same land that bore you from your primal parent stock," which Anchises initially thinks is Crete (3.130–145). When they stop at the island of the Harpies, they are again told that they are going to their "fatherland," and the Harpies prophesy that once they arrive, they will "grind your tables with your teeth" (3.349). As told by the Harpies, the prophecy is sinister, but the fulfillment is more positive: As they sit for their first meal on the shores of Italy, they use bread for plates, and, once finished with everything else, they eat the bread. Ascanius finds it humorous: "Look, how we've devoured our tables even!" (7.151). Though meant playfully, it reminds Aeneas of a prophecy repeated to him by Anchises: "when the time comes that hunger on a strange coast urges you, when food has failed, to eat your very tables, then you may look for home" (7.164–167). Pious Aeneas leads the people in a feast of home-coming (7.179–197) and sends a delegation to speak to King Latinus, while he "marked his line of walls with a low trench, they toiled away to deepen it, to throw an earthwork up with palisades, camp style, around that post" (7.209–212). We have seen Aeneas sending delegations and building before, most notably in Carthage. This time, though, he builds in the promised land. Like Abraham, Aeneas comes to a land he has never seen and calls it home.

Aeneas's arrival also fulfills another prophecy. Faunus, King Latinus's father, has warned him not to give Lavinia, his daughter, to an Italian husband. Rather, "men from abroad will come and be your sons by marriage," men who will eventually rule "as far as on his rounds the Sun looks down on Ocean, East or West" (7.125–132)—a warning that Latinus has piously heeded. When Aeneas arrives, he recognizes him as a new Odysseus, the long-awaited husband (7.341–347). The prospect of marriage is important to Virgil. While he wants to show that Rome descended from Troy, he also wants to indicate that the native Latins made their contribution to Roman character. A purely Trojan people is eastern, and has to be mixed with the hardy stock of a western race before it can produce the world-dominating Romans. A marriage of Aeneas and Lavinia is a marriage not only of Trojans and Latins, but of Orient and Occident.

Aeneas is awaited for political reasons as well. During his visit to Evander in Book 8, Aeneas is told about the tyrant Mezentius, who has been oppressing the city of Agylla. When the men of the city arise against the tyrant, they are warned to stop:

> A soothsayer of great age holds them all back,
> Forewarning them:
>     "Picked men of Maeonia,
> Flower and heart of an old heroic race,
> Though justly moved by your past suffering
> Against your enemy, and though Mezentius
> Fires you with rightful anger, no Italian
> May have command of this great people's cause,
> Choose leaders from abroad" (8.672–680).

Overthrowing Mezentius is a job for a Roman called to "impose the rule of law" and "battle down the proud."

Our examination of the Odyssean elements of *Aeneid* 7–12 has led us into the Iliadic features, which are more elaborately developed. To understand Virgil's use of the *Iliad*, however, we must recognize the variety of ways in which the situation in Italy is characterized. On the one hand, Juno sees Aeneas as another Paris:

> Hecuba's not the only one who carried
> A burning brand within her and bore a son
> Whose marriage fired a city. So it is
> With Venus' chid, a Paris once again,
> A funeral torch again for Troy reborn! (7.437–441).

The situation is also similar to Aeneas's stay in Carthage, with Lavinia standing in for Dido and Turnus for Dido's rejected suitor, Iarbas. From Juno's perspective, Virgil's main characters match up with Homer's: Aeneas is a new Paris, Lavinia a new Helen, and Turnus an aggrieved Menelaus and an avenging Achilles.

We have no reason, however, to trust Juno on this point. She thinks *every* Trojan is a Paris. From the beginning of Aeneas's approaches to Latinus, it is clear that the characters do not fit into Juno's slots so snugly. Lavinia is not, after all, either married to Turnus nor engaged to him, and Aeneas is a perfect gentleman throughout his courtship. As the story progresses, it becomes clear that the characters can be matched to Homeric counterparts in a very different way. Through much of the battle of Book 9, Turnus seems another Achilles. Raging and rioting, he drives the Trojans back and beats at the makeshift wall of the Trojan camp, finally setting it on fire. When the Trojan tower falls, "all heaven thundering with its crash," we wonder if we are witnessing another siege and destruction of Troy (9.712–759). Though Turnus initially looks like a new Achilles leading his men to destroy the new Troy, he ends up looking more like Hector firing the Greek ships. Events play out quite differently than Juno imagined: Turnus is doomed Hector defending his homeland, and Aeneas is Achilles and Menelaus, destined to win the bride.

For a time, Turnus even seems to be an Odysseus, slipping unnoticed through the open gate (9.1012–1021). Unfortunately for the Latins, Turnus has not a strategic bone in his body; he may sneak through the gate, but he has no craft, no *metis* (see chapter 3 above):

> And if the thought had come to the champion
> To break the gate-bars, to admit his friends,
> That would have been the last day of the war,
> The last for the Trojans. But high rage and mindless
> Lust for slaughter drove the passionate man
> Against his enemies (9.1051–1056).

These transformations of Homer reflect Virgil's view of war and heroism. Unlike the Greek heroes, Aeneas fights only reluctantly and defensively, only when he is attacked. Once engaged in battle, he is a formidable warrior, but his goal as a Roman warrior is the imposition of law and the establishment of peace. He does not fight for his own glory but to ensure the future glories of Rome. Related to this, Virgil's *"Iliad"* relocates the theme of wrath that plays such a crucial role in Homer. In Book 8, Aeneas is, like Achilles, an absent hero, but Aeneas withdraws from the battle not because of wounded pride but in order to find reinforcements for the beleaguered Trojans, motivated not by the sulking rage of Achilles but by a typically Roman sense of public responsibility. He withdraws not in *furor* but out of *pietas*.

Wrath and rage are located not in the hero but in the war itself. For Virgil, war is a kind of madness, a public expression of irrational fury and anger. This is evident when we examine the origins of the Trojan–Latin war. As in Book 1, Juno initiates the conflict to frustrate the Trojan plans. She sees that she has been "defeated and by Aeneas," yet intends to drag out the inevitable destiny, delay it as much as she can, and cause as much grief as possible in the process. She wants to turn the proposed wedding into a "funeral torch again for Troy reborn," and promises a dowry "in blood" to Lavinia. Just as Hecuba, Paris's mother, "carried a burning brand within her and bore a son whose marriage fired a city," so

Venus's son, Aeneas, is "a Paris once again" (7.429–441). Juno hopes to use him to ignite a conflagration of new Troy.

Despairing of help from heaven, Juno looks for "help wherever help may lie" (7.424–425), and seeks out help from one of the Furies of the underworld, Allecto:

> Grief's drear mistress, with her lust for war,
> For angers, ambushes, and crippling crimes.
> Even her father Pluto hates this figure,
> Even her hellish sisters, for her myriad
> Faces, for her savage looks, her head
> Alive and black with snakes (7.445–450).

That Juno resorts to a Fury is significant on several levels. We have seen several times already that Juno is a principle of chaos, and this is further strengthened here by her association with death and the underworld. Well does the Sibyl speak of "Juno of the lower world" (6.202). This adds yet another dimension to the chart of opposites discussed at the beginning of this chapter: Juno/feminine/*furor* and Rome's enemies are all associated with the realm "below," while Jupiter/masculine/*pietas* are "heavenly." Inspired by Allecto, the Latins become a "great sea" surging against aged King Latinus (7.805–826). He vainly tries to stand against their *furor*, but, being no Neptune, he eventually "shut[s] himself away and drop[s] the reins of rule over the state" (7.825–826). Aeneas, however, has been prepared for this trial; he has already triumphed over the sea, and he has already faced the terrors of the realm below and emerged again to daylight.

The madness of war is also indicated by the triviality of its cause. At Carthage, Aeneas killed seven stags, and Virgil used this hunt as an image of his inadvertent "wounding" of Dido. Similarly, in Book 7, Iulus inadvertently provokes the *furor* of the Latins. Allecto finds Ascanius hunting and sends his dogs into a fit, so that they start chasing a stag that belongs to Tyrrhus and is treated as a pet by his daughter, Silvia. Filled with passion "for the honor of the kill" (7.682), Ascanius shoots the stag and it stumbles back to Silvia, who incites the men of the countryside to revenge. Stirred by Allecto, the Latins turn their ploughshares to swords and come out against the Trojan invaders (7.871–873). Though Ascanius's act is inadvertent, it is not accidental that he does it while impassioned for "honor." He is acting like a Homeric hero, and Virgil believes that when people act that way, the gates of war are about to burst.

*This* war particularly is sheer madness. For starters, it is sacrilegious. Not only does it violate the will of Jupiter and the determination of Fate, but it breaks a truce. Before Allecto gets busy whipping Amata into her frenzy, Latinus has already declared that he will give Lavinia to Aeneas: "Your king's the man called for by fate, so I conclude, and so I wish, if there is truth in what I presage" (7.367–370). And he has sealed this offer with a generous assortment of gifts (7.371–385). Most importantly, the war is a fit of irrational *discordia*—not merely war, but civil war. Allecto's rampage arouses discord within the royal house of Latium, setting Amata and Turnus against Latinus. Eventually, moreover, Trojans and Latins are destined to be woven into a single people, so their conflict is between future brothers. By suppressing this conflict and restoring the order of peace, Aeneas is a prototype of Augustus, who brought an end to a century of *discordia*.

From Virgil's perspective, Homeric lust for glory is a part of the madness of war. Virgil's challenge to the Homeric heroic model is also seen in his attitude toward plunder. As we noted in chapters 2 and 3, heroes increase their reputation not only by showing prowess in battle but also by collecting a hoard of booty. In the *Aeneid*, however, everyone who seeks plunder pays dearly for it. The Nisus and Euryalus episode is an example of sacrifice, but also of the dangers of plundering. Nisus is found out by the Latins because he cannot resist taking a shiny helmet. In Book 11, the Amazon Camilla fights skillfully, but she falls when her attention is arrested by a pretty bauble (11.1133–1166). These minor episodes of plundering form a context for evaluating

Turnus's error in taking the belt from the dead body of Pallas. As with Camilla, taking plunder costs Turnus his life.

The actions of Turnus also indicate Virgil's skepticism about Achillean rage. As he attacks the makeshift walls of new Troy, Turnus boasts his superiority to the Greek hero:

> Did they not see
> The walls of Troy, built up by Neptune's hand,
> Collapse in flames? Which one of you picked men
> Is ready with his blade to breach their wall
> And rush their flustered camp with me? I need
> No arms from Vulcan, nor a thousand ships,
> To take these Trojans on (9.200–205).

Like Achilles, "high rage and mindless lust for slaughter drove the passionate man against his enemies" (9.1050–1057). But his *furor* leads him into fatal errors. He lays an ambush for Aeneas but gives up waiting just before Aeneas passes (11.1222–1224), and in the definitive battle with Aeneas, he picks up the wrong sword (12.994–1003). Homeric fury is ineffective on the shores of Italy. More subtly, Virgil shows the inconclusiveness of war when fought according to pure Homeric ideals. Book 9 tells of the nighttime raid of Nisus and Euryalus and the *aristeia* of Turnus, but neither of these episodes decides the outcome of the war. Nisus and Euryalus end up dead, and, in his Achillean rage, Turnus acts foolishly. Something more than heroic prowess is needed if *discord* is to yield to peace. That something is the *pietas* of Aeneas.

Book 8 is an interlude between the outbreak of war and its continuation in Book 9, but it is a crucial interlude in several ways. First, like Book 6, it provides glimpses of the future of Rome, which come at the beginning and end of the book:

> Aeneas at the future site of Rome
>     Alliance with Evander
> The shield of Aeneas, depicting the future of Rome

Evander's kingdom is in the location where the city of Rome will be built. He is "founder unaware of Rome's great citadel" (8.413–414), and he shows Aeneas the "altar and the gate the Romans call Carmental" (8.447–448), "the wood that Romulus would make a place of refuge" (8.451–452), and finally takes him "to our Tarpeian site and Capitol, all golden now, in those days tangled, wild with underbrush" (8.459–460). Though Aeneas will never build a city here, his presence associates him with its greatness. In Virgil's *Iliad*, further, Evander is the focus of Aeneas's *pietas*, fulfilling the role vacated by the death of Anchises. When Aeneas leaves, Evander gives his son, Pallas, into his care, like another Ascanius, whom Aeneas is supposed to teach the arts of war. Past and future meet in Evander, and Aeneas's response to these demands will be a key test of his piety.

Aeneas is also being compared to a hero of the distant past, Hercules. When he first arrives at Evander's town, the people are celebrating a feast to Hercules, and Evander tells him the story of Hercules' combat with Caucus, a half-human monster that once haunted that kingdom. When the celebration is over, Evander leads Aeneas into his hut with these words:

> In victory Hercules
> Bent for this lintel, and these royal rooms
> Were grand enough for him. Friend, have the courage
> To care little for wealth, and shape yourself,
> You too, to merit godhead. Do not come
> Disdainfully into our needy home (8.480–485).

Aeneas enters through the same portal as Hercules, just as he had followed in his footsteps through the underworld. He is a "founding hero" like Hercules before him.

A second glimpse of Rome's future comes from the shield of Aeneas. While Aeneas is with Evander, Venus becomes alarmed by the course of the war with the Latins, and seductively persuades her husband Vulcan to forge heavenly armor for her son. Though Juno and Turnus both see Aeneas as a new Paris, the fact that he receives armor straight from Vulcan associates him with Achilles. This throws an ironic light on Turnus's boast that he needs no armor from Vulcan to defeat Troy. Book 8 assures us there is an Achilles in Virgil's epic, but it isn't Turnus.

According to Aeneas's father, the vocation of Rome is to beat down the proud and establish the peace of good order. Now, his mother lays on Aeneas essentially the same burden, for the shield depicts the triumphs of Roman *pietas* over violence. At the very center of Aeneas's shield is the battle of Actium, at which Augustus defeated Antony and brought peace to Rome. Augustus appears on the stern of a ship "and from his blessed brow twin flames gushed upward" (8.919–920), and elsewhere, having defeated Antony, the Emperor is shown enthroned in Rome, watching as "conquered races passed in long procession," paying homage (8.976–977). For Virgil, the wars of Rome and especially Actium were not mere political achievements but ushered in a new age of peace and justice. Nearby, Vulcan "pictured the deep hell of Tartarus" (8.902), and above the whole scene is "Actian Apollo" (8.953). As Augustus triumphs at Actium,

> Monster forms
> Of gods of every race, and the dog-god
> Anubis barking, held their weapons up
> Against our Neptune, Venus, and Minerva.
> Mars, engraved in steel, raged in the fight
> As from high air the dire Furies came
> With Discord, taking joy in a torn robe,
> And on her heels, with bloody scourge, Bellona (8.945–952).

Heaven, hell, and everything between is involved in the wars and victories of Rome.

Though there are cosmic references, Aeneas's shield is narrowly Roman. Achilles' shield, as Jasper Griffin has pointed out, contains nothing that identifies it as specifically Greek. The cities depicted there might have been Athens or Troy. But there is no mistaking that the scenes of Virgil's shield are Roman. This again highlights a difference between the two poets. Homer's sympathies are evenly divided between Greeks and Trojans; there is no hint that the Trojan War is a struggle of civilized Greece against a barbarian Troy. For Virgil, however, the universe revolves around Rome.

When Aeneas left Troy, he was burdened with the past and leading the future by the hand. As he enters the battle that will end with the establishment of new Troy, he again bears this double burden, but the emphasis has shifted significantly. He receives the shield from his mother, and with it comes the implicit requirement to honor his parents. But Aeneas is no longer literally carrying his father; he is carrying his sons and grandsons. Honor to the past is not forsaken, but his primary duty is to realize the future. Taking up the shield means "taking up upon his shoulder all the destined acts and fame of his descendants" (8.990–992).

*Review Questions.*
1. How is the conflict of *pietas* with *furor* different in Books 7–12?
2. How is Aeneas's arrival in Italy like Odysseus's homecoming?
3. How does Juno conceive of the situation in Italy? Is this the way things really are?
4. Why does Aeneas leave the Trojans? How does this show the difference between Aeneas and Achilles?
5. How does Virgil show that war itself is a kind of madness?
6. Describe some ways that Virgil challenges the Homeric heroic ideal?
7. Where does Aeneas go in Book 8? What is significant about this? How does this figure into the structure of Book 8?
8. What is depicted on Aeneas's shield?
9. Who gives Aeneas his armor? Why is this significant?
10. Whom does Evander replace from Books 1–6? How does Aeneas's relationship to Pallas relate to this?

*Thought Questions.*

1. Book 7 begins with the funeral of Aeneas's nurse, Caieta. Why? (7.1–9)
2. How is the entrance to the Tiber River described? Why? (7.36–46)
3. Latinus is a descendant of Saturn (7.60–67). Why is this significant?
4. How does Allecto "possess" Amata? (7.466–494) What is significant about the imagery used?
5. Virgil compares Amata to a top being spun by boys (7.521–530). Who is "playing" with her?
6. What does Aeneas find on his way to visit Evander? Why is this significant? (8.108–117)
7. What story about Hercules does Evander tell Aeneas? How does this fit with Aeneas's situation? (8.269–365)
8. Who helps Vulcan make Aeneas's shield? (8.590–595). In the light of Hesiod's *Theogony*, why is this significant?
9. What were Aeneas's instructions to his men when he left to visit Evander? How does Aeneas differ from the heroes of Homer's epics? (9.54–65)
10. What do Jove and his mother talk about? What is Jove's promise? How is it fulfilled? (9.108–151)

## Fury in the Service of Piety, Books 10–12

To understand Book 10 fully, we need to recall the concentric structure that we have borrowed from Brooks Otis. Book 10 corresponds to Book 4, since each records a tragic death for which Aeneas is in some way responsible: Dido in Book 4 and Pallas in Book 10. Contrasts are, however, more important than similarities. In Book 4, Aeneas is possessed by a passion directly contrary to *pietas*, and this madness puts him on a collision course with fate. In Book 10, on the contrary, he acts from pure *pietas*, particularly his sense of obligation to Evander for the care of Pallas. Importantly, his piety toward Evander leads directly to the achievement of his fate.

In both Books 4 and 10, moreover, the role of the father is crucial, though in both cases, the father figures are absent. Evander is back home, and Anchises is already dead in Book 4. As Hamlet discovered, however, fathers are never completely dead. They keep rising from the dust to haunt their sons and impose burdens upon them. Though Anchises is absent from the scene in Book 4, Aeneas's actions are still evaluated as responses to Anchises. In his dalliance with Dido, Aeneas is *impius* toward the memory of his father, who has urged him continually to move toward his destiny. By contrast, in Book 10, Aeneas shows that he is loyal to Evander, and this loyalty to Pallas's father is also loyalty to his own father. Finally, Aeneas's response to *furor* in the two books may be compared. Dido's furious love nearly turns Aeneas from his fate, and now he faces the terrible battle fury of Turnus. In the earlier book, Aeneas was as yet unprepared to journey to Italy to achieve his destiny, but in Book 10, he takes up that destiny responsibility. He proves himself to be Aeneas reborn.

Like many books of the Aeneid, Book 10 has a tripartite structure. It opens with a council of the gods, the only one in the *Aeneid*. Its presence here serves to highlight the pivotal character of the book. As in Book 1, Venus and Juno are at odds, and here their conflict erupts into the open. At the beginning of the epic, Venus, like Thetis in the *Iliad*, asks Jupiter to help her son, and Jupiter assures her that Aeneas's fate will be achieved. Book 10 has a different result: Jupiter is so disgusted with the gods that he leaves everything to fate.

The second scene of Book 10 begins with the return of Aeneas, which is the hinge of the book and of the entire second half of the epic. Up to this point, the Latins have been making headway, forcing the Trojans behind their "walls." When Aeneas returns with reinforcements, he ensures the Trojan victory, and this reshuffles all the Iliadic roles. Before Aeneas's arrival, the Trojans have been Trojans, barely able to fend off a "second Achilles." When Aeneas appears, the Trojans suddenly take the role of Greeks. Aeneas has been called a Paris and was in danger of becoming a Hector, but his return is Achillean. This comparison with Achilles is further developed after the death of Pallas. Virgil's description of Aeneas's appearance is significant in a number of ways:

> By now, as he stood high upon the stern,
> He had the Trojans and the camp in view.
> On his left arm holding the shield ablaze,
> He raised it up now. From the walls the Trojans
> Shouted to heaven. Hope reawakened wrath,
> And they hurled missiles, clamoring as when
> The cranes that home on Strymon through the clouds
> Call back and forth as they traverse the heavens,
> Leaving the South behind with cheerful cries.
> Rutulian prince and captains of Ausonia
> Marvelled first at all this, till they turned
> And saw the sterns already nearing shore,
> The whole sea moving landward with the ships.
> Aeneas' helmet blazed; flames from the crest
> Gushed upward; the gold boss of his great shield
> Show out firelight, even as when
> Blood-red, ill-omened, through transparent night
> A comet glows, or Sirius comes up,
> That burning star that brings drought and disease
> To ill mankind, and makes all heaven drear
> With baleful shining (10.361–381).

Just as Aeneas himself was inspired by his glimpse of the future glories of Rome in Book 6, so the Trojans redouble their efforts at the first sight of Aeneas's great shield. Flames from Aeneas's head recall both the burning head of Iulus in Book 2 and the depiction of Augustus at Actium, worked into the very shield that Aeneas carries (8.914–921). Like his descendent, Augustus, father Aeneas enters the war in order to pacify the fury of discord.

The crucial event in this second section of Book 10 is the death of Pallas. Pallas is the Patroclus of Virgil's *"Iliad,"* but the differences between the two situations are important to note. Patroclus and Achilles were boyhood friends, so that

Achilles' rage and anguish at his death arises from deep personal loss. Aeneas meets Pallas only in Book 8, and has known his father only that long. Aeneas's motive for avenging Pallas's death is not Achillean passion but Roman *pietas*.

Virgil carefully sets up the battle scene to highlight the piety of Aeneas, especially by way of contrast with Turnus. The scene begins with Pallas and Lausus, the son of Mezentius, making their way toward each other across the battlefield. Both are young men getting their first taste of war, and a fight between them would be an equitable affair. As they near each other, Turnus's sister urges him to intervene and Turnus seeks out Pallas, a younger opponent. Significantly, Turnus's taunt is not mainly against Pallas but against Evander: "I wish his father stood here to watch" (10.614–615), he says before the fight, and after killing Pallas, he adds:

> Arcadians, note well
> And take back to Evander what I say:
> In that state which his father merited
> I send back Pallas. And I grant in full
> What honor tombs confer, what consolation
> Comes of burial. No small price he'll pay
> for welcoming Aeneas (10.685–691).

It is a mismatch between a powerful and experienced warrior and a young opponent. We have seen this scene before: Troilus, killed by Achilles while unarmed, and Marcellus are both "pitiable boys." In this sense at least, Turnus is a second Achilles.

As soon as Aeneas sees Pallas fall, he begins to pursue Turnus. Given Turnus's taunt, Aeneas is defending Evander's honor as much as he is seeking revenge for Pallas. At this point, Juno intervenes to take Turnus away from the battle. But Mezentius stumbles across Aeneas's way, a substitute for Turnus. Aeneas's fight with Mezentius fulfills the prophecy that Evander mentioned in Book 8 and also foreshadows the later battle with Turnus. The details of this battle are also significant. Aeneas hits Mezentius with a spear (292–293), and as he falls, Mezentius's son, Lausus, steps in to defend him. Aeneas find himself in a situation similar to that of Turnus: Turnus intervenes between Lausus and Pallas to fight Pallas; Lausus intervenes between Aeneas and Mezentius to fight Aeneas. In another sense, Aeneas is in precisely the opposite situation to Turnus: Instead of seeking out a lesser opponent, Aeneas is forced to face a young man who has sought him out.

Aeneas's response to this situation also contrasts with that of Turnus. Far from mocking the father, Aeneas warns Lausus to step aside: "Why this rush deathward, daring beyond your power?" (10.1136). Lausus will not back away, and in anger Aeneas "drove his sword through the young man's body up to the hilt" (10.1142). Virgil calls Aeneas "Anchises' son" (10.1150), for he sees in Lausus's loyalty to his father an image of his own piety. As he says to Lausus, "filial piety makes you lose your head" (10.1137). When pious Lausus lies dead, Aeneas laments:

> O poor young soldier,
> How will Aeneas reward your splendid fight?
> How honor you, in keeping with your nature?
> Keep the arms you loved to use, for I
> Return you to your forbears, ash and shades,
> If this concerns you now. Unlucky boy,
> One consolation for sad death is this:
> You die by the sword-thrust of great Aeneas (10.1154–1161).

No Turnus-like arrogance here. Even in the midst of battle, Aeneas retains his humanity. His moral superiority to Turnus has been so strongly asserted here that we have no doubt about the outcome of their eventual duel.

Clear-cut as the moral issue might seem at this point, Aeneas's reaction to Pallas's death raises questions. Throughout the epic, we have been tracing the facets of the *furor-pietas* opposition. After his journey to the underworld in

Book 6, we have seen a new Aeneas, resisting disorder in all its forms, submissive to the fates, loyal to his father and his people. Or so we have said. After Pallas dies, however, we see another Aeneas on the battlefield. When he hears the news, Aeneas "took four sons of Sulmo, four more Ufens reared, took them alive to offer to the shades in sacrifice" (10.727–730). From this sacrifice, he moves to the sacrificial arena of the battlefield. He refuses Magus's pleas for mercy and chases down the priest Haemonides until he can offer him "in sacrifice" (10.762). Imagery of fire, normally attached to Turnus, is used to describe Aeneas's rampage across the field (10.773). Virgil compares him to the hundred-handed titan mentioned in Hesiod's *Theogony*:

> As men say
> The titan Aegaeon had a hundred arms,
> A hundred hands, and sent out burning breath
> From fifty mouths and breasts when he opposed
> Jove's thunderbolt, clanging his fifty shields
> And drawing fifty swords, just so Aeneas
> Multiplied savagery over the whole field
> Once his sword-point warmed (10.794–801).

Aeneas turns monstrous as he ravages his enemies.

Aeneas's *furor* is equally intense in the climactic Book 12. Arrangements have been made for Turnus and Aeneas to end the war with a duel, but this pact is broken, and Turnus ignites his old battle frenzy. At first, Aeneas urges his men to keep the truce, but his patience finally wears thin:

> He called on Jove and called
> On altars of the broken peace to witness,
> Many times, then into the melee
> He raced, most terrible to see, with Mars
> Behind him, rousing blind and savage slaughter,
> All restraints on wrath cast to the winds (12.674–681).

His rage comes to a climax in the closing battle with Turnus. Aeneas gains the upper hand, and when Turnus goes down,

Aeneas is moved by his call for mercy, until "to his glance appeared the accurst swordbelt surmounting Turnus's shoulder, shining with its familiar studs—the strap young Pallas wore when Turnus wounded him" (12.1279–1284). All bets are off:

> For when the sight came home to him,
> Aeneas raged at the relic of his anguish
> Worn by this man as trophy. Blazing up
> And terrible in his anger, he called out:
> "You in your plunder, torn from one of mine,
> Shall I be robbed of you? This wound will come
> From Pallas: Pallas makes this offering
> And from your criminal blood exacts his due."
> He sank his blade in fury in Turnus' chest.
> Then all the body slackened in death's chill,
> And with a groan for that indignity
> His spirit fled into the gloom below (12.1287–1298).

*Furor* language is quite deliberately piled up here, as Aeneas drives his sword into a wounded and defeated foe, who pleads for clemency. The director shouts, "Cut!" The curtain falls.

What is going on here? Does Aeneas, in the end, succumb to the *furor* he has been combatting throughout the epic? Is Virgil calling into question Augustus's *imperium sine fine*, his "empire without end"? Is he suggesting that the empire is just another form of madness, motivated just as much by *furor* as the civil wars that preceded it? Some have suggested as much, but this is not Virgil's viewpoint. He has consistently associated Augustus's enemies with *furor*, indicating that in his mind, they, like Dido and Turnus, were simply resisting the inevitable. Dido and Turnus may be sympathetic characters, but their great flaw is impiety, their refusal to submit to fate.

The key to understanding the transformation of Aeneas in Books 10–12 is to see that Aeneas's actions are all motivated by *pietas*. This is true in two ways. First, he knew from

Anchises that the vocation of Rome is to beat down the proud, and Turnus had spoken and acted with arrogance (10.617). Submission to Roman destiny required Aeneas to rid the world of Turnuses. Second, Aeneas had taken charge of Pallas, and protecting him was part of his responsibility to Evander. Aeneas failed in his efforts to protect Evander's son, but piety toward this new Anchises demanded that he avenge Pallas's death. From this perspective, it is clear that the opposition of piety and *furor* is not an absolute one. There is a *furor*, a battle madness, that is an expression of piety rather than a rebellion against it. This is evident at the divine level too: Juno, the divine representative of *furor* becomes submissive to Jupiter's plan, but she is not cast from Olympus. She retains the same passionate inclinations she has always had; she simply submits, reluctantly, to necessity. Aeneas, humane and gentle as he can be, is, after all, a Roman, and his project is the establishment of a military empire. That omelet he cannot make without breaking some eggs.

According to St. Augustine's account in his *City of God*, Rome rose to dominance out of a lust for dominion, their sinful desire for supremacy. This, he contended, was also the cause of the discord of civil war, as each contender sought dominance over the others. And, this, Augustine believed, was the same principle at work in the expansion of the Roman empire. In spreading its empire throughout the Mediterranean, Rome simply carried its civil war to the four corners of the earth. In Augustine's view, Aeneas and Augustus, far from putting down the proud, were themselves among the proud; far from triumphing over madness, they were themselves mad. Virgil saw the dangers and excesses of *furor* but in the end accepted it as a necessary part of establishing empire. Augustine, with the whole church, proclaimed a true *imperium sine fine*, established not by the blood of war but by the blood of a cross, not by *furor* but by obedience to death.

*Review Questions.*
1. Explain the similarities and contrasts between Books 4 and 10.
2. How is Evander another Anchises?
3. How does Virgil describe Aeneas's return to battle? Who is Aeneas being compared to?
4. In what ways does Aeneas's battle with Lausus differ from Turnus's battle with Pallas?
5. What is Aeneas like after Pallas dies?
6. How is Aeneas's battle fury related to his *pietas*?
7. According to St. Augustine, what was the dominant motive of the Roman empire? How was the empire related to the civil strife that preceded it?

*Thought Questions.*
1. Who tells Aeneas about the battle? (10.297–338)
2. To what does Virgil compare Pallas's role in the battle? What does this epic simile mean? How does it fit with larger themes of the epic? (10.555–564)
3. What does Aeneas say as he kills Lucagus's brother? (10.833–849). What does this tell us about Aeneas?
4. What does Juno do to Turnus during the battle? Why? What effect does this have? (10.881–966)
5. What does Evander want in exchange for the death of Pallas? How does this fit with the larger issues of the epic? (11.245–250)
6. Who is Diomedes? What is his response to the Latin request for help? What does this suggest about the battle for Italy? (11.305–400)
7. What does Draces say to Turnus? (11.454–510)
8. How does Camilla fit with other characters and events of the epic? (11.721–1179)
9. Describe the procedure for oath-taking in 12.265–297. Why would oaths be taken in this way?
10. How is Aeneas healed of his wound? How are his wound and healing parallel to other incidents of the epic? (12. 562–587)

*Notes:*

[1] Line numbers follow the translation of Robert Fitzgerald (New York: Everyman's Library, 1992).
[2] This is from Robert Fagles's translation (Penguin 1996).
[3] This point was suggested by my student, Courtney Huntington.
[4] Thanks to my student, Michael Collender, for this insight.
[5] This is the translation of Rolfe Humphries (New York: Charles Scribner's Sons, 1951), p. 132. The Latin is *pugnae simulacra*.

# Section II:

# Greek Drama

## Introduction: Greek Drama

Due to the fragmentary nature of the evidence that has survived to our day, there is much that we do not know about Greek drama. Of the thousands of tragic productions produced in Athens and other cities beginning in the fifth century B.C., thirty-some, a comparative handful, have survived as whole plays, and only fragments of others remain. Any conclusions about characteristic themes and plots of Greek drama, then, are based on meager evidence. Similarly, though modern scholars can use archeological and textual evidence to determine some general features of how plays were performed, many specifics cannot be known. P. E. Easterling lists some of the unanswered questions: "What the earliest theatres, masks and costumes looked like, how the music sounded, what sort of performance-styles and dramatic conventions developed, how far the surviving [plays] are typical of the hundreds, or thousands, that must have been composed during the period, and what tragedy meant for the contemporary Athenian—and non-Athenian—audiences."

A few facts are, however, well-established. Plays were first produced in Athens around 500 B.C. at annual religious festivals, particularly the Great Dionysia, a spring feast in honor of Dionysus, the god of wine. The Dionysia was the occasion for a theatrical competition. Initially, each writer produced a trilogy, frequently drawn from mythology, to which was added a fourth, shorter drama called a "satyr play." Originally, Greek tragedies were static—we might say "boring"—productions involving a single masked actor, often the poet, and a masked chorus of as many as fifty boys or men that both sang and danced in praise of Dionysus. "Tragedy," according to some accounts, is derived from the Greek *tragoidia*, "goat-song," since the goat was sacred to Dionysus. Over time, additional actors were introduced, though the chorus continued to play a prominent role, typically singing and dancing after every scene. When it entered into dialogue with the leading characters, the chorus frequently spoke for the traditions and customs of the city against characters in danger of transgressing them.

Despite variations, theaters had certain basic features in common. The Theater of Dionysus at Athens was part of the area of the Acropolis (the "high city," which was the religious center) known as the Dionysian precinct, and it included a temple as well as a theater. The theater was an outdoor amphitheater built onto a hillside, so that the audience was seated in a semicircle around the dramatic area. Directly in front of the audience, at ground level, was a circular zone known as the "orchestra." On either side of the orchestra was a ramp, called a *parados*, by which actors entered and exited. Early dramas were staged in the orchestra, but around 460 B.C., a *skene* was introduced on the opposite side of the orchestra from the audience. The *skene*, from which we derive our word "scene," was the facade of a building with doors and could be made up to look like the front of a house, temple, or palace. Actors entered and exited through the doors, and gradually the center of dramatic action shifted to what is known as the "proscenio," the area immediately in front of the *skene*. This was a crucial development in drama, since, as Simon Goldhill points out, the arrangement "places a focus on the boundary of the door, the hidden secrets of the inside of the house, and the public space of the stage."

Each of the main playwrights studied here are known for particular contributions to drama and stage craft. Aeschylus's birth date is disputed, with guesses ranging from 525 to 512 B.C. He died in 456 B.C., credited with between seventy and ninety plays and with more than a dozen first prizes. Though often called the "creator of tragedy," Aeschylus was not the first to write or produce tragic plays. Aeschylus's innovations in staging techniques and his poetic gifts, however, made him the first of the great Greek playwrights. According to Aristotle's account, his main contribution was the introduction of a "second actor." A slight innovation perhaps, but H. D. F. Kitto explains the striking effect it has on drama:

> The second actor makes it possible, dramatically, to set the hero in a position which not only seems, but also is, innocent. Now the situation can change; messengers bring news or heralds make proclamations, and what was safe becomes perilous.... The tragic implications of the second actor are even more important than the dramatic ones. Since the situation moves, the hero must be of a certain kind; he must—if we are to have tragedy—be of such a moral constitution as to oppose himself to this movement, not to conform to it.... In other words, the moving plot was designed to display and test moral character, to give room for moral choice and for its results.

The *Eumenides*, examined in chapter 5, was the third play in the trilogy known as the *Oresteia* that Aeschylus produced in 458.

Sophocles, who lived from 496–406 B.C., is credited with adding a "third actor," which further enhanced dramatic possibilities and transformed the role of the chorus. Kitto suggests that Sophocles' main intention in adding the third actor was to "illuminate the chief character from several points of view," and this gives his characters a Shakespearean richness and complexity. Kitto further suggests that Sophocles was able to add an actor without eliminating the chorus because he always made the chorus a participant in the drama, rather than a mere observer. Seven complete Sophoclean tragedies remain, but there are fragments of between eighty and ninety others. Sophocles won a first prize in competition with Aeschylus in 468, and overall he wrote some twenty first-prize plays. Unlike the *Oresteia*, Sophocles' three plays on Oedipus were written over a long period of time. *Antigone* was produced around 441, *Oedipus Tyrannus* around 428, and *Oedipus at Colonus* was not staged until 405, a year after the author's death. Chapter 6 examines the second of these.

The last of the great Greek tragedians was Euripides, who was born around 484 B.C. and died in 407/6 B.C. in Macedonia, apparently self-exiled. Of his ninety-some plays, only five won first prizes, the first in 455 and the last after his death. Euripides was attacked during his lifetime for his innovations in tragic drama. Aristophanes, a comic playwright, criticized him for putting beggars on stage, for his hatred and fear of women, for making tragedy less lofty and morally uplifting, for subverting received morality, and for promoting unorthodox religious views. Though he is considered a transitional figure and a practitioner of "New Tragedy," it is a mistake to exaggerate the differences between Euripides and his predecessors. In many ways, he was affirming the same worldview as Aeschylus and Sophocles. *The Bacchae*, treated in chapter 7, was one of his last plays and won first prize when presented by his son after his death.

Since Aristotle wrote his analysis of Sophocles' *Oedipus Tyrannus* in his *Poetics*, certain themes have been considered typical of Greek tragedy. Though many plays do not conform to the Aristotelian pattern, familiarity with some of his concepts is important for understanding the development of drama. Tragedy, in Aristotle's view, is defined by having a certain kind of plot; in biblical terms, a tragedy is a "fall story" about a character who falls from some high position because of a *hamartia*. The concept of *hamartia* is crucial. Though translated as "sin" in the New Testament, in Aristotle the word does not have the same moral force that it does for Paul. Instead, a *hamartia* can be a tragic error, a mistake of judgment that leads to terrible and often terrifying consequences.

Sometimes the *hamartia* is a moral wrong, and many Greek plays focus on the specific evil of *hubris*, often translated as "pride." A character is guilty of *hubris* when he seeks to go beyond the limits of human knowledge and action. Human beings can rise only so far, and then the gods beat them back. Because the Greek gods are finite, their relation with human beings is a "zero-sum game"; if humans gain, then it must be at the expense of the gods. Though Christians often think and speak this way about their relationship with God, the Greek view is in fact almost the precise opposite of the Christian position. True religion, according to Scripture, requires submission to a Person who is infinitely greater in every respect than we. Yet God's existence, knowledge, and achievements are not *limits* or *barriers* to my existence, knowledge, and achievements. On the contrary, I exist only because God continually keeps me in existence; I know only because He has revealed the truth; I achieve only because He is ever at work in me. For the Bible, the infinite power of God is not a "limit" on human strength; God and His work are the necessary ground and assumption of everything we are and do. As we examine Greek tragedy, we will find that the difference between the Christian and Greek view of God has profound cultural and political implications.

Aristophanes is the one comic playwright examined below. The development of Greek comedy is frequently arranged in three phases. Old Comedy, which arose in Athens during the fifth century, was bawdy and obscene, gave a prominent role to the chorus, and commented on current political or cultural events. Plays of Middle Comedy, written between 400 and 320 B.C., were like Old Comedies in many ways but placed less emphasis on the chorus. After about 320 B.C., "New Comedy" developed, an apolitical dramatic form that eliminated the chorus altogether and took romance as its central theme. New Comedy produced plays similar to the comedies of Shakespeare; Old Comedy is closer to *Saturday Night Live*.

Considered the leading poet of Old Comedy,

Aristophanes lived from 447/6 B.C. to sometime between 386 and 380 B.C. Forty-four comedies were ascribed to him by ancient writers, of which eleven are available today. Aristophanes won a half dozen first and four second place prizes. Like other comic playwrights of his period, Aristophanes wrote political satires, at least one of which was sharp enough to provoke Cleon, the object of satire in *Babylonians*, to denounce the playwright to the Athenian council. Far from being cowed into silence, Aristophanes wrote another play, *Knights*, whose attack on Cleon was even more pointed. *Clouds*, first produced in 423 B.C., makes another prominent contemporary, the philosopher Socrates, the object of mockery. It is discussed in chapter 8.

Political circumstances in Athens are important background to tragedy as much as to Old Comedy. Paul Cartledge points out that most of our surviving tragedies were composed during the Peloponnesian War that pitted Athens against Sparta, and the plays reflect the social strains that the war produced. More generally, the plays discussed below are preoccupied with the dilemmas and dangers that faced the *polis* or city-state that was the characteristic political form of the classical period of Greek history. Written against the background of Homeric heroism, tragedy raises questions about how human beings, with all their ambitions and love of preeminence, can live together in a cohesive community. Tragedians and comic writers explore other threats to the city-state—family loyalties (the *Oresteia* of Aeschylus), disruptive religious passion (*The Bacchae* of Euripides), and skeptical philosophy (the *Clouds* of Aristophanes). Though these writers do not arrive at a Christian view of society, they effectively expose some of the flaws and dilemmas of the Greek city-state, and therefore help Christians refine our own thinking on these matters.

## Blessings of Terror:
## Aeschylus, *The Eumenides*

*The Eumenides* is the final play in the *Oresteian* trilogy and is named for Orestes, the leading character of the final two plays. In the first play, *Agamemnon*, Aeschylus dramatizes the *nostos* or "return story" of Agamemnon, focusing on his murder at the hands of his wife, Clytemnestra, a story already familiar to us from the *Odyssey* (see chapter 3). In *The Libation Bearers* (or *Choephori*) and *The Eumenides* he traces the effects of that initial murder on subsequent generations. Chronologically, Aeschylus's trilogy takes us from the end of the Trojan war to the establishment of the court of the Areopagus in Athens. Like Shakespeare's *Hamlet*, the plot of the *Oresteia* focuses on the practice of blood vengeance, the notion that murder has to be avenged by a near relative. Aeschylus explores where this custom leads and points to a way of ending it.

Though the trilogy moves from the heroic generation of Agamemnon to his son Orestes, the story actually begins a generation earlier, with a conflict between King Atreus and his brother, Thyestes. Thyestes seduces Atreus's wife, and in response, Atreus banishes his brother. Some time later, Atreus allows his brother to return and invites him to dinner, where he cuts up Thyestes' children and stirs them into his brother's stew. Before he realizes it, Thyestes has, like Kronos, eaten his own children. This violation brings a curse on the house of Atreus, and at one level, *Agamemnon* is about the revenge that Thyestes' son, Aegisthus, takes on Agamemnon, the son of Atreus, fulfilling the family curse and bringing the house of Atreus to the brink of extinction.

Another line of vengeance also finds its target in Agamemnon. When Agamemnon is preparing to go to Troy, unfavorable winds force his ships to remain at Aulis. Informed by a seer that the gods demand the sacrifice of a virgin girl, he offers his own daughter, Iphigeneia, on the altar. Winds change, and Agamemnon leads his men to Troy and to victory. Back home, however, his wife, Clytemnestra, mourns the senseless death of her daughter, and, with Aegisthus, plots revenge. Shortly after Agamemnon's return, while he is completing his rites of cleansing, they attack him, wind him tight with a robe, and kill him. Cassandra, a Trojan prophetess whom Agamemnon took as a war-bride, is also murdered. Before he ever left Argos for Troy, Agamemnon was caught in a trap, forced on him by the demands of vengeance: He is obligated to avenge the wrong that Paris had committed in seducing and taking Helen from his brother, Menelaus, yet to do that he kills his daughter, which makes him an object of vengeance.

Behind these human avengers are the gods. Early in *Agamemnon*, the chorus sees an omen: Two eagles swoop down on a pregnant hare and tear it to pieces. A seer interprets it as a prophecy of the Trojan war:

> But the loyal seer of the armies studied Atreus' sons,
> two sons with warring hearts—he saw two eagle-kings
> devour the hare and spoke the things to come,
> "Years pass, and the long hunt nets the city of Priam,
>     the flocks behind the walls,
> a kingdom's life and soul—Fate stamps them out.
> Only let no curse of the gods lower on us first,
>     shatter our giant armor
>         forged to strangle Troy. I see
>             pure Artemis bristle in pity—
>                 yes, the flying hounds of the Father
>     slaughter for armies ... their own victim ... a mother

### Blessings of Terror: *The Eumenides*

trembling young, all born to die—She loathes the eagles' feast!" (126–138).[1]

Though Agamemnon and Menelaus conquer, the seer reports, they do it without mercy, slaughtering not only the hare but its innocent and helpless young. As a result, the gods will have pity on the victims, and pity includes vengeance on oppressors. When the herald cheerfully boasts that Agamemnon has "dug Troy down, he worked her soil down, the shrines of her gods and the high altars, gone!—and the seed of her wide earth he ground to bits" (516–519), he is announcing the very acts that seal Agamemnon's doom.

This indicates that there is another epicycle on the cycle of vengeance, coming from the Trojan war. From one angle, the *Oresteia* traces the effects of the Trojan war on postwar Greece. In keeping with this emphasis, *Agamemnon* refers frequently to the sin of Paris, at times employing bird imagery connected with the omen quoted above. Menelaus and Agamemnon set out from Greece "like vultures robbed of their young" (54), crying as they soar from their nest until "someone hears on high—Apollo, Pan or Zeus . . . and drives at the outlaws, late but true to revenge, a stabbing Fury" (61–65). Thus, "towering Zeus the god of guests drives Atreus' sons at Paris" (66–67). Paris robbed the nest of Menelaus, and now he and his city are torn by the two vultures. Because Agamemnon and Menelaus act savagely, however, they too will suffer an appropriate punishment. Again, the ethic of blood vengeance traps Agamemnon; he becomes an object of the wrath of the gods in the very act of carrying out their wrath against Troy. Our expectation that they will be punished is reinforced by the storm that sinks all the Greek ships, save Agamemnon's (647–648). Since this storm arises, as the Herald says, from the anger of the gods against the Greeks, we are left wondering why Agamemnon has been spared: Greeks sin and are punished; Agamemnon sins but arrives safely home. We can expect the other foot to fall.

Sins of Atreus, the sacrifice of Iphigeneia, the Greeks'

merciless treatment of the Trojans—all these fall upon the head of Agamemnon. Yet, the cycle of vengeance cannot stop there. Hunting down her prey to the kill, Clytemnestra becomes, as all blood avengers do, someone else's prey. Thus, in *The Libation Bearers*, at the urging of Apollo, Orestes, the son of Agamemnon and Clytemnestra, kills his mother and Aegisthus in the same house in which Agamemnon was murdered. Clytemnestra netted Agamemnon on his return, but she is equally entangled in the workings of revenge. Having killed his mother, Orestes, of course, turns from hunter to prey. This brings us to *The Eumenides*, where Aeschylus brings this multi-generational family feud to an end.

Before we examine how Aeschylus ties things up, we should examine the biblical institution of the "blood avenger" (Hebrew, *go'el*), which seems quite similar to the Greek practice. Numbers 35:16–21 states that a "near relative" has the duty to kill someone who has killed his relative: "the blood avenger shall put the murderer to death when he meets him" (verse 21). Verses 22–28 emphasize that the blood avenger has this duty whether the killing was intentional (murder) or unintentional (manslaughter). The actions of Clytemnestra and Orestes seem perfectly legitimate by biblical standards.

Two features of the biblical system, however, show that the Bible establishes something different from the blood feud. First, the law not only gives the *go'el* the right to pursue a murderer, but it also emphasizes the need for a trial and provides a safe haven for those guilty of manslaughter:

> When you cross the Jordan into the land of Canaan, then you shall select for yourselves cities to be your cities of refuge, that the manslayer who has killed any person unintentionally may flee there. And the cities shall be to you as a refuge from the avenger, so that the manslayer may not die until he stands before the congregation for trial (Num. 35:10–12).

What the Bible envisions is this: Shema kills Raham accidentally. Shema then flees to a city of refuge, with Raham's brother, Rekem, hot on his trail. At the gate of the city, Shema is tried, found guilty of manslaughter rather than murder, and permitted to move into the city of refuge. If Shema leaves the city prior to the death of the high priest, Rekem can pursue and kill him (Numbers 35:26–27), but so long as he stays within the walls, he is perfectly safe. Rekem's first duty is to ensure that Shema stands trial, *not* to ensure that Shema is killed. If the rulers of the city find Shema innocent of murder, Rekem has to live with their verdict. In the Bible, the "blood avenger" is not a vigilante outside the law but part of the legal system. Second, if the blood feud rules, the cycle of violence continues indefinitely. If Rekem kills Shema, then Shema's brother would kill Rekem, then a near relative of Rekem would pursue Shema's brother, and so on. This the Bible does not permit. Blood avengers execute murderers, but they do not become objects of revenge. Justice demands the death of the murderer, but there the demands of vengeance stop. No further bloodshed is permitted.

To understand Aeschylus's solution to the blood feud, we need to see how Aeschylus sets the action of the play within a series of thematic contrasts. First, and above all, the conflict resolved in *The Eumenides* is between two generations of gods (see chapter 1, on Hesiod's *Theogony*). The play is named for the Furies (Erinyes), agents of blood vengeance who are transformed by the end of the play into "Eumenides," good spirits who bring blessing and favor to the city. Female children of "Night," the Furies are part of an older generation of deities. Against these gods are arrayed the Olympians, especially Apollo, Athena, and Zeus. The opening lines, spoken by the Pythia, the priestess of Apollo at Delphi, raise this division at the outset of the play. Though the priestess honors several generations of gods—Mother Earth, Themis, Phoebus, and finally Zeus, who inspires Apollo to speak (1–20)—above all "Athena [is] at the Forefront of the Temple crowns my stories" (21). Thus, the Pythia's words hint that the play has to do with a succession of gods, and that a younger generation, especially Athena, and hence Athens, should receive the fullest worship.

This theological shift also involves a shift in the basis of society. The question raised in *The Eumenides* is, What is the proper basis for harmonious society? What kinds of roles and relations are paramount? How is the order of society best preserved? Two answers are presented. For the Furies and the older gods, blood is the basis of society; the most sacred and inviolable connections are those established by physical birth and descent—mother-child, brother-brother, etc. Faced with a choice, I should betray my neighbor rather than my brother. Social order is strong when blood ties are honored, but collapses when they are ignored or attacked. For the Olympians, agreements, contracts, covenants, and oaths are the fundamental bases of social relations; thus, the marriage bond and the bond between a king and his people are more sacred and inviolable than the blood relation of parent and child. I should submit to my king, even if it somehow damages members of my family. Social order is strong if contractual obligations, particularly marriage, are respected.

To put this point slightly differently, the old gods preside over the "house" (Greek, *oikos*), which consists of parents and their children, those related by blood. The Olympians are gods of the city (Greek, *polis*), where contracts between unrelated people, the marriage contract, and the "social contract" between rulers and ruled order the life of the community. Agamemnon's original choice—between the public duty of attacking Troy and the private duty of protecting Iphigeneia—is one variation on this conflict: To fulfill his "civic" duty, Agamemnon transgresses his "household" duty. Orestes' choice in *The Libation Bearers* is more intensely paradoxical, for he must attack his house in order to regain it. In *The Eumenides*, the struggle is explicitly between the values of the house and those of the city. Here again we see that the *Oresteia* tracks the historical shift from the heroic society of Homer to the urban civilization of classical Greece.

The opposing sets of gods are also divided along gender lines. The Furies are horrible creatures, but recognizably female: "not women, no, Gorgons I'd call them... black they are, and so repulsive" (*The Eumenides*, 50–51, 55). Physical descent is crucially important to female deities, for mothers have a physical intimacy with their children found in no other human relation. For the Furies, Orestes' attack on his mother threatens the very existence of society. Olympians prefer the male. Apollo and Zeus are themselves male, and even Athena takes the man's part. The decision of the court in favor of Orestes is based on Apollo's view of procreation, which reduces the mother to a holding tank for the male seed that is the real source of new life. For the Olympians, Clytemnestra is guilty of a more serious transgression than Orestes, for she commits adultery, kills her king, and blurs sexual distinctions, acting like a man in the violence of her attack.

House and city differ in their conceptions of justice (Greek, *dike*, pronounced dee-KAY). For the old gods, justice is summarized by the biblical phrase, "an eye for an eye, and a tooth for a tooth." Whoever injures another will receive the same injury in return. This is the moral basis of the blood feud, as the Furies make sure that bloodshed leads to bloodshed. Athena, however, accuses the Furies of preferring the appearance of justice to true justice, and suggests that doing justice requires more than a mechanical tit-for-tat. A just ruler examines circumstances and the motivations of the accused and may show mercy rather than demand the strict letter of the law. Each conception of justice has its own institutional form. Blood revenge is, for the old gods of the household, perfectly just. If blood is the most sacred of all relations between people, then a violation of that bond must be severely punished, and it is fitting that this is carried out by a blood relative. The Olympians, by contrast, are champions of the court and the trial, where disputes are resolved by persuasion rather than by further killing. Thus, the religious transition from old to new gods involves the creation of a new form of politics, the order of democratic Greece. Fittingly, the climactic scenes of the play take place in Athens, on the Areopagus, the site of one of the oldest of Athenian law courts. As Simon Goldhill has put it, the trilogy "traces a transformation from *dike* as revenge to *dike* as legal justice."

The political dimensions of the trilogy become apparent at the end of *Agamemnon*. When the Chorus learns of the double murder of Agamemnon and Cassandra, their unified voice suddenly breaks into individual, opposed voices. The death of the king breaks the community into its individual parts, into anarchy, a system in which everyone does what is right in his own eyes: No king, no chorus. Tyranny, the oppressive rule of one, is, Aeschylus goes on to show, the flip side and product of anarchy, a point made in Aegisthus's speech to the chorus. When the chorus warns that the people will finally curse Aegisthus, that his murderous deed will come upon his own head, Aegisthus says they lack discipline:

> You say! You slaves at the oars—
> while the master on the benches cracks the whip?
> You'll learn, in your late age, how much it hurts
> to teach old bones their place. We have techniques—
> chains and pangs of hunger,
> two effective teachers, excellent healers.
> They can even cure old men of pride and gall.
> Look—can't you see? The more you kick
> against the pricks, the more you suffer (1649–1657).

Politically, the blood feud can lead only to anarchy or tyranny. More precisely, the blood feud creates anarchy that can only be controlled by a tyrant. If a city is to avoid these unhappy political extremes, some other politics is necessary. In *The Eumenides*, Athena makes it clear that the Olympians favor a system that "will eschew alike license and slavery" (722).[2] Courts and democratic assemblies are, in their view, means for avoiding both anarchy and tyranny.

Examining the structure of the play reinforces these oppositions but also introduces some important complexities. *The Eumenides* is a very short play, consisting of barely more than 1000 lines. (*Agamemnon*, for the sake of comparison, is just over 1700 lines.) It has a roughly chiastic arrangement:

Scene 1: Apollo's temple at Delphi: Orestes departs, Furies driven out, 1–232
    Scene 2: Athena's temple in Athens: Orestes contends with Furies, 233–570
    Scene 3: Areopagus: Court decides between Orestes and Furies, 571–791
Scene 4: Areopagus: Athena welcomes Furies to Athens, 792–1057

As in other chiastic texts we have studied, the first and fourth section match, as do the second and third. In the first section, Orestes must flee from the Furies, and the Furies themselves are driven out of Apollo's temple. In the matching fourth section, Orestes is freed and Athena welcomes the Furies into her city and temple. Orestes thus undergoes a kind of "resurrection," moving from the status of "pursued fugitive" to the status of "acquitted," and with Orestes' "salvation," the house of Atreus is also preserved. The Furies likewise move from being rejected by the Olympian god Apollo to being accepted and welcomed by Athena. In both cases, the change of fortune occurs in the central, pivotal scenes, especially in scene 3. With Athena presiding, the court's ruling effects a change in the status of Orestes, which leads to a changed role for the Furies, as well. Law courts are not only key institutions in the city. They also make possible the transition from house to city, from blood to contract.

Second, the outline shows that the complex transition from old to new that I have outlined above is dramatized as a geographic movement, from Delphi to Athens. Delphi, with its famous oracle, is associated with the old gods and ways of life, while Athens is the city of the Olympians and their order. Contrasting religious, social, and political systems are also associated with two forms of speech. Older gods speak riddling prophecies like Apollo's oracles, but these give way to the persuasive and public speech of the Athenian democratic assembly, where opposing arguments can be weighed and tested. Aeschylus, himself an Athenian, suggests that the Athenian way of life is superior to the old ways.

In summary, we can chart the thematic oppositions of the play as follows:

| Category | Old | New |
|---|---|---|
| Theology | Furies | Olympians |
| Sexual | Female | Male |
| Social unit | House | City |
| Basis of society | Blood | Contract |
| Resolve disputes | Feud | Court |
| Speech | Oracles | Argument |
| Geography | Delphi | Athens |
| Justice | Revenge | Law |

These oppositions are crucial to following the thematic progression of *The Eumenides*, but Aeschylus introduces a number of complexities. One of these has already been mentioned in the discussion of the structure of the play. Orestes' acquittal includes the salvation of his *house*, but it is achieved by Athena, the goddess of the *city* of Athens. Preservation of the house is impossible on the basis of pure household values. If it is to survive and flourish, the *oikos* must be "resurrected" as part of the *polis*. Along similar lines, as we shall see, Apollo's theory of procreation, which helps Orestes win acquittal, does not lay aside the primacy of blood but gives a new spin to the meaning of "blood relation." For Aeschylus, Athenian democracy safeguards the best of the earlier household-based order.

Just as the social and political transition from house to city does not destroy the former, so also the theological change does not mean that the old gods are simply rejected. At the end of the play, with perfect refinement and reasonableness, without even raising her voice, Athena persuades the Furies to play nice, and, all black and wingless and with eyes oozing discharge, they go off to find themselves a nice little place in the 'burbs. Considering the first encounter between an Olympian and the Furies, this is a surprising outcome. When, at the opening of the play, the Pythia enters Apollo's temple to find Orestes, hands still dripping with Clytemnestra's blood, surrounded by sleeping Furies, she is horrified:

> there in a ring around the man, an amazing company—
> women, sleeping, nestling against the benches...
> not women, no,
> Gorgons I'd call them; but then with Gorgons
> you'd see the grim, inhuman...
>     I saw a picture
> years ago, the creatures tearing the feast away from Phineus—
>     *These* have no wings,
> I looked. But black they are, and so repulsive.
> Their heavy, rasping breathing makes me cringe.
> And their eyes ooze a discharge, sickening,
> and what they wear—to flaunt that at the gods,
> the idols, sacrilege! even in the homes of men (48–59).

These creatures are associated with old order both by their sex and by their color—black—which indicates their impurity. To the Pythia, it is a defilement that Apollo must purge (65–66).

Apollo is even less hospitable. Threatening the Furies with arrows (177–179), he mocks them as "grey, ancient children" (73), goddesses "born for destruction only, the dark pit" who are most at home in "the world of death" (74–75) or "a lion's cavern reeking blood" (191–192). Bursting out in a horrifying litany of torture and mayhem, he says they belong in places where

> heads are severed, eyes gouged out,
> where Justice and bloody slaughter are the same...
> castrations, wasted seed, young men's glories butchered,
> extremities maimed, and huge stones at the chest,
> and the victims wail for pity—
> spikes inching up the spine, torsos stuck on spikes (183–188).

Apollo ranges himself on the side of the Olympians, who do not equate justice with slaughter. Of the Furies, he says, "They disgust me" (72).

If so, why are the Furies in his temple in the first place? Perhaps the Furies have some role even in the Olympian order, but, if that is the case, why does he treat them so savagely? The issue becomes more serious when we realize that throughout the *Oresteian* trilogy an alliance of Furies and Olympians is assumed. Zeus himself unleashes Agamemnon and Menelaus against Troy as "Furies" that take revenge for Paris's violation of hospitality (*Agamemnon*, 59). Cassandra charges that Apollo has been her destroyer and he has destroyed her by sending her to a house where the Furies have been unleashed (1079–1080). Sensing Clytemnestra's intentions, she cries, "Howl, Furies, howl, you bloody ravening pack, gorged with this house's blood, yet thirsting still" (1119–1120).[3] Zeus is further implicated by the reference to the "net" that was laid for Agamemnon (1116), which matches the net that captured Troy, flung over the city by the justice of Zeus (359–370). In *The Eumenides*, Zeus's alliance with the Furies becomes more explicit. The chorus claims that Zeus, too pure to get his hands mucky, leaves the punishment of crimes to the Furies. Though he "repels our gory presence with loathing and contempt," it is "for him" that the Furies' "dreaded footfall, launched from the height, leaps downward with keen and crushing force" (362–372).[4]

Likewise, in *The Libation Bearers*, Apollo imperiously demands that Orestes take vengeance for Agamemnon by killing Clytemnestra. Orestes tells his sister, Electra, that Apollo has demanded that he "gore [Clytemnestra and Aegisthus] like a bull" or "pay their debt with your own life, one long career of grief" (*The Libation Bearers*, 280–281). This point is not lost on the Furies, whose leader reminds Apollo, "You commanded the guest [i.e., Orestes] to kill his mother" (*The Eumenides*, 200). Apollo's close association with the Furies makes us wonder how sincere he is in assuring Orestes that he will protect him from the Furies (67–68,

232). Perhaps, when he appears to be driving the Furies from his temple, he is really urging them to chase down Orestes. After Orestes is gone, he tells the Furies, "Hound him then, and multiply your pains" (224). Some protector!

To be sure, already in *The Libation Bearers*, the initiative has begun to move away from the bloodthirsty Furies. Clytemnestra defends her murder of Agamemnon by pointing to his sins, particularly his sacrifice of Iphigeneia, but she also wants to get Agamemnon out of the way so she can continue to share her bed with Aegisthus. By contrast, Orestes and his sister, Electra, take vengeance for pure motives, to fulfill the justice of Zeus. Significantly, when Apollo cleanses Orestes and sends him on his way to Athens, he does not awaken the Furies, which suggests some division between him and the Furies. The leader of the Furies obviously does not consider Apollo an ally (198–210).

Another way to read this opening sequence is to say that Apollo, though an Olympian, is a marginal god who does not belong fully to either world. It will take an Athena, sprung from the head of Zeus, and it will take an Athens to effect the change from old to new. Though this interpretation has some value, it is too neat, for the play ends with yet another alliance of Olympians and Furies when Athena welcomes them into the city. Relations between Olympians and Furies have to be transformed, but Aeschylus is not telling a story in which the Furies are eliminated and destroyed but one in which their "gifts" are harnessed for the good the city. If the Furies reign unchecked, the cycle of revenge is unending and society is thrown into chaos. Even the house cannot survive when ruled exclusively by the goddesses of blood. Yet the terror of the bloodthirsty Furies is not simply rejected. A new social and political order must be established, which makes ample room for the Furies without being dominated by them. From a biblical perspective, Aeschylus, like Hesiod, highlights a profound flaw in the Greek worldview, for both show us that the power of the Olympians and the health of their cities depend on an alliance with the powers of darkness.

*Review Questions.*
 1. Trace the lines of revenge that meet in *Agamemnon*.
 2. How does the biblical institution of the "blood avenger" differ from the archaic Greek idea of blood revenge?
 3. Describe the transition from old gods to new.
 4. What is the Pythia's initial speech about? Why is this significant?
 5. How is the transition from old to new gods reflected in social relations? In politics? Geographically?
 6. Outline *The Eumenides*.
 7. What is the role of the court in making the transition from the house to the city?
 8. What is Apollo's attitude toward the Furies?
 9. Why is it significant that the Furies are in Apollo's temple?

*Thought Questions.*
 1. In *Agamemnon*, the chorus says that Agamemnon offers up Iphigeneia "to help a war fought for a faithless wife." What is ironic about this description?
 2. When Agamemnon returns, he promises to hold an assembly to resolve disputes among his citizens. He says "Fire or the knife shall purge this body for its good." What does he mean? What is ironic about this statement?
 3. Cassandra, the prophetess who returns with Agamemnon, asks shortly before Agamemnon's death, "will cow gore bull?" What does she mean by this?
 4. In *The Libation Bearers*, the chorus tells Orestes that Clytemnestra has dreamt that she gave birth to a snake that drew blood rather than milk from her breasts. What does the dream mean?
 5. When Aegisthus goes into the palace where Orestes is preparing to kill him, the chorus calls him a "human victim." How are they describing Orestes' vengeance? What is significant about this?
 6. According to Apollo, where do the Furies live? What

is significant about this?

7. Who wakes the Furies when they are sleeping in Apollo's temple? What is significant about this?

8. The Furies speak of "Earth's central sacred stone" being defiled. What are they referring to? How has it been defiled?

9. According to Apollo, what marriage is the seal of all marriages? How does this fit with the larger issues of the play?

## Furies Find a Home, Lines 233–1047

The new section is marked by the geographic movement from Argos to Athens. Another spatial transition is evident as well, from "inside" the temple of Apollo to the open acropolis of Athena. Agamemnon, Clytemnestra, and Aegisthus are all murdered "inside" the house, and the Furies first appear "inside" Apollo's temple. City life, however, is lived "outside," in the open squares where citizens gather for festivals and to deliberate and pass judgment. In moving to the city, Orestes is seeking freedom from the claustrophobic pressure of the *oikos*, seeking to breathe the free air of Athens.

But the Furies have followed him, and the initial scene in Athens brings Orestes to a crisis. The Furies demand "blood for blood" (262), vengeance for the mother's blood that Mother Earth has drunk, never to be brought back again (259–261). Orestes protests, "Well I know the countless arts of purging" (274–275), and he assures Athena that he has been cleansed by sacrifices. Like the Furies in Apollo's temple, "the blood sleeps" (278). Not only that, but he urges the Furies to consider his situation: "Mine is a long story if I'd start with the many hosts I met, I lived with, and I left them all unharmed" (283–284). Neither of these appeals moves the Furies. Their archaic conception of justice will not allow them to take circumstances or motives into consideration. Blood for blood is all they know on earth. Vampire-like, they intend to leave Orestes "bled white, gnawed by demons, a husk, a wraith" (302).

Orestes appeals to Athena for help, but receives no answer, and the Furies cast a spell: "the chains of song I sing to bind you tight" (306). The refrain of their binding song reveals the nature of their work:

> Mine is the overthrow of houses, yes,
>     when warlust reared like a tame beast
> seizes near and dear—
>         down on the man we swoop, aie!
>             for all his power black him out!—
> for the blood still fresh from slaughter on his
>     hands (364–369).

Ironically, the Furies are ready to destroy the house in order to protect it. Again, Aeschylus is suggesting that the house without the city is doomed. Specifically, the house of which Orestes is head is nearly fallen and needs a "savior."

Enter Athena. She comes on the scene to break up the circle tightening around Orestes, having just returned from "Scamander's banks, just claiming Troy," which the Greeks have given over "root and branch all mine, for all time to be" (409–412). Athena is introduced as an imperial queen, who conquers and brings lands under her rule. Shortly, we shall see her make another conquest, over the Furies. In her initial examination of the Furies, we see the sharp contrast between their conceptions of justice and right. The Leader submits the charge:

> Leader: he murdered his mother—called that murder just.
> Athena: And nothing forced him on, no fear of someone's anger?
> Leader: What spur could force a man to kill his mother?
> Athena: Two sides are here, and only half is heard.
> Leader: But the oath—he will neither take the oath nor give it, no, his will is set.

> Athena: And you are set
> On the name of justice rather than the act (437–443).

To the Furies it is impossible that anything could spur a man to kill his mother, so closely tied by blood. Circumstances are irrelevant. To Athena, the Furies are narrowly concerned with the form of justice, and with a mechanical application of their bloody principles. This is not, for the Olympians, true justice but only its name.

After hearing Orestes' story, Athena is caught in a dilemma. Orestes has been cleansed and he comes to Athena as a suppliant, seeking her mercy. She cannot turn him aside. Yet, she fears the consequences of deciding against the Furies: "if they fail to win their day in court—how it will spread, the venom of their pride, plague everlasting blights our land, our future" (492–494). Athena wants to give proper place to the Furies, to blood, to the house, and, importantly, she accommodates them to avoid their wrath. The Furies, she feels, have to be appeased, their pride left intact, or they will wreak havoc with the city, and the Furies agree: "one act links all mankind, hand to desperate hand in bloody license." If Orestes wins his case, "deathstrokes dealt by children wait their parents, mortal generations still unborn" (509–513). Furies are "law and order" types: Orestes needs to be punished as a deterrent to the crimes of others. Within terror, there is no order. .

This is a principle that Athena wants to preserve, but she cannot bring the Furies into the city wholesale. It must be done in justice, not merely under the appearance of justice. But if true justice is more than a name, it is also more than principles and ideas. It must be embodied in proper procedures and institutions. So, Athena proposes to "appoint judges of manslaughter, swear them in, and found a tribunal here for all time to come" (497–499). There is an important political and moral truth here. However exalted our ideas of justice, justice will not be achieved within an unjust legal and political system. Publicly, the Soviet Union was committed to freedom, equality, and brotherhood but the actual political institutions promoted the opposite—grinding slavery, radical inequalities, suspicion, and fear.

At the same time, there is also a dangerous idolatry at work in the play. Aeschylus shows the mythic origins of a venerable Athenian court, the court of the Areopagus, which tried cases of homicide in Aeschylus's day. By showing that it was founded by a goddess, he enhances its authority and dignity. This court is Aeschylus's solution to the dilemmas of the blood ethic of the "house." Feuding can be brought to an end by setting up a tribunal and appointing fair judges to preside. Athena proposes a political solution to the blood feud, a prescription for salvation through politics, much like the promises of modern politicians that they can bring happiness and prosperity to a country through their economic policies. Aeschylus apparently wants us to believe this will work. It won't.

Athena presides at the trial, Apollo testifies as an "expert" witness, the Furies act as prosecutors, and Orestes stands in the dock as the accused. As the Furies interrogate Orestes, the issue that emerges is the distinction between the father-child and mother-child relation. Orestes brings "two counts" against his mother: "She killed her husband—killed my father too," and he demands to know why the Furies never hounded her into exile (606, 608, 610). The Furies' answer is a remarkable bit of double-talk: "The blood of the man she killed was not her own" (611). This is a major qualification to their motto that "blood demands blood." Apparently, they avenge the shedding of blood only if the blood is shed by a murderer who shares the blood of the slain. Since Agamemnon and Clytemnestra were not related by blood but only by marriage, the Furies excuse her action. It does not come under their jurisdiction. Blood relations, not the marriage contract, are fundamental.

If the Furies strain at gnats, Orestes' rejoinder, supported by Apollo, swallows an enormous camel. As Apollo explains, the rights of a mother and those of a father are not the same:

> Here is the truth, I tell you—see how right I am.
> The woman you call the mother of the child
> is not the parent, just a nurse to the seed,
> the new-sown seed that grows and swells inside her.
> The *man* is the source of life—the one who mounts.
> She, like a stranger for a stranger, keeps
> the shoot alive unless god hurts the roots (665–671).

For Apollo, it does not take two to tango; the woman houses the man's seed until it develops, but she has no blood relation with her child. Blood passes directly from father to son. Apollo here does not deny that blood ties are crucial. He merely claims that mothers have no blood ties to their sons. Here again we see an Olympian incorporating the "strengths" of the old order; they want to find room for the claims of blood within the walls of the city. At the same time, Apollo is also arguing in favor of a different conception of social order: Not the biological bond of mother and son, but the covenantal bond of husband and wife is more sacred.

When the jury's ballots are counted, the vote is tied, but Athena casts the vote in favor of Orestes, explicitly agreeing with Apollo's biology lesson:

> No mother gave me birth. I am
> all for the male, in all things but marriage.
> Yes, with all my heart I am my Father's child.
> I cannot set more store by the woman's death—
> she killed her husband, guardian of their house (751–755).

She thus "raises to life a fallen house." The close vote, however, means that the Furies' claims are not wholly rejected, a fact that Athena seizes on: "No more heavy spirits," Athena says, "You were not defeated—the vote was tied . . . with no disgrace to you" (806–808). This anticipates the theme of the last scene, the incorporation of the Furies into the Olympian order.

Many modern commentators believe that Aeschylus could not possibly have taken Apollo's theory seriously, but it is quite possible that he did. If we take this as a serious proposal, we begin to see the price that is paid for the establishment of the city. It is well known that women could not be citizens of the city. From Apollo's argument, a radical subordination of women is not accidental but essential to the religious ideology of the Greek city. Being killed by an Amazon in battle is an honorable death for a warrior like Agamemnon, but being killed by a woman in a bath is an offense against order. Subordination of the Furies to the Olympians, subordination of blood feud to the court, subordination of house to city, subordination of women to men—all are part of the same process. Aeschylus would have been puzzled by Peter's claim that women are "joint heirs of the grace of life" (1 Pet. 3:7), and bewildered by Paul's statement "there is no male nor female" (Gal. 3:28). He could not conceive of a city in which women are citizens.

In her exhortation to the court, Athena urges the Athenians to avoid the political extremes of anarchy and tyranny:

> Here from the heights, terror and reverence,
> my people's kindred powers
> will hold them from injustice through the day
> and through the mild night. Never pollute
> our law with innovations. No, my citizens,
> foul a clear well and you will suffer thirst.
> Neither anarchy nor tyranny, my people.
> Worship the Mean, I urge you,
> shore it up with reverence and never
> banish terror from the gates, not outright.
> Where is the righteous man who knows no fear? (703–713).

Athens is not governed by the blood feud of the Furies, and therefore it can avoid the extremes of anarchy and tyranny. Again, however, the politics of the Furies are not wholly renounced. "Terror" is an essential support for this vision of moderate government. Without terror, the city is endangered. If the house is saved by incorporation into the city, the city can survive only by welcoming the house.

And that is precisely what Athena proceeds to do. In part, the agreement rests on mutual extortion. The Furies threaten to unleash evil on the city if they are ignored, but Athena has a bigger gun: "I am the only god who knows the keys to the armory where [Zeus's] lightning-bolt is sealed," she says, hastily adding, "No need of that, not here" (836–838). Her victory over the Furies must be through persuasion rather than violence, else the city is no different from the house and is always in danger of collapsing into violence and civil war. Athena persuades the Furies by promises of gifts; she bribes the Furies to stay, but also extracts the promise that they will never "waste our youth" or "pluck the heart of the battle cock and plant it in our people." She is perfectly content that Athens expend its violence on other lands but curses civil strife that might invade the city (856–866). The Furies agree, praying that civil strife would never rage through the city. They have been urbanized.

Bringing the Furies into the city ensures not only Athens's survival but an almost Edenic prosperity:

> No ill wind
> Shall carry blight to make your fruit-trees fade;
> No bud-destroying canker
> Shall creep across your frontiers
> Nor sterile sickness threaten your supply.
> May Pan give twin lambs to your thriving ewes
> In their expected season;
> And may the earth's rich produce
> Honour the generous powers with grateful gifts....
> City, rejoice and sing,
> Who, blest and flourishing
> With wealth of field and street,
> Wise in your hour, and dear
> To the goddess you revere (939–947, 997–1001).[5]

All this is far too easy—Eden on the cheap. Orestes is acquitted on the basis of a ridiculous and anti-feminine view of procreation. The Furies are brought into the city with promises of worship and gifts, and they in turn promise to support the city rather than fight her. What has *not* been achieved is even an appearance of justice. Athena saves Orestes and the house of Atreus by changing the rules. She is the justifier of Orestes, for she secures his acquittal; but she is not, as Paul says of the Father, just *and* the justifier (Rom. 3:26). "Blood will have blood"—or maybe not, or maybe sometimes. You can hear the gears grinding. We feel that Aeschylus has cheated, achieved a form of peace in the city by sleight of hand. Historically, this sleight of hand was far from successful, for Greek cities continually struggled to harness the explosive power of house and blood. In their studies of the ancient city, Fustel de Coulanges and Max Weber both pointed out that the Greek city was internally divided along blood (and religious) lines, and Weber argues that this segregation was not overcome until the rise of the Christian city of medieval Europe. Athens did not banish the Furies, and this made the Greek city an inherently unstable order. In Acts 19, the only New Testament reference to an "assembly" of a Greek city-state, Luke similarly exposes the deep fault lines of the Greek city. The citizen assembly of Ephesus erupts in bestial violence when their idolatries are confronted by Paul's preaching. When the gospel comes, the Furies, whom Aeschylus would have us believe had been tamed, turn savage again.

Strikingly, the Bible is more savage and "primitive" than Aeschylus, for the Bible is more insistent on the necessity of vengeance. For the Bible, "blood will have blood" is true without qualification. Mercy is not offered by setting aside this principle, by changing the rules. Instead, mercy is offered on the basis of a once-for-all, final shedding of blood that will, when all is said and done, bring an end to every cycle of blood vengeance. And this means that the Christian *polis*, the church—which the New Testament calls God's *ekklesia*, the same term used of the Greek civic "assembly"—is not the product of a compromise of the Furies and Olympians. It is founded on the blood shed once for all by Jesus Christ. A city founded on *that* blood can finally put the demands of blood to rest.

As suggested in earlier chapters, the issue of creation is deeply involved here. According to the Bible, God created man good. Had Adam not fallen, a city would have been established in which there was no sin or need for punishment. To be sure, the Bible is realistic about sin and crime and teaches that there is a legitimate place for punishment and for deterrence. Yet, unlike the Bible, the Greeks believed that the Furies were always necessary for any city. No city can exist without terror, because no human beings can exist without rivalry and violence. Because it insists that sin is not "built into" creation, Scripture holds out the hope in the new creation of a city without sin, without tears, without terror, from which the Furies are forever excluded.

*Review Questions.*
 1. What do the Furies demand of Orestes?
 2. How is Athena's character revealed in her initial appearance and speeches?
 3. What value do the Furies have, in Athena's view?
 4. Describe the importance and limits of political structures.
 5. What is Apollo's theory of procreation? How does this reflect the themes of the play?
 6. Why does Athena agree with Apollo?
 7. What political ideal does Athena put forth for Athens? What does she exhort the Athenians to avoid?
 8. Why is it important for Athena to *persuade* the Furies to stay in Athens?
 9. Describe the mutual threats of the Furies and Athena. What does this say about the stability of the Greek city?
 10. Is Athena's decision just? Why or why not?
 11. Compare the Bible's view of the demand for blood to that of Aeschylus.

*Thought Questions.*
1. How do the Furies describe their pursuit of Orestes? What is significant about this imagery?
2. According to the Furies, who rules the ways of men? Why?
3. What does Orestes promise Athens if he is acquitted?
4. Do the Furies share meals with the Olympians? What image does Aeschylus use to describe the difference between the two?
5. What is the relationship between Zeus and Apollo?
6. Explain the complaint of the chorus when they are defeated in the trial?
7. Athena asks the Furies to "sternly weed out the impious, lest their rankness choke the flower of goodness." What is significant about this imagery?
8. What kinds of conflict does Athena approve of? What does she disapprove of?
9. Agamemnon's arrival is announced by a line of torches. In the light of this, explain the significance of the procession to the Eumenides' underground residence at the end of *The Eumenides*.


*Notes:*
[1] Unless otherwise noted, I am using the translation and line numbering from Robert Fagles, *Aeschylus: The Oresteia* (New York: Viking Press, 1975). Line numbering will differ in other translations.
[2] This is the translation of Philip Vellacott (Penguin, 1959).
[3] Here I am using the translation of Philip Vellacott.
[4] Again, this is Vellacott's translation.
[5] This from Vellacott's Penguin Classics translation.

## Riddles of One and Many: Sophocles, *Oedipus Tyrannus*

As much as any other work of Greek literature, Sophocles' tragedy *Oedipus Tyrannus* or *Oedipus the King* has influenced twentieth-century thought and culture. Sigmund Freud, the founder of psychoanalysis, used the play in formulating his theory of the "Oedipal complex," the suppressed desire of a child to kill his father in order to take his mother as wife, which, according to Freud, wriggles its way into our fantasies and dreams and was even formative of the structures of ancient society. Maverick historian Immanuel Velikovsky argued, in a fascinating book, that the myth of Oedipus was based on the factual life of the Egyptian Pharaoh Akhenaton. More recently, the lovely French films *Jean de Florette* and its sequel, *Manon of the Springs*, depict a reverse Oedipus story, one in which the father unwittingly kills his son in order to seize his land.

The events that so intrigue modern writers and thinkers, however, have already taken place when the play opens. Like Homer in the *Iliad*, Sophocles begins *Oedipus Tyrannus*, which is the first of a trilogy that includes *Antigone* and *Oedipus at Colonus*, near the end of the story. The background to the play is this: When Oedipus is born to Laius and Jocasta, king and queen of Thebes, an oracle predicts that the child will grow up to murder his father and marry his mother. Frightened, Laius and Jocasta bind the boy's ankles and give him to a servant with orders to leave him to die on the mountain Cithaeron. Instead, the servant has compassion on the child and delivers Oedipus to a shepherd from the house of Polybus, king of Corinth, who in turn sends him to the childless Polybus. Raised as a prince of Corinth, Oedipus as a young man is told during a feast that he is not the son of Polybus. Though his parents vehemently deny it, Oedipus, showing early a characteristic relentlessness in seeking the truth, visits the oracle at Delphi, where he hears the same prophecy that frightened his true parents so long before. Fearing the oracle will come to pass if he returns to Corinth, and still believing that Polybus is his father, Oedipus flees the city.

Near the city of Thebes, Oedipus encounters a chariot carrying an old man at a place where three highways meet. Enraged when the chariot forces him from the road, Oedipus strikes the charioteer. The old man, who is, of course, Laius, hits Oedipus on the head with a goad, and Oedipus fights back, killing all but one of the party. Continuing toward Thebes, Oedipus meets the Sphinx, a monster with a woman's head and the body of a winged lion, who has been terrorizing the city. She asks a riddle of every traveler to and from Thebes, and if he cannot answer correctly, she kills and eats him. Oedipus solves the riddle, is proclaimed a hero and savior of Thebes, and marries the recently widowed queen, his mother, Jocasta.

Sophocles' play is about Oedipus's and Jocasta's dawning realization that the oracle had come true after all. Painfully, we watch them put together the pieces and solve the riddle, and they are driven to desperation from the picture that results. Jocasta kills herself, and Oedipus puts out his eyes with her brooches and then demands to be exiled. Revelations come in reverse chronological order, as the following outline indicates:

> Prologue: Plague in Thebes; Oedipus and Creon
> Scene 1: Teiresias tells Oedipus he is the murderer
> Scene 2: Oedipus accuses Creon of conspiracy

Jocasta tells the place of the murder, and Oedipus concludes
      he's a murderer
   Scene 3: Oedipus and Messenger from Corinth; he learns he
      is not Polybus's son
   Scene 4: Oedipus and shepherd; he learns he is Laius and
      Jocasta's son
   Exodus: Jocasta kills herself, Oedipus blinds himself; Oedi-
      pus and Creon[1]

Starting from his position as King of Thebes, Oedipus embarks on a time-reversing quest that returns him to the womb—of his wife. As this outline shows, the turning point comes at the end of scene 2, when Oedipus first suspects that he killed Laius. The reversal of fortune that he suffers is as dramatic as his unexpected rise to the throne of Thebes. As Bernard Knox puts it, Oedipus falls from tyrant to beggar, from best to worst of men, from honor to uncleanness, from sight to blindness.

No one in the play knows what has happened in the past, but readers and viewers do know, and this gives nearly every line of the play a significance that eludes the characters. At the beginning, Thebes is suffering from a plague. When Oedipus learns that the plague has come because Laius's killer is still at large, he promises to discover the killer's identity:

> And justly you will see in me an ally,
> a champion of my country and the God.
> For when I drive pollution from the land
> I will not serve a distant friend's advantage,
> but act in my own interest. Whoever
> he was that killed the king may readily
> wish to dispatch me with his murderous hand;
> so helping the dead king I help myself (135-141).[2]

Oedipus sees that investigating the death of the late king is in his own interest but has not the slightest suspicion that the vengeance he swears might fall on his own head, that he is the "filth" that must be driven out. Oedipus's fear that the man who killed Laius may do him harm is fully justified, for the same hand that killed the former king will in the end be raised against Oedipus.

Later, Oedipus insists that he will fulfill the duty of avenging Laius's death, since the late king had no chance to beget sons of his own:

> Since I am now the holder of his office,
> and have his bed and wife that once was his,
> and had his line not been unfortunate
> we would have common children—(fortune leaped
> upon his head)—because of all these things,
> I fight in his defense as for my father,
> and I shall try all means to take the murderer (259–265).

In addition to the more obvious unintended meanings here, there is that subtle little comment about "fortune" or "luck." Oedipus will later say that he is the son of "Luck" (1080). Unknown to Oedipus, Laius did have "luck" in fatherhood, though it turned out to be bad luck that "leaped upon his head."

Concentrating on the end of the story enables Sophocles to play with the double significance of what is said and done. But Sophocles' decision has some drawbacks, strewing the drama with tremendous improbabilities. When the play opens, Oedipus has long ago killed his father and married his mother but during the course of the "investigation" that takes up most of the play, Oedipus apparently learns for the first time how Laius died and begins to realize that he was present at the murder scene on the very same day. Before he begins probing, Oedipus does not even seem to know whether Laius was killed in the country or the city. Why didn't he investigate long before? Would not a man with the forcefulness and intelligence of Oedipus have looked into Laius's death immediately upon taking the throne? Moreover, one man survived from Laius's party, but instead of saying something when the Oedipus showed up at Thebes as a hero, he left the city and became a herdsman. Why did he not inform someone that the new king was a regicide? Characters comment, finally, on the strong resemblance that Oedipus bears to his father, and we wonder why Jocasta never noticed this before.

Despite these flaws, the play continues to move audiences and fascinate scholars, and the reasons are not difficult to find. *Oedipus Tyrannus* is about a spectacularly dysfunctional family, far worse even than the Danish royal house in *Hamlet*. In the twentieth century, marriage vows are taken so lightly and divorce and remarriage so common, that the relations of parents and children in a home can be very confusing. I once met a family with three children, none of whom had the same two parents; one child was the mother's from a previous marriage, another the father's from a previous marriage, and a third child had been born during the second marriage. Oedipus makes such a family look mainstream. He is husband and son to his wife, brother and father to his children. He could have a whole week to himself on Jerry Springer.

As with most Greek drama, *Oedipus Tyrannus* also operates at a political level. Some scholars have gone so far as to suggest that the play is essentially a story about Athens, with Oedipus representing that Greek city, while others have tried to match the play's characters to political figures of Sophocles' day (much as *Primary Colors* is thinly disguised tittle-tattle about Bill and Hillary Clinton). Though most doubt that *Oedipus* is so directly a political commentary, there is undoubtedly a political message that would have been understood by the original audiences. The political angle is evident in the title, for Sophocles calls Oedipus a *tyrannus*. This word does not necessarily have the same negative connotation as our "tyrant"; in tragedy it is sometimes interchangeable with "king" (hence the Latin translation of Sophocles' title is *Oedipus Rex*). But the Greek word could mean "tyrant" in a sinister sense, and even when it refers to a benevolent ruler it refers to a ruler with absolute power. Through the play we will be forced to ask in what sense Oedipus is *tyrannus*.

Related to this political theme is the cultural opposition between city and wilderness, savagery and civilization. This contrast is built into the Oedipus myth, since Oedipus's parents put him in a wilderness to die. Without city or home, this child of the wasteland becomes husband, father, and king. Yet, he remains a man of the wilderness in many ways, as his crimes indicate. To the Greeks, as we shall see more fully below, prohibition of parricide (killing one's father) and incest were basic human laws. Unlike animals, which kill and mate indiscriminately, human beings view natural blood relations as morally significant. A man who attacks his father and beds his mother has moved morally from the city into the wild. He is no longer a man but a beast.

With this attention to the contrast of savage and civilized, Sophocles is wrestling with the worldview inherited from the heroic epics of Homer. Like the hero, Oedipus is like a force of nature, towering above all other citizens, reaching toward the amoral height of the gods. He has an overpowering personality, is quick and aggressive, rages like an Achilles against obstacles, and has a nose for the slightest whiff of conspiracy or competition for his honors. Large portions of the play are like scenes from *L.A. Law*, as Oedipus rather brutally interrogates witness after witness until he finds the truth. This play, like other Greek tragedies, examines what happens when such a hero takes up residence in a house or a city. Can we expect Achilles to put on an apron to wash the dishes or Odysseus to concern himself with the details of administering a city? Can a hero survive in a city? Can a city survive a hero?

In ancient thought, religious and political concerns were not separated, and the contrast of city and wilderness are related to religious rituals and beliefs. On one level, the play is a dramatic rendering of the Greek religious rite of the *pharmakos*. In this rite, which is very close to the Hebrew rite in which the scapegoat was sent into the desert on the Day of Atonement (Lev. 16), the impurities of the city were cleansed by driving a victim outside the walls. In the play,

Oedipus is the scapegoat, the source of impurity. Accordingly, Oedipus urges Creon to exile him from the city when it is shown that he is unclean. The one who violates the principles of the city, who descends to the level of the beast, must be thrust back into the wild. In this way, the city can be purged, healed, and raised to new life.

Oedipus's return to the wild is highly paradoxical, for, though left to die on a mountain as a child, he has come to embody the highest attainments of civilization. Vigorous, intelligent, benevolent, Oedipus has ruled Thebes with skill. As Knox points out, the imagery of the play associates him with the cultural and scientific achievements of ancient Athens. Sherlock Holmes in a tunic, he interprets clues and doggedly hunts for the truth (108–110, 221–222); without training as a prophet, he unravels the riddle of the Sphinx (398–399); he is compared to a captain who can guide Thebes through her storms (103–104), to a ploughman who has caused the city to blossom like a rose, and to a physician who can heal the plague (68). Each set of imagery, however, is reversed during the course of the play: The hunter turns out to be the hunted, and Holmes accuses himself; the man who solved the riddle of the Sphinx is baffled by the riddle of himself; the captain is stricken and loses control of the ship (922–923); the ploughman ploughs where he should not and causes sterility (25–30); the physician is sick and infects everyone.

Oedipus's fall is not meaningless but has a crucial theological dimension. An embodiment of the Greek view that "man is the measure of all things," Oedipus learns through bitter suffering that, on the contrary, man is measured by the gods. Oedipus is initially hailed as one who knows the gods intimately, but as his quest progresses, he realizes that he knows nothing of their ways. The chorus leader concludes that Oedipus has been the victim of savage and cruel demons who "leaped on your life to your ill-luck—a leap beyond man's strength" (1301–1302). Agonized, he asks, "What has God done to me?" (1312; Fitts and Fitzgerald translation) but has little hope of an answer. The struggle between Oedipus and the gods centers on the reliability of prophecy, and there is a conversation among Oedipus, Jocasta, and the chorus concerning this issue throughout the play. If the gods truly rule, they must be able accurately to tell the future; if they cannot, then, as Jocasta eventually says, Chance rules all and one should live randomly (977–979). Oedipus realizes, too late, that there is no escape from the gods, and he becomes a "proof" that the gods rule, and that oracles, once pronounced, will come to pass (1193).

Interwoven with the question of the relation of the gods to Oedipus is the issue of responsibility and guilt. In his *Poetics*, Aristotle used *Oedipus Tyrannus* to illustrate his theory of tragedy. According to Aristotle, a tragedy tells of a great and noble character who falls because of some tragic fault, some *hamartia*, which is one of the Greek words translated as "sin" in the New Testament. Taking *hamartia* to mean "sin," many have searched the play for evidence of Oedipus's wrongs, pointing to his overbearing treatment of Creon and Teiresias and to his excessive self-confidence as evidence of the fault of *hubris*, a word often translated as "pride" that refers to the effort to exceed human limits. Yet, these events happen after the plague has already begun, so the plague can hardly be punishment for sins that have not been committed yet. Clearly, Oedipus's *hamartia* is his parricide and incest, but since he was ignorant of his actions, we are left wondering at the severity of his punishment.

The question of Oedipus's responsibility can be answered so long as we realize, as E. R. Dodds points out, that *hamartia* in Aristotle does not mean "sin" in the Christian sense but a mistake, a false judgment, an error. In this sense, Oedipus commits a *hamartia* when he ignorantly kills his father and marries his mother. In tragedy, according to Aristotle, the consequences of *hamartia* arouse us to pity and fear. We pity Oedipus because we feel that it is not his fault. We fear not because Sophocles warns that we will be judged by a just God but because the play reveals the unpredictable nature of fortune and the savagery of the gods. The play suggests the frightening prospect that the world is the kind of world where such horrible things happen to good and decent people like Oedipus, and that the gods are the kind of gods that spring traps like the one they laid for Oedipus.

Oedipus's pursuit of the truth may also be seen as an act of *hubris*, reinforcing the theme of the limits of human knowledge and achievement. Pursuing truth is one of the glories of man, yet once uncovered, truth brings catastrophe. Oedipus does not fall because of his weaknesses but because of his strengths. Imagery of blindness and sight, light and darkness, and hiding and unveiling reinforces this theme. To see this issue fully, we need to recall that Oedipus became king of Thebes when he successfully solved the riddle of the Sphinx. Oedipus is a hero of the mind, who finds a way to untie the knot of any riddle. Teiresias mentions this in his encounter with Oedipus early in the play, and gives him a further riddle to solve. The whole play is about Oedipus trying to solve a double mystery: Who killed Laius? and Where did I come from?

Confident of his own intellect, he pushes aside everyone who tries to conceal the truth or divert his attention. In the end, tragedy arises because both questions point to his guilt. When he has sketched the criminal's face, he finds he is looking in a mirror. In this case, truth does not set free; truth leads to despair. Oedipus's incest also plays a symbolic role in this regard. Incest is, as we will see below, an assault on a fundamental structure of the life of the city. When the sexual wall between mother and son is crossed or broken, the city dissolves and dies. There are hints that the pursuit of knowledge itself is considered a kind of incest, a breaching of limits and boundaries.

Though never explicitly mentioned in the play, the riddle of the sphinx is important background. She asks, "What creature is it who, though speaking with one voice, walks sometimes on four legs, sometimes on two, and sometimes on three, and is weakest when it has the most legs?" Oedipus correctly discerns that the answer is "man," who crawls as a baby, rises to an upright position, but must lean on a staff in old age. To the Greeks, this was more than a not-very-clever joke but represented the position of man in the universe. Humans differ from gods because men are changeable. Gods do not grow through various stages; they are born, as it were, walking upright. At the same time, the riddle distinguishes human beings in two ways from the beasts. Infants who crawl on all fours are similar to animals who go on four legs, but for the human infant this is only one stage of development. Man "evolves" beyond the beasts. Elderly humans, moreover, are known by that strange "third leg." Unlike animals, man is capable of compensating for the weakness of age through technology and invention. Thus, the riddle places man in middle earth between the gods above and the beasts below.

The riddle has a specific, ironic meaning for Oedipus himself. When Oedipus was an infant, Laius and Jocasta put pins in his ankles to keep him from crawling to safety when they exposed him on the mountain; thus, he never went on all fours. As a result of this childhood maiming, Oedipus is lame; he never fully stands on two legs, a fact evident in his name, Oedipus—"swollen foot," for which there are many puns in the play. At the end, he uses a cane because of his blindness. Oedipus himself is the "man" that answers the sphinx's riddle. Yet, when he has solved that riddle, he has solved almost nothing. Riddles still abound—riddles concerning the gods, riddles concerning himself.

*Review Questions.*
1. Tell the story of Oedipus.
2. Sophocles starts at the end of the story. Describe the ironic effect this has on the speeches in the play.
3. What are the political issues of the play?
4. How does Oedipus represent the wilderness/savagery? How is this related to the issue of heroism?
5. How does Oedipus represent the achievements of human civilization?

6. What role do the gods have in the play? Explain the issue of prophecy in this connection.
7. What did Aristotle mean by *hamartia*? What *hamartia* does Oedipus commit? Contrast the Christian idea of "sin" with Aristotle's idea.
8. How is the play a warning against the dangers of pursuing knowledge?
9. What is the riddle of the sphinx? How does this figure into the play?

## City in Confusion, Prologue and Scene 1[3]

When the play begins, Thebes is suffering from a plague. As the priest tells Oedipus, "our city [is] reeling like a wreck already; it can scarcely lift its prow out of the depths, out of the blood surf." With Thebes tossed by storms, the people appeal to Oedipus, reliable helmsman of the "ship of state" (see 923–924). Thebes has also become barren. Because of the plague, "a blight is on the fruitful plants of the earth, a blight is on the cattle in the fields, a blight is on our women that no children are born to them" (lines 25–27; cf. 151–214). Wilderness has invaded the fruitful city, which has become a wasteland, full of decay and death. The corporate dimension of the crisis is important throughout the play. Oedipus's is a journey of self-discovery, but it is played out against the background of the threat, as the priest tells Oedipus, that the State will be engulfed in the storm (51). Imagery of fruitlessness is significant, for the failure of the Thebans' ploughing and sowing owes to the illicit sexual "ploughing" and "sowing" of their king (1210–1212, 1256–1258, 1497–1499).

Oedipus warrants the trust they put in him. The priest reminds him that once before he was "savior" of the city (48), when he "loosed" the knot of the Sphinx's riddle (36). Oedipus is clearly a compassionate, good king. He considers his subjects "children" (1, 58), identifies with their anguish, and promises them all the help that they need. He is also a man of dominating action, "swift" and decisive (765, 861). The priest suggests that he consult the gods to help the city (42), but Oedipus has already done so (70–72). The fact that Oedipus consults the gods before taking action to deliver the city suggests he is a pious ruler as well.

So it seems. Yet, the early action of the play suggests a certain confusion among the citizens and with Oedipus. The first set of choral songs are prayers for healing and salvation:

> What is the sweet spoken word of God from the shrine of
>     Pytho rich in gold
> that has come to glorious Thebes?
> I am stretched out on the rack of doubt, and terror and
>     trembling hold
> my heart, O Delian Healer, and I worship full of fears
> for what doom you will bring to pass, new or renewed in the
>     revolving years (151–155).

Yet, the priest calls Oedipus "Greatest in all men's eyes" (40) and appeals to him for a "remedy" (42). Though the priest admits that Oedipus is not one of the gods, he leads the people to the altar because he is the "first of men in all the chances of this life and when we mortals have to do with more than man" (31–34). It is difficult to tell whether the people of Thebes are praying to Apollo or to Oedipus, since, as the priests tells Oedipus, they sit as supplicants around "your altar" (15, in the Greek). As king, Oedipus is expected to be not only ruler but savior.

Oedipus, especially in his blistering exchange with Teiresias, reveals a troubling strain of impiety. When Teiresias refuses to help, Oedipus responds with a series of nearly blasphemous attacks on the prophet and prophecy. Teiresias is a "juggling, trick devising quack" who has "eyes for his own gain, but blindness in his skill" (387–388). Prophecy itself, relying on entrails and the flights of birds, was no help when the Sphinx threatened Thebes, and it is no help now: "I solved the riddle by my wit alone. Mine was no knowledge got from birds" (397–399). Human ingenuity, not divine prophecy, is the measure of knowledge. Oedipus's piety is like that of nominal Episcopalians whose faith the philosopher Alasdair MacIntyre summarized as, "There is no God; and it is prudent to pray to him from time to time."

The chorus of citizens is far more conservative. Caught between their love for their king and the honor due to prophets of Apollo, they conclude that perhaps Teiresias got it wrong:

> Truly Zeus and Apollo are wise
> and in human things all knowing;
> but amongst men there is no
> distinct judgment, between the prophet
> and me—which of us is right?
> One man may pass another in wisdom
> but I would never agree
> with those that find fault with the king
> till I should see the word
> proved beyond doubt (498–507).

More insightful at this point than their king, the chorus sees that if prophecy fails, so do the gods. They are not prepared to accept that.

For those who know the story, the opening dialogue between the priest and Oedipus is full of unintended ironies. In the priest's opinion, Oedipus is the "wisest in the ways of God," but events will reveal an Oedipus who has completely failed to understand the gods. When Oedipus says that "I know that you are all sick; yet there is not one of you, sick though you are, that is as sick as I myself" (60–61), his expression of sympathy is much truer than he knows. The word "loose," used here to describe how Oedipus solved the Sphinx's riddle, is found many times in the play. His feet were bound and loosed as an infant, he has loosed Thebes once before, and the people look to him to loose them from the plague. But he is not capable of loosing the knot of the new riddle—the riddle of himself (cf. 407, 1003, 1034). The one trusted to keep the wilderness at bay is himself a product of the wilderness; the citizens turn to a healer who has caused the plague.

Choral strophes in scene 1 also include unnoticed clues to the identity of the murderer. The chorus warns the criminal that "now is the time for him to run with a stronger foot than Pegasus" (467–469) and speculates that the "unknown murderer" is lurking "in the savage forests . . . and in the caverns like the mountain bull. He is sad and lonely, and lonely his feet that carry him far from the navel of the earth" (476–480). In both sentences, the chorus uses the word "foot"—*pous* in Greek. But they do not recognize the murderer standing before them on his own "swollen feet."

Just as Oedipus tells the priest that Creon has been sent to consult the oracle at Delphi, Creon appears. Apollo's oracle "in plain words commanded us to drive out a pollution from our land, pollution grown ingrained within the land," a defilement that has been feeding on the strength of the city (96–98). We tend to think of crime and punishment in terms of "deterrence": When people see that crime is punished, they are afraid to commit the same crimes themselves; if we do not punish criminals, then more people will commit crimes. In the ancient world, crimes were often thought of in terms of dirt and cleansing, of defilement and purging. In the book of Leviticus, for example, various kinds of uncleanness are listed—skin disease, touching a dead body, certain kinds of emissions from the body—and these make a person unfit to enter the court of the Lord's house for worship. For an unclean person, drawing near to a holy place is dangerous, and Leviticus 12–15 prescribe certain cleansing rites that will make it safe for a worshiper to come near. Similar conceptions are at work in Sophocles, now applied within a city. Thebes suffers from plague because of impurity, and if she is to revive, the impurity has to be removed. Murder in itself would defile the city, but this is a particularly serious defilement because the victim is the former King, Laius. For many ancient peoples, the king was a sacred figure, and attacking him was an act of sacrilege that generated dangerous impurities.

The exchange between Creon and Oedipus that follows is significant on several levels. Like so much else, this passage is filled with double-meanings, as both characters speak falsehoods they believe to be true and make statements that say far more than they realize. Oedipus claims that "I have not seen" King Laius (105); in reality, he is simply blind to what he saw, since he was the last to see the king alive. Oedipus immediately begins interrogating Creon about the crime and asks whether any witnesses remain, without knowing that he is the chief witness. Then there is the strange inability of Creon and Oedipus to agree on the number of Laius' attackers. Creon tells Oedipus that "the robbers they encountered were many and the hands that did the murder were many; it was no man's single power" (122–123); "not just one man, but a great company" is the translation offered by J. T. Sheppard. In the next line, however, Oedipus is wondering how "a robber" could be so daring (124).

Several things may be going on here. First, Creon's insistence that there was a company of highwayman delays Oedipus's recognition of his crime and thus heightens the dramatic tension. Second, perhaps Oedipus has already begun, unconsciously, to realize that he did see Laius, and so he corrects Creon's mistaken account. Finally, and more subtly, this conversation opens the theme of the "one and many" that is important throughout the play. Creon speaks of many attackers; Oedipus speaks of one. For the audience who knows the story the "many" is the "one." Though "one," Oedipus is also "many," combining many roles. Father and brother to his children, son and husband to Jocasta—he is a whole family in one person. According to the riddle of the sphinx, man, unlike the gods, is always both one and many; he begins in a bestial stage on four legs, stands on two legs, and then relies on tools to help in old age. Similarly, every man may be both son and husband, both father and brother. In this sense, Oedipus is everyman.

Of course, the way the one and many combine in Oedipus is unique, and here we return to the issue of defilement.

Impurity, in ancient cultures, often results from crossing moral or ritual boundaries. Sometimes these boundaries are literal; an unauthorized person who crosses the threshold into a temple defiles the temple. Sometimes the boundaries are moral and social: Saying "Thou shalt not" is like drawing a line or building a fence, and a person who crosses that line to do what is forbidden causes impurity. Both of Oedipus's crimes cross a moral boundary essential to a flourishing city. Oedipus's initial crime is not only murder, not only the murder of a king, but the murder of his father. Paternal authority was to the Greeks, as in the Bible, one of the fundamental structures of civilized society. If sons do not honor their fathers, they will not receive the wisdom and skill that the fathers have accumulated. Whatever foundations the fathers laid, the sons will pull them up or ignore them and lay their own foundation. At this rate, no building can ever be completed, for each generation must begin afresh, making up the world as it goes. A civilization without honor to fathers is doomed to stagnate and stall; it will build nothing more than foundations. For a son to assault his father is like pulling down a load-bearing pillar in a house; it brings the whole building crashing down.

Oedipus's further crime was incest, and this too is an assault on a basic principle of the city's order. An organized society exists only if the various roles we play in the theater of life are protected by rules. If every man can act as a husband to every woman, then family life dissolves into chaos. No one could tell which men belong with which women or who has responsibility for which children. Like an attack on the father, therefore, incest is a source of sterility and stagnation. A man who marries his daughter or a woman who marries her son inhibits the "leaving and cleaving" that is necessary to the creation of a new home. If each father is also a brother to his sons, if each woman is sister to her daughters, then the "younger" generation has not really moved beyond the "older" generation, and no progress is possible. Oedipus, ignorant though he may have been, crosses the barrier between a mother and son and confuses the roles of son and husband. Fittingly, the whole city is dissolving and sterile as a result of the plague that these actions have brought on.

The scene between Creon and Oedipus also begins to highlight their differences of temperament. Oedipus is precisely the kind of king you want if your city is being threatened by a sphinx or a plague: Aggressive, probing, impatient, he wants to get to the truth and now. But his quickness also leads him to jump to rash conclusions. When Creon tells him about Laius's death, he muses: "How could a robber dare a deed like this were he not helped with money from the city, money and treachery?" (124–125). Sheppard again gives a more literal translation: "What brought the robber . . . what, unless 'twas pay . . . Something contrived from Thebes! . . . to such a deed?" In this translation, Oedipus interrupts his own question by pondering the possibility that someone might have planned and paid to have Laius killed. Creon says that this possibility was raised at the time, but the threat from the sphinx prevented him from pursuing it (126–128). For the quick-thinking Oedipus, this begins to smell like a cover-up. He asks the crucial political question, "who benefits?" and suspects Creon.

Oedipus goes even further in his suspicions of Creon after his sharp encounter with Teiresias (scene 2). He now suspects that Creon is "the murderer of that man" and has attempted "highway robbery of my crown" (534–536). Again, he has only the slenderest of evidence that this is true, yet he makes the accusation insistently. Creon's reaction is remarkable: "Do you know what you're doing? Will you listen to words to answer yours, and then pass judgment?" (543–544). He has just been accused of plotting murder and revolution, but he remains calm and moderate, patiently offering a defense against an outrageous slander. His essential character, and his difference from Oedipus, is summarized in a statement he makes twice in the course of the play: "when I know nothing, I usually hold my tongue" (569). Cautious to a fault, Creon is also without ambition. When Oedipus accuses him of seeking the throne, he says he prefers restful sleep to the cares and anxieties of office, as he thinks "any sane man" would (584–587; Fitts and Fitzgerald translation). If so, then his king is insane, for he relishes the responsibility of rule. In all these respects, Creon is a foil to Oedipus, a character who shows up Oedipus's strengths—and weaknesses—by way of contrast.

Teiresias, the blind seer, is not so calm as Creon. His encounter with Oedipus begins cordially. Oedipus addresses him as one "versed in everything, things teachable and things not to be spoken, things of the heaven and earth—creeping things" (300–302), high praise from a king whom the priest described as the wisest mortal in the ways of the gods. Though physically blind, Teiresias sees things that no one else does. Indeed, he sees more than he wishes to tell, and refuses at first to answer Oedipus's questions about the source of the city's plague. There is no need to reveal wisdom "when it brings no profit to the man that's wise" (316–317). For Oedipus, discovery of the truth is essential to the health of the city, and he considers Teiresias's resistance as the act of a traitor: "Would you betray us and destroy the city?" (330–331). Paradoxically, it is unveiling the truth that will bring far more serious ruin.

Mention of betrayal takes Oedipus back to his half-formed thoughts in his conversation with Creon, and he again rashly concludes that there is a conspiracy: "I would have you know I think you were complotter of the deed and doer of the deed save in so far as for the actual killing" (346–349). When Teiresias directly tells him "you are the land's pollution" (353), Oedipus concludes that Teiresias is being paid by Creon to accuse him: "Creon, friend from the first and loyal, thus secretly attacks me, secretly desires to drive me out " (385). The closing exchanges between the king and the prophet play on imagery of blindness and sight. When Oedipus says Teiresias has eyes only for money (388–389), Teiresias takes up the challenge to his prophetic insight:

> Since you have taunted me for being blind,
> here is my word for you.
> You have eyes but see not where you are
> in sin, nor where you live, nor whom you live with.
> Do you know who your parents are? Unknowing
> you are an enemy to kith and kin
> in death, beneath the earth, and in this life.
> A deadly footed, double-striking curse,
> from father and mother both, shall drive you forth
> out of this land, with darkness on your eyes,
> that now have such straight vision (412–420).

A "deadly footed" curse will light upon King "Swollen foot," and blindness lies in store for the man who prides himself for his insight. Teiresias closes the scene by predicting that the murderer of Laius will be found. Known as a stranger, the murderer will be revealed as a Theban, and then having received "blindness for sight and beggary for riches his exchange, he shall go journeying to a foreign country tapping his way before him with a stick" (454–456; note the reference to the riddle of the sphinx). On stage, there is a man without sight, but it is not the blind man. Perhaps one must become blind before he can begin to see.

Oedipus's blind spot has to do with the parenthood, and thus with his own identity. For the Greeks more than for us, "Who am I?" was very closely linked to "Who are my parents?" Oedipus is struck by the seer's continual references to his parents, but Teiresias says only, "This day will give you a father, and break your heart." Oedipus rages against his "infantile riddles," but Teiresias reminds him that "you were a great man once at solving riddles," and adds that solving the sphinx's riddle "brought about your ruin" (437–443; Fitts and Fitzgerald translation). What Oedipus and all Thebans "see" as an act of salvation Teiresias "sees" as the beginning of disaster. Unraveling this new riddle, the one concerning his parenthood and identity, will complete Oedipus's destruction.

*Review Questions.*
1. What is the situation of Thebes at the beginning of the play? Why is the city's condition important?
2. What kind of king is Oedipus?
3. Is Oedipus a pious king? Explain.
4. Why is there a plague in Thebes? Discuss the difference between our ideas of crime and Sophocles'.
5. What is significant about Oedipus's confusion about the number of Laius's attackers?
6. Why do Oedipus's crimes result in disorder in the city?
7. What does Oedipus accuse Creon and Teiresias of? What does this say about Oedipus?
8. Describe Creon's character. How does he differ from Oedipus?
9. Why is it significant that Teiresias is blind?

*Thought Questions.*
1. What imagery does the priest use in urging Oedipus to "find a remedy" for the plague? What is significant about this? (45–57)
2. How is defilement purged? (100–102). Compare Sophocles' conception to that of Aeschylus in *Eumenides*.
3. Oedipus says that he has been a "stranger" to the story of Laius's death (219–220). What is significant about this choice of words?
4. What is the curse that Oedipus pronounces against the murderer? How it is fulfilled? (269–272)
5. Who is the "real exorcist" (or "prophet") that Oedipus refers to in lines 394–395? What is significant about this statement?
6. What does the chorus predict will happen to the murderer? (462–473)
7. Does the chorus take the side of Oedipus or Teiresias? Why? (496–512)

## Pieces of the Puzzle, Scenes 2–4 and Exodus

We have already examined some aspects of the encounter between Oedipus and Creon that takes place at the beginning of scene 2. This is not merely a personal quarrel, however, and it is important to notice its political dimensions. Oedipus accuses Creon of planning to overthrow him and seize his throne, and as the quarrel proceeds, the question of Oedipus's "tyranny" is raised. Sheppard's more literal translation is again useful here:

> *Cr.* Come then. What is your will? To cast me forth...
> *Oe.* Not so! My will is death, not banishment.
> *Cr.* Still so unmoved? Can you not trust my word?
> *Oe.* No, you must prove the folly of ambition!
> *Cr.* Have *you* such wisdom?
> *Oe.*       I can play my hand!
> *Cr.* But should play fair with me!...
> *Oe.*       —who are so false!
> *Cr.* If you are blinded...
> *Oe.*       Still I must be King!
> *Cr.* Better unkinged, than Tyrant...
> *Oe.*       Thebes—my Thebes!
> *Cr. My* Thebes, as thine! Both are her citizens! (622–630).

This rapid-fire dialogue is dramatically powerful. But the artistry of Sophocles is such that he can develop significant themes in the midst of this heated argument. Our first impression has been that Oedipus is *tyrannus* in the neutral sense of being a benevolent autocrat, but these lines leave us wondering if he is *tyrannus* in the sinister sense, for he insists on being king even if blind, and he virtually claims Thebes as his own personal possession. The tyrant, not Creon, will end up "proving the folly of ambition."

As their conversation reaches a pitch of intensity, Jocasta makes her first appearance, and her arrival is the dramatic turning point of the play. She breaks up the quarrel by reminding the two men that Thebes is "sick" (636). As she speaks with Oedipus after Creon's exit, she sparks sickening memories in her husband-son. Jocasta believes she has learned from experience that oracles cannot be trusted:

> There was an oracle once that came to Laius...
> That it was fate that he should die a victim
> at the hands of his own son, a son to be born
> of Laius and me. But, see now, he,
> the king, was killed by foreign highway robbers
> at a place where three roads meet—so goes the story;
> and for the son—before three days were out
> after his birth King Laius pierced his ankles
> and by the hands of others cast him forth
> upon a pathless hillside....
> So clear in this case were the oracles,
> so clear and false. Give them no heed, I say (711–723).

Jocasta is unwilling to cover her impiety, as her husband does, with a show of public worship. For her, oracles are worth nothing.

Jocasta's rejection of prophecy is too much for the chorus. Teiresias may be wrong, but not the gods themselves. They issue a rejoinder to Jocasta:

> May destiny ever find me
> pious in word and deed
> prescribed by the laws that live on high:
> laws begotten in the clear air of heaven,
> whose only father is Olympus (864–868).

Importantly, the antistrophe responding to this passage speaks of the arrogance that leads to tyranny (874–882). In Jocasta's rejection of prophecy, the citizens see not only blasphemy but the potential for political oppression. Politically as well as religiously, it is safest "to hold God as our protector" (882).

Ironically, Jocasta's proof for the unreliability of oracles proves the opposite, for it begins to unravel the riddle of Laius's murder and Oedipus's identity. Oedipus recognizes the setting of Laius's death: a place where three roads meet.

At the very moment his identity begins to be revealed, there is another pun on Oedipus's name. Oedipus can, as we have seen, mean "swollen foot"; for the moment, he fails to make the connection with Jocasta's story about her son's bound ankles. "Oedipus," however, also puns with the Greek words for "know where" (Greek, *oida pou*), so it is fitting that Oedipus's search for himself, for his true identity and name, is bound up with "knowing the place" of his birth (see 925–926). And here, when the first dim recognition begins to flicker in his mind, it is because he recognizes Jocasta's description of the *place* where Laius was killed.

Three roads meet in one place—where have we heard something like that before? Again, we are in the realm of the one and the many. The location of the murder matches the sphinx's riddle that described man as a one "place" that is also three and also points to Oedipus himself, the one man who is son-husband and father-brother. Oedipus's discussion with Jocasta continues to revolve around the one and many. Oedipus's only hope is that the report is true that Laius was killed by a group of "marauders": "if there were several, clearly the guilt is not mine: I was alone" (841–844; Fitts and Fitzgerald). He has not yet considered the possibility that being one and alone, he was still many.

Jocasta's story, then, puts the lie to her skepticism about oracles, and Oedipus is forced to concede, "I have a deadly fear that the old seer had eyes" (746–747). The nature of the gods also begins to dawn on him. "What net has God been weaving for me?" he asks, and when the identity of the murderer is confirmed, he asks, "if I was created so, born to this fate, who could deny the savagery of God?" (738, 830–831; Fitts and Fitzgerald). Even Jocasta, for all her impiety, goes through the motions of offering branches and incense to the gods (911–917). Yet in spite of having a glimpse of the horror of knowledge, of the terrible secret that he is uncovering, Oedipus cannot leave the truth hidden; he cannot be prudent, like a Teiresias or a Jocasta. Relentless in pursuing the quarry, he calls for the shepherd who was the one survivor of the assault on King Laius.

While Oedipus and Jocasta wait for the shepherd, another messenger from Corinth, appears, looking for Oedipus. He will enable Oedipus to "know where" he comes from, and will begin to reveal the second of Oedipus's crimes. The messenger claims to have good news for the royal couple of Thebes, though the news is tinged with grief. For the messenger, the good news is that Oedipus is being asked to come to Corinth to succeed his "father" Polybus as king. But Jocasta does not rejoice because Oedipus will become king of Corinth; she is happy that her "father-in-law" is dead: "Yet this news of your father's death is wonderful" (987; Fitts and Fitzgerald). Sophocles has so skillfully developed the action and characters that we barely notice the horror of the scene. Jocasta's relief and joy at the death of a father seems perfectly natural. In her own way, she repeats the original murder of Laius: an assault on the father. Oedipus's other crime is dimly mirrored in Oedipus's reaction: "Wonderful" that Dad is dead, he agrees, "but I fear the living woman" (988; Fitts and Fitzgerald).

The message also leads Oedipus and Jocasta into another loop of the religious roller coaster they have been riding. Jocasta loses every trace of her new-found piety and mocks oracles: "O oracles of the gods, where are you now? It was from this man Oedipus fled, lest he should be his murderer! And now he is dead, in the course of nature, and not killed by Oedipus" (945–949). She draws the logical conclusion. If oracles are unreliable, then Luck (Greek, *tyche*), not the gods, governs all. If that is true, we have nothing at all to guide us and one way of living is as good as another. Trying to calculate consequences, whether from oracles or reason, is useless: "Best to live lightly, as one can, unthinkingly" (978–979). Oedipus, who shortly before had begun to believe Teiresias, now dismisses the seers who "look to the birds screaming overhead," for Polybus "has packed the oracles off with him underground. They are empty words" (964–972; Fitts and Fitzgerald).

Oracles, however, refuse to rest in peace. The messenger has another message to bring, though he seems to delight in making it difficult for Oedipus to extract it from him. Riddles are offered, until Oedipus, the solver of riddles, forces him to a clear declaration: "Polybus was no kin to you in blood" (1016). Long ago, the messenger worked as a shepherd on Mount Cithaeron and received Oedipus from another shepherd. Again we see that Oedipus's quest is bound up with places, and he must track his quarry from one place to another, from one set of hands to the other, until he "knows where" he began. Oedipus must *oida pou*.

Here arises one of the most contrived coincidences in the play. The shepherd who delivered the child to the Corinthian messenger turns out to be the very same man who escaped from the attack when Laius was killed, the man whom Oedipus has just called as witness to the crime. Jocasta here sees better than her normally insightful husband. Sensing the direction of the inquiry, she pleads with Oedipus: "For God's love, let us have no more questioning," and she wishes that he would "never learn who you are." Oedipus turns her away: "the truth must be made known" (1056–1068; Fitts and Fitzgerald). At this point, he believes that Jocasta fears he was born a commoner. Things are far worse than that; for he is about to discover he was born a prince.

When he arrives, the shepherd is of the same mind as Jocasta and tries to hide what he knows. The Corinthian messenger, however, cheerfully pushes and prods, without noticing how reluctant the shepherd is. Oedipus threatens to kill the shepherd if he does not cooperate, and in the end, the shepherd relents. Oedipus has come to the end of his search; his questions, Where am I from? and Who am I? are now answered, and they confirm the oracles that Oedipus has lately buried with Polybus. As the Chorus says, the generations of man are "equal with those who live not at all" (1187). As Charles Segal puts it, Oedipus, having found himself both "many" and "one," discovers in the end that he is "zero."

All the revelations have now taken place. Oedipus has been proved the murderer, and his marriage has been shown to be incestuous. As Oedipus himself puts it, he has been caught in "the net of incest, mingling fathers, brothers, sons, with brides, wives, mothers" (1406–1408; Fitts and Fitzgerald). This confusion threatens to bring the whole city down, and the only way to save the city is for Oedipus to leave. Oedipus is thus a double savior: First in loosing Thebes from the sphinx and now in loosing the city from the plague. Oedipus is a savior by his coming and a savior by his going.

Jocasta despairs and hangs herself over her incestuous marriage bed. When Oedipus bursts in to see, he storms about the room moaning and bellowing (1253–1255). The wording here is close to that of the chorus's early description of the murderer as a hounded mountain bull (473–482). Unveiled as the murderer he had cursed, Oedipus turns bestial and rages like a wounded bull, a tenacious hunter become the prey. Then, he "tore the brooches—the gold chased brooches fastening her robe—away from her and lifting them up high dashed them on his own eyeballs" (1267–1272). It is a fitting act for one who has "too long been blind to those for whom I was searching" (1274–1275; Fitts and Fitzgerald). Now that he sees all, he blinds himself, ending the play like Teiresias.

Miserable and pitiable as Oedipus is when he emerges from the house, blood still dripping from his vacant eyes, he still commands the situation. Typically, Oedipus apparently thought through his act before performing it:

> I do not know with what eyes I could look
> upon my father when I die and go
> under the earth, nor yet my wretched mother—
> those two to whom I have done things deserving
> worse punishment than hanging. Would the sight
> of children, bred as mine are, gladden me?
> No, not these eyes, never. And my city,
> its towers and sacred places of the gods,

of these I robbed my miserable self
when I commanded all to drive *him* out.
The criminal since proved by God impure
and of the race of Laius (1372–1383).

Deliberately transforming his body into "a tight cell of misery," Oedipus exiles himself not only from Thebes but from all human contact—from parents, children, city. There is the suggestion here that he sacrificed his eyes for the sake of the city, so that her defilement might be cleansed. Chastened though he is, he still considers the good fortune of Thebes. Later he says that he wants to "never let this my father's city have me living a dweller in it" (1450–1451). Blinded, he is still savior; he bears the pollution into the wilderness, to Azazel (Lev. 16). Though his exile will loose Thebes from the plague, Oedipus knows that his blood cannot completely purge the defilement he has caused. Instead, his sins have corrupted the whole world, and, as if his gaze brought deeper impurity, the best he can do is avoid seeing what he has done. Nor will the curse end with his death. Barrenness is transferred from Thebes to the children of Oedipus: "Who will marry you?" he asks his daughters. "No one, my children; clearly you are doomed to waste away in barrenness unmarried" (1500–1502).

Creon is now in charge; without desiring it, he is now sitting on the throne that Oedipus accused him of trying to seize. Or, he seems to be. Oedipus, so used to commanding the city, continues to speak in ironic imperatives: "Drive me from here with all speed you can to where I may not hear a human voice" (1436–1437). Oedipus, who has doubted the oracles throughout the play, now insists that its instructions be carried to the letter: Apollo's "word has been quite clear to let the parricide, the sinner, die" (1440–1441). In the final lines, Creon has to remind Oedipus, "Do not seek to be master in everything" (1522). Only with difficulty does Oedipus cease to be *tyrannus*. This is an astonishing reversal. After his initial horror of recognition, Oedipus has reassumed the stature that he had at the beginning, taking control and giving commands. It is as if man's stature is not diminished but enhanced by his encounter with the gods. Now, however, he acts with "eyes open." His "eye surgery" is successful; it brings new insight.

The final lines, spoken by the Chorus, present the closest thing to a "moral" to this story. It is a cautionary tale, not about displeasing the gods, not about sin and judgment, but about the fragility of man and his achievements and the unpredictable nature of fortune. Since man is so small and weak, and fortune so changeable, happiness cannot be judged until life is done. The only happiness that a man can have is an apparent happiness, which will often turn to misery: "None hath more of happiness, none that mortal is, than this: But to seem to be, and then, having seemed, to fail" (1189–1192; Sheppard's translation). It is a bleak picture of the world, one ruled by savage gods who spin nets for victims, a world filled with demons who leap on unsuspecting prey, a world barren and desolate, without a King whose blood can cleanse the city.

*Review Questions.*
1. What kind of king does Oedipus appear to be in his conversation with Creon?
2. What oracle does Jocasta report? What is ironic about Jocasta's report?
3. Explain the pun between "knowing the place" and "Oedipus."
4. What does the place where three roads meet symbolize?
5. How do Jocasta and Oedipus react when they hear about Polybus's death? What does this say about the effects of Oedipus's original crimes?
6. What conclusion does Jocasta draw from the fact that "luck" rules?
7. How does Oedipus find out his true identity?
8. Explain how Oedipus embodies the confusion of the whole city.

9. What does Oedipus do when he sees Jocasta dead? Why is this significant?

10. How does Oedipus treat Creon at the end of the play? What does this say about his character?

*Thought Questions.*

1. Oedipus asks Creon why the prophet did not accuse him when he first arrived in Thebes (564). Why didn't he?

2. Why is Creon content with his position? (583–615)

3. How does Oedipus want to punish Creon? What is ironic about this? (638–641)

4. Oedipus is horrified at the impurity of touching Jocasta with the same hands that killed her husband. Why does this cause defilement? (821–822)

5. According to the chorus, where does tyranny come from? How does this choral ode fit into the play? (874–896)

6. The messenger from Corinth works hard to spark a memory in the shepherd who witnessed Laius's murder. Explain how this fits with the larger action of the story (1133–1141).

7. Compare lines 1181–1185 with line 133. Discuss the imagery of "light" in these two passages and relate them to the imagery of sight and blindness.

8. In lines 1207–1209 the Chorus asks, "How, O how, have the furrows ploughed by your father endured to bear you, poor wretch, and hold their peace so long?" What does this mean?

9. How does the "second messenger" reinforce the defilement of Thebes? (1227–1232)

10. According to the concluding chorus, what is the best hope that man can have? (1529–1530). How does this fit with the themes of the play?

*Notes:*

[1] Scene numbering comes from the translation of Dudley Fitts and Robert Fitzgerald in *The Oedipus Cycle: An English Version* (San Diego: A Harvest Book/Harcourt Brace & Company, 1976).

[2] Line numbering and translation come from David Grene and Richard Lattimore, eds., *Sophocles, The Complete Greek Tragedies* (Chicago: University of Chicago Press, 1954).

[3] Again, I am using the scene divisions from Fitts and Fitzgerald's translation.

## The Contest of Fetters and Thyrsus: Euripides, *The Bacchae*

The story of *The Bacchae* takes place in Thebes, to which the god Dionysus or Bacchus, a son of Zeus and god of wine and revelry, has come to vindicate the honor of his mother, Semele. Semele was accused by her sisters—Agave, Ino, and Autonoe—of lying about having a child by Zeus. Opposed by the leading women of the city and by the Theban King Pentheus, Dionysus takes his revenge by leading the women of the city to abandon their homes and their work and enticing them to the mountains where they at first rest in a kind of paradisal leisure. Faced with this domestic and civic crisis, Pentheus arrests the "mysterious stranger" and imprisons his followers. Fascinated by his beautiful, boyish captive, Pentheus admits that he would like to spy on the women, the Bacchae, and so, at the urging of Dionysus, Pentheus disguises himself as a woman and climbs a tree to watch the rites. As soon as he is in the tree, Dionysus tells the women a man is spying on them. Led by Pentheus's own mother, Agave, the women fall on Pentheus and tear him to pieces. Agave proudly brings Pentheus's head into the city, boasting of her prowess in hunting down such a magnificent "lion." Gradually, and with horror, she realizes what she has done, and the play ends with all remaining opponents of Dionysus being exiled from the city.

On one level, *The Bacchae* is a confrontation between civilization and nature, reason and excessive raw emotion.

Pentheus represents the city and its ordered civilization and therefore cannot accept the introduction of disorderly Dionysian ecstasy. He seeks to maintain the social and moral boundaries of city life against Dionysus, under whose influence the aged act like children, and women, whose characteristic tool is the loom, hunt like men. Inspired by Dionysus, women, who normally stay indoors, frolic in the wilds of the mountainside, where they tear prey and eat raw flesh, as if they were animals. Pentheus wants to arrest the spread of Dionysus by law and especially by force, the main weapon at his disposal, but it turns out that, uncontrollable as he is, Dionysus (like Aeschylus's Furies) must be tolerated and even welcomed within the city walls. Trying to confine him to the forests only leads to greater disaster.

The threat that Dionysus poses to the order of the city is highlighted by the roughly concentric structure of the play:

A. Dionysus announces he has come to vindicate his mother
    B. Teiresias and Cadmus, dressed as worshipers of Dionysus, go to the rites, opposed by Pentheus
        C. Pentheus meets Dionysus
            D. Dionysus's escape; the collapse of Pentheus's palace
        C'. Dionysus tempts Pentheus to spy
    B'. Pentheus dresses as a woman to spy on the Bacchae
A'. Dionysus vindicates his divinity, avenges himself against Agave and Pentheus

Several of the correspondences are worth noting. First, the two A sections center on motherhood, so that the drama is framed by Dionysus's defense of his mother's honor. The B sections are related ironically; initially, Pentheus rages and mocks when he sees respectable elders dressed like Bacchae, but by the end of the play he has put aside his armor and dresses like a woman. The C sections are crucial, describing the encounters between the two main characters, and the hinge of the whole story, the scene that focuses the play most clearly, is Dionysus's escape from prison and the resulting earthquake that begins to destroy the palace of the king of

Thebes. If opposed, Dionysus will shake down palaces until not one stone is left on another.

There is a personal dimension to this conflict as well. Pentheus represents not only the forces of civilization and order but is supposed to embody the power of reason and moderation. Just as he intends to protect the city from the emotionalism of the Bacchae, so he hopes to protect himself from the power of irrational impulse. Warden of the boundaries of the city, he also seeks to guard his own soul from the passions of Dionysus, but his personal resistance is as ineffective and disastrous as his political resistance. Mainly, this is because Pentheus is not a pure representative of the realm of order and reason. When he first hears of the Bacchae, he imagines that they are indulging in sexual excesses, though the reports of their activities do not include this feature. Fascinated and captivated by Dionysus when the two meet, he quickly succumbs to the Dionysian temptation to spy on the celebrating women. Though an "opponent" of Dionysus, from the first, Pentheus is more than half a disciple. The god hooks onto the king's Dionysian core to drag him to his doom.

Two key motifs focus the conflict between Pentheus and Dionysus. The first is "wisdom" (Greek, *sophia*), closely associated with "right-mindedness" (Greek, *phronein*). As R. P. Winnington-Ingram says, "there is a competition throughout the play for the right to claim this quality." Pentheus sees the Bacchanal, the festival and rites of Bacchus, as folly and madness and laughs when he encounters old men dressed for the feast. Dionysus, by contrast, considers Pentheus a fool, and insists that the only true wisdom comes from joining with the Bacchae. When Pentheus eventually comes to accept Dionysian madness as true sanity, it is too late, for he has become a victim of that very frenzy.

He has also become a victim of the Dionysian version of "justice" (Greek, *dike*, pronounced dee-KAY), the second key word to which the two main characters give widely different interpretations. For Pentheus, justice is established by maintaining order by the use of force. Dionysus, however, uses the term mainly to describe his defense of his mother and his judgment against his opponents. When he sets his trap for Pentheus, the chorus sings,

> Justice, now be revealed! Now let your sword
> Thrust—through and through—to sever the throat
> Of the godless, lawless, shameless son of Echion,
> Who sprang from the womb of Earth! (p. 228).

Like the Furies in the *Oresteia*, Dionysus believes that justice and savage revenge are synonyms.

From another angle, the play illustrates the theories of literary critic Rene Girard. The initial predicament in Thebes is what Girard calls a "sacrificial crisis," a situation where all the normal boundaries of civilized life have broken down. Elders act like children, women like men, servants like masters, etc. When a city comes to this point, it threatens to fly apart into a thousand pieces. What can be done to glue everything back together and to put everyone back in his proper place? According to Girard, sacrifice is the means for reviving the city. Energies and hostilities from the whole community are directed toward a scapegoat, who is blamed for causing the crisis and is killed or exiled for the sake of the many. Because the whole city unites against the scapegoat, the scapegoat is credited for putting the pieces back together again. Scapegoats thus are considered the city's "saviors." Inspired by Dionysus, Thebes becomes "double," but when the women "sacrifice" Pentheus and when the other opponents of Dionysus are driven away, the city, now ordered by Dionysus, has hope of renewal.

Historically, the Greeks tried to find a place for Dionysus within the order of city life. Dionysian celebrations were part of the religious calendar of many cities. Tragedies were, in fact, first performed at Dionysian festivals. Philosophically, too, the Greeks attempted to include "Dionysian" features into their worldview, and a consideration of this dimension will deepen our understanding of

Euripides' play. Unbelieving thought goes in basically two directions. On the one hand, unbelievers try to establish a kind of eternity on earth, in which nothing really changes or develops. The ancient empires of Egypt were attempts to stop history in its tracks. Dead bodies, for example, were embalmed so that they would be eternally changeless. In Greek philosophy, the great representative of this "static" view of life was Zeno, who argued that motion is logically impossible. For an arrow to move from the bow to the target, it has first to move halfway; but before it moves halfway, it has to move halfway toward the halfway point; but before it moves halfway to the halfway point, it has to move halfway to that quarter-point; and so on. Since the arrow always has to get to a halfway point before reaching its destination, and since the segments can be divided in half infinitely, it never gets to the target.

On the other hand, unbelieving thought might claim that *nothing* stays the same. Everything is in constant flux, chaotic and random. Christian philosopher Gordon Clark clarifies Heraclitus's argument that a man cannot step into the same river twice:

> The second time he tried to step, new waters would have flowed down from upstream: the water would not be the same. Neither would the bed and banks be the same, for the constant erosion would have changed them too. And if the river is the water, the bed, and the banks, the river is not the same river. Strictly speaking, there is no river.... Worse yet, you cannot step into the same river twice because *you* are not there twice. You too change, and the person who stepped the first time no longer exists to step the second time.

Obviously, neither of these viewpoints describes the world we experience. Against the view that says that nothing changes, we have the undeniable experience of change. I have photographic evidence to prove that, once upon a time, I had hair on the top of my head and no hair on my chin, but today the proportions are reversed. If the differences between then and now are an illusion, then the world makes no sense. Against the second view, we have equally undeniable experience that the world is not random. If nothing is predictable, we cannot know if the sun will rise in the East tomorrow, or if the properties of air and water will remain the same from day to day, or if gravity will reverse itself. Clearly, science is completely impossible on such a view, for science is all about learning to predict and control natural forces. But science is possible; therefore there must be some regularity in creation.

We cannot say that everything stays the same, and we cannot say there are no regularities. What to do? Well, why not a bit of both? If we are bold, we might say that the world is *both* absolutely unchanging *and* absolutely chaotic, or, if that does not work, we can say that the world somehow moves back and forth between these two poles. Ultimately, the tendency of all unbelieving philosophy is to swing wildly between these alternatives.

These abstract philosophical considerations help us understand something about the depth dimension of Euripides' play. Pentheus represents order, regularity, civilization; he is the political and cultural counterpart to Zeno. Dionysus represents chaos, nature, excess; he embodies Heraclitean flux. Euripides does not force a choice between these alternatives. Pentheus, with his fetters and jails, is a far from ideal ruler, but Dionysus is not a wholly attractive character either. The "solution" offered by the play seems to be that, to survive, the ordered city must add a dash of Dionysian frenzy. After a week of disciplined work, citizens should have the weekend to retreat to the mountains to dismember some goats.

The Bible answers these puzzles the way it answers all the puzzles that Greek thought throws up: by insisting that a sovereign God created the world from nothing and that He sovereignly preserves, rules, and governs everything in it, from the falling star to the falling sparrow, from the light that travels from distant galaxies to the lilies of the field, from the revolutions of the moon to the mites that inhabit carpets and feed on bits of discarded human skin. If this God *is*, there is absolutely no element of chaos in the universe; nothing occurs by chance. Yet, this does not mean that everything is always the same. On the contrary, God created and rules a world that is in constant motion and change. If He ordains everything that occurs, then there must be occurrences; if He rules every event, events must happen, for He must be ruling *something*; if He dresses the lilies in glorious blossoms, then the process of blooming must be real and really be a process. Change is constant in the world—not random but governed and purposeful change. Above and behind and in it all is the God in whom there is no shifting shadow.

Culturally, the Bible teaches that there is a rhythm to human life. "Six days you shall labor, but the seventh is the Sabbath of the Lord your God" (Ex. 20:9–10). From creation, God ordained life to follow a pattern of work and rest, of labor and celebration. "Workaholism" is not a Christian ideal but this does not mean that when the weekend comes we can cut loose and do what we please. Even our eating and drinking and rejoicing take place before the face of God (Deut. 14:26), so there is no room for the amoral ecstasies of Dionysus. Disciplined labor and celebration are not necessarily in conflict but are two steps of a single dance. Yahweh, not Pentheus, builds a city of genuine order and beauty; and Yahweh, not Dionysus, is the true God of wine (Judg. 9:13).

*Review Questions.*
 1. Tell the story of *The Bacchae*.
 2. How does this play match with Aristotle's definition of tragedy?
 3. Explain how the conflict of Pentheus and Dionysus is a conflict of civilization and nature.
 4. Discuss the concentric structure of the play.
 5. Why is Pentheus such an easy target for Dionysus?
 6. What is Zeno's philosophical position? What is Heraclitus's?
 7. How do these philosophical considerations fit with the play?

8. What is the Christian response to the problems posed by Zeno and Heraclitus?

## City in Crisis, Lines 1–420[1]

The first two hundred lines of the play introduce the main character, Dionysus, first with a long monologue and then with a series of speeches from the Chorus of his Asiatic followers. We learn several things from Dionysus's opening speech. First, he has a special connection to Thebes. His mother, Semele, is the daughter of Cadmus, legendary founder of the city, and his father, as he states, is Zeus. Dionysus was born to Semele when Hera, jealous of Zeus's love for a mortal, sent lightning to destroy Semele's house. Dionysus is a son of the lightning god, and even a son of lightning itself. After his birth in Thebes, however, Dionysus toured Eastern lands, manifesting his divinity and making converts to his rituals. Historically, it seems, the worship of Dionysus was introduced to Greece from Asia, but more important, the East has symbolic overtones for the Greeks, associated with emotionalism, luxury, and excess. To the various oppositions noted above, we can add this one: Dionysus is oriental, Pentheus is occidental.

Semele's sisters have spread the story that Semele was pregnant not by Zeus but by a mortal man, and that she made up the story about Zeus to distract attention from her loss of virginity. Thus, Dionysus has come to Thebes to "vindicate my mother" (p. 193) by proving himself to be a god. When the play opens, his vindication has already begun. He has induced the leading women of Thebes to leave their homes to engage in Dionysian rites in the mountains. Power to provoke such frenzy is a manifestation that Dionysus is the "divine son whom [Semele] bore to immortal Zeus" (p. 193). Being also an act of revenge, his manifestation includes a threat to those who oppose him:

> If Thebes in anger tries to bring the Bacchants home
> By force from the mountain, I myself will join that army
> Of women possessed and lead them to battle. That is why
> I have changed my form and taken the likeness of a man.
> (p. 193)

This is what he means by "setting all in order here" (p. 193). From the first, Dionysus comes to Thebes intending harm.

His speech also provides the first description of the rites in which the Bacchae engage. The location is significant: "the whole female population of Thebes, to the last woman, I have sent raving from their homes" (p. 192) to the mountains where they "sit roofless on the rocks under the silver pines" (p. 192). They are driven from the city to the mountain, from their homes to the roofless wilds, from inside to outside; that is to say, they are driven from civilization to nature. On the mountains, the women are clothed in fawnskins, clothing that, as Winnington-Ingram points out, summarizes the double-sidedness of the Bacchic rites. On the one hand, the fawn is a proverbially gentle and harmless animal. As a herdsman later reports the situation to Pentheus, the women have achieved a peaceful harmony with nature:

> They were a sight to marvel at
> For modest comeliness; women both old and young,
> Girls still unmarried. First they let their hair fall free
> Over their shoulders; some tied up the fastenings
> Of fawnskins they had loosed; round the dappled fur
> Curled snakes that licked their cheeks. Some would have in
>     their arms
> A young gazelle, or wild wolf-cubs, to which they gave
> Their own white milk—those of them who had left at home
> Young children newly born, so that their breasts were full.
> And they wore wreaths of ivy-leaves, or oak, or flowers
> Of bryony. One would strike her thyrsus on a rock,
> And from the rock a limpid stream of water sprang.
> Another dug her wand into the earth, and there
> The god sent up a fountain of wine. Those who desired
> Milk had only to scratch the earth with finger-tips,

> And there was the white stream flowing for them to drink
> While from the thyrsus a sweet ooze of honey dripped (pp. 215–216).

Dionysus brings his devotees into a land flowing with wine, milk, and honey, where the Bacchae graze like fawns.

One cannot wear fawnskins, however, without first killing some fawns. Dressed in fawnskins, the Bacchae are also predators:

> O what delight is in the mountains!
> There the celebrant, wrapped in his sacred fawnskin,
> Flings himself on the ground surrendered,
> While the swift-footed company streams on;
> There he hunts for blood, and rapturously
> Eats the raw flesh of the slaughtered goat (p. 196).

Transformation from fawn to predator can be sudden. The same herdsman who describes the peaceful revelry of the Bacchae was discovered spying on the women, with grim results:

> Now, Agave as she danced passed close to me; and I
> At once leapt out from hiding, bent on capturing her.
> But she called out, 'Oh, my swift-footed hounds, these men
> Are hunting us. Come follow me! Each one of you
> Arm herself with the holy thyrsus, and follow me!'
> So we fled, and escaped being torn in pieces by
> Those possessed women. But our cattle were there, cropping
> The fresh grass; and the women attacked them, with their
>     bare hands.
> You could see one take a full-uddered bellowing young heifer
> And hold it by the legs with her two arms stretched wide;
> Others seized on our cows and tore them limb from limb;
> You'd see some ribs, or a cleft hoof, tossed high and low;
> And rags of flesh hung from pine-branches, dripping blood
> (p. 217).

Dionysus represents the twofold face of nature, both its peaceful beauty and its terrible, amoral violence. The sudden eruption against helpless cattle foreshadows the later eruption against Pentheus.

This double-sidedness is appropriate to a god of wine. Wine induces relaxation, peace, and contentment. Teiresias speaks early in the play in praise of wine: "When mortals drink their fill of wine, the sufferings of our unhappy race are banished, each day's troubles are forgotten in sleep. There is no other cure for sorrow" (p. 200). The chorus goes even further, attributing to wine the power to bring social harmony:

> Dionysus, son of Zeus, delights in banquets,
> And his dear love is Peace, giver of wealth.
> Savior of young men's lives—a goddess rare!
> In wine, his gift that charms all griefs away,
> Alike both rich and poor may have their part (p. 205).

True as this is, wine is potent stuff, which can make inhibited people turn rowdy, or worse. It is no accident that the Bacchae attack the heifer after lounging at a "fountain of wine."

Other than Dionysus and the chorus, the first characters we meet are Teiresias and Cadmus. Teiresias is the blind seer in Sophocles' *Oedipus Tyrannus*, and Cadmus is the legendary founder of Thebes. In *The Bacchae*, they are old men, but each is clothed in fawn skins and carries a thyrsus, an ornamented stick that is the emblem of the Bacchic reveler. They are in part objects of fun, a comic touch, but Euripides also has a more serious point in presenting these two as the first characters. Differences among roles and persons are essential to social life. Americans do not like to hear it, but it is simply impossible and wrong to treat everyone "equally." Scripture instructs us to give honor and reverence to elders and rulers, whether in families, churches, or nations. It would be wrong for us to treat a civil judge or a church elder the way we treat our friends, and treating our friends with the same deference we pay to a judge would be weird. Americans are Dionysians, devoted to the god who erases social distinctions. The first characters to appear in the play illustrate the effects of the god of wine: Old, respectable, and grave, they are dressed like children. "What joy it is to forget one's age," says Cadmus (p. 197), sounding like the countless American seniors who try, unsuccessfully, to hide their age behind red sports cars and bikinis.

Teiresias acknowledges that his behavior may be despised by the people; they will whisper that he lacks "the dignity of my age." But the god he worships "draws no distinction between young and old" because "he desires equal worship from all men: his claim to glory is universal" (p. 198). Dionysus's claim to universal glory is precisely the point of contest between Dionysus and Pentheus. When Pentheus appears a few lines later, he shows his contempt for the god. Theban women have left home to go "gadding about on the wooden mountain slopes, dancing in honor of this upstart god Dionysus, whoever he may be" (p. 198). Pentheus shows no tolerance for the new rites. He has already captured some of the women in Dionysus's entourage and is keeping them under guard. Among those still at large is "my own mother Agave," but Pentheus is confident that he can hunt down the women: "once they're fast in iron fetters, I'll put a stop to this outrageous Bacchism" (p. 199). Hopeful to capture the "foreigner" who has stirred the women "inside my walls," he plans to "cut his head from his shoulders" (p. 199). Dionysus, in the view of Pentheus, does not deserve "universal glory." His plans for Dionysus also ironically foreshadow his own future. Pentheus fancies himself the hunter, but he does not yet know that the Bacchae are themselves huntresses. Though he expects to remove Dionysus's head, his own head will be paraded in the streets of Thebes. Pentheus's attitude toward his mother is a sharp contrast to Dionysus's attitude toward Semele; while the god has returned to Thebes to defend his mother's honor and reputation, Pentheus is willing to put his own mother in fetters.

Fetters define Pentheus. If he were a member of the U.S. Congress, he would sponsor bills to build more prisons and put a hundred thousand more cops on the streets. He represents civilization, especially civilization as it is hostile to wild nature and emotion. By definition, a civilized society is an orderly society, and in a world of sin maintaining order requires the use of force. Thus far, Pentheus's political viewpoint is sound. Yet he is wrong to believe that violence and irrationality can be controlled and suppressed by force. Fetters are necessary, but something more than fetters is needed. Teiresias summarizes the point in his long speech to Pentheus: "You rely on force; but it is not force that governs human affairs" (p. 201).

In part, Pentheus's flaw is his inability to discern the nature of his enemy. Thinking that the women have been stirred up by some oriental conjurer (p. 199), he does not recognize that it is the god himself. He even denies that Dionysus is a god at all: "The truth about Dionysus is that he's dead, burnt to a cinder by lightning along with his mother, because she said Zeus lay with her" (p. 199). A different account is presented by the Chorus:

> Once, on the womb that held him
> The fire-bolt flew from the hand of Zeus;
> And pains of child-birth bound his mother fast,
> And she cast him forth untimely,
> And under the lightning's lash relinquished life;
> And Zeus the son of Cronos
> Ensconced him instantly in a secret womb
> Chambered within his thigh (p. 194).

This account reflects the rituals of Dionysian worship, which enacted his death and resurrection. Rumored to be dead, Dionysus is in fact a resurrected god.

Pentheus also fails to reckon with the power that Dionysus holds over his adherents. Ironically, he thinks he can deal with the god once he gets him "inside my walls." To feel the full weight of this, we need to recall the spatial division of the play: Dionysus and his worshipers are outside the city in the wilds of the mountain, while Pentheus seeks—using fetters—to maintain proper order within the walls. This perfectly expresses the Greek conception of the city as an island of proper order in a sea of chaotic nature. Bringing Dionysus into the walls will not, however, accomplish what Pentheus hopes; instead, it fulfills precisely the god's own plan to bring the revelries of the mountains within the walls of Thebes.

Most seriously, Pentheus, despite his attachment to fetters and despite his insistence on order, is already more than half a disciple of Dionysus. When Cadmus sees him approaching, he observes that "He appears extremely agitated" (p. 198). Representative of rational order and an opponent of all excess, Pentheus makes his entry in a state of nervous excitement. His encounter with Teiresias and Cadmus is important in this connection. On the one hand, he laughs at the old men cavorting about like youths: "Sir, I am ashamed to see two men of your age with so little sense of decency" (p. 199), and he compares them to the women whom he has just thrown into prison (p. 200). As ruler of the city, he wants to protect proper divisions of age and sex. On the other hand, his attack on the two old men is immoderate. Teiresias rebukes him: "Power and eloquence in a headstrong man spell folly; such a man is a peril to the state" (p. 200). Both Cadmus and Teiresias insist that the better part of wisdom is to accept the new god and honor him. Pentheus responds ferociously. Speaking of Teiresias, he says,

> I will punish
> This man who has been your [i.e., Cadmus's] instructor in
>     lunacy.
> Go, someone, quickly to his seat of augury,
> Smash it with crowbars, topple the walls, throw all his things
> In wild confusion, turn the whole place upside down,
> Fling out his holy fripperies to the hurricane winds! (p. 203).

Pentheus resists the rites of a god who turns everything upside down... by turning everything upside down! Fetters, in Pentheus's hands, become another form of thyrsus, another mark of the Dionysian excess. Though Pentheus accuses Cadmus of "lunacy," Teiresias is more correct when he says of Pentheus: "you were unbalanced; now you are insane" (p. 203).

Pentheus is a disciple of Dionysus also in his fascination with what he suspects are the sexual indiscretions of the Bacchae. He orders his servants to "comb the country and track down that effeminate foreigner, who plagues our women with this new disease, fouls the whole land with lechery" (p. 203). To this point in the play, all we know of the women's activities is that they are feasting in the mountains—on the raw flesh of a goat, to be sure, but there is no hint that the women are engaged in orgies. Pentheus has dreamed this up himself, and it shows how Dionysian his mind already is.

The encounter with Teiresias and Cadmus also introduces the issue of wisdom and folly. Teiresias says that Pentheus's rage is "folly" and calls him a "foolhardy man" when he announces his plans to destroy the seer's "seat of augury." He warns the king, "Do not mistake for wisdom that opinion which may rise from a sick mind" (p. 201). True wisdom is to do one's duty to the gods. This is not, for the Greeks, because the gods are attractive or even good. Rather, the gods are powerful and dangerous and will pounce on those who resist them. A prudent man will, therefore, do all he can to appease them. By refusing to acknowledge the god, Pentheus becomes guilty of the chief sin of Greek tragic figures: *hubris*. Pentheus oversteps the limits of human behavior by failing to submit to the power of this god. This becomes more explicit in the first choral Antistrophe that follows the encounter. Speaking of Pentheus, the chorus says,

> The brash unbridled tongue,
> The lawless folly of fools, will end in pain....

> To know much is not to be wise.
> Pride [*hubris*] more than mortal hastens life to its end;
> And they who in pride pretend
> Beyond man's limit, will lose what lay
> Close to their hand and sure (p. 204).

Armed with fetters and jails, thinking himself wise in his opposition to Dionysus, Pentheus is a fool. His future is precisely what the Chorus says: He will lose all that lies close at hand.

*Review Questions.*
1. Why is Dionysus in Thebes?
2. Where are the women? Why is this significant?
3. Why is it significant that the women wear fawnskin?
4. How are Teiresias and Cadmus dressed? What does this say about the condition of Thebes?
5. What is Pentheus's view of Dionysus?
6. What does Pentheus intend to do? How does he intend to do it?
7. What indications do we have that Pentheus is more like the Bacchae than he admits?
8. How is Pentheus guilty of *hubris*?

*Thought Questions.*
1. What army does Dionysus intend to use against Thebes? What is significant about the composition of his army? (p. 193)
2. The chorus prays that Dionysus will be brought from "the Phrygian hills to the broad streets of Hellas" (p. 194). What is significant about the two locations mentioned here?
3. With what does Dionysus wreath his head? Why? (p. 195)
4. Cadmus is called the builder of the walls of Thebes. What is significant about this description? How does it relate to Dionysus? (p. 197)
5. Why, according to Pentheus, is Teiresias interested in the Dionysian cult? How is Pentheus like Oedipus here? (p.

200)
    6. What gifts does Dionysus bring to man? What is the other great gift of the gods? (p. 200)
    7. What is Teiresias's explanation of the myth that Dionysus came from the "thigh" of Zeus? (pp. 200–201)
    8. What does Cadmus encourage Pentheus to do with regard to Semele? Why does Pentheus reject his advice? (p. 202).
    9. Is Dionysus a god of peace or war? How is the gift of wine related to this? (p. 205)

## From King to Disciple, Lines 421–977

    A guard begins the next section by telling Pentheus that his order has been carried out. Picking up on Pentheus's hunting metaphor, he announces, "we've brought the prey you sent us out to catch; we hunted him, and here he is" (p. 205). Instead of finding him the dangerous beast they expected, they found him "gentle"—like a fawn. More ominously for Pentheus, the guard also informs him that the prison has turned into a sieve: "those women you rounded up and put in fetters in the prison, those Bacchants; well, they're all gone, turned loose to the glens" after their "fetters simply opened and fell off their feet" (pp. 205–206). If such miracles are done for the disciples, how can Pentheus hope to restrain the master? Headstrong man that he is, he fails to take the hint, and even instructs the prince to untie Dionysus, now standing before him. A perfect image of the hopelessness of Pentheus's opposition to Dionysus, this incident symbolizes that no matter how firmly he ties the fetters, what he is ultimately doing is loosing Dionysian frenzy.
    Before, when Dionysus was at a distance, Pentheus was fascinated by him. Now seeing him face to face, he becomes embarrassingly admiring:

> Well, friend: your shape is not unhandsome—for the pursuit
> Of women, which is the purpose of your presence here.

> You are no wrestler, I can tell from these long curls
> Cascading most seductively over your cheek.
> Your skin, too, shows a whiteness carefully preserved;
> You keep away from the sun's heat, walk in the shade,
> So hunting Aphrodite with your lovely face (p. 206).

A man with a lovely, seductive, effeminate face, Dionysus embodies the sexual confusion he introduces into Thebes.

The conversation between Dionysus and Pentheus develops several themes we have already noticed. From the first, Dionysus controls the encounter, and he makes the most of it, knowing he already has a beachhead in the impetuous heart of the Theban king. Pentheus asks what rites Dionysus is introducing, but Dionysus refuses to answer: "To the uninitiated that must not be told." Pentheus recognizes that the god intends to "arouse my eagerness," but his curiosity is too much for him. He cannot refrain from the hunt that will end when he becomes the prey. Dionysus makes clear that the rites are being introduced from the exotic lands of the East. Claiming to be a "Lydian" by birth, he tells Pentheus that "every eastern land dances these mysteries" (p. 207). Connected with the Eastern origin of the rites is the fact that they are practiced in darkness and chiefly by women. Darkness and femininity are associated with the East as light and masculinity are with the West.

Wisdom and folly are also prominent points of discussion. Dionysus assures Pentheus that no prison in Thebes can hold him, since the god himself is near to help his disciples. Pentheus does not believe it: "Where is he, then? Not visible to my eyes" (p. 208). Dionysus replies that his blindness is due to his failure to honor the god; only disciples can know their master. Sight and blindness merge into sanity and madness when Dionysus adds, "I am sane, and you are mad" (p. 208). Despite the guard's report about the miraculous release of the women, Pentheus is fool enough to believe in fetters: "Take him and shut him in my stables" (p. 208). This blindness will end badly; Dionysus warns that the gods will "come in swift pursuit to avenge this sacrilege," since Pentheus is "putting him [i.e., Dionysus] in prison when you lay hands on me" (pp. 208–209).

The chorus of Dionysians calls out to the god to manifest himself and end the oppressive violence of Pentheus. From within the palace, the voice of Dionysus is heard calling for an earthquake, which tears the palace of Pentheus to pieces. As the Lord's coming and appearance shakes and melts the earth (see Psalm 18:7–15), so here the manifestation of Dionysus. At the same time, the flame before Semele's tomb burns brighter. By revealing himself as a god, Dionysus vindicates his mother, showing that she was telling the truth about the father of her child.

Much ink has been expended on the collapsing palace scene. The problem is this: Although the chorus here screams out that the palace is falling, the play proceeds as if nothing has happened. Characters move in and out of the palace as if it were still intact. As far as staging goes, the best explanation is that the earthquake shakes the house but does not topple it. Symbolically, though, the scene is powerful and important, for it shows that Pentheus's opposition to the god will lead to the downfall of his royal "house." Dionysus tells the chorus that he has left the stables of Pentheus in ruins, his prison now a "heap of rubble." This is what happens, he adds, to a man who "dared to take arms against a god" (p. 213).

Dionysus explains to the chorus how he escaped Pentheus's bonds:

> He thought he was binding me;
> But he neither held nor touched me, save in his deluded mind.
> Near the mangers where he meant to tie me up, he found a bull;
> And he tied his rope round the bull's knees and hooves, panting with rage,
> Dripping sweat, biting his lips; while I sit quietly by and watched (p. 212).

In other myths, Dionysus sometimes appears in the guise of a bull, and the substitution is appropriate here. A bull symbolizes the uncontrollable power of nature; trying to bind Dionysus is like trying to restrain a raging bull. Pentheus tries to tie up the Dionysus raging within his own soul and prevent the spread of Dionysian frenzy in Thebes. In both efforts, he is doomed to fail. Fetters cannot bind this god.

Indeed, nothing whatever binds him. As Pentheus says, Dionysus is "the god who frees his worshipers from every law," to which Dionysus responds, "Your insult to Dionysus is a compliment" (214). Dionysus is a god of liberation, freeing from all the constraints that civilization imposes—not only fetters, but all distinctions and limits. The deep irony of this is that Dionysus condemns Pentheus for not observing proper limits, while at the same time breaking down all possible limits. Dionysus is *hubris* incarnate, yet he condemns men for their *hubris*. Just as there is madness and madness, wisdom and wisdom, so there is *hubris* and *hubris*. Early in the play, the chorus warns, according to Vellacott's translation, that "There's a brute wildness in the fennel-wands—reverence it well" (p. 195), but the Greek text speaks of "holiness" in the handling of "hubristic wands." United to the thyrsus, *hubris*, the breaching of human limits, becomes "holy."

The exchange between Dionysus and Pentheus is a temptation scene, as Dionysus lures Pentheus to his death. Temptation only works, however, because Pentheus is already inclined to follow Dionysus's instructions. James 1:12–18 says that we are enticed and led into sin by our own lusts, not by the temptation itself; it is because we already desire to violate God's law that circumstances and things "tempt" us to do so. So also here. While Pentheus is putting on his armor in preparation for the sacrificial massacre of the women that he hopes will reunite the city, Dionysus asks, "Do you want to *see* those women, where they sit together, up in the hills?" He already knows the answer: "Why, yes," Pentheus replies, "for that I'd give a weighty sum of gold" (p. 220). Pentheus

## The Contest of Fetters and Thyrsus: *The Bacchae* 355

takes the bait and swallows the hook. Dionysus's question, "Shall I lead you?" is something more than an offer to show him the path into the mountains. It is an invitation to discipleship.

Becoming a disciple means putting off his armor—representing civilized order imposed by fetter and prison and sword—and putting on the garb of a Dionysian; he lays down the scepter to take up a thyrsus. Dionysus offers to dress the king like a woman: flowing hair, full-length robe, fawnskin. In part, the clothing of Pentheus is a disguise that enables him to observe the Bacchae without being seen. As a disguise, the get-up is worse than useless. More importantly, this clothing change means that he, Pentheus, the upholder of civilized distinctions, is possessed by the spirit of Dionysus, blurring the distinctions of male and female. He has become a mirror, imperfect to be sure, of his master. Becoming the double of Dionysus is, however, the beginning of his punishment for refusing to bow to the god. The same Pentheus who laughed at Teiresias and Cadmus now becomes the object of laughter, humbled from his earlier *hubris* (p. 222).

As Pentheus emerges in his outrageous costume, the issue of sight and blindness is taken up again. Dionysus says Pentheus is a "perverse man, greedy for sights you should not see" (p. 224), and this greediness has perverted his sight. He tells Dionysus that he sees everything double: "two sons, a double Thebes; our city's wall with seven gates appears double" (pp. 224–225), and he believes that Dionysus has turned into a bull. When Dionysus replies, "you see as you should see," he is not being sarcastic. Pentheus, for the first time, sees Dionysus for what he is, a powerful, dangerous beast; and he sees too that Thebes has been split in two by the Dionysian revelry. Himself double, Pentheus is inclined to follow Dionysus while at the same time he insists on maintaining civilized order. Pentheus was mad when he opposed the god; now he is sane. The sinister edge to this is that his "sanity" will lead to his death.

*Review Questions.*
    1. What happens to the jailed women? Does Pentheus notice?
    2. How does Pentheus react to Dionysus? What does this tell us about Pentheus?
    3. How does Dionysus tempt Pentheus?
    4. What happens to the palace? What does this symbolize?
    5. How does Dionysus escape from Pentheus's bonds? How is this appropriate?
    6. Explain Dionysus's relation to *hubris*.
    7. How does Dionysus clothe Pentheus? What is the significance of Pentheus's clothing change?
    8. How does Thebes appear to Pentheus? What is significant about this?

*Thought Questions.*
    1. The guard assures Pentheus that the "beast was gentle" (p. 205). To whom is he referring? What is significant about the language he uses?
    2. Pentheus lets Dionysus be untied because "he's securely in the trap" (p. 206). What is ironic about these words?
    3. Why does Dionysus hold his rites at night? Why does Pentheus think he holds his rites at night? (p. 207)
    4. The name "Pentheus" means "sorrow." With this in mind, discuss the exchange between Dionysus and Pentheus about his name (p. 208).
    5. At the end of the choral Antistrophe on p. 210, the chorus calls on Dionysus to deliver them. From what? How will he deliver them? What is significant about the "weapons" mentioned here?
    6. According to the herdsman, Agave reacts to the bellowing of cattle. Why? (p. 215)
    7. What do the Bacchae do when whipped into a frenzy? What is significant about this? (p. 218)

8. Where does Pentheus go to change into the costume of a woman? Why? (p. 221)

9. How does the choral Epode on page 224 reflect the action of the play?

10. Explain the double meanings in the dialogue between Dionysus and Pentheus on page 227.

## From Hunter to Prey, Lines 978–1392

The choral song that begins this final section of the tragedy brings up several themes we have been tracing. First, the Chorus predicts that Pentheus's mother will be the first to spot him spying on the Bacchae, and will disown him: "that lad never lay in a woman's womb; a lioness Gave him suck, or a Libyan Gorgon" (p. 228). For Dionysus, it is particularly important that vengeance be carried out by a mother, since he has come to Thebes to defend his own mother, Semele. Agave's disowning of her son will demonstrate the truth of Semele's claim that her son is a god, a thematic link brought out in the concentric structure mentioned above. Agave will concede that a "lioness" gave birth to Pentheus, for she will mistake her son's head for a lion's. Second, the destruction of Pentheus is seen as an act of justice that will "sever the throat of the godless, lawless, shameless son of Echion" (p. 228). Fetters and prisons notwithstanding, Pentheus's "reckless" and "proud" resistance to the god makes him "lawless." Dionysus's vengeance will prove that "he who unquestioning gives the gods their due, and knows that his days are as dust, shall live untouched" (p. 228). Greek gods are not lovable, and they do not ask for love from their adherents—only fear and respect for their power. Third, there is an equity to the justice that Dionysus exacts. Pentheus hunted and sought to bind Dionysus; now, the chorus calls on Bacchus to "swoop down . . . on the hunter of the Bacchae; smile at him and snare him" (928–929). Hunting in Greek culture was as much a way of initiating boys into the world of men as a way of gathering food, and therefore women and girls were normally excluded. This hunt is a Dionysian hunt, and it is suitably inverted: Pentheus goes hunting women dressed as a woman, yet it will turn out that the women hunt him.

A messenger reports the grisly details, telling how Dionysus, whom he describes always as "the foreigner," trapped Pentheus by putting him at the top of a pine tree to spy out the celebration:

> He took hold of a pine-tree's soaring, topmost branch,
> And dragged it down, down, down to the dark earth.
>     It was bent
> In a circle as a bow is bent, as a wheel's curve,
> Drawn with a compass, bends the rim to its own shape;
> That foreigner took that mountain-pine in his two hands
> And bent it down—a thing no mortal man could do.
> Then seating Pentheus on a high branch, he began
> To let the tree spring upright, slipping it through his hands,
> Steadily, taking care he should not be flung off (p. 230).

Pulling down that tree, Dionysus is fitting an arrow to the bow, readying for the kill. The emphasis on the circular shape perhaps suggests the circle of fate. Things rise, and things fall, and the world goes round and round and round. Pentheus is now high (in the tree, in Thebes) but when the wheel turns he will be crushed beneath it. In Thebes, as in the tree, it is his very height that makes him vulnerable, for at the top of the tree he is "more visible to the Maenads than they were to him" (p. 231).

At the command of Dionysus, the women attack: "Women, here is the man who made a mock of you, and me, and of my holy rites. Now punish him" (p. 231). That the women listen to the voice of the god in attacking their ruler shows that Thebes has indeed become double. One half of the city listens to the voice of the king, the other half to the voice of Dionysus. As the Chorus tells the messenger, "Dionysus commands *me*; not Thebes, but Dionysus" (p. 229). Again, the danger of accommodating Dionysus in the city is manifest, for he divides the city. Resisting Dionysus is more dangerous still, for he can shake down palaces, break fetters, breach city walls, and cast kings down from their heights. Better, apparently, a double city divided between fetter and thyrsus than no city at all.

Finally, the women bring Pentheus down, down, down, and begin the slaughter. Reflecting a strict principle of "eye-for-eye" justice, the violence of Pentheus's end matches the violence of his conduct and temper throughout the play. Because they see it as an act of divine retribution and justice, the Chorus greets the news with joy. It means salvation for them, since "not any more do I cower in terror of prison" (1036). Now the hunter of Bacchae is dead, and Dionysus again proves himself a liberator. Yet, this is no ordinary murder, but a sacrifice, described in explicitly religious language: "His mother first, as priestess, led the rite of death, and fell upon him" (232). The sacrificial imagery can be understood in the light of Girard's theories, explained above. Here, Pentheus is the scapegoat, and his sacrifice at the hands of the Bacchae reunites the city that had become "double." This sacrificial context explains the horrifying violence of the kill; Pentheus is not merely killed but dismembered:

> [Agave] grasped
> His left arm between wrist and elbow, set her foot
> Against his ribs, and tore his arm off by the shoulder.
> It was no strength of hers that did it, but the god
> Filled her, and made it easy. On the other side
> Ino was at him, tearing at his flesh; and now
> Autonoe joined them, and the whole maniacal horde....
> One of them carried off an arm,
> Another a foot, the boot still laced on it. The ribs
> Were stripped, clawed clean; and women's hands, thick red with blood,
> Were tossing, catching, like a plaything, Pentheus' flesh (p. 232).

Well does the chorus sing that this is a case of inverted sacrifice, where the Dionysian "bull" leads a "man to the ritual slaughter-ring" (p. 233). But who is the real beast here?

Dionysus has appeared in the guise of a bull, but here he is the hunter. Meanwhile, Pentheus, representative of civilization, order, and reason, is led like a sheep to the slaughter, a feast for a predatory god.

"The god filled her." Agave and the other women did not carry out this slaughter by their own wisdom. Rather, "possessed by Bacchus" she "paid no heed to him" (p. 232). For Agave too, Dionysus rather than Thebes commands. This is the "wisdom" of Dionysus, the wisdom of unrestrained nature. Possessed by Dionysus, the women become beasts, tearing the raw flesh of their king. So long as Agave is on the mountain, she sees according to Dionysian blindness-sight, but back in the city walls things begin to look different. Initially, she thinks she is carrying the head of a "lion-cub" or a young calf (pp. 234–235), and invites the city to join her in a victory feast. She recognizes that she has been an instrument of Dionysus: "The god is a skilled hunter; and he poised his hunting women, and hurled them at the quarry" (p. 235). Yet, though an instrument of the god, and a willing one, she is simultaneously being punished. Gradually, she sobers up and is able to detach herself from the mob action of the Bacchae in order to see things as a mother. After she recognizes the horror of her crime, Cadmus tells her that Pentheus "sinned like you, refusing reverence to a god. Therefore the god has joined all in one ruin... to destroy my house and me" (p. 239). Unholy *hubris* shakes down the palace.

At the end Dionysus appears in his divine glory, no longer as a man. He tells the Thebans that they have been punished for denying his divinity and then pronounces sentence against Agave and her sisters, who

> Must immediately
> Depart from Thebes; their exile will be just penance
> For the pollution which this blood has brought on them.
> Never again shall they enjoy their native land;
> That such defilement ever should appear before
> The city's altars, is an offence to piety (p. 242).[2]

Cadmus too is doomed to exile, transformed with his wife Harmonia into a snake. The scapegoat has shifted; Pentheus was the sacrificial victim that had to be slain, but now those who killed him must be driven outside the camp. All this because they refused to "choose wisdom" and "recognize" Dionysus as the son of Zeus. Purged and renewed, the city becomes the possession of Dionysus. The thyrsus replaces the fetters.

Winnington-Ingram argues that Euripides does not approve Dionysian excess or the cult of emotion that he depicts in the play. But Euripides does recognize the power of Dionysus, the effects it has on society, and the dangers it poses, and he wrote the play in order to give his audience insight into the working of this power. The chorus summarizes the insight required in the last words of the play:

> Gods manifest themselves in many forms,
> Bring many matters to surprising ends;
> The things we thought would happen do not happen;
> The unexpected God makes possible:
> And that is what has happened here today (p. 244).

It is important to notice what kind of insight is offered here. Wisdom is not related here, as Christian wisdom is, to faith and trust in God. We cannot trust this god; by definition, we cannot rely on him; what kind of man would love him? Euripides offers another kind of wisdom: He warns against the fresh and horrifying surprises he springs. Terror of an unpredictable god, not fear in the biblical sense, is the beginning of Dionysian wisdom.

*Review Questions.*

1. Why is it significant that Agave is the first to attack Pentheus?

2. How does the hunt of the Bacchae overturn the normal Greek hunt?

3. What is significant about how Dionysus places

Pentheus in the tree? Why is it important for Pentheus to be in a high place?

4. How does the killing of Pentheus illustrate the division of the city?

5. Explain how the death of Pentheus is a sacrifice. What effect, according to Girard's theory, does this kind of sacrifice have on a community?

6. What does Agave think she is carrying into the city? How does this show that Agave is possessed by Dionysian "sight"?

7. What happens to Agave and her sisters at the end? Why?

8. What moral does the Chorus draw from the play?

*Thought Questions.*

1. When Dionysus urges the women to attack Pentheus, there is a "flash of dreadful fire" from heaven (p. 231). In the light of Dionysus's origins, explain the significance of this fire.

2. Why is it significant that *women* offer Pentheus as sacrifice? (p. 232)

3. What is the first description that Agave gives to her hunting "prize"? Why is this significant? (p. 234)

4. According to Agave's speech on page 236, what is the characteristic work of women? How has she departed from that norm?

5. Cadmus tells Agave that Pentheus was killed "where, long ago, Actaeon was devoured by hounds" (p. 238). What is significant about that allusion? How does it fit with the action of *The Bacchae*?

6. Why does Agave hesitate to touch Pentheus's body? (p. 240)

7. Why must Cadmus and his daughters leave Thebes? (p. 242). Explain the parallel with *Oedipus Tyrannus*.

8. What does Cadmus say about the revenge that Dionysus has taken on Thebes? Why is Cadmus surprised by this? How does Dionysus defend himself? (p. 243)

*Notes:*
   [1] I am using the Penguin edition (1973), translated by Philip Vellacott. Unfortunately, this edition does not have useful line numbering, so I have cited the quotations by page number.
   [2] There is a large gap in the texts, so part of this quotation is conjectural.

## Sophist in the City: Aristophanes, *Clouds*

During the fifth century B.C., a new philosophical school gained prominence in Athens. Known as "Sophists," from the Greek *sophia* ("wisdom"), these men set themselves up as teachers of rhetoric and logic. The term *sophist* had been applied to poets and wise men long before the Sophist movement, but with the Sophists something new came to Athens. According to H. D. Rankin's description,

> Sophists . . . were people who professed to teach "wisdom" and "virtue" for a fee. They were a profession, but not a homogenous one. Their main points in common were that they were paid for their teaching and that they based their teaching upon developed uses of language for imparting skill in argument and persuasion. Whether an individual Sophist's claim was to teach *arete* (virtue) or merely some argumentative technique or way of arranging language in the most impressive or convincing style, his concern was with the human realm and the association of man with man in the competitive life of Greek society [rather than with natural sciences].

Sophists prospered because their methods of training met the changing needs of fifth-century Athens. K. J. Dover explains that "Persuasive speaking, in assembly and law courts, was felt to be the key to worldly success, the way to wealth and influence and power." Since the Sophists claimed "to refine and impart this technique," they had a regular supply of students and could demand substantial fees for their instruction.

Many Sophists went beyond vocational training and dabbled in philosophy, though it was philosophy of a specific flavor. Their philosophical interests were connected to their teaching of oratory in two ways. First, as Dover points out, concentration on the arts of persuasion shifted attention away from the question, "is thus-and-such true and real?" to, "how can I make it *seem* that thus-and-such is true and real?" Pressured by their concern for rhetoric, sophistic philosophers thus tended to teach a "skeptical" worldview. To say that a philosopher is "skeptical" is to say that he questions received social customs and political institutions, doubts the truth of tradition and religion, and suspects that man is finally incapable of knowing what is true. One key theme in this skeptical outlook was the Sophistic interest in the relation of "nature" (Greek, *physis*) and "law" or "custom" (Greek, *nomos*). Rules that govern the life of the city are based, they said, on mere agreement among citizens, not revealed by God or somehow rooted in the nature of reality. Thus, in Rankin's words, the Sophists "released their pupils from the inner need to conform with the traditional rules of the city state." At several points in *Clouds*, Aristophanes puts typically Sophistic arguments into the mouths of his characters.

Second, as William Arrowsmith points out, the Sophists were capable of questioning the basis of Athenian society only because they were paid for teaching rhetoric. Philosophers associated with Socrates always refused payment, but many of them, including Plato, were wealthy members of the upper class. By charging for their teaching, the Sophists were freed both from financial pressures and from too-close an attachment to the entrenched ruling classes of Athens. Financial and social autonomy, in turn, freed them to be revolutionaries.

In *Clouds*, the leading Sophist is, surprisingly, Socrates. The play focuses on Strepsiades, a farmer who has been forced by war to move into Athens. His son, Pheidippides, has run up tremendous debts racing horses, and Strepsiades wants desperately to evade his creditors. Hearing about the "Thinkery," the Socratic academy whose students learn to argue their way out of any jam by making bad arguments triumph over good ones, he tries to convince Pheidippides to join. When this fails, Strepsiades becomes a student of Socrates himself, but Strepsiades is too dull to make any progress and Socrates gives up in disgust. Strepsiades then forces Pheidippides to enter the school, and the son, by observing the contest of Philosophy and Sophistry (or, in other translations, Good and Bad Argument or Right and Wrong), learns how to argue for the wrong side of a case. He demonstrates his new skills to his father, who gleefully applies them to his creditors. In the end, however, Strepsiades' dishonest evasion of his obligations returns on his own head, when Pheidippides uses Sophistic arguments he learned from Socrates to justify beating his father. Outraged, Strepsiades renounces Sophistry and burns the Thinkery to the ground.

In contrast to Aristophanes, Plato depicts Socrates as an inveterate critic and enemy of the Sophists. In one dialogue, Socrates encounters the Sophist Gorgias, a teacher of rhetoric. Typically, Socrates argues Gorgias into a corner, until he is forced to admit that his rhetoric requires no knowledge of the subject matter:

> *Socrates*: . . . the rhetorician need not know the truth about things; he has only to discover some way of persuading the ignorant that he has more knowledge than those who know?
> *Gorgias*: Yes, Socrates, and is not this a great comfort?—not to have learned the other arts, but the art of rhetoric only, and yet to be in no way inferior to the professors of them?

Aristophanes' portrait of Socrates differs from Plato's and Xenephon's in several other respects as well. Unlike Plato's Socrates, Aristophanes' is interested in natural sciences, as were the Sophists. Aristophanes presents Socrates as an atheist, but, as Dover says, "the Socrates of Plato and Xenephon is not only a pious man, who participates in the observances of the society in which he lives..., but displays an unwavering faith in the reality of the gods." Plato's Socrates would never encourage people to act unjustly or argue untruthfully for gain, but in *Clouds* Socrates cooperates fully with Strepsiades' efforts to evade his creditors.

Plato's presentation of Socrates notwithstanding, Athenians did consider Socrates and the Sophists to be part of the same philosophical school. One source of the popular association of Socrates and the Sophists was *Clouds* itself. First written and produced in 423 B.C., the play was still on Socrates' mind during his trial in 399. In his *Apology*, he quoted the charges against him:

> "Socrates is an evil-doer, and a curious person, who searches into things under the earth and in heaven, and he makes the worse appear the better cause, and he teaches the aforesaid doctrines to others." Such is the nature of the accusation: it is just what you have yourselves seen in the comedy of Aristophanes, who has introduced a man whom he calls Socrates going about and saying that he walks in air, and talking a deal of nonsense concerning matters of which I do not pretend to know much or little.

As G. B. Kerferd points out in his book on the Sophist movement, Socrates' defense implies that he was considered a Sophist.

Whether Aristophanes deliberately distorts Socrates' teaching cannot and probably need not be answered. Aristophanes was a playwright, not a philosopher, and like many, he probably balked at the niceties and details of philosophical debate, regarding the fine distinctions of different philosophical positions as trivial. More importantly, it is clear that he is writing a spoof, a satire on the character of Socrates and philosophy in general. Douglas MacDowell provides a fine summary of the probable reasons he used Socrates as the leading intellectual in the play:

Aristophanes wanted to write a play ridiculing intellectuals and their pretensions; for practical dramatic reasons he needed to have one character representing the intellectuals; most of the leading intellectuals were not suitable for this purpose because they were foreigners not well known to the Athenian public...; Socrates on the other hand was familiar to most Athenians because he had lived in Athens all his life, his appearance was noticeable and mildly comic (snub nose, prominent eyes, thick lips), and he frequently engaged people in conversation in public; Aristophanes therefore chose Socrates to be a character in his play and simply assigned to that character all the intellectual theories and activities which he wished to ridicule.

To make a satire of this kind work, however, it is essential to make the object of satire believable. If Aristophanes accused Socrates of plotting to blow up the Parthenon, the satire would not hit home; there would be no connection with reality. Satirists must make their objects recognizable but distort some feature of the portrait in order to make the point.[1] Aristophanes' Socrates is thus not only an easy target for an attack on philosophy, but he is, as Dover points out, close enough to the Socrates of Plato to be recognizably the same person. Aristophanes and Plato both refer to Socrates' indifference to cold and hunger, his mannerisms, and some of his terminology. Though "the characteristics of the individual Socrates which are common to Aristophanes, Plato, and Xenephon appear to fall entirely within the limits of the physically obvious," this is enough for Aristophanes' purposes. A member of the audience, hearing the name Socrates and seeing some of Socrates' personal characteristics in the actor on stage, would associate the two. Through Socrates the theatrical character, Socrates the philosopher (and through him, all philosophers) are held up as objects of satire.

How biting is the satire? Aristophanes appears in some of Plato's dialogues, and appears to be in a friendly relation with Socrates and Plato. *Clouds*, however, is not friendly.

English classicist Gilbert Murray argued that the satire of Socrates is fairly mild, pointing out the ways in which the character resembles the real Socrates and the fact that Strepsiades rather than Socrates is the butt of most of the jokes. Though Murray's comments keep us from reading *Clouds* as a vicious satire, they cannot change the ultimate suspicion and hostility toward Socrates that the play, in its extant version, arouses. At the end of the play, Strepsiades burns the Thinkery because he believes that Socrates undermines respect for tradition and threatens the order of the city. Even here, Strepsiades is the object of satire as well, for he joined the Thinkery to escape an economic and social obligation. An Athenian play about a prominent citizen that ends in this way, however, has gone beyond the realm of light entertainment, for real people, Socrates not least, were prosecuted in Athens for undermining the morals and religion of the city.

So far as we can tell from this play, Aristophanes is a "cultural conservative" fearful of the "new philosophy" that Socrates represents. To say he is "conservative" does not at all mean that Christians will find his play congenial. This is not only because the play includes a great deal that is vulgar and obscene. More fundamentally, Aristophanes is conservative in the same way that the pagan opponents of the early church were conservative. Just as Celsus and Julian the Apostate did not want to give up their old gods in favor of the Christian gospel, so Aristophanes vindicates the old gods against philosophical criticism.

Aristophanes reinforces this "conservatism" by structuring the play around a number of thematic oppositions. Strepsiades used to be a farmer (p. 13) who has come to the city because of the war (p. 11).[2] Immediately, we have two key oppositions introduced: City and Country, War and Peace. Since Strepsiades has come to the city because of the war, city and war are associated, as are the countryside and peace. Strepsiades describes his life as a farmer in lyrical terms: "the sweetest life on earth, a lovely, moldy, unspruce, litter-jumbled life, bursting with honeybees, bloated with sheep and olives" (p. 13). Like the war, the philosophers who inhabit the city tear apart the happy life of the countryside; war has "ruined Athens" (p. 11), and Strepsiades will eventually conclude that Socrates poses as great a danger. War is thus linked with the innovative thinking of Socrates, who battles custom and tradition with his new logic. Extending these polarities, we can diagram the thematic structure of the play as follows:

| *Old* | *New* |
|---|---|
| Country | City |
| Peace | War |
| Tradition | Innovation |
| Respect | Disrespect |
| Custom | Philosophy (Nature) |
| Strepsiades | Socrates/Pheidippides |

It would be a mistake, however, to take these oppositions too rigidly. Though a farmer and an old man, through most of the play Strepsiades is not an advocate of the old ways of custom, law, and piety to the gods. He is eager to accept Socrates' philosophy, if it can deliver him from his creditors. Despite this complexity in the main character, Aristophanes' sympathies are largely on the left side of the chart. *Clouds* is a comic exploration of what happens when the values associated with the right side of the chart invade a city.

*Reviews Questions.*
   1. Who were the Sophists? What was characteristic of their teaching?
   2. Explain the debate concerning *physis* and *nomos*.
   3. In Plato's writings, what is Socrates' attitude toward the Sophists?
   4. What charges were laid against Socrates by the Athenians? How is Aristophanes connected to these charges?

5. Briefly summarize the story of *Clouds*.
6. How are the Socrates of Plato and Aristophanes similar? In what ways are they different?
7. Is Aristophanes' portrait of Socrates accurate? Why or why not?
8. How is Aristophanes a "conservative"?
9. Why is it important that Strepsiades was once a farmer?

## Teaching an Old Sophist New Tricks

Strepsiades is lying on stage when the play opens, thrashing sleeplessly while his slaves and son, Pheidippides, snore nearby. Strepsiades' name, which means "twisting" or "wriggling," is doubly significant: He twists and turns in his sleep because he is preoccupied with finding a way to wriggle out of his debts. Strepsiades' early morning ruminations immediately raise the social and political concerns of the play:

> And listen to those slaves. Still snoring away!
> By god, things around here were a long sight different
> in the good old days before this war! Drat
> this stinking war anyway! It's ruined Athens.
> Why, you can't even whip your own slaves any more
> or they'll desert to the Spartans (p. 11).

Historically, Strepsiades is referring here to the Peloponnesian Wars, during which the Spartans frequently invaded Athenian territory, giving disgruntled Athenian slaves a chance to escape. From a thematic perspective, Strepsiades' complaint is significant in several directions. Ironically, Strepsiades wants slaves to submit to masters, while he dreams of ways to avoid paying his debts. As noted above, Strepsiades is already a dishonest hypocrite before he ever meets Socrates, for he favors the established order only if it benefits him. Though he lacks rhetorical training, morally he is an instinctive sophist, without any sense of obligation to keep his promises or pay his debts. Insubordination of slaves to masters is, moreover, one variety of the social upheaval that Strepsiades will later attribute to the teaching of Socrates. Reference to "whipping" slaves foreshadows a later scene. Near the end of the play, the chief effect of Sophistry is that Strepsiades no longer beats but *is* beaten.

Pheidippides, for his part, eats, drinks, and, especially, sleeps horses, but the same horses have left his father sleepless. Full of anxiety about his creditors, Strepsiades is kept awake by the "blasted bedbuggering debts and bills and stable fees" (p. 12). As MacDowell points out, the problem here is not that Pheidippides loses money betting on horses, but that he races horses, a hobby that comes with extravagant expenses. His son's indulgence has gotten Strepsiades into serious financial problems, and he thinks initially that there can be nothing worse than hedonism. By the end of the play, he will realize that hedonism can get worse; it can become philosophical. The generational tension with which *Clouds* opens symbolizes the various other conflicts of the play. As a member of the younger generation, Pheidippides will be associated with everything new and innovative, everything his "old man" comes to loathe.

As he watches Pheidippides sleep, Strepsiades reflects on his marriage and son. Remembering the happiness of his country life prior to marriage, he blames the "meddling matchmaker who prodded me on to marry your mother" for all his problems (p. 13). The main problem is that she is a "city girl" and niece of the prominent Athenian aristocrat "Megakles who was son and heir of old Blueblood Megakles himself" (p. 13). She came to the marriage longing for luxury and ease: "the whiff of spices, pure saffron, tonguekisses, Luxury, High Prices, gourmandizing, goddess Lechery, and every little elf, imp, and sprite of Intercourse." Sexually aggressive, after days working "at her loom and shoving in the wool," at night she "works on me" until her husband is entirely "shorn" (pp. 13–14).

Their disagreement over the name of their son is not, we suspect, their first argument, but it highlights the contrast between them:

> She, of course, wanted something fancy,
> some upperclass, high-horse handle with *hippos* [horse]
>     in it—
> Xanth*ippos* or Char*ippos* or Kall*ippos*—while I naturally
> wanted to give him the fine old name of Pheidonides ["skin
>     flint"]
> in honor of his thrifty grandfather (p. 14).

Including *hippos* gave a name an aristocratic sound, since only the aristocracy joined the cavalry. Strepsiades reached an uneasy compromise with the name Pheidippides, which means, in Arrowsmith's translation, "the Scrimping Aristocrat." Compromise or not, he is definitely his mother's son, more *hippos* than *Pheid*.

Strepsiades, however, thinks he has found a loophole, and he wants to push Pheidippides through it. Awakening his son and pointing to a door, he explains that it opens into the Thinkery, where intellectuals live who can prove "that the whole atmosphere is actually a cosmical oven and we're not really people but little bits of charcoal burning away" (p. 16). His interest is not, however, in the scientific pursuits of the Thinkery: "For a fee" they offer a course in winning lawsuits, whether "honest or dishonest, it's all one" (p. 16). If he learned "Sophistic, or Socratic, Logic," Strepsiades would not "have to pay a penny of all those debts you've saddled me with" (p. 17). Pheidippides will have none of it, preferring his horses to the "filthy charlatans . . . those frauds, those barefoot pendants with the look of death" (p. 17).

Having failed to convince his son, Strepsiades decides to try his own hand at learning Socratic logic. Entry into the Thinkery is like an initiation into a secret society. The student he meets at the door tells him the latest discovery is "top secret" (p. 18) and that "our researches are solemn mysteries" (p. 19), and the last word probably has a religious as well as a scientific connotation. When Socrates inducts him, he sprinkles him with flour, demands that Strepsiades strip his old clothing, and forces him to endure the torments of a bug-infested bed. It is worth everything, for it comes with the promise that "you shall be reborn, sir, as the perfect flower of orators, a consummate, blathering, tinkling rascal" (p. 27). Strepsiades professes he is willing to accept starvation, thirst, freezing, so long as "when the ordeal is completed, a new Strepsiades rise," famous for cheating and getting away with it. Initiated into the Thinkery, Strepsiades is born again of flour and gas.

Research at the Thinkery is absurd, but we must be careful to see exactly what makes it absurd. Socrates has been able to measure how far a flea can jump. In itself, this is a legitimate scientific pursuit, similar to research that might be conducted by entomologists today. Socrates' method, however, is ludicrous: He dips the flea's feet in hot wax and makes tiny flea-sized boots with which to measure the jump (p. 19). Further, the flea has jumped from one of Socrates' students to Socrates, which implies that sanitary conditions in the Thinkery would not meet code. Similarly, the students who crowd the Thinkery are engaged in geology, but their method—bending over to stare at the ground—makes it ridiculous. Strepsiades notices some students bent double, staring at the ground: "Those are graduate students doing research on Hades," Strepsiades' guide helpfully explains (p. 21).

Socratic cosmology would not be as inane to an ancient audience as it seems to us. Though Socrates teaches that everything operates according to the "convection principle, like the pot-bellied stove that serves as a model of the universe (p. 36), most of the theories that Socrates propounds have some parallel in serious scientific theories of antiquity. Anaxagoras, according to one account, claimed that thunder came from clouds bumping into each other, a theory similar to that of Socrates. Skilled satirist that he is, Aristophanes' play includes material that is familiar and seriously believed in order to mock it. However closely he follows the scientific theories of his day, however, the point remains a comic one: Just as for the philosopher, the gods are as airy as clouds, so for Aristophanes, philosophers are bloated with hot air.

Socrates himself hangs overhead in a basket (p. 25), symbolic of his ability to "walk upon the air and look down upon the sun from a superior standpoint" (p. 25). He further explains:

> only by being suspended aloft, by dangling
> my mind in the heavens and mingling my rare thought
> with the ethereal air, could I ever achieve strict
> scientific accuracy in my survey of the vast empyrean.
> Had I pursued my inquiries from down there on the ground,
> my data would be worthless. The earth, you see, pulls down
> the delicate essence of thought to its own gross level (p. 25).

That Socrates literally has his head in the clouds is significant in more than one way. It lampoons his philosophical interests, for, like a pietistic Christian, he is so heavenly minded he is no earthly good. Earth is quite explicitly beneath Socrates' concern: it "pulls down the delicate essence of thought to its own gross level" (p. 25). This is a parody of Greek thought, but it is rooted in reality. For Platonic philosophy, earthly and material things are contemptible. Though the common man takes the sensible world for reality, the philosopher knows they are mere shadows of the Forms flickering on the walls of a cave. Through philosophy, one is set free from the bondage to material reality. Socrates' suspension in midair symbolizes his lack of concern with what goes on among mere mortals. This is the nub of Aristophanes' charge against Socratic Sophistry: Heads in the clouds, it tears apart the earthly city and doesn't care a whit.

As Strepsiades notices, from his position in the clouds, Socrates can even "sneer at the gods" (p. 25). Socrates' position in the basket is thus a sign of his atheism, which becomes explicit in the following dialogue. When Strepsiades swears by the gods that he will pay whatever Socrates asks, the philosopher responds, "By the gods? The gods, my dear simple fellow, are a mere expression coined by vulgar superstition" (p. 26), for "There is no Zeus" (p. 34). The only real divinities, in Socrates' thinking, are the "majestic Clouds" (p. 28), who have taken over the rain and thunder from Zeus (pp. 34–35). Their special objects of attention are

> men of leisure
> and philosophers. To them we owe our repertoire of verbal talents:
> our eloquence, intellect, fustian, casuistry, force, wit, prodigious vocabulary, circumlocutory skill (p. 30).

All "chiropractors, prophets, longhairs, quacks, fops, charlatans, fairies, dithyrambic poets, scientists, dandies, astrologers and other men of leisure . . . walk with their heads among the clouds and base their inspiration on the murky Muse" (p. 31).

Strepsiades immediately accepts the new divinities and prays that they will make him a "new Strepsiades" who will be renowned as a successful cheat and swindler. Before they grant his request, however, Socrates has to test his abilities. Though his memory is weak, his talent for speaking is nonexistent, and his skill in reasoning is highly questionable, Socrates accepts him into the Thinkery. Stripping his robe, Strepsiades is initiated into the cult of philosophers that worships the clouds. Before following him into the Thinkery, Socrates makes sure that he takes Strepsiades' cloak as payment (p. 42).

The next time we see Strepsiades, he is again lying on stage, as he was at the beginning of the play. Now, however, he believes he is being trained in the wisdom that will relieve his debts. Little, in fact, has changed; he is still "wriggling" on a bug-infested mattress. Socrates is not impressed with his new pupil: "Never in all my days have I seen such peerless stupidity. . . . I no sooner teach him the merest snippets of science than he suffers an attack of total amnesia" (p. 49). Socrates is trying to teach him a sense of measure or rhythm, which "confers a certain ineluctable social *savoir-faire*" (p. 50), but Strepsiades willfully misunderstands everything. When Socrates tries to pin down some definitions and categories, Socrates as much as Strepsiades becomes the object of ridicule. He woodenly forces language to behave in prescribed ways, even if it means making "duchess" the feminine form of "duck" (pp. 52–53).

Strepsiades, though he seems to be learning nothing, learns that strained logic is the order of the day in the Thinkery. Lying on a mattress, he conceives a plan to rid himself of debt:

> Strepsiades: Just suppose I rented one of those witchwomen
>     from Thessaly
> and ordered her to charm down the moon from the sky.
>     And then
> I snatch up the moon and I pop her into a box,
> and polish her face until she shines like a mirror.
> Socrates: And what would you gain by that?
> Strepsiades: What would I gain?
> Why, think what would happen if the moon never rose.
> I wouldn't have to pay interest.
> Socrates: No interest? But why?
> Strepsiades: Because interest falls due on the last day of the
>     month,
> before the New Moon, doesn't it? (p. 59).

Socrates is impressed: "A superlative swindle" (p. 59). But the session ends badly. When Strepsiades suggests he could avoid his creditors by hanging himself before the case comes to trial, Socrates resigns (pp. 60–61).

Though his training is a failure, Strepsiades becomes an evangelist for Socratic atheism. As he drags Pheidippides to the Thinkery, his son protests, "Almighty Zeus, you must be mad!" (p. 62). Strepsiades lets loose a barrage of Socratic philosophy: "there is no Zeus" but only "Convection-Principle" (p. 63), and he even repeats the duck-duchess gag. Reluctantly, thinking his father mad, Pheidippides joins the Thinkery, though the son prophetically warns "someday you'll be sorry" (p. 65). Strepsiades' hope to use his son as a weapon against his creditors is destined to backfire; he forgets that the Socratic weaponry can be turned against him.

*Review Questions.*
  1. Why can't Strepsiades sleep?
  2. What is significant about Strepsiades' marriage?
  3. What does the name "Pheidippides" mean? Why is this significant in the play?
  4. What procedure is used to induct Strepsiades into the Thinkery? Why is this significant?
  5. What kind of research goes on in the Thinkery? What is Aristophanes trying to say?
  6. Where is Socrates when we first see him? Why is this significant?
  7. Does Strepsiades show any talent for philosophy? Why does Socrates accept him into the Thinkery?
  8. What is Strepsiades' plan for avoiding his debts?

*Thought Questions.*
  1. To what does Strepsiades compare his debts? Why? (p. 13)
  2. How does Xanthias, Strepsiades' slave, treat his master? How does this fit with the themes of the play? (p. 14)
  3. By whom does Pheidippides first swear? Why does Strepsiades object? By whom does Pheidippides swear the second time? What is significant about this second oath? (pp. 15–16).
  4. What effect do the Clouds have on Strepsiades? How does this fit with Aristophanes' portrait of Sophistic philosophy? (p. 30)
  5. What causes thunder, according to Socrates? How does this fit with the rest of the play? (pp. 35–36)
  6. In the midst of the play, Aristophanes (or, the chorus speaking for him) gives a lengthy speech. What is the thrust of that speech? (pp. 43–46)
  7. How does Strepsiades describe the personal habits of the students in the Thinkery? (p. 64)

## Second-Generation Sophistry

Pheidippides' training is not carried out by Socrates himself. Instead, Philosophy (traditional logic) and Sophistry (Socratic logic) stage a debate. The contest is an intergenerational debate, anticipating the conflict of values that will later emerge between Strepsiades and his son. Philosophy and Sophistry fight for the soul of the younger generation of Athens. Philosophy calls Sophistry a "repulsive whippersnapper" and a "parricide," since he attacks his "father," and Sophistry calls his opponent a "disgusting fogy" (p. 70). When Sophistry claims to welcome abuse, Philosophy is appalled:

> Philosophy: *Welcome* it, monster?
> In my day we would have cringed with shame.
> Sophistry: Whereas *now* we're flattered. Times change.
> The vices of your age are stylish today. (p. 70)

This initial sparring is comic, but it has a thematic point: Aristophanes wants to stuff the revolutionary words of the Sophists into the mouth of Socrates.

Koryphaios, the Chorus leader and chief Cloud, intervenes to stop the petty bickering and asks each of the contestants to describe his philosophy of education. Education (Greek, *paideia*) here has a wider sense than our modern concept, including not only the communication of basic knowledge and skills but the transmission of the entire way of life of a civilized people. Students in Greek schools would not have been trained for "jobs" but would have been formed into mature Greeks. Greek education inculcated the values of the city into the next generation, and thus educational methods and goals determined the moral climate of life in the future. Thus, the form of education shapes the form of culture.

Philosophy goes first, describing the educational methods of the old days. Education, he says, should seek to produce the three Ds—discipline, decorum, and duty—in both body and soul. Music and gymnastic are the means for achieving this result. Greek "gymnastic" is similar to our modern practice, involving vigorous physical exercise. Gymnastic was designed to train boys with sound bodies. "Music," however, had a much broader meaning than it does today. Arrowsmith explains:

> By Music was meant the education of the inward man; the schooling not merely of the mind, but of the emotions, the "soul," the feelings and the thoughts in their rational ensemble. The basic instrument of this inward education was poetry joined to music, a blend in which poetry taught by means of example and emulation and was sustained by music which was believed to inculcate the moral virtues.

The poetry involved, it should be noted, was the poetry of myth and epic, which provided examples of the heroic virtues of self-control, piety, courage, and dignity.

According to Philosophy, this hardy curriculum produced "a generation of heroes, the men who fought at Marathon," while Sophistic methods produce "vanity and softness, and the naked beauty of the body muffled in swirling clothes, gross and unmanly." Because of the new education, Athens is dominated by "contentious disputations," "cheap, courtroom cant," and the "corrupting softness of the bath" (pp. 73–74). One emphasis here is on producing manly men: "True athletic prowess, the vigor of contending manhood in prime perfection of physique, muscular and hard, glowing with health" (p. 75). Philosophy also emphasizes on the respect for elders that this mode of education generated:

> At table courtesy and good manners
> were compulsory. Not a boy of that generation would
> have dreamed
> of taking so much as a radish or the merest pinch of parsley
> before his elders had been served (p. 74).

Among the chief virtues are "deference toward one's elders; respect for one's father and mother," especially "scrupulous obedience" to one's father and the duty to "honor his declining years who spent his prime in rearing you" (p. 74). A city that trained its youth according to the dictates of Philosophy would raise a new generation to honor the gods, maintain traditional hierarchies, and follow the customs inherited from the past.

Though Sophistry has no positive program of his own, he states the goals of his *paideia* with shocking honesty:

> Now then, I freely admit
> that among men of learning I am—somewhat pejoratively—
>     dubbed
> the Sophistical, or Immoral, Logic. And why? Because I first
> devised a Method for the Subversion of Established Social
>     Beliefs
> and the Undermining of Morality. Moreover, this little
>     invention of mine,
> this knack of taking what might appear to be the worse
>     argument
> and nonetheless winning my case, has, I might add, proved
>     to be
> an *extremely* lucrative source of income (p. 76).

This summarizes the popular perception of Sophists, and the fact that Socrates employs Sophistry in his training means he too endorses this program.

Sophistry takes aim at a number of Philosophy's claims. If the gods support justice and honor to fathers, he asks, why was Zeus never punished for imprisoning his father? (p. 69). If, as Philosophy claims, hot baths undermine manhood, then the hot baths of Hercules must have made him "both flabby and effeminate" (p. 77). If debating is so vicious, he asks, why is Nestor, the wise old man of the *Iliad*, a politician? In each of these arguments, Sophistry shows that the mythology on which Philosophy's training heavily relies is full of contradictions. Homer's epics were virtually equivalent to the Bible for the ancient Greeks, so Sophistry's appeal to the *Iliad* to refute Philosophy is, as Arrowsmith says, like Satan quoting Scripture. However distorted Aristophanes' depiction of Socrates, he listened carefully to the Sophists, for they were fond of discovering contradictions in the sacred texts of Greek mythology.

Turning directly to Pheidippides, Sophistry lists the pleasures he must renounce in order to follow the program of Philosophy: "Sex. Gambling. Gluttony. Guzzling. Carousing. Etcet." His hedonistic advice is "what on earth's the point of living, if you leach your life of all its little joys." If a man who professes to follow virtue sins, he has no defense, but a sophist can "romp, play, and laugh without a scruple in the world" (p. 78). Philosophy has no real answer, for if one is caught in adultery,

> you simply inform the poor cuckold that you're utterly innocent
> And refer him to Zeus as your moral sanction. After all, didn't he,
> a great and powerful god, succumb to the love of women?
> Then how in the world can you, a man, an ordinary mortal, be expected to surpass the greatest of gods in moral self-control?
> Clearly, you can't be (pp. 78–79).

Pheidippides, we may imagine, is paying close attention; Sophistry gives him the philosophical ammunition to defend the hedonism that he has pursued from the beginning.

Sophistry finally silences Philosophy with a grotesque argument. Philosophy reminds him that a man following his advice may commit adultery and be subjected to the horrible punishments sometimes carried out in Athens. The one he mentions is that a radish would be pushed up the back end of the adulterer so that the adulterer was made a "bugger." Sophistry proves that this is not a disgrace by reminding Philosophy that all lawyers, tragic poets, and politicians are also buggers. If so many are buggers, there can be nothing evil in it (pp. 79–80). Philosophy is forced to agree and is removed from the scene. Pheidippides enters the school, with

Socrates' promise to "send him home a consummate little sophist" (p. 81).

On the day that Pheidippides is due to return home, Strepsiades is anxious: "Today's Dueday" for Pheidippides' debts (p. 84). Fortunately, his "little sophist" provides an absurd argument to escape paying: "Today's two days? Or two Duedays? But how can one day be two days?" Since one day cannot be two days, the creditors will "forfeit their bond" (p. 84). Arrowsmith's translation here is loose. MacDowell explains that interest payments on loans were due monthly. Ancient Greeks reckoned the month by the phases of the moon, so that each month ended with the waning of the old moon and the waxing of the new moon. Between the old and new moon was a transitional day known as "Old and New," and it was on this day that interest had to be paid. Literally, Pheidippides argues that paying interest on "Old and New" day is absurd, since no one day can be both Old and New. (The pun on "old and new" is no doubt related to the conflict between old and new throughout the play.) Strepsiades thinks it is an airtight case. When Pasias comes to collect, Strepsiades is indifferent not only to paying his debts but to perjury. Convinced there are no gods, he swears to falsehoods without fear. Amynias, another creditor, he threatens with a whip. Without the gods, without customs, nothing can constrain Strepsiades to pay up.

That whip, however, comes back to haunt him. Strepsiades hopes the acid of Sophistic logic will dissolve his duty to pay creditors but then lose its potency. But if Sophistry dissolves one social obligation, it dissolves all. If it enables Strepsiades to escape his debt obligations, it equally frees Pheidippides from his obligation to respect his father. Thus, when Strepsiades asks Pheidippides to sing an old song at the table, the son refuses and instead recites some modern poetry. Escalating into a fight, this disagreement ends with Pheidippides beating his father and defending himself using his new-found rhetorical skills. Since in the past Strepsiades has licked Pheidippides out of love, the son now has the right to repay that love by licking his father (p. 104). Strepsiades, once enamored of Socrates' attack on custom, finds that *nomos* provides his only escape from beating: "It's . . . illegal," he objects.

Pheidippides' response is worth quoting at length, since it captures the essence of Aristophanes' view of Sophistry:

> The *law*?
> And who made the law?
> An ordinary man. A man like you or me.
> A man who lobbied for his bill until he persuaded the people
>   to make it law.
> By the same token then, what prevents me now
> from proposing new legislation granting sons the power
>   to inflict
> corporal punishment upon wayward fathers?
> Nothing vindictive, of course.
> In fact, I would personally insist on adding a rider,
> a Retroactive Amnesty for Fathers, waiving our right to
>   compensation
> for any whippings we received prior to the passage of the
>   new law.
> However, if you're still unconvinced, look to Nature for
>   a sanction.
> Observe the roosters, for instance, and what do you see?
>   A society
> whose pecking-order envisages a permanent state of open
>   warfare
> between fathers and sons. And how do roosters differ
>   from men,
> except for the trifling fact that human society is based
>   upon law
> and rooster society isn't? (pp. 104–105).

Pheidippides employs the typically Sophistic opposition of *nomos* and *physis* to show that conflict between sons and fathers is more natural than respect. Behind his argument is the notion that law is merely a matter of agreement. If that is true, then the law can be changed from moment to moment, and if this is true, then the city is a site of "open warfare between fathers and sons." Each new generation will tear down the achievements of the previous generation, the sons will reject the customs and logic of their fathers, and the city will become a pit in which cocks fight for control, like the contest between Philosophy and Sophistry.

Once his premises are granted, Pheidippides' argument is compelling. By what purely logical argument, after all, can you prove that children should respect their parents? Is it because parents are bigger, stronger, older, wiser? But sometimes only one of those is true, and why should one respect an older person in any case? For Christians, these questions are answered by reference to God's Word, which requires honor to elders, especially parents, but on Pheidippides' atheistic premises, appeal to God's commandments is out of the question. Instead, one is left with the rule of brute force and the shifting whims of public opinion. Strepsiades sees the force of the logic and the result: If there are no gods, and laws and customs are purely human inventions, then "the kids have proved their point; naughty fathers should be flogged" (p. 106). Which is to say that if that is true, the city is turned upside down.

Yet there is one chink in Pheidippides' case. Strepsiades may not have graduated from the Thinkery, but he sees through his son's argument from *physis*. If the natural behavior of cocks is the guide, Pheidippides should eat dung and sleep on a perch at night. His son has no answer to this rejoinder and ironically can only appeal to the authority of his teacher: "If you don't believe me, then go ask Socrates" (p. 105). Forced into a corner, the Sophist falls back on the "customary" teaching of his school. The conflict between *nomos* and *physis* reduces, in the end, to a conflict of different *nomoi*.

Seeing the result of Sophistic logic, Strepsiades embraces traditional beliefs. And this, the Clouds inform him, is precisely what they intended to achieve. They accuse him of wanting to use them for the sake of gain. Like Sirens, the Clouds lure "foolish men through their dishonest dreams of gain to overwhelming ruin," so that, "schooled by suffering, they learn at last to fear the gods" (p. 107). Through his sufferings, Strepsiades is converted. This, not the Strepsiades produced by the Thinkery, is the truly "new Strepsiades." Had he succeeded with his dim-witted pupil, Socrates would only have given philosophical "rigor" to Strepsiades' ingrained tendency to flout his responsibilities. Now, for the first time in the play, Strepsiades, trained by the Clouds, genuinely accepts the rule of custom and law. Strepsiades' is hardly an admirable conversion, however, for he approves the old ways mainly because he dislikes being on the business end of a whip.

Having been brought to fear of the gods, Strepsiades becomes an instrument of divine vengeance. When Pheidippides denies Zeus, Strepsiades finds a ladder and an axe and begins to dismantle and burn the Thinkery. This scene apparently was added after the play was first produced in 423 B.C. Originally, MacDowell speculates, the play probably ended with Strepsiades escaping his creditors through the use of Sophistic rhetoric. Audiences "thought that the play implied approval of sophistry," though the playwright's real intention had been to satirize. The final scene was added to make his opposition to Sophistry explicit.

Even if added later, the ending is fitting. Socrates and his students believe that the universe is like a pot-bellied stove, and Strepsiades ironically turns their Thinkery into an oven. Like the gods, Strepsiades descends upon the Thinkery from above, and in doing so he repeats Socrates' boast to "walk upon the air and look down upon the sun from a superior standpoint" (p. 112). But it is no longer Sophistry, but the old paths and traditions, that provide this superior standpoint. In the last scene, Strepsiades, with the encouragement of the Clouds, thrashes Socrates and his followers for their crimes, "but most of all because they dared outrage the gods of heaven" (p. 113). Aristophanes takes the side of the old gods against the atheists, the side of *nomos* against the corrosive appeal to *physis*.

Christians must refuse to make a choice between Sophistry and Philosophy. On the one hand, Sophistry, which questions all customs and traditions from atheistic assumptions, threatens, as Philosophy perceives, all moral order. As Dostoevsky put it, If God is dead, all is permitted. But Christians must agree with Sophistry that Greek mythology provides no sound guidance for living a righteous life. How, as Sophistry asks, can we expect mortals to exercise self-control if the chief of the gods is a philanderer? Moral order cannot be established by just any old god, certainly not by an adulterer like Zeus. Though he pointedly shows up the weaknesses of various viewpoints, Aristophanes provides no ultimate wisdom or vision of human life. For that Christians must turn to their own book and their own city. As St. Augustine recognized, only that city that worships a holy, trustworthy, and faithful God can flourish.

*Review Questions.*
1. Who trains Pheidippides in philosophy?
2. How does the conflict between Philosophy and Sophistry mirror the conflict between Pheidippides and Strepsiades?
3. What is Philosophy's educational method? What kind of men does Philosophy's educational system produce?
4. What is Sophistry's agenda?
5. How does Sophistry win the debate?
6. After returning from the Thinkery, what argument does Pheidippides' use for evading debts?
7. Why does Strepsiades turn from Sophistry? What is the role of the Clouds in his "conversion"?
8. What effects does Sophistry have on the life of the city?
9. What ultimately happens to Socrates and the Thinkery? Why is this significant?

*Thought Questions.*

1. According to Philosophy, what effect does Sophistry have on the youth of Athens? How does this fit with later charges against Socrates? (p. 71)
2. How should boys dress at school, according to Philosophy? Why? (pp. 73–74)
3. Why does Sophistry consider moderation and decorum absurd notions? (pp. 77–78)
4. How does Strepsiades escape paying Pasias? (pp. 88–90)
5. Why did Strepsiades ask his son to sing at the table? What does Pheidippides want to recite instead? Why does his father object? How does this fit with the themes of the play? (pp. 100–101)

*Notes:*

[1] Thanks to my student, Matthew Greydanus, for clarifying this point concerning satire.

[2] I am using the translation of William Arrowsmith in Aristophanes, *Three Comedies* (Ann Arbor: University of Michigan Press, 1969). Unfortunately, this edition contains no line numbers and is too freely translated to match up well with the Greek, and therefore I have cited quotations by page number.

# For Additional Reading

I have not listed all the books I consulted and used in writing *Heroes of the City of Man*. Those listed below are included either because they were cited in the text or because they proved especially helpful. Advanced students may find them useful, though I should point out that none of them takes the explicitly Christian approach that I have taken here.

### Hesiod, *Theogony*

Vernant, Jean-Pierre. "At Man's Table: Hesiod's Foundation Myth of Sacrifice," in Marcel Detienne and Jean-Pierre Vernant, eds., *The Cuisine of Sacrifice among the Greeks* (trans. Paula Wissing; Chicago: University of Chicago Press, 1989).

Walcott, Peter. *Hesiod and the Ancient Near East* (Cardiff: Wales University Press, 1966).

West, M. L. "Prolegomena," in M. L. West, ed., *Hesiod: Theogony* (Oxford: Clarendon Press, [1966] 1997).

### Homer, *The Iliad*

Edwards, Mark. *Homer: Poet of the Iliad* (Baltimore, MD: Johns Hopkins University Press, 1987).

Lewis, C. S. *A Preface to Paradise Lost* (Oxford: University Press, 1942).

Owen, E. T. *The Story of the Iliad* (Wauconda, IL: Bolchazy-Carducci, [1946] 1989).

Redfield, James M. *Nature and Culture in the Iliad: The Tragedy of Hector* (Chicago: University of Chicago Press, 1975).

Schein, Seth. *Mortal Hero: An Introduction to Homer's Iliad* (Berkeley: University of California Press, 1984).

Weil, Simone. *The Iliad, or, The Poem of Force* (trans. Mary McCarthy; New York: Politics Press, 1947).

Whitman, Cedric. *Homer and the Heroic Tradition* (Cambridge, MA: Harvard University Press, 1958).

### Homer, *The Odyssey*

Berry, Wendell. *The Unsettling of America: Culture and Agriculture* (San Francisco: Sierra Club, [1977] 1986), pp. 123-131.

Clarke, Howard W. *The Art of the Odyssey* (Wauconda, IL: Bolchazy-Carducci, [1967] 1989).

Frame, Douglas. *The Myth of Return in Early Greek Epic* (New Haven, CT: Yale University Press, 1978).

Griffin, Jasper. *Homer: The Odyssey* (Landmarks of World Literature; Cambridge: Cambridge University Press, 1987).

Knox, Bernard. "Introduction," in Robert Fagles, trans., *Homer, the Odyssey* (New York: Penguin, 1996).

Schein, Seth. "Introduction," in Seth Schein, ed., *Reading the Odyssey* (Princeton, NJ: Princeton University Press, 1996).

Segel, Charles. "Kleos and Its Ironies in the Odyssey," in Seth Schein, ed., *Reading the Odyssey* (Princeton, NJ: Princeton University Press, 1996).

Thalmann, William G. *The Odyssey: An Epic of Return* (New York: Twayne, 1992).

Vidal-Naquet, Pierre. "Land and Sacrifice in the Odyssey," in Seth Schein, ed., *Reading the Odyssey* (Princeton, NJ: Princeton University Press, 1996).

### Virgil, *The Aeneid*

Anderson, William S. *The Art of the Aeneid* (Wauconda, IL: Bolchazy-Carducci, [1969] 1989).

Gransden, K. W. *Virgil: The Aeneid* (Landmarks of World Literature; Cambridge: Cambridge University Press, 1990).

Gransden, K. W. *Virgil's Iliad: An Essay on Epic Narrative* (Cambridge: Cambridge University Press, 1984).

Griffin, Jasper. *Virgil* (Past Masters; Oxford: University Press, 1996).

Otis, Brooks. *Virgil: A Study in Civilized Poetry* (Norman, OK: University of Oklahoma Press, [1964] 1995).

Poschl, Viktor. *The Art of Virgil: Image and Symbol in the Aeneid* (Ann Arbor: University of Michigan Press, 1962).

Slavitt, David R. *Virgil* (New Haven, CT: Yale University Press, 1991).

### Aeschylus, *The Eumenides*

Goldhill, Simon. *Reading Greek Tragedy* (Cambridge: Cambridge University Press, 1986).

Kitto, H. D. F. *Greek Tragedy* (London: Routledge, [1939] 1966).

Murray, Gilbert. *Aeschylus: The Creator of Tragedy* (Oxford: Clarendon, 1940).

### Sophocles, *Oedipus Tyrannus*

Dodds, E. R. "On Misunderstanding the Oedipus Rex," in Michael J. O'Brien, ed., *Twentieth-Century Interpretations of Oedipus Rex* (Englewood Cliffs, NJ: Prentice-Hall, 1968).

Knox, Bernard. *The Heroic Temperament: Studies in Sophoclean Tragedy* (Berkeley: University of California Press, 1964).

Knox, Bernard. *Oedipus at Thebes: Sophocles' Tragic Hero and His Time* (New Haven, CT: Yale University Press, [1957] 1998).

Segal, Charles. *Tragedy and Tradition: An Interpretation of Sophocles* (Cambridge, MA: Harvard University Press, 1981).

**Euripides, *The Bacchae***

Girard, Rene. *Violence and the Sacred* (trans. Patrick Gregory; Baltimore, MD: Johns Hopkins University Press, [1972] 1977).

Winnington-Ingram, R. P. *Euripides and Dionysus: An Interpretation of the Bacchae* (London: Bristol Classical Press, [1948] 1997).

**Aristophanes, *Clouds***

Dover, K. J. "Introduction," in K. J. Dover, ed., *Aristophanes: Clouds* (Oxford: University Pres, 1989).

Kerferd, G. B. *The Sophistic Movement* (Cambridge: Cambridge University Press, 1981).

MacDowell, Douglas M. *Aristophanes and Athens: An Introduction to the Plays* (Oxford: University Press, 1995).

Murray, Gilbert. *Aristophanes, A Study* (Oxford: University Press, 1933).

Rankin, H. D. *Sophists, Socratics, and Cynics* (London: Croom Helm, 1983).